Investment Industry Claims Debunked

Robert P. Kurshan

Investment Industry Claims Debunked

Smart Personal Finance Management For Ordinary Folks, Before and After Retirement

Robert P. Kurshan
Distinguished Member of Technical Staff, Bell
Labs Research (retired)
Fellow, Cadence Design Systems (retired)
New York
NY, USA

ISBN 978-3-030-76708-2 ISBN 978-3-030-76709-9 (eBook)
https://doi.org/10.1007/978-3-030-76709-9

© The Editor(s) (if applicable) and The Author(s), under exclusive license to Springer Nature Switzerland AG 2022
This work is subject to copyright. All rights are solely and exclusively licensed by the Publisher, whether the whole or part of the material is concerned, specifically the rights of translation, reprinting, reuse of illustrations, recitation, broadcasting, reproduction on microfilms or in any other physical way, and transmission or information storage and retrieval, electronic adaptation, computer software, or by similar or dissimilar methodology now known or hereafter developed.
The use of general descriptive names, registered names, trademarks, service marks, etc. in this publication does not imply, even in the absence of a specific statement, that such names are exempt from the relevant protective laws and regulations and therefore free for general use.
The publisher, the authors, and the editors are safe to assume that the advice and information in this book are believed to be true and accurate at the date of publication. Neither the publisher nor the authors or the editors give a warranty, expressed or implied, with respect to the material contained herein or for any errors or omissions that may have been made. The publisher remains neutral with regard to jurisdictional claims in published maps and institutional affiliations.

Photo credit: Artwork depicted on the cover is by Tom Otterness.
Cover photo credit: Katvan Studio, NY.
Jacket photo of the author credit: Miri Ben-Shalom.

This Springer imprint is published by the registered company Springer Nature Switzerland AG
The registered company address is: Gewerbestrasse 11, 6330 Cham, Switzerland

Dedicated to my longtime friend, colleague, and mentor
B. Gopinath

Preface

I have written this book for people who want to know what to do with the money they save: so that it's there when they need it (to buy a home, pay for college, etc.), but also grows enough so they don't outlive it.

Although the book is written to be accessible to those with little or no prior knowledge of finance, the studies and conclusions presented here can benefit a multitude of investors who may consider themselves financially sophisticated, but never have bothered to sanity-check their basic investment assumptions. *Unfortunately, much mainstream financial advice is simply incorrect.*

The investment industry spins self-serving yarns. Foremost among them is that engaging with financial advisors and investing in actively managed funds will increase your wealth beyond what you could do on your own.

The industry is fixated on the importance of maintaining a "balance" (some chosen ratio) of stocks and bonds, shifting to more bonds as one ages. In fact, what's important is to have just enough bonds and cash to support spending needs from a stable source, and to replenish these through the sale of stocks at propitious times (when the stock market is not depressed). This is a central point of the book.

In contrast to the industry advice, this leads to a "balance" of stocks and bonds that is dynamically changing, in response to spending and market conditions. In fact, it's common sense that stock holdings should be maximized, beyond spending needs, on account of their better return, while spending should come from more stable assets (bonds and cash) in order to avoid the unrecoverable loss from selling depressed stocks—a loss that can be counterproductively forced by the industry standard to maintain a chosen balance. This industry standard also will degrade portfolio growth when stocks

viii   Preface

(depressed or not) are sold to cover regular expenses (a largely overlooked issue).

The investment industry touts investments like annuities and, for the US investor, rollovers to Roth IRAs, without providing accurate measures of their possible benefits—and often there are none, except to the brokers.

Industry fairy tales come in place of cogent analysis, delivering intuitively plausible advice that happens to be wrong. This includes the common advice on how best to use tax-advantaged funds: "bonds in tax-advantaged, stocks not." The reality is more complicated, and at least for the US investor, the best solution by far involves putting stocks in an IRA, rolled over to a Roth, as a simple calculation shows. This opportunity apparently has been completely overlooked by the investment industry.

They get it completely wrong when advising to preserve the benefits of tax-advantaged funds by drawing them down last. Another simple calculation shows that the correct rule is to draw down last the investment giving the best returns, irrespective of whether it is tax-advantaged, while retaining enough bonds and cash to cover expenses. They tout dollar cost averaging, while widely available research shows that it's disadvantageous.

The banking industry has created a fog of confusion over interest rates (APR, APY, IRR, ...). This is easy to clarify once one understands the definitions. While it is tempting to accuse the banks of intentional deception, and that may be a part of it, a level of cluelessness also seems apparent. As I show, they simply may have confused themselves.

This book is a compilation of cogent information from published sources together with conclusions based on simple calculations. It derives from my investigations after I retired on how best to manage my own finances. With a degree in mathematics, I had no preconceived notions, no axe to grind and, frankly, little knowledge of or interest in finance. I wish I had bothered to look into these issues long before—I'd be wealthier if I had.

I spent most of my career at Bell Labs, where I worked in the Mathematics Research Center. While there, I took leaves to teach (at The Technion, U.C. Berkeley and NYU). In my research, I developed a mathematical model for which I received two awards. It now is used commercially to check the correctness of integrated circuits. Related to that model, I am the inventor on a number of patents.

During my career, I never gave much thought to finance. My attitude toward money was: earn, save, spend. Before I retired, I made a rough calculation to see if with the money I had saved, I could afford to retire, and concluded that I could. As I later figured out that calculation was based on bogus assumptions, and in the end I was just lucky, saved by the recent big market up-swing.

Only in retirement, with no more salary, did I finally decide to take a closer look at managing my finances. I began to realize that it wasn't so simple. I spent months simply to understand the rudiments of how best to manage my investments while drawing on them for expenses; also learned: how to optimize Social Security, and how to handle healthcare.

My first realization was that since my investments would be fluctuating in value, if I made a withdrawal when the markets are "down," it constitutes a larger proportion of my savings than the same withdrawal when the markets are "up." Although the general market trend is "up," in the face of regular withdrawals, the "ups" fail to counterbalance the "downs" (the relationship is non-linear). Hence, periodic drawdowns from a volatile investment degrade its nominal growth rate—something to be avoided. Thus, *how* I managed drawdowns of savings for expenses would be important.

The industry recommendation to maintain a balance of stocks and bonds not only doesn't address this, but can be counterproductive, as already mentioned. However, the alternative mentioned above provides a more fruitful and possibly new way to manage savings in retirement. While consistent with mainstream microeconomic analysis, this strategy has not been made explicit in print, that I could find.

Drawing expenses from bonds and cash, back-filled from stocks at propitious times, the prime investment question becomes not what to invest in, not even in what proportion to hold stocks and bonds, but how far in advance to prepare to shift funds from stocks to bonds and cash.

Personal finance has not generally been subject to rigorous analysis. Instead, it is guided by "common wisdom" and financial nostrums that too often, when analyzed mathematically, turn out to be wrong.

Much of what is wrongly reported is known correctly by some, but their voices go largely unheard. In seeking answers, I became dismayed by professional advice, too often patently nonsensical, self-serving, and ignorant. Searching for sound published advice proved fruitful, but it was tedious and laborious to separate out the nonsense.

So, this book is a sharing of my discoveries, to save the reader the need to repeat my tedious learning process—or worse, to retire without understanding that there *are* issues, and pay a price of a shorter supportable retirement.

You might think it's all just not worth the bother, and for a bit of money lost to fees, you'll just put it all in the hands of your trusty financial advisor. About this I warn: that's like lunching with an alligator. Those small fees compound and after a number of years can represent a very substantial loss. But what is

x   Preface

even worse, that expert financial advice often is wrong (for you—self-serving for your advisor). That can cost you much more than the lost fees. I know this is a brash claim, and I devote Chap. 1 to making this case. You and the alligator have different views of what's for lunch.

Chapter 1 considers the value of an investment advisor and managed funds in general, as well as various ways that investors seek to "beat the market." Given that, Chap. 2 considers what are the best all-around investments for most people.

Risk is an inescapable component of investment, just as it is in every walk of life (including crossing the street). How to assess and manage risk in investment is addressed in Chap. 3.

If you lack the time or interest to follow the detailed guidelines given in this book, at least do this: keep enough cash in a money market fund to cover anticipated expenses for the next few years, with the rest of your savings in a broadly diversified stock index fund. Then, when it comes time to pay for the expenses, pay from the money market fund if the stock price is depressed, else pay from the stock fund. From time to time, when the stock fund value is near an all-time high, replenish the money market fund from the stock fund. Following this seemingly self-evident advice at least will save you from the counterproductive, portfolio-degrading investment industry advice to maintain a fixed balance of stocks and bonds. How best to do this is explained in Chaps. 4–5: Chap. 4 describes how to tune one's holdings in bonds and cash to near-term expenses; and Chap. 5 explains how to calculate when to replenish this fund. A simple method to calculate one's expenses—non-discretionary and discretionary—is given in Chap. 6.

One way to mediate risk is through insurance. However, there are limits to how much one should be willing to pay, in order to reduce various risks. How to assess the cost-effectiveness of insurance is discussed in Chap. 7.

Even if you have done perfectly with your investments, if someone robs you, it can have the same effect as having done poorly. Some simple measures to safeguard assets are described in Chap. 8.

A number of general investment issues such as the importance of avoiding high fees; the cost of discretionary spending from depressed equity; the value of a mortgage, even if you don't think you need one; and dollar cost averaging are covered in Chap. 9.

Chapter 10 shows how to answer the question "Can I afford to retire?"

Chapter 11 covers investment issues that are particular to retirement, including the degradation inherent in a regularly drawn down volatile investment (an issue that apparently has been overlooked by the investment industry) and tailoring for retirement the strategy for covering expenses with *fixed income*

Preface xi

investments described in Chaps. 4–5. Other retirement issues are addressed here as well, including the notorious "4% rule" and what to do if savings become insufficient.

The essential conclusions of this book are independent of tax laws and other government regulations, applying to all investors internationally. In addition, I have added considerations that are specific to the US investor, in Chaps. 12–18. The issues and calculations given there may apply to other jurisdictions as well, but with varying specific details.

For the US investor, the issue of how best to manage tax-advantaged accounts like 401(k)s and IRAs, pre-retirement is covered in Chap. 12, and post-retirement in Chap. 13. Chapter 14 looks at tax relief for education and charitable contributions. Chapter 15 covers optimizing Social Security.

Important US healthcare considerations, both before and after retirement, are discussed in Chap. 16.

Pension concerns such as "Will I receive my full pension?" depend in large part on your workplace sector. Most (but not all) private sector pensions tend to be in good shape, while the opposite is true of many public sector pensions. Your risks and protections are described in Chap. 17, as well as how to decide whether to accept a pension buy-out offer.

General funding for retirement is in crisis in the USA. How we got there and what can be done is discussed in Chap. 18.

Finally, in an extended Appendix, the simple (high school level) math is derived that is needed for the various conclusions based on calculations that are presented in the book. It covers how to calculate the value and yield of bonds and bond ladders; how to evaluate a mortgage, annuities, and the buyout value of a pension; and how to compute the amount needed to be set aside in savings to compensate for inflation, payouts from pensions, annuities, and the like that do not adjust for cost of living.

All claims in this book that are not supported directly by market data or external studies are justified through elementary mathematical calculations. While these involve no more than a high school level of math, many readers may consider them tedious. Therefore, I have isolated them in subsections titled "*let's do the calculation*" that may be skipped by those willing to accept the claims that precede them.

And now, the lawyerism: nothing in this book should be construed as legal or financial advice (!). While every effort has been made to portray facts accurately, in the end, what is presented here is only the personal opinion of the author, which is not represented as being necessarily factually accurate (although the author has made every effort within his ability to assure that all is accurate). Government rules and regulations that may have been true

xii   Preface

at the time of writing, could change. Therefore, before acting on any advice conveyed in this book, it is the reader's responsibility to decide if the advice is accurate, relevant, and useful. The author hereby disavows any responsibility for readers' actions that may have been influenced by reading this book. (But if you save a bundle and credit the book, the author may not reject donations given in gratitude!)

New York, NY, USA   R. P. Kurshan

Acknowledgments

I thank Olivier Humblet, Tom Kramer, Peri Kurshan, Tom Liptay, and Rick Van Ness for their very helpful feedback.

The daily price data of the S&P 500 are taken from *Yahoo!* Finance (*finance.yahoo.com/q/hp*), S&P 500 dividend data from an invaluable data set compiled and posted by Robert Shiller,[1] filled in by readily available recent data. Daily yield data for 10-year U. S. Treasury constant maturity rates are taken from the Federal Reserve (FRED 2015a) and priced using Robert Shiller's methodology (Shiller 2015), calculated through a calculator maintained by DQYDJ.[2] The Federal Funds Rate data was taken from FRED (2015b) (from 1950 to June 1954, the Federal Funds Rate was not defined, and in its place, the Federal Discount Rate was used, which it closely approximates).

Statistical computations and resulting plots were made using R from The R Foundation for Statistical Computing.

The artwork depicted on the front cover is by Tom Otterness. Photo credit: Katvan Studio, NY.

Credits for portrait photos are as follows: Mayer Rothschild–Elbert Hubbard; Daniel Kahneman–Johan Mackenbach; John Bogle–The Vanguard Group, Inc., used with permission; Warren Buffett–Shuji Kajiyama/AP; Andy Tobias–Victor Jeffreys II; Leonhard Euler–Jakob Emanuel Handmann; Ron Lieber–with permission of Ron Lieber; William Sharpe–Larry D. Moore CC BY-SA 3.0; Paul Samuelson–Innovation & Business Architectures, Inc.; James Simons–Gert-Martin Greuel, Cropped version of image from

---

[1] econ.yale.edu/~shiller/data.htm.

[2] dqydj.net/treasury-return-calculator/.

xiv   Acknowledgments

Oberwolfach Photo Collection, CC BY-SA 2.0 de; Søren Kierkegaard–sketch by Niels Christian Kierkegaard; Robert Merton–Massachusetts Institute of Technology; Joshua Slocum–Hollinger Co; Nassim Taleb–Nassim Nicholas Taleb; John von Neumann–Los Alamos National Laboratory; Edward Thorp–Mark Jordan, with permission of Edward Thorp; Scott Walker–Gage Skidmore; William Bengen–with permission of William Bengen; and Euclid-twentieth-century statue by Joseph Durham in the Oxford University Museum of Natural History.

Contents

1 How to Get Richer — 1
- 1.1 Exploiting Market Inefficiencies — 2
- 1.2 Newsletter Advice — 6
- 1.3 Andy Tobias' Veal Parmesan — 7
- 1.4 Actively Managed Funds — 7
- 1.5 Research on Active Management — 9
- 1.6 Persistence — 14
  - 1.6.1 Can Anyone Consistently "Beat the Market"? — 16
  - 1.6.2 Vanguard Persistence Study — 18
- 1.7 Claims of "Outperforming" Funds — 19
- 1.8 How to Underperform — 23
  - 1.8.1 Market Timing — 23
  - 1.8.2 Stock Picking — 25

2 Deciding What to Invest In — 27
- 2.1 Investing for Earmarked Expenses — 28
- 2.2 Stocks — 29
- 2.3 Bonds — 30
  - 2.3.1 Bond Types, Terminology, and Considerations — 31
  - 2.3.2 Yield Curve Inversion — 36
  - 2.3.3 Bond Ladders — 36
- 2.4 Stocks vs. Bonds — 39
- 2.5 What Domestic/Non-domestic Balance Is Best? — 40

xvi   Contents

2.6		Index Funds	41
	2.6.1	Vanguard Index Fund Study	42
	2.6.2	Value of Index Funds Is Consistent with Research	43
2.7		ETFs or Mutual Funds?	44
	2.7.1	Setting Up a Limit Order	45
2.8		CDs	46
2.9		And Then There's Cash	46
2.10		Annuities	49
	2.10.1	Variable Rate Annuity	50
	2.10.2	Fixed Rate Annuity	51
	2.10.3	Risk of Default	53
	2.10.4	Annuities for Portfolio Diversification?	54
	2.10.5	Evaluating an Annuity	55
	2.10.6	Annuities Are Expensive!	56
2.11		Real Estate	58
2.12		Are Solar Panels a Good Investment?	63
2.13		Finally, Some Specific Advice	64
3		**Understanding Risk**	**67**
3.1		Risk vs. Uncertainty	68
3.2		Managing Risks	69
3.3		Sharpe Ratio	72
3.4		Expected vs. Worst-Case Return	73
	3.4.1	Expected Return	73
	3.4.2	A Worse Worst Case	74
	3.4.3	Extreme Worst Case	74
	3.4.4	Samuelson Example	75
	3.4.5	Powerball	81
3.5		Maximize Expected Portfolio Longevity: Is That Enough?	81
3.6		Does Stock Risk Diminish with Time Held?	82
3.7		Risk Aversion	84
	3.7.1	Reverse Engineering to Find Its Meaning	85
	3.7.2	Another Possible Meaning	86
	3.7.3	Economists Optimize Risk-Reward Tradeoff	87
	3.7.4	The Goal of Financial Planning	89
3.8		Liquidity Risk	90

		Contents	xvii

4 How Much to Hold in Fixed Income Investments? — 93

4.1	Stability vs. Growth	96
4.2	Fixed Income Buffer as Shock Absorber	102
4.3	Funding Schooling (and the Like)	105
4.4	Buying or Repairing a Home	107
4.5	How About an Emergency?	107
4.6	Saving for Retirement	109
4.6.1	Front-Loading Discretionary Spending	110
4.6.2	Back-Loading Discretionary Spending	111
4.6.3	Hold Enough in Fixed Income Investments at the Start	112
4.7	Investment Industry Recommendations	113
4.8	Target-Date Funds	115

5 When to Exchange Equity for Fixed Income Investments — 117

5.1	Historic Lengths of Market Downturns	120
5.2	Times Between Market All-Time Highs	122
5.3	Shortfall Exchanging Stocks for Bonds	125
5.4	Optimal Transition Window Length	126
5.4.1	Catching the Trigger Condition	133
5.4.2	Decreasing Expense Allocation	134

6 Calculating Spending — 137

6.1	Calculating Spending Needs	138
6.2	Recurring Non-discretionary Expenses	141
6.3	Recurring Discretionary Expenses	143
6.4	One-Time Expenses	144
6.5	Tallying the Expenses	144

7 Insurance Mediates Risk — 147

7.1	Protection from Catastrophic Loss	147
7.2	Making Insurance Cost-Effective	150
7.3	Longevity Insurance	150
7.4	Life Insurance	151
7.4.1	Term Life Insurance	151
7.4.2	Whole Life Insurance	152
7.4.3	Write Your Will!	152

xviii   Contents

	7.5	Health-Related Insurance in the United States	153
		7.5.1 Medical Insurance	153
		7.5.2 Long-Term Care Insurance	154
		7.5.3 Disability Insurance	156
	7.6	Summary	156

8 Fraud Deterrence 159

8.1	In the United States, Freeze Your Credit Reports!	159
8.2	Strong Passwords?	162
8.3	Frequently Change Passwords?	163
8.4	Two-Factor Authentication?	164
8.5	In the United States, IRS Identity Protection	165
8.6	Sadly, You're on Your Own	166
8.7	And Then There's Robocalls…	169
8.8	In the End…	169

9 General Investment Issues 171

9.1	Make a Budget	171
9.2	Fees	172
9.3	Let's Buy a Boat	174
9.4	Pay Off a Mortgage Early? Pay All Cash?	175
9.5	Is Dollar Cost Averaging a Good Idea?	177
9.6	Don't Buy a Dividend or Coupon	179
9.7	Stocks and Bonds Often Move Inversely	180
9.8	Rebalancing	180

10 Can I Afford to Retire? 183

11 Investments After Retirement 187

11.1	Regularly Drawn Volatile Savings		188
	11.1.1	Degradation	189
	11.1.2	The Math of Degradation	192
	11.1.3	Market Example of Degradation	194
	11.1.4	Degradation Seen with a Commercial Market Forecaster	196
11.2	Retirement Portfolio Shock Absorber		198
11.3	Retirement Discretionary Spending		202
11.4	The 4% Rule		202
	11.4.1	Is the Rule Reliable? Useful?	203
	11.4.2	Some Famous Economists Weigh in	204

11.5	Will Your Taxes Decrease in Retirement?		208
11.6	Most Important: Monitor Your Spending		209
11.7	If Savings Becomes Insufficient		210
	11.7.1	Earning Money in Retirement	212
	11.7.2	Move to Less Expensive Housing	213
	11.7.3	Decreasing the Retirement Period	217

For the U.S. Investor

219

12 Pre-retirement Investment

221

12.1	Traditional 401(k) Plans	222
12.2	Roth 401(k)	223
12.3	IRAs	224
12.4	401(k)/IRA Regulations Worth Knowing	226
12.5	Roth IRA	227
12.6	Deferred Compensation	230
12.7	Federal Taxation	230
12.8	Tax-Deferred vs. Ordinary Investment	234
12.9	Roth vs. Ordinary Investment	238
12.10	Traditional 401(k) or IRA vs. Roth	239
12.11	Rollovers	242
12.12	Bonds Go in an IRA, Equity Doesn't?	244
12.13	"Swap" Tax-Advantaged and Ordinary	247
12.14	Actively Traded Equities Go in an IRA?	247

13 Tax-Advantaged Savings in Retirement

249

13.1	RMD	250
13.2	Roll over a Traditional IRA to a Roth?	252
13.3	What to Keep Where	253
13.4	What Account to Draw First	253

14 Tax Relief for Education and Gifts

255

14.1	529 Education Fund	255
14.2	Charitable Contributions	258

15 Optimizing Social Security

261

15.1	Deciding When to Start	262
15.2	Deferring Benefits	262
15.3	Reversing a Benefit Election	263

xx   Contents

15.4	Divorcee Benefit	264
15.5	Goodbye to "File and Suspend"	264
15.6	How Much Social Security Benefit Is Taxed?	265
15.7	COLAs	265
15.8	Is Social Security Going Broke?	265

16 Healthcare   269

16.1	Before Retirement	270
16.2	After Retirement	272
16.3	Medicare	273
	16.3.1 Deadlines: Important!!	275
	16.3.2 Choices	276
	16.3.3 IRMAAs	277
16.4	Dental? Vision?	278
16.5	Long-Term Care Ratings and Rates	278

17 Pensions   281

17.1	Workplace Sectors	284
17.2	Private Sector Pensions	287
	17.2.1 Single-Employer Plans	287
	17.2.2 Multi-Employer Plans	289
	17.2.3 The Pension Benefit Guaranty Corporation	292
	17.2.4 Uninsured Benefits	295
	17.2.5 Single-Employer Pension Fund Termination	295
	17.2.6 Multi-Employer Pension Fund Termination	298
	17.2.7 How to Find Out if Your Pension Plan is Underfunded	299
	17.2.8 The PBGC Itself is in Trouble	302
	17.2.9 Should You Take a Pension Buyout Offer?	303
17.3	Public Sector Pensions	307

18 The Looming Retirement Crisis   313

Appendix A   Some Simple Math   319

A.1	Zero-Coupon Bonds	319
A.2	Straight Bonds	321
A.3	Geometric Series	322
A.4	Pricing Straight Bonds	324

| | | Contents | xxi |

	A.4.1	Coupons Issuing More Frequently than Annually	325
	A.4.2	Financiers' Interest Rate Confusion	326
	A.4.3	Calculating Bond Price Between Coupons	328
	A.4.4	Computing Yield, Given Price	330
A.5	Mortgages		331
A.6	Drawing Down a Savings Bank Account		334
A.7	Bond Ladders		335
	A.7.1	Building a Zero-Coupon Bond Ladder	335
	A.7.2	Building a General Bond Ladder	338
A.8	Preferred Stock		338
A.9	Annuities		339
	A.9.1	Computing the Value of an Immediate Annuity	339
	A.9.2	Computing the Value of a Deferred Annuity	344
A.10	Inflation Compensation for Flat Payouts		345
A.11	Buyout Value of a U.S. Pension		347

References 351

Index 355

1

How to Get Richer

The best way to get richer is to be already very, very rich, say with $1 billion in disposable cash. Then you might invest in an ultra-high-speed fiber link from New York to Chicago, beating out the existing links by a millisecond, and deterministically reap as much money as you can push through the system, trading on commodity price differences between the two locations.

If that's too much trouble, you can just take over an underpriced, poorly managed company in an area in which you happen to be an expert and, by running it better, turn a nice profit.

Or, if you've forgotten how to do real work yourself, just hire a team of quants to dream up esoteric speculative algorithms to ferret out market inefficiencies for you (Sect. 1.1).

If you're merely very rich, say with $100 million to flash at your bank, you can get them to install a computerized trading system on which you can run your own simple trading algorithms to troll for minute market timing inefficiencies and trade on them.

But if you have a mere $10 million in wealth, then you're in league with all the rest of us, who have much less. In this case, your best bet is simply to invest in the financial markets as a whole. This is best done through low-fee diversified index funds, especially ones that track the S&P 500 or even broader "total" stock funds that are indexed to a larger class of U.S. and/or foreign stocks, as well as classes of bond index funds (intermediate-term is a favorite class) that invest mostly in "risk-free" U.S. Treasury bonds along with some top-grade commercial bonds.

The rest of this chapter is devoted to justifying these claims.

© The Author(s), under exclusive license to Springer Nature Switzerland AG 2022
R. P. Kurshan, *Investment Industry Claims Debunked*,
https://doi.org/10.1007/978-3-030-76709-9_1

1.1 Exploiting Market Inefficiencies

A financial market is said to be *efficient* if its prices reflect all available information. A Nobel Prize was awarded to Eugene Fama for work related to his *efficient market hypothesis*[1] that a typical investor cannot outperform a market because any market inefficiencies quickly are erased through *arbitrage*—simultaneous buying and selling of assets that reflect differing information and thus different prices. However, the hypothesis does not preclude the possibility of exploiting inefficiencies before they disappear. If momentary inefficiencies are ubiquitous, then so are arbitrage opportunities to the first to discover them.

Mayer Rothschild c1775

Moreover, the efficient market hypothesis itself applies less and less as technological advances provide the capability to ferret out insights hidden from the general marketplace, for those with the resources to pay for them. An example of how such technologies can be used to private advantage is given by The New York Times:[2] "Foursquare received much attention in 2016 after using its data trove to predict that after an E. coli crisis, Chipotle's sales would drop by 30% in the coming months. Its same-store sales ultimately fell 29.7%." Although this example may not have been used to private advantage, it clearly shows the potential.

Financial legends of the past succeeded by treading where no man before had gone, like Mayer Rothschild, credited with establishing international finance and J.P. Morgan credited with organizing American business through

---

[1] Fama (1970).
[2] nytimes.com/interactive/2019/12/19/opinion/location-tracking-cell-phone.html.

strategic mergers. Both became fabulously wealthy through their exploits. Warren Buffett is a legend on account of his early successes in turning around inefficiently run companies and later just buying great businesses with great management and staying out of the way.

Edward Thorp

However, there is another type of financial wizard more comprehensible on account of operating single-handedly, picking up financial nuggets—market inefficiencies—overlooked by the rest. Unlike the others, we can almost imagine ourselves achieving some prowess in this direction. Edward O. Thorp, the inventor of the algorithm to beat blackjack through card-counting (and other casino-beating wonders including exploiting minute biases in the balance of roulette wheels), was able to spot market inefficiencies without an internet connection (there was no internet-connected market back then). Most famously, he discovered and exploited market inefficiencies in—don't worry about what these are—warrants, options (before Black-Scholes[3] said how to price these), futures contracts, and convertible securities. Through his acumen, he managed to reap millions before the rest of the world caught on. He said he kept his options pricing formula secret to maximize what he could earn from mis-pricing, before others figured it out.[4]

---

[3] This is a 1973 Nobel Prize-winning option pricing model that followed Thorp's market exploitations by 6 years.
[4] Poundstone (2006).

James Simons 2007

James Simons, no less brilliant, if lesser known, and unquestionably more wealthy, established the most consistently successful fund (see Sect. 1.6.1) by applying algorithms to search for market inefficiencies.[5] The fund is fueled by an army of mathematicians, physicists, statisticians, and computer scientists, who use their prowess to continually invent new ways to find and mine the inefficiencies. However, since the effort doesn't scale, the fund is open only to the employees and owners.

Another form of "market inefficiency" (and a new perspective on the concept) is the increasingly popular move by hedge funds to look for inequities in the marketplace that result from specific actions by a company believed to be involved in an illegality or tort[6] and then to bet against the value of that company's stock (by selling it short[7]). Once the bet is placed, then the bettor may release information to the press about the suspected illegal activity or hire a team of lawyers to pursue the company through a class action lawsuit against a tort, each of which, by themselves, before any final determination of guilt or culpability, may result in a drop in the price of the company's stock and a profit for the short seller.[8]

While some have argued that this practice serves a salutary purpose of punishing illegal activity, an analogous strategy applied to debt may be harder to justify. This is where the hedge fund buys some debt from a troubled company and then covers that liability with credit default swaps in amounts that far exceed the debt liability. They effectively over-insure against loss of

---

[5] The algorithms were developed not only by James Simons, who was a famous mathematician (a geometer and former code breaker) before he was attracted to finance, but also by algebraists Leonard Baum and James Ax and algebraic coding theorist Elwyn Berlekamp (a former colleague of mine at Bell Labs).

[6] A *tort* is an infringement of rights that produces a civil legal liability.

[7] A common practice whereby shares of a stock are "borrowed" and then sold at the current market price, with the expectation that when it becomes time to pay back the borrowed shares, the price will be lower, resulting in a profit of the price difference.

[8] wsj.com/articles/hedge-fund-managers-next-frontier-lawsuits-1425940706, also bloomberg.com/news/articles/2015-03-18/hedge-fund-betting-on-lawsuits-is-spreading.

1 How to Get Richer 5

the debt. Then they take actions that seek to force the troubled company into bankruptcy, enabling the hedge fund to collect on the swaps.[9]

Finally, there are stock traders who discover profitable ways to exploit tax loopholes and technical deficiencies in electronic payment systems. The most notorious example is the European states' $80 billion loss to *cum-ex* trading.[10] Through clever timing and manipulation of associated electronic payment systems, one allowed tax refund is converted into two. Presently, its legality is being hotly contested in European courts. During its reign (2006–2011), hundreds of bankers and investors, including many Americans, participated in the scheme, which state prosecutors have characterized as a form of organized crime. However, the perpetrators claim it was entirely legal, the fault lying with poorly written lax laws and inadequately controlled refund mechanisms that supported the scheme.

So, what's left for the rest of us? Some enjoy gambling, even knowing it's a losing proposition. Others mistake gambling luck for skill.[11] Some believe that by "studying" the performance of a company or, even more broadly, a "trend" across the entire market, that they can discover a secret missed by everyone else. That allows them to pick "a winner" or to know when is a better than average time to buy or sell. Studies have shown how counterproductive such exploits tend to be (Sect. 1.8). Even a CEO has a hard time predicting where his (or, occasionally, her) own company is headed, accounting for frequent disappointing quarterly earnings reports. But the fact that among any collection of gamblers there always are some winners engenders the fallacy that if I try hard enough, "I too" may become a winner. Losses are taken simply as motivation to keep trying harder.

William Poundstone[12] recounts a 1984 speech by Warren Buffett, in which he asks his listeners to imagine that Americans have paired off and each pair bets $1 on the outcome of a coin toss. The winners then pair off and bet their combined winnings—$2—on another toss. And so on, in each round, the bettors betting the combined winnings from the previous round. After 20 tosses, 215 people will be left, each with over a million dollars in winnings. Some of these winners, Buffett said, will write books on their "methods:" *How I Turned a Dollar into a Million*, deriding the theorists who said "winning 20 consecutive even-odds bets is virtually impossible."

---

[9] nytimes.com/2019/03/18/opinion/wall-street-risk-debt.html.

[10] nytimes.com/2020/01/23/business/cum-ex.html.

[11] nytimes.com/2019/04/05/business/investing-risk-in-retirement.html.

[12] Poundstone (2006).

1.2 Newsletter Advice

One study that analyzed the advice in 237 investment newsletters has shown that over 75% gave advice that produced negative returns.[13] That study cited a 1994 article by John R. Graham and Campbell R. Harvey that stated "For example, the (once) high profile Granville Market Letter-Traders produced an average annual loss of 5.4% over the last 13 years. This compares to a 15.9% average annual gain on the Standard & Poor's 500-stock index."

The same study cited a 2012 Morningstar analysis of tactical asset allocation funds that concluded that on the average they performed more poorly and at higher cost than a simple low-fee Vanguard index fund. Warren Buffett is quoted as saying "The only value of stock forecasters is to make fortunetellers look good." Other quotes included in the study include: "A decade of results throws cold water on the notion that strategists exhibit any special ability to time the markets" (The Wall Street Journal) and "Far more money has been lost by investors preparing for corrections, or trying to anticipate corrections, than has been lost in corrections themselves" (Peter Lynch, long time manager of the Magellan Fund at Fidelity Investments).

Jeff Sommer of The New York Times has been compiling statistical studies of stock market forecasts for years. His continued conclusion: "many Wall Street strategists are flagrantly inaccurate. ... The more specific forecasts—like how high or low the market will go in a given year, and whether it will lose half of its value or rise 30%—should be treated as fiction".[14]

The AAII (American Association of Individual Investors) is essentially a newsletter that claims "investment returns that are consistently higher than those of the stock market as a whole." This claim has been met with some ridicule,[15,16] together with "compliments" for the business behind the newsletter, for making a handsome profit without concrete evidence of providing any actual consistent value.

---

[13] nytimes.com/2014/01/28/your-money/forget-market-timing-and-stick-to-a-balanced-fund.html = tinyurl.com/y9c3y3u6.

[14] nytimes.com/2019/12/23/business/retirement/index-fund-investing.html.

[15] mymoneyblog.com/american-association-of-individual-investors-aaii-the-numbers-behind-the-non-profit.html = tinyurl.com/yb2to4k6.

[16] henrywirth.com/LIESandSTATISTICS.html = tinyurl.com/ybfxwo77.

1.3 Andy Tobias' Veal Parmesan

The famous investment guru Andy Tobias wrote: "The odd thing about investing—the frustrating thing—is that it is not like cooking or playing chess or much of anything else. The more cookbooks you read and pot roasts you prepare, the better the cook—within limits—you are likely to become. The more chess books you read and the gambits you learn, the more opponents—within limits—you are likely to outwit. But when it comes to investing, all these ordinarily admirable attributes—trying hard, learning a lot, becoming intrigued—may be of little help, or actually work against you. It has been amply demonstrated …that a monkey with a handful of darts will do about as well at choosing stocks as most highly paid professional money managers. Show me the monkey that can make a decent veal parmesan."[17] To which the Nobel Prize-winning Daniel Kahneman added: "Many individual investors lose consistently by trading, an achievement that a dart-throwing chimp could not match."[18]

Andy Tobias 2016

1.4 Actively Managed Funds

The performance of an actively managed fund generally is measured relative to a target benchmark, say, the S&P 500, or the Russell 2000 small-cap index, for example. The benchmark is a target the fund is meant to *outperform*, stated in the fund's prospectus. (In finance lingo, the extent to which it outperforms

---

[17] Tobias (2016).
[18] Kahneman (2011).

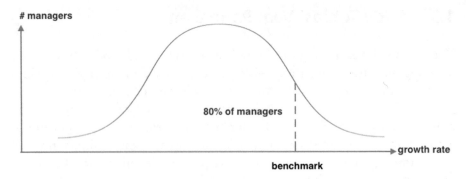

Fig. 1.1 Active fund manager performance net fees. For fund managers who seek to outperform a given benchmark, the plot shows the predicted shape of the function that gives, for each average annual growth rate, the number of fund managers who achieve that rate, net their fees. Most fail their goal—those to the left of the "benchmark" line, although some succeed, a few by a lot—those on the right end "tail").

is called the fund's *alpha*. And while we're in lingo-land, its *beta* is a measure of its volatility. This is related to its risk of doing poorly, a factor that offsets its measure of performance.[19])

The point of Warren Buffett's bettors tale (Sect. 1.1) is that an event that may seem very unlikely from one perspective can in fact be inevitable or highly likely. With a million monkey-propelled darts, it's actually highly unlikely that none hit the bulls eye. Likewise, with so many funds out there, it's highly unlikely that a few won't outperform ("beat the market"), even by a lot, in a given year. Likewise, it's highly unlikely that of those that do, a few won't do so for a number of successive years. Which ones will be the winners, though, despite media-fueled ballyhoo, is essentially unpredictable (Sect. 1.5). And the few exceptions, as mentioned, aren't available to us common folks. Just think: if they were, then everyone would invest in them, leaving no one to beat, driving to zero their advantages.

Without analyzing a single fund, this story can be told in simple probabilistic terms. Figure 1.1 shows the average annual performance in terms of fund growth rate, net fees, for fund managers who seek to outperform the growth rate of some given benchmark. While a few succeed—the ones to the right of the dashed line—most fail. In fact, for some benchmarks, a staggering 80% fail, and this is similar, more or less, for all benchmarks, as we'll see in Sect. 1.5 (Figs. 1.3 and 1.4 give the details.)

---

[19] Bodie and Merton (2000), Malkiel (2015).

For the active managers, if they worked for free and their performance were random, on account of general market efficiency, half would be expected to outperform their benchmark, and half to underperform since the benchmark represents the average of the chosen market segment.

But, active fund managers and, more generally, financial advisors[20] make their money off the fees they charge their investors. And these fees are structured like "heads I win, tails you lose" bets: they get their fees (your money) no matter how your investment has fared. Pretty sweet deal! They don't need a successful strategy to beat the market; they only need a successful strategy to make their clients think they have one. Once their fees are added, they shift the distribution to the left as shown, with most underperforming. Recently undercut consumer protections "enable financial advisers to resume recommending products that yield high commissions for them while exposing retirees to risk",[21] so poor financial advice is not always merely hapless.

What about persistence? Some managers will do well for a year or two simply by chance. But, if a manager outperforms the target benchmark year after year, must that be a sign that the manager really has something going? No. Again, simply on probabilistic terms, while it's very unlikely that a *particular* manager will exhibit long-term superior performance, similar to Buffett's bettors, it's extremely *likely* that *some* managers will, as illustrated in Fig. 1.2. More on this in Sect. 1.6.

1.5 Research on Active Management

The research is unequivocal: most managed funds underperform their market benchmarks. As many as 80% or more of managed funds underperform their benchmarks after fees are assessed (it doesn't matter how much they gross before fees, but even gross, they mostly underperform their benchmarks, which is a perverse feat worth noting).

Each year, S&P releases their SPIVA (S&P Indices Versus Active) scorecard that gives the percentage of actively managed U.S. funds that are outperformed by their target benchmarks, net fees, for a variety of "styles": the benchmark that the fund is targeted to outperform. The general story is quite consistent from year to year, although some narrower sectors go in and out of favor in

---

[20] Michael Kitces observed that despite the 1940 Investment Advisers Act, today "advisor" is the more common spelling.

[21] newyorker.com/magazine/2020/10/26/trumps-labor-secretary-is-a-wrecking-ball-aimed-at-workers = tinyurl.com/y244v95h.

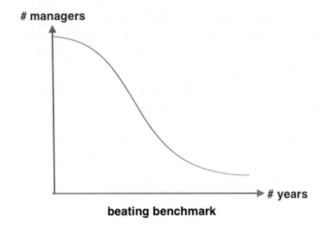

Fig. 1.2 Active fund manager persistence. Of those from Fig. 1.1 who outperform their benchmark, this graph shows that the number expected to persist in outperforming in successive years grows smaller with each successive year and, in practice, vanishes after about a decade.

terms of how well the managed funds perform in them (these ups and downs are said to be random, and the SPIVA scorecard report warns against assuming that a narrow sector that outperformed its benchmark is a good bet). The reports for 2015 for managed equity (stock) and fixed income (mostly bond) funds are given in Figs. 1.3 and 1.4, respectively. They're sobering. The reports are largely the same, year after year.

By contrast, for a ("passively" managed[22]) index fund (Sect. 2.6), its performance is expected to *track* some index. This is usually achieved in large part by buying a cross section of the securities that the index tracks. Thus, it is not expected to outperform the index it tracks. The extent to which it underperforms the index could be a result of poor management but, more than anything else, is a result of the fees the fund charges. Why, you might well ask, would anyone invest in an actively managed fund over an index fund?

---

[22] The terms "actively managed" and "passively managed" are misnomers, as both types of funds are actively managed, just differently. As Vanguard has explained, "indexing strategies use quantitative risk-control techniques that seek to replicate the benchmark's return with minimal expected deviations." An index fund manager may hold a broad cross section of the target market, changing over time, and may even invest (usually only a small proportion) in unrelated products like derivatives.

1 How to Get Richer 11

Report 1: Percentage of U.S. Equity Funds Outperformed by Benchmarks					
Fund Category	Comparison Index	One-Year (%)	Three-Year (%)	Five-Year (%)	Ten-Year (%)
All Domestic Equity Funds	S&P Composite 1500	74.81	80.85	88.43	83.18
All Large-Cap Funds	S&P 500	66.11	75.81	84.15	82.14
All Mid-Cap Funds	S&P MidCap 400	56.81	61.64	76.69	87.61
All Small-Cap Funds	S&P SmallCap 600	72.20	81.73	90.13	88.42
All Multi-Cap Funds	S&P Composite 1500	73.64	79.61	88.56	88.32
Large-Cap Growth Funds	S&P 500 Growth	49.30	76.34	86.54	93.63
Large-Cap Core Funds	S&P 500	73.82	83.70	88.26	82.84
Large-Cap Value Funds	S&P 500 Value	59.16	78.70	82.17	61.00
Mid-Cap Growth Funds	S&P MidCap 400 Growth	79.89	65.91	81.48	91.23
Mid-Cap Core Funds	S&P MidCap 400	67.88	62.59	76.51	87.76
Mid-Cap Value Funds	S&P MidCap 400 Value	32.35	48.68	70.27	82.56
Small-Cap Growth Funds	S&P SmallCap 600 Growth	88.43	85.59	91.89	92.39
Small-Cap Core Funds	S&P SmallCap 600	77.62	86.62	91.44	89.16
Small-Cap Value Funds	S&P SmallCap 600 Value	46.56	79.51	92.31	86.36
Multi-Cap Growth Funds	S&P Composite 1500 Growth	68.02	79.00	90.57	90.44
Multi-Cap Core Funds	S&P Composite 1500	86.68	86.81	91.16	88.25
Multi-Cap Value Funds	S&P Composite 1500 Value	52.42	61.24	76.87	77.71
Real Estate Funds	S&P US Real Estate Investment Trust	61.90	76.22	82.64	86.08

Source: S&P Dow Jones Indices LLC, CRSP. Data as of Dec. 31, 2015. Table is provided for illustrative purposes. Past performance is no guarantee of future results.

Fig. 1.3 Managed stock funds outperformed by their benchmarks. The percentage of managed U.S. equity (stock) funds that were outperformed by the benchmarks that they sought to surpass, over the last 1, 3, 5, and 10 years. SPIVA scorecard chart; reprinted with permission.

proponents of active management answer

Proponents of active management do not disagree with the research. Those selling actively managed funds or active management services merely say that they strive to be among the top 20% that outperform their benchmarks.

Indeed, some actively managed funds can consistently outperform their benchmarks for a number of consecutive years, some giving jaw-dropping returns: 20%, 30%, or even more — as much as 72% for a fund that is unavailable to the general public.[23]

but...

The research shows that for funds open to the general public, which fund will outperform its benchmark cannot be predicted in advance, even if it has shown a past record of doing so, even for an impressive number of years. Eventually, virtually every outperformer available to the general public becomes an underperformer, without warning.

---

[23] The closed Medallion Fund of Renaissance Technologies, LLC, has earned an average return since 1994 of 71.8%; see Sect. 1.6.1.

Report 11: Percentage of Fixed Income Funds Outperformed by Benchmarks					
Fund Category	Comparison Index	One-Year (%)	Three-Year (%)	Five-Year (%)	Ten-Year (%)
Government Long Funds	Barclays Long Government	41.46	100.00	98.89	95.56
Government Intermediate Funds	Barclays Intermediate Government	93.10	85.29	68.29	77.08
Government Short Funds	Barclays 1-3 Year Government	90.70	86.36	63.64	74.36
Investment-Grade Long Funds	Barclays Long Government/Credit	12.90	68.50	96.27	93.94
Investment-Grade Intermediate Funds	Barclays Intermediate Government/Credit	93.90	54.17	42.11	54.24
Investment-Grade Short Funds	Barclays 1-3 Year Government/Credit	74.78	63.64	29.63	60.81
High Yield Funds	Barclays High Yield	33.61	57.99	79.23	93.97
Mortgage-Backed Securities Funds	Barclays Mortgage-Backed Securities	73.02	80.00	64.52	81.25
Global Income Funds	Barclays Global Aggregate	56.07	49.34	51.24	60.42
Emerging Markets Debt Funds	Barclays Emerging Markets	89.90	92.96	94.29	81.25
Loan Participation Funds[1]	S&P/LSTA U.S Leveraged Loan 100	13.04	25.00	41.67	N/A
General Municipal Debt Funds	S&P National AMT-Free Municipal Bond	62.62	47.06	43.48	70.00
California Municipal Debt Funds	S&P California AMT-Free Municipal Bond	42.11	54.05	42.11	87.50
New York Municipal Debt Funds	S&P New York AMT-Free Municipal Bond	58.06	75.00	61.76	91.43

Source: S&P Dow Jones Indices LLC, CRSP. Data as of Dec. 31, 2015. Outperformance is based upon equal-weighted fund counts. All index returns used are total returns. Table is provided for illustrative purposes. Past performance is no guarantee of future results.

Fig. 1.4 Managed fixed income funds outperformed by their benchmarks. SPIVA scorecard chart; reprinted with permission.

How much of the performance of an outperforming fund is the result of cogent management strategies, and how much is pure chance? Undoubtedly, the successful fund managers believe it's the former. The Nobel Prize-winning economist/psychologist Daniel Kahneman[24] shows that it's human nature to believe so. However, although it may not be possible to debunk the value of a given investment strategy, it can be noted that the number of outperforming funds can be more or less predicted by pure chance. The distribution of fund performance forms a bell curve, with the target index around the 80% mark, showing most funds underperform, as illustrated in Fig. 1.1.

In the end, for much of investing, there is no magic formula, but only subjective value judgements. The sobering platitude is that every time you strategically buy or sell a stock, there's someone on the other side of the transaction doing the opposite, thinking that the opposite is the better strategy. Why, Kahneman asks, is it that buyers and sellers, who generally share the same information, come to opposite conclusions about which action is more favorable?

It's not only individuals investing on their own behalf that deceive themselves. Recently, the Chief Investment Officer of the City of New York issued

---

[24]Kahneman (2011) shows that humans are evolutionarily predisposed to snap judgments that are then guarded overconfidently, resisting reevaluation even in the face of conclusive evidence to the contrary. "Overconfidence arises because people are often blind to their own blindness," he writes.

Daniel Kahneman 2004

a report[25] that finds that by investing in privately managed funds, the City not only failed to beat the market, but through these investments, the City pension funds lost billions of dollars. The report concludes that the worst performers of all were "private equity, hedge funds and real estate [which] fell $2.6 billion short of target benchmarks after fees" over a 10-year period. The gross investment performances were often ok, but the net returns were killed by astronomical fees. The report's conclusion: "external managers failed to add substantial value to the five NYC pension funds over the 10-year period studied. The results in private asset classes, where fees are higher, are much worse than in public asset classes, relative to their respective benchmarks."

The economics Nobel Prize laureate William F. Sharpe wrote a paper[26] that analyzes the effects of fees on savings, in which he demonstrated that
"a person saving for retirement who chooses low-cost investments could have a standard of living throughout retirement more than 20% higher than that of a comparable investor in high-cost investments." Sharpe concludes "Although a long-term investor may be able to find one or more high-cost managers who can beat an appropriate benchmark by an amount sufficient to more than offset the added costs, the reality is that 'compared with the readily available passive alternative, fees for active management are astonishingly high' (Ellis 2012, p. 4). Managers with extraordinary skills may exist, but as I argued in this publication many years ago (Sharpe 1991), another exercise in arithmetic

---

[25] comptroller.nyc.gov/wp-content/uploads/documents/BAM_Report_Impact_of_Management_Fees.pdf = tinyurl.com/yc2vp5wl.
[26] Sharpe (2013).

William Sharpe 2007

indicates that such managers are in the minority. And as Ellis has reminded us, they are very hard indeed to identify in advance. *Caveat emptor.*"

1.6 Persistence

Taking the 20% of actively managed funds that succeeded to outperform their benchmarks, Fig. 1.2 plots them according to the number of consecutive years that they consistently outperformed. This plot too forms a half bell-like curve. While most don't last on this "honor roll" for more than a few years,[27] simply by the laws of chance, a few will last there for a long time, lying on the tail of the curve. The bitter truth is that *which ones* cannot be predicted in advance, as detailed in a Vanguard study (Sect. 1.6.2).

For the decade since its inception in 2004, the Pershing Square hedge fund succeeded to "double the stock market returns," returning over 20% a year on average (compared with the S&P 500, which returned under 8%). Then, in 2014, its manager, William A. Ackman, "one of Wall Street's brashest and most self-assured hedge fund managers,"[28] hit a snag. In the following 2 years, his fund lost almost a third of its value, in large part to a bet on Valeant Pharmaceuticals, which Ackman conceded "was a huge mistake." This was possibly not so bad for investors who were there from the beginning. However, in 2014, for those investors who were finally attracted to invest in the fund on account of its decade-long stellar performance, their experience would be to immediately lose almost a third of their investment. To make matters worse, a

---

[27] pionline.com/article/20161216/INTERACTIVE/161219895/low-persistency-of-active-managers = tinyurl.com/yaagtwuy.

[28] nytimes.com/2017/03/19/business/william-ackman-pershing-valeant.html.

federal lawsuit initiated in that year for violating security laws could result in $2 billion damages for the $11 billion firm.

Around this same time, it was announced that Eric Mindich, "a Wall Street wunderkind,"[29] is closing down his Eton Park hedge fund, as a result of recent poor performance. It had managed as much as $14 billion, and its assets under management had lost half their value since 2011, 7 years after the fund's 2004 inception.

Other well-known hedge funds that shut down recently included Perry Capital and Eaglevale Partners, as reported by the same *Times* article, which cited research from Hedge Fund Research Inc. that "1057 hedge funds closed or were liquidated in 2016, compared with 729 openings." All in all, the *Times* reported "For eight consecutive years, hedge funds have disappointed, underperforming a roaring stock market. In addition, some managers have lost billions of dollars through wrong-footed bets." At the same time, they reported "The 25 best-paid hedge fund managers earned a collective $11 billion in 2016." Of these, "Nearly half of the top-25 earners made single-digit returns for their investors, a lackluster sum in a year when the Standard & Poor's 500-stock index was up 12%, accounting for reinvested dividends."[30] Belief dies hard, it would seem, even among billionaire investors.

Warren Buffett has long railed against the hedge fund industry's claims that they can outperform the market, despite the large fees that they charge. In 2007, he made a famous $1 million wager with a hedge fund manager that over the following decade, the S&P 500 will rise higher than any selected basket of hedge funds. The hedge fund manager selected the basket, and Buffett selected a Vanguard index fund that tracked the S&P 500 as his benchmark. When the wager ended, a decade later, the S&P 500 index fund had realized an average annual gain of 7.1%, while the hedge fund basket realized an average annual gain of only 2.1%—not even close. Buffett contributed his winnings to charity.[31] His adversary complained that the S&P 500 was over-valued and that another decade would tell a different story. (So far, though, the following decade tells the same story—even more so: while the S&P 500 roars, hedge funds have experienced one of their worst performance runs.)

---

[29] nytimes.com/2017/03/23/business/dealbook/eton-park-hedge-fund-closes.html = tinyurl.com/ybdbd556.

[30] nytimes.com/2017/05/16/business/dealbook/best-paid-hedge-fund-managers.html = tinyurl.com/mhpowkj.

[31] blogs.wsj.com/moneybeat/2017/12/30/biggest-winner-of-famed-buffett-bet-girls-inc-of-omaha/ = tinyurl.com/y3czf72o.

1.6.1 Can Anyone Consistently "Beat the Market"?

All this is not to say that it is impossible to consistently "beat the market." There is a general sense—not without its skeptics regarding its significance—that inevitably there are at least transient inefficiencies in the market that can be exploited with less risk than the market in general. Remember Edward Thorp and James Simons (Sect. 1.1)? They may be two of the few who have demonstrated this possibility. However, inefficiencies are like dollar bills dropped on the sidewalk: they are few and far between and require vigilance to find. What made Thorp special was that he was able to use mathematical computations to determine market practices that were inefficient and then exploit them. However, exploiting inefficiencies did not scale without bound. He became rich, but not a multi-billionaire (his net financial worth was estimated in 2012 to be $800 million). Why? Because, like dropped dollars on the sidewalk, there is a limit to the rate at which market inefficiencies can be exploited by a single person.

There is also the matter of diminishing returns: each successive inefficiency tends to be less valuable than the ones before. Thus, as an actively managed fund grows in size, any success it may have had can be expected to diminish: there are not enough exploitable inefficiencies to advance the holdings of an ever larger number of clients.

James Simons' Medallion hedge fund, often deemed the most successful hedge fund in history, has generated "average annual returns after fees of an astounding 40%" over almost three decades, according to Bloomberg News,[32] 72% since 1994. However, the Medallion fund is limited to its employees, closed to outside investment since 1993, with assets capped at around $10 billion, according to Bloomberg News. This limitation is deemed necessary in order to preserve the efficiencies of its trading algorithms.

Other funds run by Renaissance Technologies, the parent company of the Medallion fund, are open to outside investment, but have not done as well. Simons explained this to The New Yorker[33] by saying that it was a result of their size: "large amounts of money cannot be traded as quickly, and longer-term trading makes algorithms less useful." Indeed, in 2020, two Renaissance Technology funds open to the public lost 22.62% and 33.58%, respectively.[34]

---

[32] bloomberg.com/news/articles/2017-04-25/renaissance-mints-another-billionaire-with-two-more-on-the-cusp = tinyurl.com/mmk8tdd.

[33] newyorker.com/magazine/2017/12/18/jim-simons-the-numbers-king.

[34] institutionalinvestor.com/article/b1q3fndg77d0tg/Renaissance-s-Medallion-Fund-Surged-76-in-2020-But-Funds-Open-to-Outsiders-Tanked = tinyurl.com/y43ckwdg.

what about Warren Buffett?

Warren Buffett 2012

Even the estimable Warren Buffett is not immune to failure. At the end of 2008, his Berkshire Hathaway sustained a 77% drop in earnings. In a 12-month period, his personal fortune dropped by $25 billion—almost half his net worth. He dropped from being the richest man in the world to being the third richest (second in the United States, after Bill Gates). The drop exaggerates the reality, because at the same time, he contributed billions of dollars to charity (contributing to his loss of wealth). But he has had a number of notable investment failures, including ConocoPhillips. Over the decade that followed the Great Recession (2009–2019), Buffett's Berkshire Hathaway (slightly) underperformed the S&P 500 (dividends reinvested).

Many, including Warren Buffett, have said that making money (especially in the market but even elsewhere) is a combination of three circumstances: a good idea, good timing (being in the right place at the right time), and good luck. Buffett has said that without all three—including especially, luck—one is unlikely to become rich. There aren't many Warren Buffett's in the world.

As the world sees him, he became so wealthy through buying into undervalued companies, in sectors where he felt he had expertise—something he emphasizes—and managing or influencing them to increase their profitability. For him, wealth bred wealth, and the more companies he bought or was able to influence, the more he could then afford, achieving an economy of scale in ownership and influence. He famously never bought Apple stock (until he did), because he said he didn't understand technology stocks (and yet, to the surprise of many, he did buy a very significant stake in IBM and, later, in Apple). In 1999, he astutely (and accurately) predicted that low interest rates and inflation will lead to a drop in aggregate equity returns from 11% to 6% "over the next 17 years." Wow!

1.6.2 Vanguard Persistence Study

Vanguard has a white paper,[35] updated periodically, with the title "The case for index-fund investing." It provides a relentless drubbing of actively managed funds based on in-depth statistical analyses. One of their three main conclusions is highlighted in the introduction: "persistence of performance among past winners is no more predictable than a flip of a coin." They go on to conclude that the total of fees charged by an actively managed fund "is one of the largest factors driving ...deviations relative to the target index." They concur with the SPIVA finding that "the relative underperformance of actively managed funds versus their style [target] benchmarks has been consistent across asset classes (both equity and fixed income)."

Not only did they find that active managers underperform, but their managed funds also tended in many cases to have higher volatility. Nonetheless, they acknowledged, "even over a relatively long period, some actively managed funds survived and outperformed their benchmarks." However, they pointed to studies over the past 40 years that have concluded that there is "no evidence of persistence in fund outperformance" after adjusting for "the influence of the equity market, fund size, and fund style, as delineated by Eugene Fama and Kenneth French in 1993".[36] Finally, they describe their own study in which they conclude that the levels of persistence in managed U.S. equity funds "do not appear to be significantly different from random." They found one exception to this: "persistence has tended to be stronger for previous losers" (i.e., they persist in losing). They also warn about jumping from the frying pan to the fire, saying "the temptation to change managers because of poor performance can simply lead to more disappointment." They cite a "well-reported" 2008 study by Goyal and Wahal[37] that finds that "when sponsors of U.S. institutional pension plans replaced underperforming managers with outperforming managers, the results were far different than expected," in the sense that "the fired managers actually outperformed the managers hired to replace them by 49 basis points in the first year, 88 basis points over the first 2 years, and 103 basis points over the first 3 years" after switching.

---

[35] pressroom.vanguard.com/nonindexed/Updated_The_Case_for_Index_Fund_Investing_4.9.2014.pdf = tinyurl.com/y4car3vq.

[36] Fama and French (1993); in Fama and French (2010), they report results of a 22-year study that indicates that it is "extremely difficult for an actively managed investment fund to regularly outperform its benchmark."

[37] Goyal and Wahal (2008).

what about in bear markets?

They debunked the commonly held view that while managers may not perform well in bull markets,[38] they do in bear markets (by definition, a drop of at least 20%), "because, in theory, active managers can move into cash or rotate into defensive securities to avoid the worst of a given bear market." To the contrary, what they actually found was that "the probability that these managers will move fund assets to defensive stocks or cash at just the right time is very low. Most events that result in major changes in market direction are unanticipated. To succeed, an active manager would not only have to time the market but also do so at a cost that was less than the benefit provided." In fact, "In four of seven bear markets since January 1973, and six of the eight bull markets, the average mutual fund did not outperform its target index."

well, but what about in inefficient market sectors?

Vanguard went on to analyze claims that while active management for broadly diversified funds may underperform, that for inefficient market sectors, managers do better. To the contrary, they found "a significant majority of actively managed funds in so-called inefficient sectors such as mid- and small-cap[39] stocks, high-yield[40] bonds, and emerging market stocks underperformed their benchmark." They conclude that "a common myth is that actively managed funds have a leg up in market segments perceived as inefficient."

1.7 Claims of "Outperforming" Funds

Investment literature is replete with examples, "notwithstanding all the studies," of particular managed funds that "consistently outperform their benchmarks." A commonly cited example is Fidelity's managed fund FLPSX that has "consistently significantly outperformed its target benchmark": the Morningstar mid-cap value index, even outperforming the S&P 500 (except for a few years at the end of the century, when it matched it), and the Russell 2000 small-cap index, all "for the past 26 years." The graph shown in Fig. 1.5 is impressive indeed. What about *this* fund? Seeing is believing, is it not?

---

[38] A *bull market* is simply one in which stock prices have been consistently rising.

[39] The "cap" or *market capitalization* of a stock is the market value of its outstanding shares, and "small" here generally means under $2 billion.

[40] The *yield* of an investment is its rate of return.

Well, yes and no. If you invested in FLPSX in 1989, indeed you would have done very well. But simply because the FLPSX graph is consistently above the others in Fig. 1.5 does not mean it outperformed those indices in *each* year of that time span. Unfortunately, we cannot return to 1989 to invest in FLPSX. What if instead, we invested in FLPSX starting in another year, say, 2014? Figure 1.6 tells a rather different story. In that year, and subsequently, it significantly *underperformed* those benchmarks. (Fidelity makes this clear on its website, in its performance plots for the fund. It's others—the business defenders with a stake in promoting the false idea, but having no legal liability—who tell the deceptive story.) Throughout the 26 years, if one invested in some years, the investment outperformed its target index, investing in other years, it underperformed.

You cannot assess the performance of a fund by looking at its performance from a single start year. Any fund inevitably does better when measured from one start year than when measured from another. I have no doubt that FLPSX may be a very fine fund, but to say that Fig. 1.5 shows that it "consistently outperforms its benchmarks" is deceptive.

Vanguard also—in seeming contradiction to its central philosophy that investors should buy only lowest-fee broadly based index funds—sells a

Fig. 1.5 Fidelity's managed fund FLPSX. The performance of FLPSX over 26 years, from 1989, compared with the S&P 500, the Morningstar mid-cap value index and the Russell 2000 small-cap index.

1 How to Get Richer   21

Fig. 1.6 FLPSX starting in 2014.

number of actively managed (non-index) funds: in fact, more than they sell index funds. They sort of say these funds can sometimes outperform index funds on account of Vanguard's exceptionally careful choice of managers (although a careful reading reveals that their recommendation of these actively managed funds is nuanced). They also show that in some cases these funds have outperformed their target benchmarks. However, using Vanguard's plotting tools, one easily sees the many cases where the funds underperform their benchmarks, and when they outperform, it's often not by very much at all (Fig. 1.7). In fact, in the example shown—chosen from Vanguard's own web page recommending actively managed funds—over shorter periods looking back from the present, they underperform their benchmarks and finally, after 10 years, are almost equal to their benchmarks—but not quite.

What's going on? I don't know. Perhaps they just see the demand for actively managed funds as a business opportunity that there is no point to miss. As for me, I'll stick with their reasoned, researched recommendations of passively managed index funds, which as far as I can tell are the best-performing and most cost-effective investments available to an average investor.

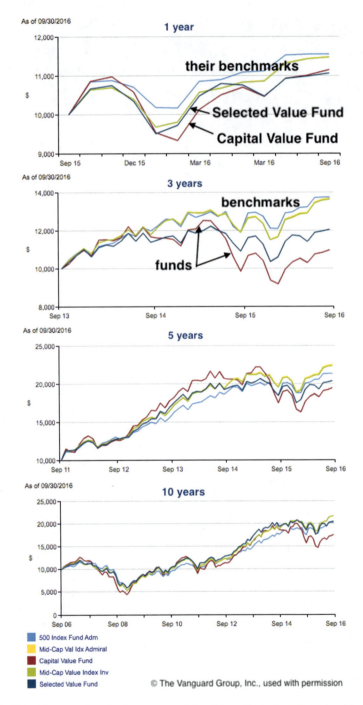

Fig. 1.7 Two Vanguard actively managed funds vs. their benchmarks. The actively managed funds are the capital value and selected value funds.

1.8 How to Underperform

It's easy to do much worse than the market overall. Good ways to do worse than the market include buying high and selling low. These are common exploits of novices who panic about missing a surge or getting swallowed by a crash, instead of simply hanging on and doing nothing.

1.8.1 Market Timing

A very popular way to do worse than the market is to try to "time" the market. That means that you think you can predict when the market will rise or fall and act accordingly. This is a quest shattered by numerous studies showing that all those time series analyses don't really work.

Nobel laureate William F. Sharpe shows that market timing would need to be correct three quarters of the time in order to beat a (perfectly efficient) market index fund.[41] Vanguard writes "Market timing rarely turns out well, as the best and worst days often happen close to each other. In many cases, timing the market for re-entry simply results in selling low and buying high,"[42] a view echoed by Michael Edesess in his book The Big Investment Lie.[43]

Vanguard did a study[44] of how well professional managers did at stock picking and stock timing. Looking at the record of market-timing mutual funds since 1997, they found lackluster results. They wrote: "Presumably most such funds are run by sophisticated investment managers with data, tools, time, and experience on their side. Generally speaking, their common objective is to outperform a benchmark in any market environment. To do this, the managers may be authorized to invest in any asset class or sub-asset class of their choosing, at any time." The results? In only one of five "bull" (sharply rising) or "bear" (sharply falling) market periods did a majority of the flexible allocation funds outperform a broadly diversified benchmark of 60% stocks and 40% bonds. And of those that did outperform, fewer than half carried their success into the following period.

Vanguard found that a failure in the ability to time markets extends at least to asset allocation funds, investment clubs, pension funds, investment

---

[41] Sharpe (1975).

[42] institutional.vanguard.com/VGApp/iip/site/institutional/researchcommentary/article/
NewsPerspectiveMktDownturns = tinyurl.com/y6xbc7hs.

[43] Edesess (2007).

[44] https://personal.vanguard.com/pdf/ISGPRINC.pdf.

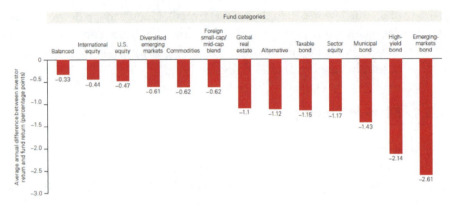

Fig. 1.8 Individual investor average losses from timing attempts.

newsletters, mutual funds, and professional market timers, as documented in nine independent studies. "The lesson?" asks Vanguard. It's "If market-timing is difficult for professional managers with all their advantages, investors without such advantages should think twice" about trying this on their own.

When investors try it on their own, indeed they do worse. Figure 1.8 shows the average annual difference between individual investor return and an associated benchmark fund return, for a number of sectors. The chart is from Vanguard, using data from Morningstar. Vanguard found that "investors tend to buy highly rated funds even as they underperform." Others move in and out of the markets on their own, but more than not are driven by emotions, leading them to buy high so as not to miss a surging market and then sell low in order to avoid being swept away in a crash.

But the temptation to time the market can be a siren, hard to resist, luring even the savvy who know better. Someone whom I know very well to scorn market timers nonetheless could not refrain from holding a substantial position in cash, in anticipation of a recession, strongly predicted by the 2019 yield curve inversion (Sect. 2.3.2). However, that recession never came, and as a result, he conceded that he lost $400,000 by not simply investing that cash in the stock market, as he knew he should have done.

1.8.2 Stock Picking

Last but not least of likely to fail investment exploits is stock picking. Some think, by reading many investor newsletters (Sect. 1.2) and business magazines, that they can pick stocks that likely will be "winners." Implicit in this thinking is that their picks somehow are superior to all the professionals in the market, who after all, had they felt the same about the stock, would already have bought it and driven up its price to the point that it no longer would be a "winner." Thus, a true "winner" wouldn't stay that way for long. But, in reality, no stock can be a "winner" in this sense of being truly underpriced, as no one, not even the CEO, has the crystal ball needed to predict its future. In fact, the CEO of a company is more clueless than many imagine, about where the company is going financially—hence, all those "corrections" to quarterly earning calls.

No simple investigations can uncover what the market doesn't already know. With the possible exception of utilizing insider information, which is illegal, if there were any tea leaves out there that foretold the future, the market would have picked up on them and already corrected for them.

The market is awash with theories—tried, tested, and discarded—for how to foretell the market future from the market past. Although there is some evidence that buying losers and selling winners gives a short-term benefit,[45] there also is evidence to the contrary.[46] For most of us, it may be fair to assume that any prospective "winner" is as good as any other random pick.

So is now a good time to buy Apple? Sure, as good a time, after adjusting for risk, as buying any other stock.

---

[45] Bondt and Thaler (1985).

[46] Jegadeesh and Titman (1993).

2

Deciding What to Invest In

Oddly, this most basic investment question turns out to be the easiest to answer. If you already know that the answer is broadly diversified index funds and cash, then after reading this introduction, you can skim the intervening sections and skip down to the final section (Sect. 2.13).

Three of the most common types of investments are in stocks (or funds of these), bonds (or funds of these), and *cash*, best saved in a money market fund, CDs (bank certificates of deposit), or a savings bank.

Stocks comprise a type of *equity*, in which the owner owns a piece ("shares") of the issuing corporation. The value of a share of stock follows the current perceived value of the corporation, changing second by second, not infrequently with large swings up and down. Even funds that diversify by holding shares in many different types of companies are volatile, as stock prices also are sensitive to daily external economic and political events—actual or perceived. This volatility makes equity an especially risky investment in case one has an intention to use it to cover non-discretionary expenses that must be paid at particular times irrespective of the equity value. Paying for an expense by selling assets that are depressed in value means paying a larger portion of one's savings for that expense than would be paid were the assets not depressed. If this practice happens with some frequency, it can lead to a significant diminution of savings. On the other hand, investing some portion of savings in equity is important to do on account of its rate of growth, which generally is superior to that of bonds and cash.

© The Author(s), under exclusive license to Springer Nature Switzerland AG 2022
R. P. Kurshan, *Investment Industry Claims Debunked*,
https://doi.org/10.1007/978-3-030-76709-9_2

Bonds, money market funds, CDs, and savings bank investments are types of *debt*, wherein you, the owner of the debt, have made a loan and received a promise from the issuing entity (e.g., the bank) to pay back the loan with interest. These types of investments are also known as *fixed income investments,*[1] which is the term we'll use going forward to refer to this group of investment vehicles. One main risk of holding bonds or funds of bonds is their price sensitivity to general interest rates—changing or anticipated to change—as well as to the fairly unlikely possibility the issuing entity fails to pay its debts. However, the volatility of fixed income investments generally is much less than that of equity, as is its rate of growth when its interest is reinvested. (Its growth is then primarily generated by the interest it gives.)

Thus, we generally think of investments in equity to be well-suited for long-term growth, given that we have the opportunity to wait out any period in which the equity value is depressed, before selling it. We use fixed income investments as a more stable means to hold savings earmarked for near-term expenses. However, holding more savings than needed in fixed income investments for such near-term expenses can lead to a significant shortfall that results from its inferior growth rate, compared with equity.

2.1 Investing for Earmarked Expenses

While we are working and generating income, we generally invest our savings so that they grow, in order to end up with as large a pool of savings as market conditions and our acumen allow. However, the point of increasing savings is to have more money to spend. If we have plans about when we want to spend portions of our savings, these plans can guide how we invest. We can think of separating savings into buckets that we call *short-term, intermediate-term* (if we have it), and *long-term*. We treat these three buckets very differently with regard to investment. Generally, we can pour from one bucket into the other as conditions change.

Short-term savings are earmarked for near-term purchases in the next couple of years: a car; a big vacation, maybe; living expenses if one is unemployed (or retired). *Intermediate-term* savings are earmarked for 3–15 years out: school, a house. *Long-term* savings are for retirement, while one is still working and retirement is far away.

---

[1]"Fixed income" also includes annuities (Sect. 2.10), which are not forms of debt.

The goal for *short-term* savings mainly is not to lose the money. However, money under the mattress is not a good idea: it is sure to lose to inflation (not to mention risk of theft, if you mean it literally). A money market fund, CD, or savings bank can be the best choice.

If you know exactly how long before you need the money, buying U.S. Government bonds that mature on the date you need the money can be the best way to save for an *intermediate-term* expense. Another simple alternative could be a CD from your bank, with a matching term. Insurance companies sell limited term "MYGA" annuities (Sect. 2.10.2—not to be confused with the more familiar annuities that provide a lifelong stipend). While these could be competitive, their conditions may be complicated, and there's always the risk that the insurance company could default (insurance companies, like bonds, are rated in terms of the likelihood of default, so it's a real—if seemingly remote—possibility). Generally, it's not a good idea to invest in stocks or stock funds for a short- or intermediate-term investment, as their value could be depressed when you need the money.

When one is far from retirement, it's virtually impossible to make a meaningful estimate of post-retirement expenses—too many factors can change in the intervening years. Instead, investments for retirement often are driven by external opportunities such as employment savings plans. However they are motivated; long-term savings mostly should be optimized for growth in the early years before retirement (meaning investment in equity) and then optimized to provide a stable source for expenses as one comes closer to retirement, as described in Chaps. 4 and 5.

Investing for unforeseen emergencies, while seemingly prudent, can be counterproductive, as discussed in Chap. 4.

2.2 Stocks

Since a company's stock price is subject to considerable volatility, an individual investor is best served by investing in a diversified selection of stocks from a broad variety of companies. The easiest and safest way to do this is through a broadly diversified stock fund.

The most diversified are the so-called *index* funds whose values track an index. One such index is the S&P 500 that represents the average value of the 500 largest corporations listed on the New York Stock Exchange or Nasdaq. Their values are measured by their respective market capitalization. The CRSP U.S. Total Market Index represents the average value of almost all the investable U.S. stock market. There are other widely used indices as well, such as the Russell 3000 Index and Wilshire 5000 Total Market Index that track broad segments of the U.S. stock market. As explained in Sect. 2.6, the most profitable index funds, on average, are the ones with the lowest fees.

There are different classes of stocks—mainly *common* stock and *preferred* stock (Appendix A.8). These distinctions are irrelevant if one invests in stock funds: the fund manager deals with the choice of classes, and thus for the ordinary investor who has optimized an investment in equities by holding them in a diversified fund, the issue stock class can happily be ignored.

Many stocks give dividends (which are passed through to funds that hold them). However, the value of an investment in stocks derives mainly from growth in the stock price, not the dividends it produces.

Some investors prefer a stock that produces few or no dividends, as dividends are taxed as ordinary income, whereas long-term (over more than a year) gains in stock value are taxed at the much lower long-term capital gains tax rate—15% for most investors (see Sect. 12.7) and, then, only when sold.

If instead of paying dividends, the amounts are reinvested in the company, that enhances the stock price. In this case, the investor in effect defers the income and receives in return better growth and lower taxes.

Since funds continually buy and sell assets, a holder of an equity fund likely experiences some taxable gains, although the investor has not sold any shares of the fund.

2.3   Bonds

Some people incorrectly think that the only risk with a bond or bond fund is default of the issuing agency or corporation. This is true for a bond that is held to *maturity*—the date when the loan is repaid. However, if interest rates change in response to changing market conditions, especially, a rate change declared by the Federal Reserve, the current value of a bond or share of a bond fund changes. If interest rates rise, then the interest rate given by a bond becomes relatively less valuable, so the bond's value falls. Correspondingly, if interest rates fall, a bond's value rises. Accordingly, the share price of a fund that holds bonds can rise and fall.

For an individual bond, barring insolvency of the issuer, none of these market conditions can affect its value at maturity, called its *face value*. However, there are many reasons to want to sell a bond before it matures.

Before a bond matures, irrespective of interest rates, its value can change on account of changing supply and demand. This, in turn, can change as a result of many externalities, such as world events. If economic conditions seem to threaten a recession, then stock prices could fall. This threat can cause some investors to sell stocks and put the proceeds into more stable bonds, possibly increasing the demand for bonds and thus increasing their value. Conversely, if the stock market is soaring, investors could sell bonds to buy stocks, decreasing bond demand and lowering their value.

Hence, bond prices, like stock prices, can be volatile. However, the degree of bond price volatility is generally much less than that of stocks, because a bond's interest rate and face value are fixed.

To avoid the problems of bond price volatility, one could insist on holding a bond until its maturity. However, such a policy would introduce *liquidity risk* (Sect. 3.8): the risk of its unavailability when you may need it. You may *plan* on holding a bond to maturity, but unforeseen needs may necessitate selling it, and when you do, you lose more if the value of the bond has decreased (even though its face value is unchanged).

2.3.1 Bond Types, Terminology, and Considerations

A *straight* bond promises to pay a fixed rate of interest, usually twice a year, throughout a period called its *term* that ends on its maturity date. Its face value is also called its *par* value. Each payment of interest is called the bond's *coupon*,[2] and its interest rate is called the bond's *yield*. So a $1000 face value straight bond with annual coupons of $50 has a yield of 5% and promises to pay back its face value of $1000 at maturity.

The *present value* of any bond (its current value, mid-term) depends on the relationship between the bond's yield and prevailing interest rates. (If the bond's yield is less than today's prevailing rates, say, then it is worth less today than it otherwise would be.) The present value of a straight bond can be calculated using a formula derived in Appendix A.4.

While a straight bond is the most common type, there are many other types of bonds. A *zero-coupon* bond in effect pays all its interest at maturity. (Its purchase price is discounted.) Some bonds have a variable coupon that is tied to some index, an example being U.S. Treasury Inflation-Protected Securities (TIPS), whose coupon is tied to inflation.

---

[2]The term "coupon" is a hold-over from days when one received a paper bond with coupon attachments that were like little post-dated checks, to be torn off and redeemed for the successive interest payments.

There are variations on bonds that affect their price, such as whether the bond is "callable," meaning that the issuer can redeem the bond before the end of its term, or "convertible" meaning that the holder can convert the bond into shares of the issuing company's stock under certain conditions. Some bonds come with a feature that allows the holder to redeem the bond before the end of its term. All these features add complexity to an analysis of the bond's initial price (which may be different from its face value as a result of its features or even market conditions) and of its present value, mid-term.

As a general rule, the price (present value) of bonds with shorter terms fluctuate less than those with longer terms (there is less time for events that could affect a bond's price). On account of this benefit, the issuer can sell shorter-term bonds with a lower yield. Normally, everything else equal, the longer the term, the higher the yield, to compensate the investor for the greater risk of holding the bond longer. However, if there is an expectation that interest rates will fall, then it's possible for this to be reversed, with longer-term bonds yielding less than shorter-term bonds. This is called a "yield curve inversion": see Sect. 2.3.2. With a lower long-term yield, the buyer in effect pays a premium to lock in a long-term rate that is expected to fall. The expectation of falling rates is much less common than the expectation of rising rates. It is usually accompanied by an expectation of a recession, in which the Federal Reserve would be expected to lower rates in order to stimulate employment and economic recovery by making money less expensive. This may happen in stages, with a succession of rate decreases and associated decreases of long-term yields.

As a matter of terminology, while I have been calling all debt securities with a stipulated term and yield a "bond," technically, a U.S. Government "bond" with a term of under a year is called a "bill," 1 to 10 years, a "note," and over 10 years, a "bond." I'll mostly just call them all "bonds."

bond risk

Bonds carry a risk of default by the issuer. This risk is generally considered nonexistent for bonds issued by the U.S. Government, which has never defaulted (although it recently came close, as a result of political maneuvering). With sanguine confidence, U.S. Government bonds thus are termed "risk-free".[3] Corporate and municipal bonds carry higher risk and are graded by various rating services according to their perceived risk of default.

---

[3] "Risk-free" is used generally to mean "lower risk than can be calculated through conventional statistical market analysis" and is reserved for U.S. Treasury debt. Its only risk is a default by the U.S. Government, which is set to "probability 0." However, when the Republican Congressional Caucus turned to

Recently, the impartiality of these services has been called into question after the default of highly rated securities during the Great Recession of 2008–2009. That's when it became public news that the rating agencies are paid by the bond issuers to rate their bonds (that's how they make their money), creating an obvious conflict of interest. Nonetheless, presented with no better option, the markets continue to rely on these ratings.

Highly rated corporate bonds (having negligible risk of default) are termed "investment-grade." "Speculative-grade," or more colloquially "junk" bonds, are lower-rated bonds that offer very high interest for very high risk. There are some who feel they can avoid the downside and earn a good return on investment with these, especially with broad diversification, spreading the risk. However, "spreading the risk" only can work as a strategy if you believe that the potential default of one is independent of the potential of default of another. In some cases this can be true, but the economic forces that lead one to default can have the same effect on many others, so "spreading the risk" is not a fail-safe strategy.

risk affects yield

The higher the risk, the lower the rating and the higher the yield (interest rate) the bond issuer must pay to market the bond. So, comparing two otherwise identical bonds with different yields, one can usually assume that the one with the higher yield has a lower rating or for some other reason is considered riskier. A bond can drop in value if the issuer suddenly is considered to be at risk. The only "bargains" are bonds that are improperly rated too low. However, it takes some hubris for a casual investor to suppose having a better gauge of the risk than the rating agencies (which, if malfeasant, can only be suspected of rating too high).

If a bond defaults, the issuer may fail to pay some or all of the promised coupons and/or return of principal (the bond's face value) or may delay promised payments. Such failure is almost exclusively the result of bankruptcy, and municipalities are not exempt, although municipal bankruptcy is extremely rare.

---

threatening default on U.S. Government debt in 2011, Standard & Poor's downgraded their rating of long-term Treasury bonds from AAA to AA+; this may call into question this definition of "risk-free."

zero-coupon bonds

One can buy a bond that pays no interest: *zero-coupon* bonds. Zero-coupon bonds pay only their face value, at maturity. Since they pay no interest, they are sold at a significant discount off their face value (cf. Appendix A.1).

"STRIPS" are an example. This acronym for a class of U.S. Government bonds stands for "Separate Trading of Registered Interest and Principal of Securities," aptly named because the bonds are "stripped" of their coupons. STRIPS refers both to the resulting ("stripped") bond and its separated coupons. Both are sold as zero-coupon bonds. The bond retains its original maturity date, and the coupons mature at their original redemption dates.

Once the coupons are stripped from a bond, the two products are functionally the same: they each promise to pay a given amount at a given time. The only differences come from the fact that the coupons are more numerous and in lower denominations than the stripped bonds, and thus supply and demand might affect the prices slightly differently. The yield of a bond stripped of its coupons is a bit less than that of the original bond, because the stripping is an added value. (The stripped bond together with its coupons can be reassembled, producing a bond with separable and individually salable coupons, something clearly more flexible and hence more valuable than the same bond with inseparable coupons.)

There are tax consequences for zero-coupon bonds. Since sold at a discount off face value, it's as if interest were accruing through the bond's term, paid at maturity. The IRS has decided that income tax shall be paid annually on a zero-coupon bond's imputed ("phantom") interest even though no income is actually distributed until maturity.

TIPS

U.S. Treasury Inflation Protected Securities (TIPS) are a type of bond with inflation-adjusted coupons. However, their inflation adjustment may not compensate for the particular level of inflation experienced by a given individual, as explained in Sect. 2.10. The market could expect a higher rate of inflation than what is built into the cost of a TIPS, resulting in a very small or even negative rate of return. This can occur during a period that the Federal Reserve has set interest rates very low to stimulate employment ("quantitative easing"). A final concern for TIPS is that inflation adjustments are considered "income" by the IRS, thus reducing their benefit. For such bonds, it is not possible to compute their present value without guesses about the future.

municipal bonds

Municipal bonds—issued by municipalities and states—often are "triple tax-free," meaning that they are exempt from federal, state, and local taxes. They are issued by states and municipalities, free of state and local taxes as an incentive to purchase, while the U.S. constitution bars the federal government from taxing interest on loans to municipalities and states. However, this allows the yield offered to be significantly less than for the comparable taxed rate. Thus, these are good investments mostly for those in high tax brackets.

bond duration

The "duration" of a bond or a bond fund is a number, expressed in years, that expresses an estimate of its sensitivity to changes in interest rates. Specifically, it expresses the time required to recover half the present value of all future cash flows from the bond or bond fund. There are various models for computing duration. For a bond mutual fund or index fund, its duration is normally stated, given by an appropriate model. The higher the duration, the higher its price volatility.

The most useful thing to know about duration is that it gives a rule of thumb for estimating the effect of a rise or drop in interest rates (for U.S. bonds or bond funds, the interest rate set by the U.S. Federal Reserve). The rule of thumb: for each year of duration and percent rise or drop in interest rates, the price of the bond or bond fund will fall or rise 1%. For example, if the duration of a bond is 10 years, and interest rates rise 1%, then the value of the bond will drop by approximately 10%.

long-term bonds

There are long-term bonds—bonds whose term exceeds 15 years—and funds that invest in them. However, the longer the term of a bond, the more sensitive it is to interest rate fluctuations (and consequent risk of loss when selling the bond before its maturity). The same applies to bond funds that invest in longer-term bonds.

For long-term bonds, duration can be around 25 years. Therefore, a 1% rise in interest rates can result in a drop in value of 25%. If everything else were unchanged, it could take close to 25 years for the bond to recover its lost value. For this reason, long-term bonds, despite their generally higher yields, are not considered appropriate for most people, even young people (since their long-term financial needs are uncertain) and certainly not for older people who may not live long enough to see a bond loss recover.

By contrast, the bonds in Vanguard's total bond market index ETF, BND, are mostly intermediate-term with an average duration of around 6 years and term of around 8 years, rendering it less sensitive to interest rate changes, and quicker to recover.

broker fees

Buying bonds is rife with abuse of the gullible, it seems. Forbes[4] warns of brokers taking advantage of the ill-informed to reap unconscionably large markups on trades. This is especially true of OTC (over-the-counter) trades of bonds bought between coupons (Appendix A.4.3).

For small-time investors (investing less than millions of dollars), these fees can be significantly higher than the fees associated with buying a mutual fund or ETF. The money lost to fees is money that cannot grow, with the loss compounding over time (cf. Sect. 9.2). Brokerage fees are not regulated, bond trades can be complex (time to the next coupon must be taken into account), and an unscrupulous broker can hide high fees in bond transactions (Appendix A.4.3).

2.3.2 Yield Curve Inversion

Occasionally, the yield of long-term bonds falls below that of short-term bonds. When this happens, the resulting *yield curve inversion* is thought to signal a recession. In the last 60 years, every recession has been preceded by an inversion (although two earlier ones were not), and but for twice, conversely, see Fig. 2.1. The curve is the difference between long- and short-term yields: 10-year Treasuries yield minus the Federal Funds Rate (Sect. 2.9). The points at which it falls below 0 are the yield curve inversions. The shaded bars are periods of recession.

In 2019 there was an inversion (the last shown: June–October 2019). But, guess what? No recession. In 1966, the economist Paul Samuelson quipped "The stock market has forecast nine of the last five recessions."

2.3.3 Bond Ladders

If you seek a stable, dependable source of income generated at predetermined times, either sporadically or regularly (like every month), then a bond ladder can produce this (at least in theory).

---

[4]forbes.com/2009/02/26/munis-spreads-markups-personal-finance_investing_ideas_bond_brokers.html = tinyurl.com/rvulsuf.

Fig. 2.1 Yield curve inversions signaling coming recession?

Bonds are purchased that mature at the predetermined times—the ladder rungs. This avoids the risk of price volatility that occurs when a bond is sold before its maturity. (Callable bonds or bonds with other features generally would not be used in a ladder, because their features can break the ladder or distort the ladder yield.)

However, a bond ladder does have a number of risks. The most obvious is the *counterparty risk*: the issuer of a bond may default. A bond ladder can be risk-adjusted, by choosing bonds with a range of ratings, from "investment grade" commercial bonds to U.S. Government bonds that are as "risk-free" as you can get. By mixing a range of risk levels, a ladder's overall level of risk can be fine-tuned. Risk can be further decreased by using bonds from a variety of companies, chosen to reduce the likelihood that all the bonds might fail together.

If the rate of inflation increases significantly, the rate of return of the ladder is depreciated by the inflation. A 4% average rate of return from a ladder may look good at a time that the rate of inflation is only 2%. However, if the rate of inflation rises to 5%, that 4% return constitutes a loss. Moreover, with increasing inflation, interest rates also rise and thus the value of the bonds in a ladder falls. This affects the sale price in case you need to break the ladder and sell some bonds before they mature. The risk of inflation can be countered to some extent with TIPS (**TIPS**, Sect. 2.3.1).

Then there is liquidity risk (Sect. 3.8): the ladder holds its guaranteed value only if the ladder is not broken. If you need to sell some bonds in the ladder before they matured, say, for an emergency, they could have lost value if interest rates rose since you bought the bonds.

When building a bond ladder, there are brokerage fees that need to be paid to buy the bonds and later to sell them. Many when not all transactions will need to be OTC (over the counter), between coupons. These fees are unregulated, are subject to abuse for small investors, and can have a significant negative impact on savings (see **Broker Fees**, Sect. 2.3.1).

Another issue with a bond ladder is that it generally is not possible to extend its term past 30 years, as most bonds have a maximum term of 30 years. This may not be terribly significant, though, as the ladder can be extended over time.

Finally, it may not be possible to fill every rung of the ladder with the desired bonds, on account of unavailability. This can be compensated for by increasing the values of preceding rungs (Appendix A.7), but leads to inefficiencies in the ladder, manifest as a reduction in yield.

Bond ladders can be arbitrarily complex. For example, in an environment of rising interest rates, it is popular to construct ladders with a mixture of short-term and longer-term bonds, with the idea that when the short-term bonds mature, they can be rolled over into longer-term bonds that take advantage of the increasing yields. (Of course, if what was expected to be "rising" changes to "falling," then this strategy can backfire.)

Despite the complications, a ladder of bonds can solve the problem of providing a steady predicable guaranteed return from a bond portfolio. As such, it is an alternative to an annuity (Sect. 2.10).

Details on how to construct a bond ladder and compute its yield are given in Appendix A.7.

For investment, a ladder may not be competitive with and much more bother than a simple intermediate-term bond index fund (or ETF).

However, even if a bond ladder is not desired for actual investment, a theoretical ladder (one constructed only on paper) can be used to evaluate an annuity (Sect. 2.10) or a pension buyout (Sect. 17.2.9). The ladder construction also can be used to compute the required size of an earmark for annuity or pension inflation compensation (Appendix A.10).

2.4 Stocks vs. Bonds

On average, the growth of stock prices significantly outpaces the return from bonds, which primarily is the interest they give. For example, the S&P 500 annualized return for the 20-year period 1995–2015, dividends reinvested,[5] was 9.6%,[6] while over the same period, the annualized return of 10-year Treasury notes, interest reinvested, was 4.97%.[7] This doesn't take into account taxes, which generally lowers the return for bonds more than for stocks. This is since bond interest is taxed annually at the ordinary income tax rate, while stock growth is taxed only later when sold, at the lower long-term capital gains tax rate (see Sect. 12.7).

High-quality intermediate-term bonds are inherently less volatile than stocks, because they have a known interest payout and a relatively short time to a guaranteed redemption payout at maturity. This makes them less sensitive to interest rate fluctuations and, since they are high-quality, to the risk of default. Their volatility comes mostly from changes in the market interest rate and supply and demand (see introduction of Sect. 2.3). If you hold a bond to maturity, there's no volatility whatsoever (assuming no default).

Bonds in a bond index fund generate some volatility in the share price of the fund as the fund continually buys and sells its holdings in order to optimize its value and to supply cash to investors who redeem shares.

Some volatility in supply and demand arises due to changing political and economic conditions, affecting both stocks and bonds, but bonds tend to be less sensitive to these than stocks.

Stock price, on the other hand, varies as a result of myriad factors, including how the business of the issuing company is perceived and worldwide economic conditions that are perceived as potentially affecting this business. These factors are constantly changing and, with them, stock prices. Collectively, these factors change the value of a stock index fund in an unpredictable fashion, leading to considerably more volatility than for bonds, bond indices and bond funds.

---

[5] Although it is more common to cite growth rates that exclude reinvestment of dividends and interest, for an investment this makes no sense. How can one evaluate the worth of an investment without taking into account the income it provides? In this book, unless stated otherwise, investment growth is given in terms of total return: dividends and interest reinvested, net fees where possible.

[6] dqydj.com/sp-500-return-calculator/.

[7] dqydj.com/treasury-return-calculator/.

2.5 What Domestic/Non-domestic Balance Is Best?

The investment industry recommends that for the U. S. investor, around 10%–50% of investments should be international—using the same balance chosen for domestic equities and fixed income investments. The current EU situation may set a bias for the lower end of that range. Some experts suggest that the foreign balance for bonds should be a bit less, proportionally, than for stocks on account of many considerations that surround foreign bonds.

While these recommendations may be based less on economic theory than intuition, perhaps "10%–50%" is a wide enough range not to go wrong. It makes sense that some non-domestic holdings are good for diversification. While the United States may be dominant in the world market today, there are plenty of reasons this could change. If the change is gradual, we'd have time to adjust. But changes can be abrupt—in the last decades, we've seen how sudden ground-shaking financial upheavals can be.

On the other hand, the esteemed John Bogle (see Sect. 2.6) writes:[8]

> I am not persuaded that international funds are a necessary component of an investor's portfolio. Foreign funds may reduce a portfolio's volatility, but their economic and currency risks may reduce returns by a still larger amount. The idea that a theoretically optimal portfolio must hold each geographical component as its market weight simply pushes me further than I would dream of being pushed.

John C. Bogle

---

[8] Bogle (2010), p. 137.

2.6 Index Funds

John C. Bogle created the first index mutual fund at the end of 1975, a year after he founded The Vanguard Group investment company. That first fund tracked the S&P 500 index and remains a central Vanguard fund (Nasdaq ticker symbols VFINX and VFIAX). Initially, although praised by theoreticians (Sect. 2.6.2), it was ridiculed by the investment community for producing only average returns when the goal was to "beat the market." It took decades for the idea of an index fund to gain traction in the market.

Over time, the investment world has been slowly catching on. By 2015, almost two thirds of the assets in U.S. equity funds were actively managed. As of 2019, the assets of "passively" managed U.S. equity (index) funds surpassed the assets of the actively managed funds (Fig. 2.2).

Warren Buffett argued in 2017 that $100 billion had been lost to money managers, mainly by pension funds and wealthy individuals, over the previous decade. His conclusion: these investors would have done much better simply by investing in low-fee, broadly diversified index funds.[9] Figure 2.2 suggests that investors increasingly have shared this view.

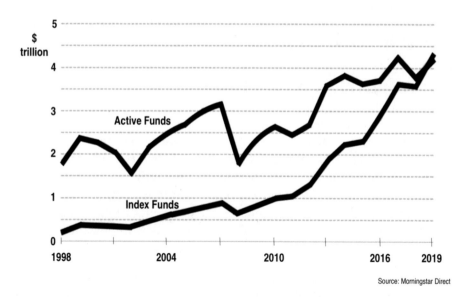

Fig. 2.2 Active vs. index market share. U.S. equity funds, including ETFs.

---

[9] nytimes.com/2017/02/27/business/dealbook/buffett-asks-big-money-why-pay-high-fees.html = tinyurl.com/j8py7m5.

Recently, Bogle has expressed concern that his idea has become too big, putting too much control of corporate ownership in too few hands, and he argues for some government regulation and possible divestiture (although the benefit to investors of index funds remains unquestioned).[10]

There is some concern for a hypothetical future when almost all of corporate America is owned by index funds—who then provides shareholder control of the companies?[11] I think there are many reasons to reject this concern, foremost being that the shareholders who own significant shares in a company do so for strategic financial reasons and are unlikely to want to switch to index funds.

Concern has also been expressed that specialized index funds leave room for collusion over what stocks are represented in the index.[12] This may be a reason to avoid specialized indices and stick with only broadly diversified, well-defined indices.

"Low-fee" is an important fund attribute, as loss to fees compounds over time. That means that the loss grows exponentially—see Sect. 9.2. It's a tribute to snappy marketing that there are so many brokerage houses and banks in this business. Logically, The Vanguard Group should have put all the others out of business, having effectively cornered the low-fee market.[13,14] But marketing is a wondrous thing that lets a hundred flowers bloom (at a cost). However, competitive pressure over low fees is indeed being felt, and recently Fidelity Investments began offering four *no-fee* index funds, seemingly besting Vanguard (but, see Sect. 2.13).

2.6.1 Vanguard Index Fund Study

In contrast to actively managed funds, Vanguard found (in their same study described in Sect. 1.6) that some index funds consistently came very close to matching their target benchmark, while others did less well. They found that "a fund's expense ratio [i.e., fees charged] was the most reliable predictor of its future performance, with low-cost funds delivering above-average performances in all of the periods examined." They cite another study that found that "expense ratio was the only significant factor in determining future alpha"

---

[10] https://wsj.com/articles/bogle-sounds-a-warning-on-index-funds-1543504551.

[11] bloomberg.com/news/features/2020-01-09/the-hidden-dangers-of-the-great-index-fund-takeover = tinyurl.com/t9mmlpe.

[12] nytimes.com/2019/02/18/opinion/index-fund.html.

[13] Vanguard is a mutual company owned by its funds, which in turn are owned by their shareholders (investors), allowing Vanguard generally to maintain much lower fees than their competitors.

[14] about.vanguard.com/what-sets-vanguard-apart/the-benefits-of-lower-costs/.

(performance relative to the target benchmark). They cite yet another study that found that "using a fund's Morningstar 'star' rating as a guide to future performance was less reliable than using the fund's expense ratio."

There also is a tax advantage to index funds: "Because turnover is much lower in an index fund, there is less need to distribute capital gains."

The conclusions of this Vanguard study form the core of Vanguard's widely lauded philosophy: index funds perform significantly better than most managed funds and almost universally better over time; the best index funds are the ones with the lowest fees (expense ratio). And Vanguard, as the discount house of investing, generally has the lowest fees available, by far—except for the two Fidelity funds just mentioned. (No, I have no affiliation with Vanguard, nor have I received any benefits from them beyond their generally available discounted investments that I use for my personal savings.)

2.6.2 Value of Index Funds Is Consistent with Research

Long before Vanguard, analyses by Harry Markowitz[15] and later, building on that, by William F. Sharpe[16] led to the creation of the Capital Asset Pricing Model (CAPM) and a Nobel Prize in economics (shared with Merton Miller, for work on the corporate side). One of the most important contributions of the CAPM is its theoretical justification for investing in index funds as an optimal strategy for balancing risk and growth. It gives a formulaic justification to the intuition that by combining many somewhat independent risky assets, the combined risk decreases, because a failure of one does not necessarily result in the failures of others. The more assets, the lower the combined risk.

An index like the S&P 500 combines assets with high growth rates to reduce risk through such diversification while maintaining a weighted average of the high growth rates of its components. A "total" stock index sacrifices some growth by diluting the pool with lower growth assets but at the same time further reduces risk with a larger and thus more diversified pool. It's hard to say which is better, and empirically the two appear very similar in their growth over time.

Normally, an equity investor would be concerned about the possible failure of an investment relative to average market performance. In the case of equity in a single company, such failure could be caused by mismanagement of the company. For investments in an equity sector (such as "small cap"), financial

---

[15] Markowitz (1952).
[16] Sharpe (1964).

shifts in perceptions of the sector can result in such underperformance. With an investment in a broadly diversified equity index fund, the bases for these concerns are diminished.

A detailed description of CAPM that is accessible to the layman can be found in the excellent readable book *Finance* by Zvi Bodie and Robert Merton.[17] A very accessible summary of the theoretical underpinnings of the better value of index funds over actively managed funds is given by Mark Hebner[18] (who is in the business of selling index funds).

2.7   ETFs or Mutual Funds?

Exchange-Traded Funds (ETFs) are like mutual funds but are traded like stocks. They are listed on exchanges and repriced continuously (like stocks) according to supply and demand. Mostly, they track an index such as the S&P 500 but could invest in industry sectors or utilize other strategies.

ETFs began in 1993 and by 2018 captured over $3.4 trillion in assets,[19] yet less than 20% of the $18 trillion mutual fund market[20] and 7% of the $50 trillion in assets invested in stocks and bonds. Nowadays, an index mutual fund and index ETF with the same target benchmark are often very similar, differing mostly in technicalities.

In the past, when ETFs were newer and had less volume, their fees tended to be slightly higher than for the corresponding index mutual fund, to cover slightly higher operating costs. However, now that they are more popular, the resulting economies of scale have brought their fees down to be virtually the same as the matching index fund. Before you buy, look for both the mutual fund version and ETF version of the index you wish to consider, and compare. Sometimes funds take lower fees in case you invest some stated minimum amount, like $10,000. If the amount you plan to invest exceeds this minimum, you should use that better cost factor in your comparison with the corresponding ETF.

The expense ratios of an ETF can be lower than a corresponding mutual fund because ETFs can reduce administrative costs by trading through brokerage firms, but often they are the same. When it comes to trading (buying or selling), there are some differences that can be significant. A mutual fund

---

[17] Bodie and Merton (2000).

[18] Hebner (2006).

[19] statista.com/statistics/295632/etf-us-net-assets/.

[20] https://mordorintelligence.com/industry-reports/us-mutual-funds-industry.

sometimes has a "load" fee: a commission paid to the vendor. This fee may be assessed at purchase ("front-end load"), upon sale ("back-end load"), or even as long as they are held ("level load"). ETFs have no such fees, and many mutual funds do not as well: "no-load" funds. On the other hand, sometimes a vendor charges a transaction fee for buys and sells (but often not). Unlike mutual funds, as ETFs trade like stocks, there are different prices when one buys (the "ask" price) or sells (the "bid" price). The difference (the "ask-bid spread") goes to the broker handling the transaction and typically is very small.

While ETFs trade like stocks, at the price of the moment, mutual funds trade according to their closing price at the end of the day. Often mutual funds support automated trading, for example, transferring a given amount to your checking account once a month. ETFs do not. There also are differences in how long it takes for transfers to settle, before they can be used for trades (mutual funds tend to be faster). ETFs often allow one to set up a limit order for sale or purchase of shares, triggered by the instant the ETF price hits a specified limit price. This can be very helpful in managing one's savings, as described next in Sect. 2.7.1. Mutual funds do not support limit sales and purchases, because they are priced only at the end of the trading day, thus without a continuum of price values.

On account of their amenability to a limit order, I recommend buying an ETF over an equivalent mutual fund, all else being equal, except in the case that you want to set up automated periodic transfers in or out—supported only by mutual funds.

2.7.1 Setting Up a Limit Order

There is a very handy mechanism that applies to the sale and purchase of individual securities and ETFs, called a *limit order*. It allows you to specify a price and number of shares that you seek to buy or sell at that price. Once set, the transaction completes automatically if the set price is ever reached, even if only for an instant during the trading day. (There are some technical limitations, such as if there are not enough shares available for a purchase, but these mostly apply only to huge transactions.)

Typically, you can set up your account so that you receive an email if the transaction completes. If you wish to exchange the proceeds of a limit sale for another security or ETF, often you also can do this immediately, either manually or as an automatic "exchange," without a need to wait for the sale to "settle." It's really simple and requires no monitoring of your asset.

This is a great mechanism to use to exchange a stock ETF for a bond ETF when the stock ETF reaches a designated high price, as counseled in Sects. 5.4 and 11.2.

As a practical matter, limit orders need to be renewed periodically (often, every 2 months).

2.8   CDs

Certificates of deposit (CDs) are sold by banks and credit unions. In a sense they lie between a savings bank deposit and a bond. Like a savings bank deposit, CDs are insured by the FDIC (up to the savings bank limits). Like bonds, CDs offer better rates of interest than a savings bank deposit, but unlike bonds, they cannot be resold. They impose strict limitations on withdrawal, and this restricted liquidity (cf. Sect. 3.8) should be fully appreciated when considering the purchase of a CD.

CDs are offered with stated terms, from a few months to several years. Usually, the longer the term, the higher the interest rate. Interest compounds within the CD and is paid along with the return of principal at the end of the term.

Like bonds, CDs can be laddered (Sect. 2.3.3), and like bond ladders, there might not be CDs available to fill all desired rungs of a ladder.

Although interest is paid only at withdrawal, the IRS treats it as annual income taxing it accordingly (much like zero-coupon bonds—Sect. 2.3.1).

2.9   And Then There's Cash

The paper money in your wallet is a Federal Reserve Note—technically, a sort of interest-free bond issued by a Federal Reserve bank, backed by U.S. Government assets. In practice, the value of currency in circulation exceeds those assets. The difference is made up by borrowing—issuing bonds.

The Notes carry no promise to be redeemed in gold, as paper money once did. The United States finally abandoned the gold standard under policies initiated in 1971 under President Nixon. That continued in stages until 1976, after which there was no connection between the U.S. dollar and gold. This was done in part to counter double-digit inflation caused by the economic policies of the time. However, it caused enormous consternation to some who feared it actually would exacerbate inflation (it did not). Earlier, in the 1930s, President Roosevelt eliminated the ability of private individuals to

2 Deciding What to Invest In   47

exchange dollars for gold, largely to stem gold hoarding that was accelerating the deflation of the Great Depression.

A highly "risk-averse" individual might be tempted to liquidate all assets and divide them into $250,000 chunks ($500,000 if married with a joint account)—the limits for FDIC insurance. Then each chunk could be invested in a different FDIC-insured savings bank and be fully insured by the U.S. Government. While at the time of this writing, savings bank interest rates are low (under 2%), they can be expected to rise with inflation. For a fee and CD withdrawal limitations, CDARS (Certificate of Deposit Account Registry Service) does the chunking for you. CDs have restrictions on when the funds may be withdrawn without penalty—generally, only at the end of the term.

A government-insured investment may seem reassuring. However, putting all one's assets in a savings bank may not be a prudent policy, as I explain at length in Chaps. 3 and 4, even for the highly "risk-averse."

Nonetheless, holding *some* assets in a savings bank can provide a very convenient mechanism for managing one's cash flow needs. For example, say you anticipated needing to draw monthly a fixed amount for expenses. The annual total can be transferred from stocks and bonds to a savings account, at times deemed advantageous for selling those. The savings account can be set up to implement automatic monthly transfers to a checking account, of the required monthly amounts. Savings account interest is orders of magnitude greater than checking account interest (e.g., 2% vs. 0.01%).

Some people prefer credit unions over savings banks. A credit union is a "not-for-profit" cooperative financial institution owned by its depositors. As a result of its reduced operating expenses and preferential tax status, in the past, credit unions generally have given somewhat better rates than savings banks. With the advent of online banks and their inherent efficiencies, this generality no longer holds. Credit unions are insured up to the same limits as savings banks, by the National Credit Union Administration (NCUA), which is analogous to the FDIC for savings banks. Generally smaller than savings banks, credit unions have a reputation for offering more personalized service.

It's worth shopping around for a good rate, as savings bank and credit union interest rates can vary considerably—one can be twice as much as another. (What happened to the "efficient market"?)

Similar to an investment in a savings bank or credit union is an investment in a money market account or fund.

The "money market" is a loosely defined concept that refers to very short-term institutional loans with high liquidity and low risk that are used by financial institutions to maintain their cash holdings at desired levels in order to facilitate conducting their daily business. Its interest rates largely track the *Federal Funds Rate*, set by the Federal Reserve, which often acts as an intermediary for such inter-bank transfers.

Commercial banks and other financial institutions offer investments in this money supply at rates that generally are slightly lower than the Federal Funds Rate. These rates can be slightly higher than what one can get from a savings bank, as they are not FDIC-insured.

On account of its backing, investments in the money market have high liquidity and low risk. Often, they can be drawn or deposited at any time, with any desired frequency. However, offered interest rates fluctuate much more than do those of savings banks and credit unions and, in some (very rare) cases, can be negative.

It is possible for an uninsured money market investment to lose money. This happens if the money market fund "breaks the buck" in investment lingo. (It refers to the price per share, normally set at $1, falling below that.) This is a very unlikely occurrence. It happened last during the 2008 financial crisis at Lehman Brothers—where the losses were around 3%. The only other such loss since money market funds were introduced in the 1970s was 6% in 1994, at Community Bankers.

Money market accounts offered by savings banks and credit unions are insured by the FDIC and NCUS (up to the savings bank limits). They are limited to six payments and six withdrawals per month, with some exceptions, and may have minimum deposit requirements and caps on single withdrawals.

Money market funds come in a number of varieties, mostly related to what the fund invests in. If mostly in U.S. Government Treasury Bills and obligations, then the investment is pretty much as safe as one in a savings bank where it is insured by the FDIC, but without the caps on the insured amount. Funds backed by other (low-risk) obligations as well can offer slightly higher yields (along with a small added risk).

The best money market interest rates offered by low-fee financial institutions like Vanguard should be slightly better than the best interest rates offered by online savings banks, on account of economies of scale and lack of FDIC insurance. However, at any given time, the rate offered by one may be better than the rate offered by the other on account of external factors. Over a span of time, the average rate to date may also be slightly different. For example, in October, 2018, the 7-day SEC yield[21] for Vanguard's "Federal" money market fund VMFXX was 2.05% (annualized), while that for Ally, an online savings

---

[21]A standardized measure developed by the U.S. Securities and Exchange Commission (SEC) for money market interest rates that is net fees.

bank, was 1.9%. However, YTD (year to date), the Vanguard annualized rate was 1.23%, while Ally's was 1.62%.

Vanguard also offers money market funds with slightly higher yields: 2.25% SEC 7-day yield and 1.42% YTD for the day in question, for VMRXX with a minimum investment of $5,000,000. But the risk with VMRXX is slightly higher, since it invests in non-U.S. Government obligations (including foreign bonds). For this reason, it is not a fair comparison with an FDIC-insured investment.

All of these rates are below the rate of inflation, so not a good idea for long-term investment. However, for short-term investments (where liquidity is essential), the loss to inflation can be substantially less than the expected loss on account of volatility (needing to sell when the investment value is depressed).

You can transfer an IRA (Sect. 12.3) into a savings bank, credit union, or money market IRA.

Although such investments in cash have the worst growth rate among conventional investments, when drawn down regularly, they experience no degradation of growth rate, as does a regularly drawn-down volatile investment (Sect. 11.1). This can make them competitive with a regularly drawn-down higher growth, more volatile investment such as in bonds (Sect. 11.1).

2.10 Annuities

Annuities come in several varieties, their unifying feature being that they are sold by insurance companies (often through brokers). The most common annuities are presented as an answer for the "risk-averse" in that they promise a guaranteed stipend, usually monthly, usually for the remaining lifetime of the annuitant. Many people who are afraid of investing in the securities markets are sold on this as a very comforting alternative to active investment—annuity sales staff are often quite effective in casting this reassuring message.

However, an annuity without an inflation adjustment loses its value over time. An "inflation-adjusting" annuity costs significantly more, lowering its effective yield—the measure of its value. It has the additional risk that it will not in fact keep up with the rate of inflation experienced by the annuitant. Indeed, even for inflation adjustments based on the CPI-U (the U.S. urban Consumer Price Index), it has been observed that the expenses of many groups—especially, the elderly—grow at a faster rate.[22] For the elderly, this

---

[22] Huang and Milevsky (2011).

is largely on account of their disproportionate need for healthcare with its rapidly growing costs. Moreover, this inflation index has become degraded. For Social Security, it has been replaced by the more slowly growing chained CPI-U (the C-CPI-U). All this reduces the ability of an annuity to keep up with the level of inflation experienced by the annuitant.

And with a simple annuity, there is nothing left for heirs no matter when the annuitant dies. Some annuities do allow for some value to be passed to heirs—at an additional expense that rarely makes financial sense.

Lastly, but certainly not least, with a lifetime annuity, one loses forever the premium paid for the annuity, so one loses liquidity. As a practical matter, this may dominate the list of deficiencies of an annuity. Unlike an investment in the securities market, you almost never[23] can retrieve your investment (the premium you paid), no matter how badly you may need it for an unforeseen emergency or just for a change in life style.

What if, under pressure from increasing financial failures in the retirement community (Chap. 18), the government began to offer a cost-effective liquid inflation-tracking annuity (a combination of government-issued inflation-protected bonds and a deferred inflation-adjusted annuity) as has been proposed?[24] If one had already purchased a commercial annuity, this putatively better opportunity would likely be lost.

Let's examine the various types of annuities individually. There are two main varieties: "variable rate" and "fixed rate."

2.10.1 Variable Rate Annuity

Variable rate annuities are a (typically, opaque) amalgam of a fixed rate annuity (Sect. 2.10.2) and a market investment. They would be hard to analyze even if their composition and operation were truly transparent. Although in the offering brochures of those that I have examined, an effort is made to *appear* transparent, their actual governing details are hard to fathom and are actually disclosed only in dense, often 100-page or more legal-jargon-filled "disclosures" that mostly defy comprehension by laypersons (if not anyone else). In fact, they seem to be constructed in order to avoid the degree of transparency needed to evaluate their actual value. One particularly egregious version, called an *indexed annuity*, guarantees protection against down markets (and may or may

---

[23]There are some complex "variable rate" annuities (Sect. 2.10.1) that do allow for some retrieval of the premium paid, but these may be terrible financial investments.

[24]Waring and Siegel (2015).

not have a fixed rate annuity component). These have been widely panned[25] and seem aimed at the fearful and gullible.

Ever wonder about those free steak dinners followed by an investment pitch[26,27] for a variable rate annuity? Someone is paying for that steak!

There are many accounts of how variable rate annuities have been used by hucksters to reap large commissions at the expense of clueless clients.[28,29,30] You can check on a broker or brokerage at FINRA, "an independent, non-governmental regulator for all securities firms doing business with the public in the United States."[31] Thanks to Ron Lieber of the *The New York Times* for these links.

The variable rate annuities that I looked at, after properly interpreting numbers that appear to show promising value, in fact give a relatively poor effective rate of return (Sect. 2.10.5). Compelling marketing, it seems, can compensate for a host of deficiencies.

2.10.2 Fixed Rate Annuity

Fixed rate annuities come in several sub-varieties, mainly fixed term and variable term—immediate and deferred.

How to compute the value of a fixed rate annuity in terms of its effective yield is explained in Appendix A.9.

MYGA

The easiest annuity to understand is one that is not often even associated with the term "annuity." It is called a "Multi-Year Guaranteed Annuity" (MYGA) or sometimes just "fixed-term annuity" and pays a fixed compounded interest rate each year for a fixed term—usually, 1–10 years—after which it returns the principal and interest. It comes with rules covering early withdrawals (which in some cases incur penalties that decrease with time). MYGAs are similar to CDs (Sect. 2.8), but unlike CDs, a MYGA is taxed only at the end of its term, when all its interest (together with the principal) are returned to the holder.

---

[25] e.g., fidelity.com/viewpoints/retirement/considering-indexed-annuities.

[26] nytimes.com/2018/11/30/your-money/retirement-annuities-steak-dinner.html.

[27] sec.gov/spotlight/seniors/freelunchreport.pdf = tinyurl.com/y9boshy6.

[28] nytimes.com/2017/08/04/your-money/401ks-and-similar-plans/when-brokers-want-to-move-your-money-out-of-a-very-good-thing.html = tinyurl.com/ybmr2dyj.

[29] https://assets.aarp.org/rgcenter/consume/freelunch.pdf.

[30] https://www.finra.org/investors/alerts/variable-annuities-beyond-hard-sell.

[31] brokercheck.finra.org.

A MYGA may be an attractive option under certain circumstances. Like any annuity, it is subject to the counterparty risk (default of the issuer—Sect. 2.10.3). It also may be subject to a hidden "fee" at the time of withdrawal. Although not a fee *per se*, it has the same effect, and works like this. As you may know, banks require a few days for a check to "clear," as allowed by the Expedited Funds Availability Act of 1987. Thirty years ago, allowing a few days for a check to clear made some sense, since most transactions were paper-based and took a while to verify. Today, however, such verifications are largely instantaneous, since they are handled electronically. Nonetheless, as you may imagine, banks are in no hurry to shorten the period, since in the time they take to "clear" your check, they are holding your money and investing it for their own purposes, with no compensation to you. Any attempts to shorten this period would be met with corresponding resistance from the banks, and given their immense political clout, this has not happened.

Ok, so you lost the use of your money for 3 days—no big deal, you say. But with a MYGA, that's just the beginning. Rather than use electronic funds transfer to disburse the funds, they may insist on sending the disbursement by paper check, via the U.S. Postal Service. Another week. And they can sit on your disbursement request for a week before they put the check in the mail: 2 more weeks. The result can be 2–3 weeks from the time your MYGA has come to term to the time that you receive the funds—a hidden "fee" of around 0.5% lost on what you could have earned on your money, had it not been retained instead by the insurance company for their own use.

In at least one case (Brighthouse Financial), they do allow for expedited handling: they send your funds (after their 3–5-day holding period) by electronic funds transfer—but only if you have set that up at least *30 days earlier*. As this 30-day requirement is not something that many investors would anticipate (in other cases, it's only 1 day), it's a pretty fair bet that they get to use your money for at least 2 extra weeks, with no benefit to you.

immediate annuity
The most common type of fixed rate annuity is called an "immediate annuity." It pays a fixed periodic stipend, usually monthly, for the life or joint life of the annuitant(s). For extra fees that may not be cost-effective, it can have a life insurance component (possibly the most cost-effective among the not-cost-effective add-ons), a buyer's remorse pay-back feature, and features that cause the stipend to increase periodically at a given rate or track an index such as the S&P 500 or CPI-U.

deferred annuity

A variation on the immediate annuity is a "deferred annuity." It is an annuity that you buy now but which starts paying its stipend after a deferral period. If you die during the deferral period, the entire premium generally is lost to the insurance company.

Sometimes these annuities are called *longevity insurance* because in fact that's their function: to insure you against living too long. Like fire insurance that pays nothing if your house doesn't burn down, these pay nothing if you die soon—which is "OK" in a financial sense, because then you won't outlive your savings. (You're not sorry your house didn't burn down after you paid for fire insurance.) But if you live longer than expected, they pay a stipend so that you won't end retirement penniless. It seems like a reasonable principle, as long as it's not too expensive. (Somehow, people don't like to think about insuring against living "too long," so the term "longevity insurance" has gone out of favor.)

2.10.3   Risk of Default

There is one annuity "benefit" that may be oversold. It is the selling point often most heavily stressed by the seller (the broker or the insurance company). That point is that "only an annuity can be guaranteed to give you a predictable stream of income for the rest of your life."

First of all, it is false, if the insurance company goes bankrupt—and a number have and others, even very big ones, have come close: think AIG—then your policy may be taken up voluntarily by other insurance companies (or even by an exceptional act of the U.S. Government, as in the case of AIG). But, aside from a federal bailout, the extent of such coverage differs from state to state, is not guaranteed, and may only pay another 5–10 years on your policy.

Thus, buying any annuity places a very long-term faith in a company that may default: the counterparty risk. Insurance companies, like bonds, are rated, and one pays more for an annuity sold by a more highly rated insurance company. But, even if you purchased your annuity from the most highly rated insurance company, there is a possibility that the obligation is sold to what ends up being a company with a much lower rating—it can happen, especially in recent times when high finance is run by algorithms aimed at optimizing a company's stock value, and the moral obligation of repaying a debt is not even a factor.

For example, in the first year after MetLife divested its annuity business to a new company it formed called Brighthouse Financial, Brighthouse's stock plummeted over 40%, and its ratings dropped from what they had been at MetLife. Standard & Poor's rating of MetLife was "Very Strong"; at the time of this writing, their rating of Brighthouse was "Strong," which still doesn't sound too bad, but they gave Brighthouse a "Negative" outlook. What is a holder of an annuity to do if it was bought from MetLife at a premium cost, thinking the investment thus to be very safe, and now finds it in the hands of Brighthouse?

Bankruptcy is not necessarily the end of the line, as a company's liabilities may be acquired along with its assets by another healthy company. However, the past rarity of insurance policy-holders losing value cannot guarantee the future. For Lehmann Brothers, the king of bankruptcies, after the dust settled, over $270 billion was lost forever. In fact, according to the National Organization of Life & Health Insurance Guaranty Associations,[32] since 1987 there have been over 70 failures of multi-state insurance companies. The risk is there and it's real even if it's hard to measure.

The SECURE Act of 2019 provides incentives for employers to include annuities in a 401(k) retirement plan (Sect. 12.1). These incentives include protection for the employer in case the annuity provider defaults. While this has been viewed as a great boon to the annuity industry by increasing the likelihood that an employer offers an annuity in a 401(k), the protection provides no benefit to the annuitant. It just means that if the provider defaults, the annuitant cannot hold the employer liable.

To state it emphatically: an annuity inherently is *not* risk-free.

2.10.4 Annuities for Portfolio Diversification?

Potentially, it could be reasonable to invest a portion of one's savings in an annuity as a means to diversify one's savings portfolio. Analytical arguments[33] have been given in support of this.

However, there would be a cost at which such a decision could make sense, and a cost beyond which it wouldn't make sense.

The point is: it all comes down to the yield of the annuity—its effective return on investment (the premium that you pay). For a commercially available annuity, if its yield is high enough, the diversification potential provides a valuable option, while if the yield is too low, the value disappears.

---

[32] nolhga.com.

[33] Horneff, Maurer, and Stamos (2008).

Somehow, when people consider the value of an annuity for portfolio diversification, they often fail to take into account its yield. This is simple enough to do (Sect. 2.10.5).

2.10.5 Evaluating an Annuity

Given that the main selling point of an annuity—that it is "risk-free"—is bogus, its value should be measured against the values of other options such as a bond ladder (Sect. 2.3.3).

Like a bond ladder, an annuity can be risk-adjusted too, by buying several from different companies. But with fewer choices, there is a coarse granularity, and in practice, for a given product, it may be possible to choose among only two or three companies with different risks and commensurate product prices. While market forces can be counted on to adjust bond prices fairly as a function of issuer rating, it is hard for a layman to understand the meaning and potential consequences of an insurance company's rating. Therefore, there is no market force to ensure that an annuity's price fairly reflects the risk of default by the issuing company, as captured by its rating.

Without a costly rider that indexes an annuity stipend to inflation,[34] an annuity may be worth much less after a number of years of high inflation. A bond ladder may be indexed to inflation, using TIPS (Sect. 2.3.1), or include, *at cost*, a growth factor that is estimated to track inflation.

Moreover, what about liquidity risk (Sect. 3.8)? Let's say you have a health emergency, a grandchild's vital need, a dramatic life change that requires money that you do not have? If you have a ladder of bonds, you can break the ladder by selling some bonds, in effect, borrowing against the future. With a simple annuity, its premium is *gone*. (Annuities that retain some cash value tend to be very expensive.)

There is also some liquidity risk with a bond ladder, in that the price that you get from an early sale may constitute a loss. But, at least you get something, and under favorable conditions, you might even get a lot more than you paid.

To evaluate an annuity, various term lengths are chosen, corresponding to different annuitant longevities (how long you will live). You can compute the yield of the annuity if you live to some given old age, or to your actuarially expected longevity, or for a premature death. You can weigh the likelihoods of these different terms, based on your health and life style (risk-taking). For

---

[34]What I found increased the cost by almost 50%, whereas the correct increase for a 24-year additional life expectancy is around 30%.

each term length, you then can compute the effective yield of the annuity. The details of how to do this are given in Appendices "A.9.1" for an immediate annuity and "A.9.2" for a deferred annuity.

As the chosen term increases, the annuity yield increases. You can find the term for which the annuity yield is competitive with that of other types of investment. A bond ladder provides one measure for comparison. Alternatively, you may decide that an investment in an intermediate bond fund is a good enough proxy for the bond ladder, and compare its range of yields over time with the yields computed for the annuity.

For a deferred annuity, it's daunting enough to contemplate that you are giving away a pile of money with the likelihood that you will not live long enough to see any benefit from it. But in addition, you need to keep your fingers crossed, hoping that the company won't go out of business before you die. Why isn't there federal insurance coverage for annuities like what the FDIC provides for savings banks? (There is some limited coverage provided *voluntarily* by state insurance cooperatives. The coverage varies from state to state. But the most likely circumstance for an insurance company to fail is a general financial catastrophe such as the one we experienced in 2008—or worse. In such a case, many insurance companies could be adversely affected, leaving insufficient funds in the ones that remained solvent to cover the obligations of those that failed.)

2.10.6 Annuities Are Expensive!

The annual payout rate (payout as a fraction of the premium) for a fixed rate annuity in December, 2015, for a 65-year-old couple was around 5.5%–6% of its cost (depending on the insurer's rating) for 100% spouse survivor payments. However, this rate is highly deceptive, as it neglects the fact that you never get the premium back!

For a 30-year term, an annual payout of 6% of the cost of the annuity corresponds to an annual yield of 4.3% on the investment (Appendix A.9.1). If the second spouse to die lived to age 105, the corresponding yield is 5.2%. Based on actuarial calculations,[35] for a 65-year-old couple, the expected age of the second spouse to die is 89, or after 24 years from the start of the annuity. For that 24-year term, the corresponding yield is 3.1%.

By comparison, in 2015, it was fairly easy to construct a ladder of high-grade bonds that lasted for 24 years with a yield of 4%–5%. Moreover, unlike with

---

[35] E.g., Vanguard (2000), pgcalc.com/pdf/twolife.pdf = tinyurl.com/yagkcyw5.

an annuity, with a bond ladder, heirs receive any surplus after the death of the second spouse to die. With a ladder, if there are unexpected expenses, the ladder can be invaded.

A deferred annuity *should* be the most cost-effective of the fixed rate annuities, because you're trusting the insurance company with your money and get nothing back during the deferral period.

For the insurance company, a deferred annuity also seems like a good bet: if the deferral period ends after your expected death, then they pay you nothing. As a result, they should be able to offer this annuity at a really great price: for what should be a small premium, you'd get the assurance that if you live longer than expected, you're covered. That's a proper use of insurance—coverage for an unlikely but catastrophic event: outliving your savings.

They do pay out more once they start paying, on account of the fact that the insurance company has been holding your premium without payment during the deferral period. However, for some odd reason, of the ones I examined, comparable immediate annuities gave almost the same yield, as calculated in Appendix A.9.2. This renders deferred annuities non-competitive with immediate annuities, an odd situation. Indeed, the insurance company should compensate you with a better yield for receiving nothing during the deferral period and for taking the risk that they go bankrupt in the interim. In addition, you have no access to the cash corresponding to the payments that you would have received with an immediate annuity.

Thus, unfortunately, the deferred annuities/longevity insurance products that I was able to find were not cost-effective.

When I asked a broker about this peculiarity, he agreed and said it looks like the insurance companies haven't figured out how to price them competitively.

It could also be that since they do pay more when they start paying, that the insurance companies hope their clients don't notice that their yields are almost the same as for the less risky immediate annuities.

Charupat et al.[36] demonstrate that annuity pricing is sluggish with respect to interest rate changes and thus may not reflect a fair market value.

Huang et al.[37] give a dollar cost averaging strategy for deferred annuities, with the potential to make them more cost-effective. But the typical consumer likely just wants to buy a fairly priced product, not one that must be "gamed."

---

[36]Charupat et al. (2015).
[37]Huang et al. (2017).

Some analysts[38] suggest that fixed rate annuities are inherently non-competitive products, simply because, after all, an annuity is a product marketed by an insurance company, with all the associated costs of marketing, corporate management, processing, selling, and obligations to shareholders that inevitably siphon off value.

2.11 Real Estate

Investment real estate comes in two flavors and many sub-flavors. The two main flavors are:

1. Real estate partnerships that you buy into, which are managed by a professional manager
2. Real estate that you own (and thus manage) completely, yourself

While there are many advantages to 1., including deferred taxation and a potential for high yields, each instance is different and, moreover, for the little guy, *highly* risky: there's lots of "fine print," many fees (explicit and hidden) and the only version of 1. that I think a rational little guy should consider are real estate investment trust (REIT) index funds, specifically (and perhaps only) the ones at Vanguard: Vanguard's VGSIX (or its ETF version VNQ), which are index funds of real estate. They're "safe," because they're index funds, but for the same reason, their performance is bland—they just follow the real estate market as a whole. You can invest here a (small) component of your portfolio in the name of "diversification," just as you can invest in a commodity index fund, a utility index fund, etc. But then: how much? in what proportion? There's little available research to answer this, and whether it ends up well or poorly may just be the luck of the draw. I'd say: just stick with broad equity index funds: the simplest, the easiest, and likely the best.

In the end, my advice is to forget 1., except possibly for time-shares in a ski house or beach house that you can actually get some pleasure from, to justify what otherwise could easily turn into a losing proposition. Even for time-shares, you need to be *very* careful: who is responsible for what? What happens when the manager (or partner who handles the bills) leaves town or otherwise drops out? What happens when someone wants to sell? What happens when a member stops paying common charges? What happens when

---

[38] Marotta (2012).

2 Deciding What to Invest In 59

the city says your sewer connection has a code violation and must be upgraded? When the state slaps a fine on you for some violation that nobody remembers ever getting a notice for, and now you must hire a lawyer? Having a professional manager doesn't necessarily solve these problems. The manager could leave or be inadequate. If the property is owned by a corporation, then the fate of your time-share is tied to the health of the corporation, which can change over time.

As for those shopping center partnerships with the 30-page glossy brochure and (unwritten) promises that you'll shelter taxes and in 2 years double your money—avoid them like the plague! There are more scandals involving such deals than I can count. Does the place even exist? Have you been there and inspected it (in the middle of far-away-wherever)? But the documents show it's been in operation for 10 years and turned handsome profits each year! Then why are you even being offered such a "good deal"? Insiders should already have gobbled it up! Oh—could it be that in 2 years that tax abatement expires and then profits go south? Or, in 2 years the parking lot will need to be redone, and expenses will eat up all the profits? Or, the biggest employer in town is moving to Mexico and then there will be no one to shop there and the shopping center will be given up for taxes? Do you have the bandwidth for the due diligence to truly assess this offer? No? Then *avoid!*

For a particular piece of real estate, it's unclear whether owning it purely as an investment is better on average than simply putting the same money into the S&P 500. It's hard to quantify such investments statistically, because their circumstances are so varied. However, since 1950, until the sub-prime bubble of 2000, U. S. home prices on average barely out-paced inflation (Fig. 2.3). This is significantly worse than the S&P 500, which grew in the same period, with dividends reinvested, at an annual rate of 10.6%, or 6.9% on top of inflation. But prices in different geographies have behaved very differently, so this average may not be terribly informative regarding a particular investment interest or region.

One of the most acclaimed real estate developers of our time is Donald J. Trump. According to an extensive investigation by *The New York Times*,[39] "Had Mr. Trump done nothing but invest the money his father gave him in an index fund that tracks the Standard & Poor's 500, he would be worth $1.96 billion today," while according to a Bloomberg estimate, his current net worth is $2.8 billion.[40] Of the $840 million difference, his tv show "along with

---

[39] nytimes.com/interactive/2018/10/02/us/politics/donald-trump-tax-schemes-fred-trump.html = tinyurl.com/y4u336wr.

[40] bloomberg.com/news/articles/2018-05-31/trump-s-net-worth-slides-to-2-8-billion-lowest-since-campaign = tinyurl.com/y327hvpk.

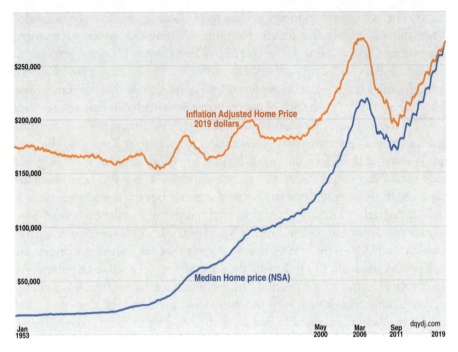

Fig. 2.3 U.S. median single family home prices 1953–2019 (not seasonally adjusted).

the licensing and endorsement deals that flowed from his expanding celebrity, brought Mr. Trump a total of $427.4 million".[41] At least some of the remaining $413 million (if not even more than that) must be attributed to his book sales and licensing deals to put his name on properties he didn't own. These were separate from his real estate transactions. But even if not, then a life of real estate investments and all the rest of the wheeling and dealing increased his net worth less than 50% over just investing the money in the S&P 500 and playing golf all day long. On the other hand, if his net worth is only the $788 million reported by Deutsche Bank,[42] then it would seem an index fund investment would have made him into the billionaire he claims to be.

Regarding 2., if you have a pile of cash that you'd like to use to buy an apartment in New York City, say—because "in NYC, real estate only goes up in value"—then consider this: it doesn't only go up. In the 1970s the bottom dropped out of the coop market in NYC and took decades to recover. The bursting of the housing bubble in 2007–2008 brought misery, misfortune,

---

[41] nytimes.com/interactive/2020/09/27/us/donald-trump-taxes.html.
[42] nytimes.com/2019/03/18/business/trump-deutsche-bank.html.

2 Deciding What to Invest In   61

"You can replace the tank, switch to natural gas, or huddle in a corner and cry as you ask yourself why you ever thought buying a house was a good idea."

Fig. 2.4 Home ownership. The New Yorker ©Condé Nast.

and destitution to many, all around the country. The factors that affect real estate prices are varied, complex, and not completely understood.[43]

Moreover, you need to *manage* your holding. That means get the heater fixed when it breaks (Fig. 2.4), hire a lawyer to evict your tenant when he defaults. And what happens when there's a gas leak in the basement of the building, and every apartment is assessed $20 thousand to make the needed repairs?

You'll need to find tenants, fix stuff that breaks, deal with tenants that don't pay their rent, deal with taxes, assessments, etc. Is it really worth it? That amazing park view gets blocked when the building next door is demolished and a high-rise is built in its place—what happens to your investment then?

---

[43] Sutton (2002), Tsatsaronis and Zhu (2004).

62   R. P. Kurshan

Nonetheless, there can be compelling reasons to own real estate: for starters, the home where you live. Despite the risks, you may be better off owning than renting, if you can afford it. Owning guarantees that you can stay in your home even if market conditions change. There's no way I could afford to rent (or buy) today the apartment that I live in, bought years earlier for very little. (But that was a matter of luck, having been in the right place at the right time. And at the time, I didn't even know it.)

On the other hand, if you own your home and it appreciates greatly in value, you may be locked in your castle. Say you want to sell, to down-size when the kids finally leave home, or simply to move to a different neighborhood. You may find that the capital gains taxes prevent you from moving, if you want to live in the same area. If you bought your home 40 years ago, its value today may have quadrupled, simply as a result of inflation. Selling it can entail paying capital gains tax on a large portion of its current value, despite the $250,000 exemption for a primary residence ($500,000 for married couples). With the proceeds of a sale, after capital gains tax, you may not be able to afford to buy another home in your neighborhood.[44] A renter generally is in a worse position, though. When home prices rise, so do rents. An exception is a renter in a rent-controlled apartment. Like the homeowner, that renter is locked in because leaving results in losing the benefit of the rent control.

Even under normal circumstances, real estate can become a high-stakes gamble. If you are buying a home, no matter how diligent you feel you have been, there are many adverse undisclosed circumstances that can lower a home's value. A factory could be planned, across the street. The wonderful school just down the block, which boosted the value of the home, could be scheduled to close. The local tax structure could be revamped, leading to a stiff increase in taxes. On the selling side, say you enter into a contract to sell your home and take a deposit as a down-payment. You may be forgiven if you think that in the worst case, the buyer can default, but then you get to keep the deposit. With the deposit, you are that much better off to sell your home again. However, the buyer can sue you using any bogus reason, in order to intimidate you into returning the deposit. The buyer can place a lien on your home, preventing you from reselling it, until you return the deposit or until you fight the suit in court and ultimately, after years and thousands in legal fees, prevail. Unless you have funds to fight the law suit, and time to stay with your

---

[44]It seems very unfair that when computing capital gains tax, inflation is not taken into account—especially, for a primary residence.

home unsold, you are left with no choice but to return the deposit, possibly together with additional "damages" that the unethical buyer has concocted.

There are other good reasons, though, to own real estate outright. Some city families invest in a "country" house to give their kids a weekend experience that isn't city life. The up-front cost is an investment that can, in theory, be recouped by selling the house, and it facilitates a style of life that otherwise might not be possible. Therefore, if you can afford the buy-in, there are compelling justifications for this sort of real estate investment, as long as you're aware of the risks and able, in the worst cases, to absorb them.

Of course, when it comes time to sell, the price can be way up, way down, or anything in between. Since the bursting of the housing bubble in 2007–2008, there are fewer subscribers to the previously popular mantra that "real estate prices only go up." But, although highly risky as an investment, it can be justified on life-style terms.

If you have a property that you have rented out that has appreciated significantly in value, and you want to exchange it for a different real estate investment, you may be able to avoid paying any capital gains tax. You do that through a strategy called a "1031 exchange."

2.12 Are Solar Panels a Good Investment?

Thinking about investing in solar panels to offset your electric bills, but don't know if it's cost-effective? There's a very simple way to decide. An investment in solar panels is exactly like a simple annuity. You pay for the installation, which is like the annuity premium. The annual saving in electric bills is like the annuity stipend. Its term, like the annuitant longevity, is how long you expect the system to last before it needs to be substantially replaced.

You compute the yield of the investment, exactly as with an immediate annuity, using the mortgage formula (Appendix A.9.1).

As an example, suppose the total cost of installing the solar panels is $20,000 and the calculated savings in electrical bills is $1,800 per year. This is 9% of the cost, but doesn't take into account the sunk cost of the panels—which you never get back. The mortgage formula gives the yield r of the investment in terms of the number of years n that the panels last. If $n = 15$, $r = 4\%$; if $n = 25$, $r = 7.5\%$; if $n = 30$, $r = 8.1\%$.

This is your actual return on your investment. In the given example, it looks comparable to a good bond. And, you're doing something good for the environment.

Of course, it's important to vet the solar panel company to assure they and their product are reliable (just like checking the rating of an insurance company selling an annuity, or a company issuing a bond).

2.13 Finally, Some Specific Advice

My favorite investments are Vanguard's lowest-fee index ETFs (Sect. 2.7):

- VOO (tracking the S&P 500)
- VTI (tracking the CRSP total U.S. stock market)
- VXUS (tracking the FTSE Global All Cap ex-U.S. international stock index)
- BND (tracking the U.S. intermediate-term bond market)
- BNDX (international intermediate-term bond index ETF that seeks to track the Bloomberg Barclays Global Aggregate ex-USD Float Adjusted RIC Capped Index)

All of these are also available as mutual funds with similar performance, and similar fee structures when bought in sufficient quantity. However, ETFs can be bought and sold through a limit order (Sect. 2.7.1), making them much easier to manage with regard to the strategy presented in Chaps. 4 and 5. Therefore, I recommend investing in ETFs, all else being equal.

Although Vanguard has essentially cornered the low-fee index fund market,[45] recently Fidelity Investments has apparently sought to undercut Vanguard by offering a *no-fee* total stock market index fund (FZROX) and three other no-fee index funds. However, it was revealed[46] that Fidelity makes up for the loss of fees by holding its dividends for up to a year before distributing them to the investors. The resulting loss to the investor, it was reported, exceeds Vanguard's expense ratio (fee) for its analogous fund.

Depending on your tax situation, especially for those in a high tax bracket (Sect. 12.7), a tax-free bond index fund like VWIUX also can be a good investment.

Vanguard has a handy tool for comparing the costs and performance of up to five different investments (including non-Vanguard offerings) that is reached from the page that describes a particular fund, through a "compare"

---

[45] see Sect. 2.6, footnotes 13, 14.

[46] personalfinanceclub.com/fzrox-vs-vtsax-the-hidden-cost-of-fidelitys-zero-fee-index-funds/ tinyurl.com/y8fs3co6.

2 Deciding What to Invest In   65

button. As a point of information, the SEC yield (30-day yield, for most funds) is computed by an SEC-mandated formula that projects the current rate of earnings, net fees, based on the last 30 days. It excludes capital gains, so only gives a partial picture of a fund.

There are other total market funds. For example, the Schwab Total Stock Market Fund and the Blackrock iShares Russell 3000, both of which track the Russell 3000 U.S. equities market, another U.S. equities market index. The Wilshire 5000 Index Investment Fund seeks to track the Wilshire 5000 Index, yet another U.S. equities market index. One more total stock market index is the MSCI U.S. Broad Market Index.

The Schwab fund has an expense ratio that is two times that of Vanguard's Total Stock Market Index ETF, BlackRock's is 4 times as much, and the Wilshire Fund is over 12 times as much, at the time of this writing.

Historically, all the total stock market indices track one another pretty closely—to which I can add the S&P 500 index, which is not a total market index, but rather tracks the 500 largest publicly traded U.S. companies.

There's no good data on "total" stock market vs. S&P 500. Some experts argue that the S&P 500 is too narrow and that the stocks it tracks give an overly optimistic view of the market in order to satisfy its Wall Street patrons. During the not-so-long history of total stock market funds (Vanguard's goes back only to 1992), they are all pretty close to the S&P 500, though.[47] You can choose "total" based on principle (it's broader), S&P 500 based on history (it has a long and reasonable track record), or some mix of the two—say, a bet-hedging 50%–50%.[48]

The S&P 500 index and the CRSP index (tracked by Vanguard's Total Stock index), for example, are so close to one another because each stock in the index is weighted proportionally to its market capitalization. As a result, although the CRSP is influenced by many more stocks, there is something like an 80% overlap between the two after weighting.

---

[47] seekingalpha.com/article/4391002-voo-vs-vti-smackdown-know-how-differ-you-invest.
[48] https://stockanalysis.com/voo-vs-vti/.

3

Understanding Risk

What does *risk* have to do with managing finances? A lot.

Simply because a choice is "risky" doesn't mean it should be avoided, because its alternative is also likely to be risky. One needs to be able to compare risks. Understanding and comparing the risks associated with an investment and its alternatives can help to make the most beneficial choice.

Every time we climb out of bed, take a shower, boil an egg, or cross the street, we engage in decisions that on some, mostly intuitive, level involve an assessment of risk. We know that people slip and break bones in the shower—it may even have happened to us. Yet, we still go to the shower. Why? We believe that the risk is worth the benefit. This is especially true when the benefit is palpable, even if small (like feeling fresh), while the risk—even if grievous, like broken bones—seems remote.

We also take risks that are less remote. The most infamous common risk is driving. If we drive, we generally are comfortable with its risks, and again, at least at an intuitive level, have decided that the benefits outweigh these risks. After all, we know it's dangerous, and yet we drive—mostly, without giving it a second thought.

Is that the "right" decision, or merely the result of a possibly bad habit? I think that most people, if forced to consider the decision carefully, would conclude that unless an individual is an alcoholic or otherwise habitually impaired, it is a reasonable decision. The intuition was right.

© The Author(s), under exclusive license to Springer Nature Switzerland AG 2022 **67**
R. P. Kurshan, *Investment Industry Claims Debunked*,
https://doi.org/10.1007/978-3-030-76709-9_3

3.1 Risk vs. Uncertainty

It is worth distinguishing between *risk* and *uncertainty*. In life, nothing is certain (well, ok: death and taxes). Modern physics has taught us that even events that we commonly understand to be deterministic, like returning to the ground if we jump in the air, have in theory some (in this case, vanishingly small) chance of not happening.

If we can assign a probability to uncertainty, we call it *risk*, and we then characterize that risk according to its probability. If the risks and expected returns of two equity investments are unequal, economists have given us models to adjust the returns for their risks[1] (Sect. 3.3), helping to decide which investment is better.

Lacking a theoretical model for computing a risk, it still is possible to assign a probability to an outcome provided there is sufficient data to do so "reliably." However, what is deemed "reliable" or "statistically significant" is arbitrary and decided by convention. The levels of "reliability" differ for different types of events. For example, in order for an experiment in particle physics to show the existence of a new particle, the level of reliability required is much higher than the level of reliability required to show that a drug alleviates a disease.

Many classes of events have insufficient data to assign a probability of risk by any generally accepted level of statistical significance. For example, we have enough data to reasonably assign a probability to the mortality risk of driving a mile, even narrowed by age and sex. We also have the data to conclude that in general, taking a bus is 60 times safer than driving. But the data we have may be insufficient to further narrow the outcome according to weather and geographical location. It likely is safer to drive if the weather is good and the location is rural. But does it bring the risk below the risk of taking a bus? Without adequate data, this is an "uncertainty."

---

[1] For this purpose, the "risk" of an equity investment is cast in terms of its volatility: the risk of having reduced value when needed for an expense (although there are other risks, such as a diminishing effectiveness of the governance of the company). For fixed income investments, the "risk" is mostly the counterparty risk of default, although bonds are sensitive to interest rate changes and other market pressures too (Sect. 2.3) and their present value shows some volatility (but mostly, significantly less than equity).

3.2 Managing Risks

How do we deal with risk? For example, we know how to lower the risks of driving. But sometimes, we are unwilling to pay even relatively small sums to reduce these risks. Ample data showed the benefits of seat belts and air bags. The automotive industry lobbied the government to resist these safety measures, arguing that the small increased costs would reduce sales. Initially, we seemed to agree, by giving no support to regulations that would require the safety measures.

For decades, through sustained weak penalties, we showed an indifference to reducing the devastating effects of drunk drivers, and now more recently, the equivalent effects of texting while driving. We appear indifferent to the 10% of traffic fatalities caused by truck drivers who continue to drive without adequate sleep, bowing instead to pressures from the trucking industry.

And yet, we obsess over much, much lower risks, like death or injury from terrorism, or like deciding to cancel a flight on an airline that has just experienced a crash. What's going on?

We commit hundreds of billions of dollars to fighting "terrorism." If we spent a small fraction of that to improving driving safety, we would save many, many more lives. If 100 million dollars spent to save one life from terrorism saved 10,000 lives from drunken, texting, or overtired drivers, one could argue that the priority to spend it fighting terrorism is inefficient. This could hold even if one deducted the cost of military actions to show the world that the United States is not a country to be trifled with. Dying from a terrorist may seem "terrifying," while dying from an auto crash may seem "routine." However, a life lost is a life lost, and it's hardly more comfort to lose a child to a texting driver than to a terrorist.

There are many mechanisms that work to skew our evaluations of risks. Using the "terrorism" example, there is an evolutionarily engendered genetic drive to defend one's territory. This surely makes sense even today. An adversary could displace or conquer our society by force.

But context and the way a risk is presented and understood can significantly alter our reaction to it. While we prepare hair trigger responses to a military incursion, our response is very different when an adversary attacks us economically, even when the essential threats to our nation are no less grievous.[2] Why do we respond to threats so differently, when the actual

---

[2] I am in perpetual awe of how ardently we have defended our beachheads from a feared military attack by China, all the while allowing China almost unfettered access to our technologies and even our industrial and military secrets. We have voluntarily closed down most of our manufacturing, exporting much of it,

risks are comparable? Is prioritizing national defense over economic defense justified? The strong instinct driving national defense sometimes leaves us defending against big shadows of small threats (cynically exploited by the military-industrial complex), while leaving economic threats unaddressed.

So, what's going on? Our perception of a particular risk is shaped by media representations, advertisements, politics, social attitudes, and emotions. Did we really want to export our manufacturing to China, after all?

Finance is no exception. We are vulnerable to deceptive media hype about the risk of inflation[3] that can cause unjustified shifts of investments to gold.[4] To sell more annuities (Sect. 2.10.6), some brokers distort the risk of volatility (Chap. 4). We are responsive to risky lures of wealth (Chap. 1) despite all the expert warnings. We are willing to commit significant resources to a risky investment in real estate (Sect. 2.11) without performing even the level of diligence that we apply to choosing a restaurant for dinner.

Bond ratings can be associated with the probability of default.[5,6] This probability can vary slightly from year to year, but highly rated corporate bonds consistently have a probability of default that is close to zero (about 0.6% across 10 years). Even after adjusting their yields for the probability of default, the results are significantly higher than the yields of ("risk-free") U.S. Treasury bonds.[7] Thus, highly rated corporate bonds, even after adjustment for default, are a better investment, on average (cf. Sect. 3.4), than U.S. Treasury bonds. Likewise, lower rated corporate bonds with their yields adjusted for default, even down to "junk"-level ratings (Sect. 2.3.1), in some cases can be better investments—on average—than more highly rated bonds. Default risk can be lowered through diversification, as achieved with a total intermediate-term bond fund. The risk of counterparty loss with such a fund is essentially 0, putting it for all practical purposes in the same "risk-free" category as U.S. Treasury bonds, but providing significantly better yields than Treasuries. Fear of default can play an oversized role, leading investors to worse outcomes.

Indeed, in finance as in the rest of life, we have great difficulty evaluating, comparing, and managing risks in a rational, cost-effective manner.

---

along with most of our manufacturing capabilities and expertise to China. If they came in shooting, we would be at war; if they come in with trade deals, we smile and give them the crown jewels of our society.

[3] nytimes.com/2009/05/29/opinion/29krugman.html.

[4] tiphero.com/12-ways-to-fight-back-against-inflation.

[5] https://moodys.com/sites/products/DefaultResearch/2006200000425249.pdf

[6] spratings.com/documents/20184/774196/2018AnnualGlobalCorporateDefaultAndRatingTransition-Study.pdf = tinyurl.com/y6f4a7ha

[7] Altman (1989).

In some cases, this is unavoidable. In evaluating a pension buyout offer (Sect. 17.2.9), how does one decide between the uncertainty of being able to invest the buyout lump sum so that its returns will match the pension, and the liquidity risk (Sect. 3.8) in choosing to keep the pension? In deciding to keep the pension, one forgoes the opportunity to in effect draw on future pension payments, as one could with a buyout lump sum. Without a way to compare an uncertainty and a risk (Sect. 3.1), there may be no reasonable way to decide. Even if we believed the liquidity risk to be great, the imponderable uncertainty of being able to invest the buyout lump sum effectively, remains.

In other cases, we evaluate risks improperly. We assume that Treasury bonds are really risk-free because everyone calls them so (although the U.S. Government came so close to defaulting that its long-term bond credit rating was downgraded (**bond risk**, Sect. 2.3.1)). Thus, we invest in Treasury bonds with lower yields than a total intermediate-term bond fund that also is "risk-free" at least to the same extent (Sect. 3.2).

We have tools to compare equities with different expected risks and growth rates (Sect. 3.3). Therefore we should neither be averse to a risky equity investment with a high enough expected return, nor complacent with an equity investment with a low risk. In either case, however, for whichever is deemed the better investment, the risk of loss, no matter how big or small, needs to be considered (Sect. 3.4).

And sometimes, we fail in evaluating risks simply because we neglect to perform the required due diligence (Sect. 2.11).

Psychologists have led us to understand this. Natural selection guided our evolution to make simple snap judgments like running when we hear a rustle in the grass—because it could be a tiger, but it left us inadequately prepared for the more complex judgments required by the social and technological advances of the past several centuries.[8] Given another 100,000 years, evolution may provide us with innate risk evaluation facilities that allow us intuitively to compare risks with some accuracy. Until then, we need to make such judgments through a learned process.

---

[8] Kahneman (2011).

3.3 Sharpe Ratio

Nobel laureate William F. Sharpe proposed a measure to compare investments with differing volatility—one with higher volatility having a higher risk of being depressed in value when needed for expenses.

The measure is the ratio of the difference between the expected growth rate of the investment and the expected growth rate of a "risk-free" investment,[9] with the investment's volatility. Thus, as a formula, the ratio is

$$\frac{R_p - R_f}{\sigma_p}$$

where R_p is the expected growth rate of a given investment, R_f is the expected growth rate of a "risk-free" investment, and σ_p is the standard deviation of the given investment. The standard deviation is a measure of its volatility: how far its actual values deviate from its mean value R_p.

There are many technical and practical complaints about this measure, as well as numerous variations that seek to adjust for the concerns. Frank Sortino proposed to measure σ_p only on the "downside" deviation, measuring the volatility of points that lie below the mean R_p, considered to be the investment's "bad" risk.

Both measures are very popular, and given all the other uncertainties surrounding an investment, not the least of which is how to value R_p (dependent on the period of time over which it is computed), it is hard to make the case that the differences in measures stand above the other uncertainties.

The way to use the measure is to compute the ratio for two investments—the one with the larger ratio is considered a "better" investment, delivering a better return for a unit of volatility. Thus, an investment with a lower mean growth rate and lower volatility, by this measure, could be deemed a "better" investment than one with a higher mean growth rate, but higher volatility.

It is important to note that the ratio analyzes only one aspect of an investment: its *presumed* growth rate relative to its *past* volatility. There are many issues pertinent to the anticipated performance of an investment, such as the reliability of the company, its governance, and its economic and political environment, all of which are harder to compare between investments.

Furthermore, when confronted with a choice between a higher expected rate of return but also a higher volatility, or a lower expected rate of return

---

[9] often the yield of a 90-day Treasury bill.

3 **Understanding Risk**   73

and lower volatility, the latter may sustain periodically drawn-down savings longer, irrespective of the Sharpe ratios, on account of the effect of degradation (Sect. 11.1.1). An example of this based on historical market data is given in Sect. 4.1.

3.4 Expected vs. Worst-Case Return

When making decisions in the face of risk, we often fail to consider the full picture. Sometimes, we only consider the expected (i.e., average) outcome, neglecting the worst-case outcome. For example, we may be attracted to an investment like "junk bonds" that gives an expected high rate of return, without considering the potential for loss (**bond risk**, Sect. 2.3.1). Sometimes, we consider only the worst-case outcome, neglecting to evaluate the benefits of the expected outcome. For example, a very "risk-averse" investor may view the potential for equity prices to crash as a reason to invest only in U.S. Treasuries, without considering the expected loss from their shortfall versus equities (Sect. 5.3). Even famous economists can have difficulty calibrating an appropriate response to low probability loss (Sect. 3.4.4).

Such myopia is ubiquitous in the social realm, where legislative actions commonly are driven by views that emphasize extreme risk without considering their expected costs. For example, at some considerable expense, penal laws have gravitated toward protecting society from miscreants without evaluating whether the expected benefits warrant the costs (which extend way beyond the cost of incarceration, to the loss of productivity and costs associated with reentry to society, including caring for the indigent). (Recent awakening to poor benefits has started movement across the political spectrum in the other direction (Chap. 18)).

No surprise that the same attitudes bleed over to finance. We are gulled by overly optimistic predictions of expected investment growth, without carefully considering the inevitable worst-case downsides. Likewise, we are cowed by dire (worst-case) predictions of inflation and an unsettled economy, lured to investments in gold, without putting the predictions in the context of expected behavior (or even checking their veracity).

3.4.1 Expected Return

The expected return on a bet is the sum of the possible payoffs, each multiplied by its probability of happening. Thus, if you roll a fair die and get in dollars the number that comes up, your expected return is $(1/6)\$1 + (1/6)\$2 + \cdots + (1/6)\$6 = \$3.50$. If charged \$2 to play this game, it is reasonable to play, because you're expected to end up \$1.50 ahead. In the worst case, you stand to lose \$1, which I'll guess is of no consequence to you, and your odds of losing nothing are 5:1. You'd likely accept this bet.

3.4.2 A Worse Worst Case

Now, let's multiply everything by 100,000. Would you write a check for \$200,000 (after transferring that amount to your checking account) to cover the bet? The probabilities and odds haven't changed, and now your expected net return is \$150,000. Unfortunately, now, in the worst case, you can lose \$100,000. Since you are reading this book, this presumably is no longer pocket change for you. While it is still most probable that you lose nothing, the risk of losing \$100,000 is likely a risk you do not want to take, even for a best-case profit of \$400,000 and expected profit of \$150,000. Although the potential to get an extra \$400,000 and the expected outcome of profiting by \$150,000 are very nice, losing \$100,000 might materially set back your retirement. I predict that you would not accept this bet.

3.4.3 Extreme Worst Case

Now, let's return to the original bet, but alter it by adding that if you roll a "1," I get to flip a fair coin 20 times, and if I get 20 heads, you must pay me \$100,000; else the bet is as before. Your expected net is essentially unchanged (\$1.48). However, there is a chance that you lose \$100,000. The chance is minuscule (less than 1 in a million), but why on earth would you take such a risk for an expected benefit of \$1.48 or even the best-case net benefit of \$4? What if we reduced the minuscule risk further: say, the chance you lose \$100,000 is less than the chance that the earth is hit by a killer astroid this year (30 consecutive heads flips)? For most practical purposes, that chance is "essentially" 0; but in fact it's not 0, so why take even this infinitesimal risk for a mere \$3? You say "no thank you" (or possibly something less polite).

On the other hand, in the second bet, if instead of multiplying by 100,000, we multiplied by 1,000, then the worst-case loss is \$1,000, while the expected gain is \$1,500. This may be appealing as a worthwhile bet with a tolerable downside. A succession of such bets would likely increase wealth, while an extremely unlucky (and unlikely) succession of losses would be manageable: at some point, with some moderate loss, just leave the game.

3 Understanding Risk 75

The point is that, for each bet, one needs to consider two numbers: the *expected return* and the *worst-case return* (including a possible loss). Even if the expected return is attractive, the worst-case return must be tolerable, when considered together with its likelihood.

3.4.4 Samuelson Example

When the worst-case return is a substantial loss, but with very low probability, it can be hard to weigh against an attractive expected gain. Oddly, mathematically based economic theory that could be hoped to help resolve such quandaries, in some cases, can leave one only scratching one's head.

The esteemed Nobel Prize-winning economist Paul Samuelson set forth the following example[10] (the bets here increased by an order of magnitude to adjust for inflation since the example was posed in 1963). A colleague with no special background in mathematics is offered a bet on a fair coin: heads, he wins $2000, tails he pays $1000. The colleague declined the bet, stating "I would feel the $1000 loss more than the $2000 gain. But I'll take you on if you promise to let me make 100 such bets." When asked why, the colleague answered "One toss is not enough to make it reasonably sure that the law of averages will turn out in my favor. But in a hundred tosses, the law of large numbers will make it a darn good bet. I am, so to speak, virtually sure to come out ahead with such a sequence, and that is why I would accept the sequence while rejecting the single toss."

Samuelson then invokes *expected utility theory* to show that answer in fact is "irrational." He proves that if the single bet is unacceptable (independent of wealth,[11]) then any sequence of such bets must likewise be unacceptable. Expected utility theory posits a formal way to express preferences using a mathematical formula called a *utility function*. The class of "reasonable" utility functions was formalized (axiomatized) in a landmark book by one of the most profound and prolific mathematical luminaries of the twentieth century: John

---

[10] Samuelson (1963).

[11] Ross (1999) shows that this seemingly innocuous constraint is very strong, implying that if the utility function is "well-behaved" (mathematically, twice differentiable), it must be constant or a negative exponential, and without the constraint, the theorem fails. Although it is argued that the single bet would be undesirable mostly for those with minimal wealth, who could not afford to lose $1000, while the wealthy would be unconcerned by such a loss and would accept the single toss on account of its favorable expected return, I disagree. I think that it's not unreasonable to imagine that the single toss would be rejected, independent of wealth, because to lose $1000 on single coin toss would make anyone feel foolish (and for the wealthy, the $2000 possible gain would be inconsequential). Would you take this favorable single-toss bet?

Paul Samuelson 1997

von Neumann, working together with the economist Oskar Morgenstern.[12] A "reasonable" utility function must satisfy some basic intuitive properties like transitivity: if A is preferred over B, and B is preferred over C, then A must be preferred over C. This axiomatization forms a pillar of modern economics.

John von Neumann Los Alamos 1940s

The Samuelson example generated a flood of papers that sought to explain the result in various complexions. Samuelson himself tried to explain the result, although not terribly convincingly. He wrote that "if it hurts to lose \$1,000, it must certainly hurt to lose $100 \times \$1,000 = \$100,000$. Yet there is a distinct *possibility* of so extreme a loss. Granted, that the probability of so long a run of losses is extremely low: less than 1 in a million (or $1/2^{100}$)."

In fact, $1/2^{100} = 1/10^{30}$ is astronomically smaller than 1 in a million, and in fact, astronomically smaller than any event, we can reasonably contemplate. Although it remains a theoretical possibility, it is less than dust compared with

---

[12] von Neumann and Morgenstern (1944).

the level of risks with which we are accustomed (Sect. 3.2). Figure 3.1 shows the probability $P(n)$ of any cumulative loss after n coin flips.[13] ($P(n) = P(n, 0)$ in the footnote.) $P(100) = 0.04\%$ or about twice as likely as dying from the flu in a given year. The expected upside[14] of 100 bets is to win $50,000. If this bet also feels too risky, you can insist on 291 flips. Then the odds of any accumulated loss is 1 in 300 million, the odds of winning the Powerball lottery. By increasing the number of flips in the bet, you can get the chance of losing anything as low as you like. With 1000 flips, the chance is 10^{-26}. That's about as likely as me choosing at random an atom in your head, and you then guessing correctly which atom I selected.[15]

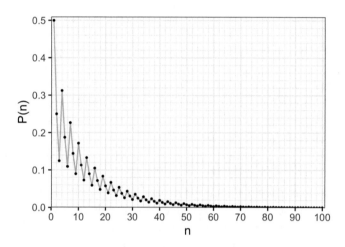

Fig. 3.1 Probability of a cumulative loss after n coin flips.

---

[13] When a winning flip wins twice as much as a losing flip loses, the probability of any loss after n flips is

$$P(n) = \frac{\sum_{k=0}^{\lceil \frac{n}{3} \rceil - 1} \binom{n}{k}}{2^n}$$

$\lceil \frac{n}{3} \rceil$ is the smallest integer great than or equal to $\frac{n}{3}$. $\binom{n}{k}$ is the probability of k heads in n flips.

[14] When a winning flip wins twice as much as a losing flip loses, the expected win for a bet with n flips and loss B of losing a flip is

$$E(n) = B \frac{\sum_{k=0}^{n}(3k-n)\binom{n}{k}}{2^n}.$$

[15] education.jlab.org/qa/mathatom_03.html.

78   **R. P. Kurshan**

Does it make sense to be concerned about such improbable events when we routinely bathe, cross the street, and drive, without a second thought?

We are not beholden to the rules of expected utility theory. In fact, *prospect theory*,[16] developed by the behavioral psychologists Daniel Kahneman and Amos Tversky, is an alternative that was the basis for another Nobel Prize in economics. Prospect theory baffles economists, because it posits that in the face of risk and uncertainty, decisions are made in a manner that is dependent on context and history.

In fact, these dependencies are well-known to the advertising and public relations communities, and their utilization has been in effect for generations. The perceived value of soap increases if the buyer identifies with an actor who presents the product. A buyer who is offered two similar products at different prices will tend to choose the less expensive one; however, if a third similar product is offered as well, at a price that is inflated to be higher than the other two, the buyer will tend to choose the middle-priced product: the one rejected when it was but one of two possibilities. Hence, preference need not be transitive, and preferences can be circular. Echoing Samuelson's colleague, people in general tend to fear loss more than they favor gain. None of this comports with expected utility theory.[17]

The collective brain power invested in "normative" mathematical models: how people *should* (rationally) behave in the face of risky decisions is daunting. But what good are they if they don't explain how people *do* behave, explanations found in "descriptive" models like prospect theory? It could be argued that at least for those who wish to make rational decisions, the normative models are useful. But does that mean that if I am (understandably!) reluctant to make the bet on a single coin flip, because another $2000 won't materially improve my life, while losing $1000 will make me feel foolish, then "rationally" I should forgo the 300 flip bet, with its virtually certain win?

Samuelson warns that although the expected value of the bet is tempting and the risk of a loss is very small, it is never zero. That leaves the possibility of a worst-case loss of $100,000 for 100 flips, or $1 million for 1000 flips. In Sect. 3.4.3, we shrank from betting with favorable odds, because the possible loss is large, while its very small risk (1 in a million) is imaginable, and the expected benefit is too tiny to make it worth considering. However, for Samuelson's bet, the expected gain is meaningful ($150,000 for 300 flips, $500,000 for 1000 flips), and with many flips, the risk of a loss is infinitesimal.

---

[16]Kahneman and Tversky (1979).

[17]See also Sect. 3.7, footnote 29.

3 Understanding Risk 79

I'll repeat Samuelson's warning: *infinitesimal is not zero.* True indeed, but let's put that infinitesimal risk in perspective. A real estate developer may invest a million dollars of his own money into the construction of an office tower. If an earthquake struck during uninsured construction, his million dollar investment could be lost, and put him out of business. Nonetheless, if an earthquake is unlikely in that location, it would not be surprising if he decided to decline earthquake insurance, to save its cost. It's just another risk/benefit assessment, like deciding to take a bath or cross the street.

But there's an even clearer way to evaluate the Samuelson bet. Betting on 1000 tosses, one could easily buy insurance against the infinitesimal risk of loss. Indeed, one can purchase $1 million of personal liability insurance coverage for under $1000 per year, thus insuring a much greater risk than that of a loss after 1000 tosses. Take Samuelson's 1000 toss bet, buy insurance against any loss, and subtract the $1000 insurance premium from the expected $500,000 winnings. In the worst case (assuming the insurance company doesn't default), with vanishingly small probability, one loses only $1000 (the insurance premium).

Samuelson seeks to explain the logic behind why if the single-toss bet is rejected, so then rationally should any longer sequence of bets be rejected. The explanation uses mathematical induction. "If you cannot accept one toss, then you cannot accept two—since the latter could be thought of consisting of the (unwise) decision to accept one plus the open decision to accept a second. Even if you were stuck with the first outcome, you would cut your further (utility) losses and refuse the next. By extending the reasoning from 2 to $3 = 2+1$ and so on, we rule out any sequence at all." However this may work in expected utility theory, it fails in real life. If someone offers you a single penny, you may decline to take it (who needs a penny in the pocket or purse?). Likewise for 2 or 3 pennies. But if offered a sequence of 100 million pennies,[18] you may be willing to confront the logistical issues and accept.[19] The Samuelson bet does not consist of offering a single-toss bet today, then returning by surprise tomorrow with another single-toss bet, and so on. (Samuelson's induction argument would work for that case.) The Samuelson bet consists of offering a bet whose number of tosses can be stated at the outset. In real life, these two are very different.

In summary, risk analysis based on sophisticated mathematical models may not lead to a useful conclusion. A simple probabilistic analysis and

---

[18] There are 130 billion in circulation.

[19] Moreover, contrary to utility theory, it's unlikely that there's a specific minimal number of pennies that one finds worthwhile to accept. The number likely changes with one's mood and the weather.

personal preference can lead to a more satisfying decision. As always, risk can be mitigated, but not entirely avoided. Even with the very practical $1000 insurance premium solution, there remains the theoretical risk of an insurance company default. As stated at the end of Sect. 3.4.3, we must weigh the expected return against the worst-case loss, considered together with its likelihood. We are left to evaluate this intuitively, in the context of all the other risks of life that we accept, such as driving.

epilogue

In illustrating the conflict between expected utility theory applied to this sort of risk analysis, and human nature, did Samuelson, at some intuitive level, anticipate Kahneman and Tversky's prospect theory? It is daunting to contemplate the enormous body of profound mathematics that sits in contrast to prospect theory. Mainstream economists notice prospect theory and then turn away, back to their usual practice. Sadly, this is consistent with the pervasive human tendency to ignore data that conflicts with strongly held beliefs—what in psychology is termed *confirmation bias*.

Profound changes from firmly established theory are tremendously hard and take time. The geocentric theory that the earth was the center of the universe prevailed for two millennia before it was gradually replaced by the heliocentric model, placing our sun at the center of our solar system. The replacement was gradual, taking the better part of a century. Geocentric proponents provided ever more elaborate mathematical justifications for challenges from the heliocentric view, inventing the very clever notion of *epicycles* to explain observed deviations from the basic geocentric model. When epicycles also proved inadequate, they posited epicycles of epicycles, entailing quite sophisticated mathematics. Recently, it was shown[20] that a sufficient hierarchy of epicycles on epicycles could bring the geocentric theory arbitrarily close to astronomical observations. However, calculations by Johannes Kepler based on the heliocentric model proved compelling and were reinforced by Isaac Newton's presentations of the effects of gravity. But even as the geocentric view faded away, adherents remained. As of 2014, a quarter of Americans believe that the sun revolves around the earth.[21]

---

[20] Saari (1990).

[21] https://www.livescience.com/43593-americans-ignorant-about-science.html

3.4.5 Powerball

Let's say that for $2, I give you a 1 in 300 million chance to win $100 million (or more). Your expected net return on this bet is −$1.66: a negative number. On the other hand, the worst-case loss ($2) is negligible, while a win is life-changing. Should you accept this bet? Almost half of America does—it's called "Powerball."

Economists generally argue against a bet with a negative expected return. The argument to play is that in a practical sense, $2 is like $0 (assuming you buy only one ticket), so the expected return is "really" positive. But it's not for a $.35 expected return that you play. It's for the essentially no-cost possibility, however remote, for a life-changing benefit. The argument against play is that the cost is not the cost of the ticket, but the cost of your time to buy the ticket, the waste of time dreaming pointlessly about winning, and the induced temptation to buy many more tickets. Although the benefit of pleasant dreams can be viewed as the whole point and well worth the $2.

You might decide that buying one ticket can't hurt and then apply mathematical induction to conclude that since one ticket can't hurt, buying one more ticket also can't hurt, so therefore you keep buying tickets. Many people do. It's the same as saying that since one penny is negligible, likewise one more penny must be negligible, and therefore continuing the argument a penny at a time, 100 million pennies must be negligible. It ain't so! A large number of small amounts can add up to a large amount. That's why it's unwise to buy many lottery tickets in your lifetime.

3.5 Maximize Expected Portfolio Longevity: Is That Enough?

No! It is not enough to maximize the *expected* longevity of savings. An expected longevity of 40 years means (by definition) that savings have a 50–50 chance to last 40 years. That doesn't sound very reassuring.

Although an investment in equities (stocks) gives the best *expected* return, its high volatility makes it a risky investment in retirement, if it is needed to cover expenses, on account of its susceptibility to significant downturns.

As discussed in Sect. 3.4, one also needs to take into account the *risk*, as a probability, that one outlives savings. That is, one should consider not just the length of time that savings are *expected* to last, but also the *probability* that they last for a given length of time.

Are you willing to invest in a way that likely supports your retirement until age 120, but runs a 30% risk of running out by age 80?

You may be most comfortable with an investment strategy that gives your savings a 90% probability of lasting until age 92 (say), regardless of its expected longevity.

The probability of a portfolio lasting a given number of years can be estimated using a (free) commercial retirement calculator such as ones from Vanguard[22] and Fidelity.[23] The calculators also can calculate the *expected* portfolio longevity: the number of years it will last with probability 50%.

3.6 Does Stock Risk Diminish with Time Held?

A widely disseminated and broadly accepted view of the investment industry is that the risk of a loss from holding stocks diminishes with the length of time they are held. The reason given is that over time, growth overtakes volatility. Although the value of a share of a broad-spectrum stock fund may be expected to be highly volatile when measured over a small number of years, over longer periods, the swings in cumulative growth rate tend to even out, relative to the average growth rate over the period. This effect is called "reversion to the mean." After 15 years, decreasing variability in expected overall growth rate leaves an S&P 500 investment positive throughout its range of variability.[24]

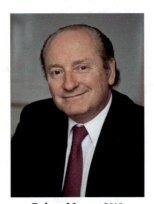

Robert Merton 2010

---

[22] retirementplans.vanguard.com/VGApp/pe/pubeducation/calculators/RetirementNestEggCalc.jsf = tinyurl.com/yazve7s.

[23] fidelity.com/calculators-tools/overview.

[24] Malkiel (2015), Chapter 14, Section 2.

3 Understanding Risk 83

This claim can be found in literature from investment houses including the highly esteemed Vanguard, the mega-best-seller *A Random Walk Down Wall Street* by B. G. Malkiel (*op. cit.*) and in the management policies of the pension plan guarantor PBGC (Sect. 17.2.3) where it is assumed that holding stocks provides a hedge against a loss of the insured benefits.[25]

In fact, Bodie (1995) shows that the opposite is true: the risk of a loss from holding stocks *increases* rather than *decreases* the longer they are held. This has been observed by many economists, including the Nobel Prize winners Paul A. Samuelson and Robert C. Merton.[26] Bodie measures this risk by looking at the expected shortfall from a stock investment compared with a benchmark investment in "risk-free" zero-coupon U.S. Treasury bonds, over the same period. For typical models of market behavior, including random-walk and mean-reverting processes, the risk of a loss is shown in fact to *increase* with time.

The apparent source of confusion stems from the fact that the *probability* of a shortfall does indeed decrease over time. After all, the substantial expected growth rate builds up a base that over time gets harder for market downturns to destroy. This is growth overtaking volatility. However, as illustrated in Sect. 3.4, *probability* is only half the story. The other half is the *amount* (cf. Sect. 3.4.3).

Even with an *expected* gain, an (unlikely) *possible* loss can be devastating. The expectation is the gain multiplied by its probability. Even a large probability of gain can hide an enormous loss potential. Although the probability of a devastating loss may be small enough to leave the expected gain big, if the loss occurs, it is . . . well, devastating. In 1998, the Long-Term Capital Management hedge fund, guided by the Nobel Prize-winning Black-Scholes-Merton formula, managed to lose $4.6 billion in 4 months, and had to be bailed out by the Federal Reserve in order to forestall an international financial meltdown, largely because in the application of the formula, a very small probability of a loss hid the catastrophic effect of the loss, should it occur.[27]

In the same way, Bodie points out, stocks cannot be viewed as a hedge against inflation (although the real return of stocks *is* uncorrelated with inflation).

---

[25] Bodie (1995).

[26] *op. cit.*

[27] thebalance.com/long-term-capital-crisis-3306240.

84   R. P. Kurshan

Not unsurprisingly, Bodie (1995) received substantial pushback from the investment industry. There were complaints about his model, complaints about its applicability, and complaints about its inferred conclusions.

Nonetheless, it is amply clear that although the probability of a shortfall in the value of stocks held for many years may be low, there always remains the possibility that at the moment the funds are needed, the market could be severely depressed. A 50% depression, while extreme, has occurred in recent memory. Searching farther back in history, one can find a 90% depression. It's not so unlikely that it can be ignored (Sect. 3.4.3), and when it occurs, the effect can be devastating.

Does this mean that stocks should not be held long term? No! It just means that before liquidating stocks, ample time should be allowed, in order to wait out a market depression (Chap. 5). And at any given time, with probability increasing with time held, their good expected growth will show.

3.7   Risk Aversion

There is an odd parameter that routinely is used to drive investment advice. It is one's degree of "risk aversion," as it is called. In fact, risk aversion is a basic notion in economics, defined as a concave utility curve. In the same context, risk-reward tradeoffs can be analyzed precisely within Modern Portfolio Theory (MPT) developed by Harry Markowitz in 1952.[28] and subsumed into the Capital Asset Pricing Model (CAPM) mentioned in Sect. 2.6.2 (see also below).

However, the very notion of utility in economics bears some questioning.[29] Experimental evidence behind prospect theory[30] (an alternative to expected utility theory for analyzing decisions with risks—see Sect. 3.4.4) shows that in reality, imputed utility is relative to context. Extensive human behavioral evidence, both in the lab and in the street, shows that utility can change from moment to moment and depend on context and how the relevant questions are framed. For the lay investor, utility can be perplexing. Thus it is rarely explained in the context of ordinary investment decisions. One's degree of "risk aversion" is left as a primitive concept, as if requiring no definition.

---

[28] Markowitz (1952).

[29] British economist Joan Robinson criticized "utility" itself as being circular: "Utility is the quality in commodities that makes individuals want to buy them, and the fact that individuals want to buy these commodities shows that they have utility." Robinson (1962).

[30] Kahneman and Tversky (1979).

In practice, the investor is asked simply to give an indication of "risk aversion" (on a scale of 1 to 10). Com'on—you like to take risks or not? If so, how much? The well-considered reply would be "What do you mean?"

3.7.1 Reverse Engineering to Find Its Meaning

In this context, the question of one's degree of "risk aversion" can be reverse-engineered to find its meaning. Simply look at the financial advice given in response to the answer. The more "risk-averse" are directed to lower volatility investments.

Based on the resulting guidance, the "risk aversion" question simply is equivalent to "what is your preferred level of volatility?" This question is at least well-defined and bears some resemblance to the economists' definition.

But, how on earth is a lay investor to answer that?

When looking to retirement, the answer may be the answer to the question: "What level of volatility will support the longest possible retirement?" However, this is a question whose answer is not simply a function of portfolio volatility. It depends on current savings, anticipated expenditures, and what and how investments are drawn for expenses (Sect. 13.4). Moreover, the answer is nuanced, in terms of probabilities for different retirement lengths.

When looking at a trust set aside for heirs, the answer may be a high level of volatility (to maximize expected returns), but depends on how much leeway there is in disbursing the trust. (Can disbursement wait for the market to reach a high level?)

So, the answer to the volatility question has more to do with the function of the investment than with the emotional sentiment of the investor.

Nonetheless, often the investment industry drives its advice based on that parameter alone. Perhaps they don't worry about whether the given answer is useful as long as it's easy to generate.

Indeed, this advice may be counterproductive even for the most financially conservative investment-phobic individual who simply wants savings to last. That individual, although self-identified as "highly risk-averse," still needs some more volatile—"riskier"—investments, to provide adequate investment growth to counter inflation and meet investment goals.

Generally, the *salient* risk is that you won't have the money you need, when you need it. In retirement, the most salient risk is outliving savings, and that risk is usually *reduced* by investing sufficiently in more volatile ("riskier") securities.

As Vanguard has written, "Stocks are risky, but avoiding stocks is also risky." *Savings that appreciate too slowly can lead to a worse loss than the sale of depressed stocks.* One needs some "happy medium" that balances the growth of equities with the stability of fixed income investments—the latter to provide a stable source for expenses—in order to maximize the longevity of savings. How to do this is described in Chap. 4.

Play with investment industry retirement simulation engines (Sect. 3.5, footnotes 22, 23). You will find that for a given level of drawdowns, as you decrease your level of "risk aversion" from its maximum level (thus, willing to accept more volatility), the expected longevity of your portfolio at first *increases.* Yes: initially, your portfolio's expected longevity increases, the more "risk" you are willing to take. Then after some point, it decreases. There's a sweet spot for volatility. Moreover, this sweet spot *increases* (more volatility) as drawdowns decrease.

The simulation engines thus indirectly confirm that you should want some of your investment to be in equities, for their better growth, and some in fixed income investments, for better stability (for less potential loss from drawdowns). As drawdowns decrease, so should the optimal stable source. But such a line of reasoning is rarely if ever presented explicitly by the investment industry.

3.7.2 Another Possible Meaning

A more benign possibility of what the investment industry actually means by "risk aversion" is: "How likely are you to be spooked into buying high/selling low, as a result of fearing to miss a surge or lose in a crash?"

Since the more "risk-averse" are counseled to invest in less volatile products (e.g., more bonds), whether or not doing so has a beneficial effect on portfolio goals, one cannot rule out this alternative meaning.

In fact, this possibility is consistent with Vanguard research[31] that states that the most valuable benefit to individual investors of working with a financial advisor is to prevent panicked reactions to market movements. Despite Vanguard's aggressive stand against wasteful fees that working with an advisor add, they consider that working with an advisor may nonetheless be worthwhile if the advisor is able to prevent rash buys and sells.

However, for an advisor to recommend investments that minimize volatility simply in order to protect a client from rash behavior seems irresponsible. It

---

[31] vanguard.com/pdf/ISGQVAA.pdf.

would diminish the overall expected growth of the client's portfolio, and go counter to the client's overall financial objectives.

The more conscientious advisor advises the client against rash transactions, while recommending an objective-guided investment plan.

3.7.3 Economists Optimize Risk-Reward Tradeoff

As mentioned (Sect. 2.6.2 and above), microeconomics is heavily invested in the Capital Asset Pricing Model (CAPM) and Modern Portfolio Theory (MPT). CAPM provides a formulaic basis to demonstrate the benefits of diversification, while MPT gives very specific stability vs. growth investment balance guidelines in terms of "risk-reward" tradeoffs based on [*drumroll*...] "one's level of risk aversion" (yup!). Ok, fine. Economists define this in terms of one's utility curve. It is the incremental expected reward required to accept additional "risk" expressed as the standard deviation of investment growth rate, that is, its volatility.[32] Yes, that's a mouthful.

Is this helpful? How does an investor determine this? Is this something that an investor or investment advisor can measure? Is it constant from day to day for a given investor? The question requires a precise numerical answer, as any differences in the answer lead to differences in the recommended portfolio. And how does one relate a chosen level of "risk aversion" to what may be the only financial risk that really matters: outliving one's savings?

Conversely, though, the MPT risk-reward tradeoff model can be used to derive the level of "risk" (i.e., volatility) required in order to meet a given investment growth requirement. This sounds more useful: if I cast my spending needs in terms of a required savings growth rate ("I need my savings to grow at this rate in order to be able to spend at that rate"), then—by increasing volatility in order to increase expected growth rate—I can use the MPT risk-reward tradeoff model to determine a mix of investments that on average satisfies that required growth rate.

---

[32] "Risk," meaning volatility, makes most sense for equity, as the volatility of fixed income investments is relatively low and correlates with duration (Sect. 2.3.1); for fixed income investments, "risk" in the sense of the money not being there when you expect it is measured by *rating* (as in Moody bond rating), not represented as a standard deviation (as used in the CAPM)—cf. footnote 1 in the beginning of this chapter. Therefore, it's a bit of a discombobulation of the word "risk," to compare, as in Sect. 3.3, a "risky" investment in equity, measured by its volatility, with a "risk-free" government bond investment, with "risk" measured by rating—the two uses of the word "risk" mean completely different things. In this context, "risk-free" should merely be considered the shorthand name of a useful benchmark for comparison: U.S. Government Treasury bonds. Which bonds, must be specified.

88   R. P. Kurshan

But then what? The larger the required growth, the higher the volatility and thus the greater the chance that when I need to draw the funds, they are depressed in value, returning less than needed. How did that help me? I got the *average* growth I needed, but also a greater chance of outliving my savings. The implied promise of being able to dial up risk to meet spending needs seems, as one might intuitively expect, to be misleading.

The model doesn't tell me *how much* my probability of outliving my savings has increased with increased volatility (although there are some simulation models that can: Sect. 3.5, footnotes 22, 23, but they depend on guesses about the future). At best, it gives a way to present a choice: either accept some unknown increase in the probability of outliving savings, or reduce spending. (But, isn't this obvious?) The risk-reward optimization is elegant; its utility is questionable.

In fact, the MPT risk-reward tradeoff model[33] is of limited use to help an investor organize a portfolio. The reason is twofold, depending upon the investor's financial needs.

For an investor who anticipates needing the funds shortly (say, within 2 years) to cover expenses, the investment should be in fixed income investments or cash in order to avoid the possibility that when needed, the investment is depressed in value. For a shorter period, the risk of having to sell depressed equity outweighs the expected shortfall from the lower growth rate of fixed income investments (Sect. 5.4).

For an investor who seeks long-term growth of an undrawn investment, a low-fee broadly diversified equity index fund is optimal (Chaps. 1 and 2, and, especially, Sect. 2.6). This intuitively natural conclusion can be derived from the CAPM, and it is reassuring to have a theoretical basis to justify the choice to invest in broadly diversified index funds.

However, given this choice, there is no risk-reward tradeoff to optimize. Volatility is irrelevant—*not* for the fallacious reason that "in the long term equity value reverts to its mean" (Sect. 3.6), but because over a long enough span of time, the equity market is highly likely to experience a period of high growth, when equity can be sold, realizing its mean growth rate. At its most basic level, this is based on the inevitable growth of commerce along with population growth. If COVID-19 decimates the planet, all bets are off. Barring that, one can seek to plan sufficiently far in advance of needing to draw down

---

[33] While arguably "risk-reward tradeoff" is snappier than "volatility-growth tradeoff," to me the latter is more honest. While "risk" in this context *could* be expected to include structural risks like risk of bankruptcy, here it refers only to volatility: it is represented in terms of the standard deviation of the investment value, as it fluctuates over time.

the investment, to await a high growth period of equity. Then, at that time, exchange the equity without loss for the more stable fixed income investment, to be used for the forthcoming expenses (Sect. 5.4).

The length chosen for this transition waiting period may be a function of one's "risk aversion" (ha!) in the sense that the longer the period chosen, the less likely the eventual need to sell depressed equity; but then also the *more* likely to lose out on required portfolio growth—a risk that the "risk-averse" should hate equally.

Indeed, it is *more* risky to portfolio goals to invest too much in low volatility bonds than to invest an appropriate portion in higher-volatility stocks that provide a "growth" factor and some protection against inflation (Sect. 4.1).

Even for their most "risk-averse" clients, financial advisors rarely advise to invest everything in bonds—although, alarmingly, as we will see, some very prominent economists in some sense do (Sect. 11.4.2).

Thus, in neither case—long- or short-term investment—is there a "risk-reward" tradeoff to be analyzed. The goal of financial planning should be to organize finances so as to have the best chances to meet spending needs (Chap. 6). Such organization indeed requires balancing assets like stocks that provide growth with assets like bonds and cash that provide a stable source for expenses (Sect. 4.1). However, the organization needs to be dynamically adjusted to spending needs and organized around a plan based on market performance to determine when to make the transition from higher growth equities to more stable fixed income investments (Chap. 5).

3.7.4 The Goal of Financial Planning

In view of the apparent confusion over "risk aversion," it is worth reflecting on what may be a major misconception in personal finance: except possibly for the very wealthy and very narcissistic, the goal of financial planning is *not* as in a marathon, where the financial winner is the one who has accumulated the greatest wealth. (The best way to compete in that marathon is to spend nothing, eat in soup kitchens, live on the sidewalk, and invest all income in an S&P 500 index fund—cf. Sect. 1.6.)

Instead, a reasonable goal of financial planning is to seek a plan that has the greatest likelihood to support desired feasible spending throughout life (meaning not outliving savings). This includes set-asides for bequests. Maximizing wealth vs. maximizing the longevity of a portfolio drawn down for expenses: these are two very different goals with two very different solutions.

3.8 Liquidity Risk

This section could be titled "The Risk of 'Risk-Free' Annuities, 'Risk-Free' Bonds, and Other Long-Term Investments."

Risk, as we have seen, mediates investments in many different ways. One more way is the risk associated with loss of liquidity. Largely overlooked, *this risk often turns out to be more significant in its likelihood than all the other risks associated with a longer-term investment.*

Let's say you have perfectly prepared for your retirement cash needs with a ladder of TIPS (Sect. 2.3.3). This guarantees a risk-free inflation-adjusted cash flow that was determined to cover all your needs (in theory—ignoring the issues raised in Sect. 2.3.3). But what happens if a new, unpredicted need arises that exceeds your allocated cash flow? Perhaps it's even just a temporary need, one that you can pay back to yourself later. For example, your grandchild (or you) needs emergency medical intervention. Even if the cost is reimbursed by insurance, for now it may require an out-of-pocket payment. What will you do? Well, you have all that money in laddered TIPS, and TIPS are liquid, so— easy—just sell one. But when it comes time to replace it, the price likely has changed, either for better or worse. So much for your "risk-free" investment.

By liquidating a portion of your risk-free investment, even if only temporarily, you have just introduced risk. It now becomes like any other investment. If a bond needs to be sold before maturity, value can be lost. But liquidation is at least possible, at worst, introducing an unanticipated penalty. Liquidity risk can be much more pronounced with semi-liquid investments like real estate and ultimately so with non-liquid investments like most annuities. It's a major factor when considering whether to take out a mortgage or pay "all cash" (Sect. 9.4).

If real estate needs to be liquidated to meet an unanticipated expense, the selling price may be substantially lower than its longer-term price average. This can be a result of a local or short-term market depression, or simply on account of needing to price it low for a quick sale.

With a common annuity (Sect. 2.10), one pays an insurance premium for a guaranteed life-long monthly stipend. Unlike an investment, once paid, the premium is gone. While an annuity often is termed "risk-free," as we already have seen, this is not true (Sect. 2.10). But probably greater than inflation and the counterparty risk is the risk that you will need the money that you paid for that annuity premium (and can't get back). Had you simulated your annuity with a bond ladder (Sect. 2.3.3), then at least you could break the ladder.

Since the risk of unanticipated expenses is hard to quantify, economists simply ignore it. But look over your past major expenses: how many could you have predicted in advance? How far in advance? One year? How about 10 years? How about 30 years? That's the time scale that economists require for their formulaic retirement planning (Sect. 11.4.2).

4

How Much to Hold in Fixed Income Investments?

This chapter examines the question of how much value to hold in fixed income investments (with the rest of savings held in equity), as a function of anticipated expenses.

For our purposes, *fixed income investments* means bonds, bond funds, CDs, fixed-term annuities, *and cash*. Sometimes, I'll redundantly write "fixed income investments and cash" as a reminder of the cash component.

The conclusion given here is iconoclastic. Almost universally (I know of no exceptions), the investment industry advises investors to hold a mix of stocks and bonds in some proportion that increases in favor of bonds as one ages. (They often advise that the chosen proportion be determined by one's level of "risk aversion"—Sect. 3.7—assumed to increase with age.) The *2 trillion* dollar industry of "target-date funds" (Sect. 4.8) is predicated on this assumption.

In this chapter I present a significantly more beneficial alternative to this industry standard.

The primary adverse effect of the industry recommendation is to irrationally restrict growth. The central benefit proposed here allows more growth by holding in equities all funds not needed for expenses.

This alternative also avoids other deleterious consequences of the industry recommendations. These are the need to sell equities when depressed in value, in order to attain or maintain a chosen balance, and a (widely overlooked) degradation of growth rate that accompanies a regularly drawn-down volatile investment (Sect. 11.1), whether depressed or not.

To follow the industry recommendation to attain a designated balance of stocks and bonds can require selling stocks that are depressed in value. This

---

© The Author(s), under exclusive license to Springer Nature Switzerland AG 2022
R. P. Kurshan, *Investment Industry Claims Debunked,*
https://doi.org/10.1007/978-3-030-76709-9_4

can occur when setting up an account or simply to increase the proportion of bonds as one ages. The latter case occurs when the required increase is proportionately greater than the depression. A target-date fund can require a 20% increase in the proportion of bonds held (at once, or over time), while the value of stocks held are depressed by 15%. Likewise, the industry recommendation can require selling stocks (and bonds, in the balance proportion) to cover expenses. This can cause a degradation of growth rate from the regular sale of volatile stocks, as just stated.

Simply to maintain a given balance, the industry forcefully recommends periodic *rebalancing*: selling what is in excess to buy what is insufficient (Sect. 9.8). In some cases, this too can require selling stocks while their value is depressed. But, even if rebalancing is benign in this respect, it misses the central point that equity holdings should be maximized for best portfolio growth, after allocating the funds required to cover anticipated expenses. Rebalancing only makes sense if the original balance, presumed optimal, remains optimal over time. This is a virtual impossibility, as we will see.

The investment industry usually doesn't explain the reason for their recommended mix, but I think they would agree that the investor should hold some stocks for growth and some bonds for stability. That doesn't explain increasing the proportion of bonds as one ages, except that in retirement, suddenly, more stable savings may be needed to support living expenses.

However, there are many occasions in life when one draws from savings (to buy a house, go to college, health emergency, etc.), and for all such occasions, a stable source for expenses is important in order to avoid the possibility of needing to sell stock when the market is depressed.

I suspect that the investment industry reasoning went like this: at any time, you hold some stocks and some bonds. There must be some proportion that's best. Whatever you figure is best, fine. But then you need to maintain that proportion through rebalancing, else you lose your "best" proportion. Indeed, Vanguard has a white paper that argues that *not* rebalancing is equivalent to maintaining a *different* balance. The fallacy is the implicit assumption that the best balance stays constant in time (or just increases in favor of bonds, as one ages). As shown here in what follows, the best balance continually changes (in both directions) along with changing near-term expenses and market conditions.

At any given time, holding more in fixed income investments than required to cover expenses risks a shortfall from reduced growth, while holding too little risks a loss from needing to sell depressed equities. But nothing in that says that the best proportion stays constant in time (it does not). And, as already explained, maintaining a balance has by itself its own additional risks and costs.

Therefore, I claim that the investment industry's advice not only is irrational but also counterproductive. The proposed alternative, on the other hand, concurs with standard economic utility models.[1]

If you are young, very secure in your employment, live simply, and feel covered for most contingencies by the balance you maintain in your checking account, then you may not need much or any savings held in fixed income investments, and can direct most or all of your savings to a low-fee broadly diversified equity index fund, thus enjoying its superior expected growth. However, you may not stay young forever, the number of those dependent on you may increase, the pressure of significant expenses may loom larger, and the time may come to reevaluate these considerations.

Your employment, health, and family circumstances invariably change over time. So then should the amount that you hold in fixed income investments.

What is key is an absolute amount targeted to be held in fixed income investments that adjusts with changing circumstances, *not* the ratio of fixed income investments to equity. This target amount is governed by one's anticipated near-term expenses that are not covered by income. When this is a very small fraction of total savings (as it normally is for the gainfully employed or the very wealthy), a high proportion of savings invested in stocks is appropriate. This is exemplified by Warren Buffett's advice to his wife, to invest after his death 90% of their fortune in a low-fee S&P 500 index fund (e.g., Vanguard's VFIAX) and 10% in short-term government bonds.[2]

Thus, if your savings or income increases while your expenses hold constant, the target amount of your savings to be held in fixed income investments should stay the same, while the investment in equity increases (contrary to investment industry recommendations to maintain a chosen balance through rebalancing).

---

[1]Cf. Bodie (1995), Section 5.

[2]Wismer (2014).

4.1 Stability vs. Growth

A common investment industry recommendation is to maintain a balance of 50% stocks and 50% bonds. Figure 4.1 illustrates a tradeoff between a portfolio that maintains this balance and a 100% stock portfolio. Here, "stocks" tracks the S&P 500 index, and "bonds" tracks the price of 10-year Treasury notes. As expected, the balanced portfolio exhibited more stability, while the all-equity portfolio shows better growth. Both starting with the same value at the peak of the real estate bubble on October 9, 2007, 17 months later, at the bottom of the crash on March 9, 2009, the all-equity portfolio had lost half of its value, while the balanced portfolio had lost only a bit less than a quarter of its value. However, by 7 years after the bottom, the two portfolios were at par with one another, and after another 2 years, the all-equity portfolio was 30% ahead of the balanced portfolio. This clearly illustrates the tradeoff between stability and growth.

If one has an investment whose purpose is to create an endowment in the next 20–30 years, then the optimal simple investment class for it is 100% in a broadly diversified equity (stock) index fund, enabling it to achieve the

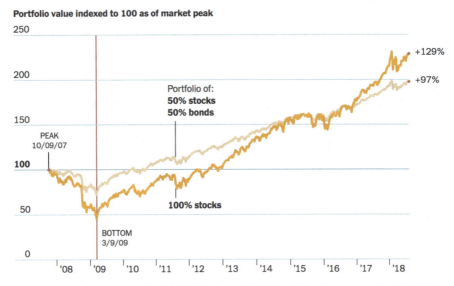

Fig. 4.1 Undrawn portfolio growth, 2008–2018.

maximum possible growth rate of the market as a whole (cf. Sect. 1.6). Then, at some propitious time, as soon as the market reached an all-time high value 20 to 30 years from now, the fund could be sold and passed on to the endowment. No "balance" with other asset classes such as bonds can help this investment do any better.

In the more common case that one has an investment to be used to support expenses, the solution changes. Let's consider the case of retirement, in which the investment is to be drawn down regularly for expenses. This case provides a clear demonstration of the general need to maintain some dynamically adjusting "balance" between stability and growth, as we see next. In fact, though, this need extends to every period in which savings are used to cover expenses (not just during retirement, but throughout life, whenever savings are to be used to buy a house, for school tuition, an expensive vacation, and so on). This may cover most of life.

The S&P 500 stock index in the period 1950–2015 has given an average annual rate of return of over 11%, with dividends reinvested (7.6% without dividends). Ten-year U.S. Treasury notes (bonds) in the same period, with interest reinvested, have given an average annual rate of return of 5.8% (constant maturity rate yield, not seasonally adjusted). Both of these rates include an adjustment for Vanguard-level fees and take into account the daily price fluctuations. Investing $102,053 in 1950 (worth $1 million in 2014) grew to over $103 million by the end of 2014 if invested in the S&P 500 (dividends reinvested) and to around $4 million if invested in 10-year Treasuries (interest reinvested). What a difference a few percentage points make in growth! Less than twice the growth rate produced more than 25 times the total growth after 65 years. This is because of the exponential nature of compounding. Looking at this, one might wonder "Why would anyone invest in 10-year Treasuries instead of an S&P 500 index fund?"

But now look at Fig. 4.2, which applies to a retirement that began in 1973, during which savings was drawn down monthly for living expenses. Over the 30 years subsequent to 1973, the average annual rate of return for the S&P 500 (dividends and interest reinvested) was 10.6%, still considerably ahead of the 8.5% for 10-year Treasuries. Neither rate of return was hugely different from the average over the 65-year period starting in 1950. However, consider a portfolio that was drawn down monthly at an inflation-adjusted annual rate that initially was 4.75% of 1973 savings (i.e., withdraw 4.75% of savings in 1973 and then the same amount adjusted for inflation in each subsequent

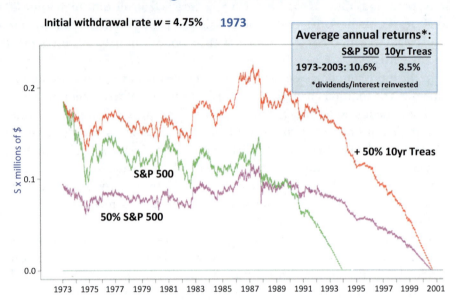

Fig. 4.2 Retirement begun in a 2-year downturn. While a portfolio invested in the S&P 500 stock index had an *expected* return that was 25% higher than that of 10-year Treasury notes, the stock portfolio supported only 21 years of retirement—just keeping up with inflation—whereas a portfolio that maintained a balance of 50% stocks and 50% bonds supported a retirement that was 33% (7 years) longer.

year). If that portfolio had been invested 100% in the S&P 500,[3] it would have lasted only 21 years (the middle curve), just keeping up with inflation ($100/4.75 = 21$).

Alternatively, a portfolio invested 100% in 10-year Treasuries (with a 2.1% lower mean growth rate than the S&P 500), drawn down at the same rate, lasted 27 years—6 years (29%) longer than the S&P 500 investment. This demonstrates the point made in Sect. 3.4 that a lower growth, less volatile asset has the potential to sustain a portfolio longer than a higher growth, more volatile asset.

As already mentioned, it is an investment industry standard to choose a "balance" (ratio) of equity and fixed income investments as a function of one's "risk aversion" (Sect. 3.7) and then *maintain* that balance through rebalancing (Sect. 9.8), whenever the chosen ratio drifts. A ratio of 50% stock (S&P 500)

---

[3]One cannot actually invest in the S&P 500 index, but one *can* invest in an index fund that tracks the S&P 500, which is essentially the same thing as long as the index fund fees are low enough.

and 50% bonds (10-year Treasuries) is a commonly recommended portfolio balance. A portfolio that maintained this balance lasted a bit longer than the all-bond portfolio: just short of 28 years, as shown in Fig. 4.2. That includes accounting for Vanguard-level fees and bid-ask spreads for buys and sells. The lower curve shows the value over time of the 50% stock investment, and the upper curve shows the combined value of that together with the 50% bond investment.

What's going on? In a word: *degradation*, an effective growth diminution caused by periodic withdrawals from a volatile investment (see Sect. 11.1 for details). Its essence is this. When a stock's price per share is below its recent mean value, a withdrawal of some dollar value constitutes a larger proportion of the portfolio than the same dollar value withdrawn when the stock's price is above its mean (which constitutes a smaller portion of the portfolio). But, over time, the market continually rises. Therefore, you might imagine that for periodic withdrawals of fixed dollar value, the gains in market "up cycles" more than balance the losses in market "down cycles." However, this is wrong, as shown in Sect. 11.1.2: non-linearity nonetheless causes a bias in favor of the "down cycle" losses. This bias degrades the effective rate of return for a periodically drawn-down volatile investment, even when the investment value is generally increasing over time. The investment industry has widely overlooked this very significant effect.

Although the all-stock fund appreciated almost 25% faster, on average, than the all-bond fund, it also was much more volatile, and the periodic withdrawals degraded its effective rate of return much more than for the less volatile bond fund.

With a large market downturn at the start of retirement, as there was in 1973, degradation was amplified by the unrecoverable loss from selling depressed stock at the beginning of the retirement period (cf. Sect. 9.3). When the market recovered (only three and a half years later for the S&P 500), the depressed stocks were spent, and thus those retirement savings could not likewise recover.

Even without regular drawdowns, just a one-time unrecoverable loss from selling depressed stock compounds over time, causing the effect of the loss to grow exponentially throughout the life of the portfolio. Thus, the earlier such a loss occurs, the more destructive it is.

With a stable source (say, cash) to cover expenses during a stock market downturn, the need to draw down depressed stocks can be avoided, and depressed stocks can remain in the portfolio—in the above example, to recover three and a half years later.

R. P. Kurshan

The protection against the need to sell equity during a market downturn and, more generally, the degradation of a periodically drawn down volatile portfolio, is to have available lower-volatility investments like bonds and cash to cover drawdowns. These can be replenished once the stock market recovers. This allows the depressed (and now, undrawn) stock investments to recover along with the stock market. Such protection is partially in place with the 50% stock/50% bond portfolio, which hence did better than the 100% stock portfolio, but the requirement to maintain the 50%/50% balance forced the sale of some depressed stocks, nonetheless. A 50%/50% balance turns out to be close to the optimal balance, on average, for the 65 30-year retirement periods between 1950 and 2015, if one insists on maintaining a balanced portfolio, as the investment industry counsels.

The 100% bond portfolio did less well for a different reason: it lacked the better growth rate of the S&P 500.

Instead of adhering to the investment industry advice to maintain some particular balance of equity and fixed income investments, let's see what happens if we seek to hold just enough of the latter to cover expenses. In the following example, depicted in Fig. 4.3, the fixed income investment is held as cash in a savings bank (simulated by using the Federal Funds Rate as its growth rate), and it is replenished by selling equity when the equity value is not depressed. All drawdowns are taken exclusively from the cash, as long as the cash balance suffices. While this condition was met, the stock fund was left alone and downturns then fully recovered.

Figure 4.3 compares the results of two portfolios for a retirement, as above. One is the industry standard balanced portfolio shown in Fig. 4.2. The new one (top curve) began with enough cash to cover 6 years worth of expenses, with the rest held in equity (S&P 500). In retirement, the replenishment of the cash buffer optimally occurs at a decreasing rate (Sect. 11.2). This is because as the retirement period progresses, the advantage of the better growth potential of equity begins to outweigh the cost of possibly having to sell depressed equity. This is reflected in the bottom curve in Fig. 4.3, which shows the value of the cash buffer, which lasted only 15 years (half way through the retirement period). After that, the condition to replenish it from the stock fund never was met. Nonetheless, the cash buffer gave the retirement portfolio a sufficient boost to significantly outperform *every* balanced portfolio for that retirement period.

The cash-buffered portfolio lasted 37 years, 35% longer than the investment industry's preferred equi-balanced portfolio. The details of how to manage a retirement cash-buffered equity portfolio are given in Sect. 11.2.

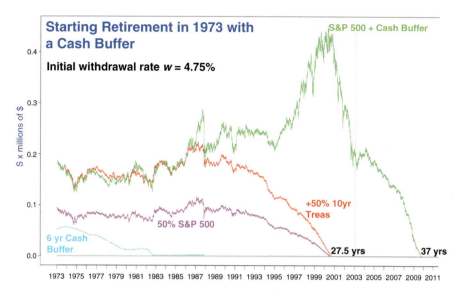

Fig. 4.3 Balanced vs. cash-buffered retirement portfolio. This is the same market data as in Fig. 4.2, with the cash buffer fund data superimposed. (The graph is rescaled to accommodate the new data.) Whereas the value of the portfolio that maintained a balance of 50% stocks and 50% bonds went to $0 after 27.5 years, the portfolio managed with a cash buffer lasted 37 years, 35% longer than the investment industry's preferred equi-balanced portfolio.

This example illuminates the basic flaw in the investment industry edict to maintain a balanced portfolio. In fact, over every 15- to 40-year retirement period in 1950–2015 (measured period lengths in 5-year increments), the cash-buffered equity portfolio outlasted or at worst matched[4] *every* maintained balance of S&P 500 and 10-year Treasuries, as well as any such balance that changed linearly over time (increasing or decreasing the ratio).

Thus, the question "what's the best balance" of equity and fixed income investments is the wrong question. The salient question is how best to cover expenses with low-volatility fixed income investments and cash. These provide a buffer that protects the portfolio from the long-term loss associated with selling depressed equity. Likewise, it protects the portfolio from the degradation associated with regular drawdowns of a volatile investment. This

---

[4] The performance metric is the portfolio longevity within the retirement period. It does not include the end balance for portfolios that lasted the full period, as the stated goal is to avoid outliving savings, not to maximize savings at the end of retirement. In some cases, a portfolio invested 100% in equities had an end balance exceeding that of the cash-buffered portfolio. Of course, this cannot be predicted in advance. So, longevity alone, to the end of the stated period, excluding the end balance, is the right metric to use.

buffer should be no larger than necessary, so as to avoid an unnecessary sacrifice of portfolio growth. Growth is driven by the rest of the portfolio, invested in equities.

Note that this example also belies the industry recommendation to increase the balance in favor of bonds, over time. As explained above, usually there is an advantage in retirement to *decrease* over time the amount held in fixed income investments.

It was mentioned earlier that by the same arguments, the utility of maintaining an equity portfolio buffered with fixed income investments also applies before retirement, to every period in which there are likely to be withdrawals from savings to cover expenses. How generally to establish and maintain the required fixed income investment buffer is a central conclusion of this book, explained in detail in the rest of this chapter and Chap. 5.

4.2 Fixed Income Buffer as Shock Absorber

In what follows, I give guidelines for how much to hold in fixed income investments (the rest in equity), based on expenses that are to be covered by savings. These fixed income investments provide a buffer that acts like a "shock absorber" (Fig. 4.4), absorbing the "shock" of a stock market depression by reducing the likelihood of needing to sell depressed equities to pay for expenses.

Thus, instead of holding equity and fixed income investments in some magical proportion as advocated by the investment industry, hold just so much in fixed income investments as is required to absorb the "shock" of a stock market depression. Holding too much compromises portfolio growth.

The main issue for maintaining a fixed income investment buffer is to decide how far in advance of an expense to prepare to set aside the required funds. Sufficient time needs to be allocated to wait out an equity market

Fig. 4.4 Fixed income buffer as shock absorber. Fixed income investments absorb the shock of temporarily depressed equity by covering expenses that are paid from savings. Once equity value restores, the fixed income investment is replenished.

downturn. The required buffer is obtained from the sale of equity as soon (within the allocated period) as the equity value is no longer depressed. If the allocated period is too short, there is an increased risk that the equity remains depressed throughout the period. If it's too long, there's a likelihood that an unnecessarily early exchange of equity for fixed income investments compromises portfolio growth.

The optimal waiting period length is different before and after retirement. Before retirement, one might after all need to sell some depressed equities for expenses (having underestimated the actual length of an equity market downturn). At the same time, though, one typically is augmenting savings— say, in a tax-advantaged retirement plan like a 401(k). Thus, the loss from the sale of depressed equity is somewhat offset by the purchase of equity at the same depressed price. Therefore, one can afford to be a bit more "aggressive" than in retirement, in optimizing the timing for exchanging equity for fixed income investments.

Pre-retirement, the optimal lead time to prepare to exchange equity for fixed income investments is around 2 years prior to the expense (Sect. 5.4). In preparation for retirement, the optimal lead time is around 10 years (Sect. 11.2).

All the optimal lead time calculations are based on historical market behavior, assuming that the general market behavior of the past half-century will continue into the next. If you have a better basis for predicting future market behavior, then use that (in Sects. 5.4 and 11.2) to determine the optimal lead times. These chapters describe a concept; they do not purport to predict future market behavior.

If the time span allocated for exchanging equity for fixed income investments is 2 years, then starting 2 years before the expense, (for example, a school's first year tuition), one waits for a "trigger" condition, signifying that the equity value is not depressed. When the trigger condition is met, the required equity is sold, and the proceeds are used to buy fixed income investments (or simply kept as cash) to be used at the end of that time span for the expense.

The trigger condition proposed in Chap. 5 is that the level of the S&P 500 is within 10% of its all-time high (an event that historically has occurred, on average, many times a year, and in the worst cases, mostly within 4 years— Sect. 5.2).

The size of the fixed income buffer typically varies over time, rising and falling according to expenditures, the equity market value, and the amount of investments earmarked for expenses. Although this might be correlated with age, I'd expect that on a macro level it increases during the second half of one's pre-retirement life, as "big ticket" expenses increase for costs like children's college, then decreases as children finish college, and finally increases again in retirement, when many expenses are paid from savings. On a micro level, I'd expect expenses drawn from savings to continually rise and fall following changes in the stock market, life circumstances, and resulting spending needs. The value of the fixed income investment buffer then rises and falls accordingly. Thus, as time passes and needs change, one should revisit the earmarked fixed income investment allocations and adjust them accordingly.

The fixed income investment itself should be organized so that for those expenses to be paid from savings, the more immediate expenses, say, those due within a year, are covered by "cash": non-volatile completely liquid vehicles like a money market fund or savings bank account. Longer-term expenses with some precise due date can be covered by zero-coupon bonds, CDs, and fixed-term annuities (MYGAs—Sect. 2.10.2). These three types of investments are attractive because at maturity, you receive a precisely known amount. Taxes on the bonds and CDs are due annually, whereas MYGA income is taxed only at maturity. The rest of savings earmarked for fixed income investments can be invested in an intermediate-term broad-spectrum bond fund. While such funds normally give a somewhat better yield than the other possibilities, they are subject to some daily price volatility (although, much less than for equity). Additionally, they are subject to some (typically small) potential losses if interest rates rise, as explained in Sect. 2.3.

There is another way to absorb the shock of needing to sell depressed equity, using a mechanism called "portfolio insurance" (cf. Sect. 11.2). It is considerably more difficult to implement than the strategy proposed here, and it is unclear if its performance is any better. Moreover, it only addresses isolated needs to sell depressed equity, not the general degradation that accompanies regular drawdowns of equity (Sect. 11.1). Its description and analysis are beyond the scope of this book.

In the following sections, I give examples of how to support anticipated spending from savings.

4.3 Funding Schooling (and the Like)

Preparing funds for schooling (and the like) is one of the easiest cases, because one likely knows of the need years in advance.

Say you have an approximately known payment due some years to come, which is too significant to support from income. A prudent action is to plan to hold the required amount in fixed income investments (rather than equity), some time prior to the expense. This is so that when needed for payment, the earmarked funds are less likely to be depressed in value.

Aside from funds required to cover expenses, savings should be invested in equity, on account of its superior growth rate (Sect. 4.1). In Chap. 5 we calculate how far in advance of an expense one needs to prepare to transfer the required funds from equity to fixed income investments. (One exchanges the funds within the allocated time span as soon as the trigger condition is met—Sect. 4.2.) If the funds are needed in annual amounts over a number of years (say, in four successive amounts, for 4 years of college), then prepare for the transfers to fixed income investments in four successive years, treating each year's tuition separately.

The optimal time span to allocate to the exchange of equity for fixed income investments is around 2 years (Sect. 5.4—based on assumptions stated there). It entails an expected "transfer *loss*" of 17% relating to the range of uncertainty (inherent any probabilistic model). This means that one can expect to use only 83% of the amount transferred. So, for a tuition of $10,000, earmark $12,000 to transfer to fixed income investments. If the expected trigger presents, then transfer only $10,000 (retaining the extra $2000 in equity). Otherwise, apply the $2000 to the depressed equity sale loss.

However, it may be difficult to provide additional funds to further cover a loss from needing to sell depressed equity in an unexpectedly long market downturn. In this case, for a large, critical payment like school tuition, one may choose a longer transfer time span, as insurance. If instead of the optimal 2 years, one chooses 4 years, that reduces the chance by 2/3 of needing to sell depressed equity on account of an unusually long market depression. The "premium" for this insurance is a 4% increase in transfer *cost*: the expected increased shortfall from holding fixed income investments longer (Sect. 5.4). The 4% is only 1% per year. If you worry about being able to find an alternative source of funds to compensate for an exceptionally long downturn, this may be considered a worthwhile premium to pay. It provides increased protection against ending up with insufficient funds. Another way to think of this: 4 years is optimal for a more conservative model that looks at only the 30% of years with the worst performance (Sect. 5.4). If you choose the more conservative model, then there is no cost "premium." However, it has a higher expected transfer cost. The first model with the premium costs about the same as the second model. But in the second model, the expected transfer *loss* is only 12% (so less needs to be earmarked for the transfer). Choice of model won't change the future, only one's expectation. But the 4-year window does add real protection against ending up with insufficient funds.

Let's suppose we choose to allocate a 4-year time span to exchange equity for fixed income investments earmarked for college tuition. Then 4 years before the start of college, begin to wait for the trigger condition, and perform the transfer for the 1st year's tuition as soon as the trigger condition is met within that 4-year window. Do likewise in successive college years. If the trigger condition is first satisfied, say, in the 3rd year of the first 4-year window (Fig. 4.5), then the first three transfers of equity to fixed income investments are triggered together. The result is that the funds in fixed income investments earmarked for the 1st year of college last for 1 year and a bit before being spent, those for the 2nd year of college last 2 years and a bit, and those for the 3rd, 3 years and a bit. (The "bit" is the time from the trigger to the end of the current year.) The window for funding the last year opens in the 4th year of the 1st year's window.

If the trigger condition fails to be met in some window, then one is left with no choice but to fund the expense through the sale of depressed equity. On average, the depression is slight and covered by the added "loss" earmark described above. Else, one must make up the difference with other funds. This

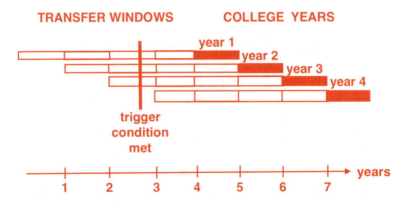

Fig. 4.5 Tuition transfer windows. In this example, the trigger condition is first met in the 3rd year of the transfer window for the 1st year's tuition. It then also triggers the transfer for the next 2 years as well.

possibility is a risk worth taking, on account of the shortfall from holding fixed income investments instead of faster-growing equity. If fixed income investments are held too long, the shortfall can make the cost of protection greater than the protected loss.

However, if you have enough value in equity now to fund the 4 years of college and could not afford the college tuition if that value decreased, then transition today the entire amount for all 4 years—*to cash*, despite any loss and expected shortfall. It's the only absolute insurance.

4.4   Buying or Repairing a Home

If you plan to buy, repair, or renovate a home, one financial strategy is to wait until the stock market is high and then cash out the needed funds. If the stock market is depressed when you make your plan, and you feel that you can't wait, you might want to compute the financial consequences (as in the boat example, Sect. 9.3) and see if you are really willing to pay the extra price to do it now rather than wait until the market has restored at least some of its value.

Alternatively, if you want to plan ahead, with a target date for spending the savings, then apply the plan of Sect. 4.3.

4.5   How About an Emergency?

Emergencies, by their nature, are unpredictable. They also can be very costly: say, a health emergency, a divorce, a bail bond, a lawyer, an unplanned wedding, and so on. What if you are hit by such a costly emergency when the stock market is depressed, and you have no option but to sell depressed stocks at a loss to cover the expense? That loss is unrecoverable.

Shouldn't you hold some bonds to cover such a case, and thus protect against the possible need to sell depressed stocks?

Generally, no. Since emergencies are unpredictable and more likely not to happen, if you held fixed income investments as "insurance" against needing to possibly sell depressed equity in an emergency, the expected shortfall from holding those investments (Sect. 5.3) would likely exceed the expected loss from needing to sell depressed equity. And how could you know how much to hold?

An exception is if you expect, with high likelihood, to have some unanticipated expense or other of $X annually that you cannot support from income. (You can guess $X now and adjust $X in succeeding years based on the

108   R. P. Kurshan

experience of the previous years, new circumstances, and any amounts left over.) How many future years worth of emergencies should one cover with fixed income investments? This question in fact is the same as the question for funding college (Sect. 4.3), except instead of funding 4 years of tuition (Fig. 4.5), fund $X[5] every year.

What about the case of an $X emergency, unsupportable by income, expected to occur at some random time within the next t years? An example: a change in one's employment situation, leading to the belief that there is a good chance of being laid off in the next few years. Then $X (per footnote 5) is what would be required to cover expenses (after unemployment insurance) until the next job.

If t is large, then the shortfall from holding fixed income investments until the emergency could be greater than the expected loss from selling depressed equity (Sect. 5.3). For what value of t does covering $X with fixed income investments make sense? The answer, based on assumptions given in Sect. 5.4, is around 4 years or less. As in Sect. 4.3, if there is concern about being able to support the expense $X for $t > 4$, in case equity is depressed, one can consider (suboptimally) increasing the number of years above 4 (or even exchanging $X worth of equity for fixed income investments now—keeping in mind that the expected resulting shortfall will be worse than the expected loss from selling depressed equity).

let's do the calculation

For an expense that occurs at a random time within the next t years, then on average one would need it after $t/2$ years (it's just as likely to be needed sooner as later). To fund that expense with fixed income investments, as always, one assigns an optimal length transfer period within which to transfer the required amount from equity. The optimal transfer period length is around 2 years before the expense (Sect. 5.4). So, as for any other expense, an emergency expense expected to occur in $t/2$ years has a transfer period window of 2 years before expected. For the random emergency expense, 2 years before it is expected to occur is 2 years before $t/2$. This means that one should fund now a random emergency expense expected to occur within $t = 4$ years, while for $t > 4$, optimally, one (in effect) perpetually awaits the opening of the transition window (so the emergency expense is never supported by fixed income investments).

---

[5]Technically, reduce $X by multiplying it by its probability p to occur. If that is unknowable, then either reduce $X slightly, based on intuition, or just assume $p = 1$.

4.6 Saving for Retirement

The investment industry is replete with advice to implement a pre-retirement spending diet to save such-and-such percent of income per year in order to have enough for retirement. Such advice in fact can be close to worthless. It can result in saving more than needed for retirement (Sect. 11.4), at the expense of enjoying more of one's income while younger. Or, it can result in being lulled into not saving enough, because far-off expenses are impossible to predict. Mostly, such advice just creates unnecessary anxiety.

I expect that these sentiments will earn me great disapprobation from financial specialists who, incidentally, have a vested interest in getting us to save more for retirement—and thus, invest more with them. The government too has an interest in increasing saving for retirement. At the very least, the U.S. Government can see the looming retirement crisis it has helped create (Chap. 18) and is terrified at the increased demand for public assistance projected for our broken retirement system.

But, when young, speculations on retirement needs are only wild guesses, and whatever is predicted likely will turn out to be wrong.

While working (receiving income), financial planning is less important to one's present financial state, because whatever mistakes are made mostly can be rectified in the years to come.[6] This ceases to be the case in retirement, when savings need to be sufficient to last. Therefore, managing investments while working is mostly about preparing to have enough in retirement.

While it's best to start thinking about retirement finances while working, if you've never given retirement finances much of a thought and are now about to retire—or are already retired—it's ok. The benefits of financial planning are back-weighted, becoming increasingly important the closer one is to retirement, and then most important once retired.

In the United States, for people with an employment-based savings plan like a 401(k) or an IRA (Chap. 12), saving something for retirement is automatic. These plans are retirement savings plans, since they have penalties for early withdrawal. Especially when young, this may suffice for retirement saving. This is not because it's the "right" amount to save—the "right" amount is unknowable. But this produces *some* savings. Moreover, it has other advantages, namely, deferring tax on the saved income and, in many cases, generating an additional employer contribution (Sect. 12.1).

---

[6]If you're unable to make ends meet, it's definitely time to have a serious conversation with yourself—or with a sympathetic friend, parent, or sibling. There are many ways out (some mentioned below), but mostly you don't find them unless you look.

110   R. P. Kurshan

In fact, trying to save more than this for retirement can be counterproductive. If income doubles in later years, then the amounts one might save through sacrifice while income is low get dwarfed by the amounts saved in later years. This render the early sacrifices superfluous. In any case, with children in school and other normal living expenses, saving more for retirement may hardly even be an option.

Young people have realized this intuitively all along. That vacation is real and will give pleasure now. Saving for retirement is only a concept. Retirement is so far into the future that its demands and ramifications are most likely different from anything imagined when young. The young may spend what they feel that they need to or want to or can, and plan that when they retire, they will spend what they can then.

So, I think that up until, say, a decade before retirement, a U.S. 401(k) or IRA savings plan, or other equivalent, is a good-enough retirement plan. As retirement approaches, it is time to give more focused thought to what style of retirement is affordable (Chap. 10) and how to prepare funding for retirement (Sect. 11.2).

Nonetheless, it's worthwhile to give some early thought to your philosophy regarding front-loading vs. back-loading discretionary spending, as explained next. The choice is related—but not identical—to the choice to live beyond your means or below your means.[7] And whichever it is, it's better if it's the result of a conscious decision than a behavior that just rolls over you and can lead to later regret.

4.6.1 Front-Loading Discretionary Spending

Let's suppose you are a passionate skier (I am), and you have had many wonderful skiing vacations with your family. Recently, skiing has become obscenely expensive, while my family continues to grow in size. A few skiing vacations with my ever-growing family has definitely cut into my savings, and not only whatever I have spent is gone, but its potential to appreciate is also gone—in particular, it all is lost to retirement savings.

I made the calculation that if my remaining investments did well, I could afford to continue this expensive practice into my retirement. If not, or if other unanticipated spending priorities arose, then I may need to cut back on this or other discretionary spending. But my calculation was that it could be ok. In the very worst case, I could sell my home and move to less expensive housing,

---

[7] Stanley and Danko (1996).

Joshua Slocum 1899

which would save a lot. It doesn't take a lot of energy to have that sort of conversation with yourself.

Therefore, I decided to indulge my family while we were younger. It provided many great memories and bonding with children and grandchildren. I was willing to pay the price, if necessary, down the line. But I made that decision based not on a hope, but on a calculation (Chap. 10) that showed me that there was a reasonable chance that my retirement savings could survive the hit. And that if they did not, I had an acceptable fallback.

4.6.2 Back-Loading Discretionary Spending

On the other hand, perhaps you harbor a dream of, after many decades of hard work, buying a boat in retirement and sailing around the world as Joshua Slocum did. Boats have become increasingly expensive too. In this case, your priority may be the reverse: be very frugal with discretionary spending prior to retirement, saving as much as you can—and hope you live to enjoy it in retirement.

4.6.3 Hold Enough in Fixed Income Investments at the Start

Once you retire, based on assumptions in Sect. 11.2, you should be holding enough in fixed income investments (like bonds and cash) to cover the first 6 years of those living expenses that are to be drawn from savings.

If the required transfer from equity to fixed income investments has not happened by retirement and depressed equity must be sold to support retirement expenses, the impact of the loss, coming at the start of retirement, can have a catastrophic effect on retirement savings. Such a loss creates a lost earning opportunity that compounds through the rest of retirement (cf. the middle curve in Fig. 4.2, representing a 100% investment in the S&P 500 at the start of a retirement that began in a bear market).

Therefore, it is cost-effective to guard against a very unlikely but catastrophically long market downturn far out in the tail of the downturn length distribution. This, despite the likely shortfall from holding so much in fixed income investments for a number of years (Sect. 5.3). However, for a 30-year retirement, the amount of fixed income investments required to cover 6 years of expenses represents only 20% or less of savings, much less than the 50–70% that the investment industry recommends to hold there (Sect. 4.7).

In order to avoid the risk of missing a trigger condition, one should begin to wait for the trigger as much as a decade prior to retirement (cf. Sect. 5.1). The trigger condition is the same as the one chosen for all pre-retirement transfers: when the S&P 500 is within 90% of its previous all-time high value.

This means that you need to attempt to anticipate retirement expenses a decade in advance of retirement. As this is probably not possible to do with much accuracy, a best estimate must suffice. Calculate current spending as described in Chap. 6, and then estimate how that will change in retirement. Once retirement begins, the size of the fixed income buffer is adjusted for actual spending needs.

If you have control over your retirement date and can wait to retire until a trigger condition is realized, you can make the transition of equity to fixed income investments then, enough to last 6 years. You can retire the next day.

4.7 Investment Industry Recommendations

Professional recommendations for a portfolio ratio of stocks to bonds include "50%/50%," "60%/40%," "40%/60%," "percent bonds equal to your age," "your age minus 28,"[8] "70% equities for a 20-year retirement,"[9] and more.

Recommendations to hold more in stocks when young and then less as one ages may be motivated by the widespread fallacious notion that the riskiness of stocks diminishes with the length of time held (Sect. 3.6).

Let's see how these recommendations comport with historical data, in retirement. Table 4.1 gives the minimum and average longevities for a portfolio that maintains a balance of bd percent bonds (10-year Treasuries), the rest stocks (S&P 500). Interest and dividends are reinvested, and Vanguard-level fees and ask-bid spreads are applied. The portfolio is drawn down monthly at an initial annual rate of w as a percent of the initial portfolio value, thereafter adjusted annually for inflation. The minimums and averages are over all N-year retirement periods between 1950 and 2015 and are based on daily stock prices and monthly bond prices.

Note that while the initial withdrawal rate w significantly affects the average portfolio longevity, the choice of portfolio balance within the middle range has only a slight effect on the averages. This may explain the wide range of advice about what is a good balance: they all are "right"!

Table 4.1 Balanced portfolio longevity. Based on market data between 1950 and 2015, for each bd, the percent of bonds maintained in the portfolio (the rest being stocks), initial annual withdrawal rate w, and retirement period length N, the pair of numbers in the table is the minimum and average portfolio longevity, in years, taken over every retirement period in that span. The best for each w is shown in bold.

$bd\backslash w$	$N = 25$				$N = 30$						$N = 35$	
	5%		4.75%		4.5%		4.25%		4%		3.75%	
100%	20.4	23.7	22.1	24.4	23.9	27.6	26.1	28.8	28.4	29.8	30	34
70%	**21.0**	**24.4**	**22.9**	**24.9**	**25.2**	**29.3**	28.1	29.9	30	30	35	35
50%	20.5	24.1	22.5	24.8	24.9	**29.5**	**28.3**	**29.9**	30	30	35	35
30%	19.7	24.4	21.6	24.7	23.9	29.4	27.2	29.9	30	30	35	35
0%	16.9	24.1	18.7	24.4	20.8	29.0	23.8	29.5	28.3	29.9	35	35

---

[8] Bengen (1996).
[9] Sholar (2018).

114 R. P. Kurshan

Table 4.2 Portfolio longevities for $w = 4.25\%$, $N = 30$.

bd	min	ave	fails	suc	set
100%	26.1	28.8	19	47%	210
90%	26.7	29.5	10	72%	211
80%	27.4	29.8	5	86%	212
70%	28.1	29.9	2	94%	213
60%	28.5	29.9	2	94%	214
50%	28.3	29.9	2	94%	215
40%	27.8	29.9	2	94%	216
30%	27.2	29.9	4	89%	217
20%	26.3	29.8	4	89%	218
10%	25.3	29.6	4	89%	219
0%	23.8	29.5	4	89%	219

Table 4.2 gives the results for one column of Table 4.1 with greater granularity, for a withdrawal rate of $w = 4.25\%$. The number of periods in which the portfolio value went to 0 before the end of the 30th year is given in the *fails* column, and the *suc* column gives the percentage of the 36 periods that did not fail. (Note that *fails* and *suc* are not very informative indicators, as they do not distinguish between a failure by a day or a decade. However, they are favorites in the investment industry.)

On this historical data, the balance that maximizes the minimum portfolio longevity is seen to be around 60% bonds, 40% stocks, giving a minimum longevity of 28.5 years, and average longevity of 29.9 years (of 30). This concurs with claims published by Bengen (1996) for a different time period. It also aligns with results from the Vanguard retirement simulator (Sect. 3.5, footnote 22), using a larger time range of historical data, which computes that a balance with 50% to 80% stocks achieves a success rate of 85% for a drawdown rate of 4.25% over a 30-year retirement. In the data set examined here (covering the years from 1950 to 2015), such a success rate was achieved by any balance with at least 20% stocks—and 40% stocks was optimal. The much more detailed Fidelity retirement simulator (Sect. 3.5, footnote 23) gives similar results. One should expect variations between data sets, but it seems that on the historical data over the last 90 years, for a large enough data set, the variations may not be large.

These results illustrate a disconnect between investment industry recommendations. On the one hand, they recommend to maintain a stock/bond balance based on "risk aversion" (Sect. 3.7) or some magic ratio as listed at the beginning of this section. On the other hand, the results of their own simulation engines compute the best balances for portfolio longevity—the amount of time your money will last—as a function of drawdown rate and retirement period. The investment industry's left hand and right hand offer conflicting advice!

The recommendation of Sect. 4.2 to maintain no "balance," but hold only as much in fixed income investments as is required to cover expenses, does significantly better than these investment industry recommendations (Sect. 11.2).

4.8 Target-Date Funds

The pervasive investment industry strategy to maintain a balance of stocks and bonds, shifting to more bonds with increasing age, has given rise to a 2 *trillion* dollar business: the *target-date funds*.[10] These funds shift investment from stocks to bonds as one approaches a target retirement date. Just because that's the prevailing advice doesn't make it worthwhile. These funds are counterproductive, as explained above, but even if you bought into their strategy, they are poor investments. If you want to follow their strategy, you can do better on your own.

Although attractive for their mindless simplicity, by construction they cannot adjust to an individual's financial circumstances.[11] For this they command hefty fees that make them poor investments.

The main problem with target-date funds is their strategy, as has already been explained in the previous sections. So, here, let's just examine their value for what they do. It's easy to see that any investor can easily mimic the behavior of a target-date fund and avoid its fees.

Let's compare one of Vanguard's own target-date funds against its own components. Let's say you're in your 40's, so you've chosen Vanguard's Target Date 2045 Fund. At the time of this writing, Vanguard advertised that, with its expense ratio of 0.16%, it has a "59% lower than the average expense ratio of funds with similar holdings," so it looks like a good bet. Vanguard stated that at the time, its composition was as follows: 54% Vanguard Total Stock Market Index Fund Investor Shares (VTSMX), 36% Vanguard Total International Stock Index Fund Investor Shares (VGTSX), 7% Vanguard Total Bond Market II Index Fund Investor Shares (VTBIX), and 3% Vanguard Total International Bond Index Fund Investor Shares (VTIBX). "Investor

---

[10] https://plansponsor.com/research/2019-target-date-fund-buyers-guide/2/.

[11] Bodie (1995) discredits the notion that the younger should always hold more in stocks.

116 R. P. Kurshan

Shares" generally have higher fees than "Admiral Shares" (which require a minimum deposit of $10,000). However, the corresponding ETFs generally track Admiral Shares and have no minimum investment requirement.

For example, the Admiral Shares version of VTSMX is VTSAX, and the corresponding ETF is VTI, with respective expense ratios: 0.15%, 0.04%, and 0.04%.

The Admiral Shares version of VGTSX is VTIAX, and the corresponding ETF is VXUS, with respective expense ratios: 0.18%, 0.11%, and 0.11%.

VTBIX is "available only as an underlying investment in Vanguard funds" but seems very similar (if not identical) to VBMFX, with Admiral Shares version VBTLX and the corresponding ETF BND, with respective expense ratios: 0.15%, 0.05%, and 0.05%.

Finally, the Admiral Shares version of VTIBX is VTABX, and the corresponding ETF is BNDX, with respective expense ratios: 0.15%, 0.12%, and 0.12%.

If you rolled your own, by constructing a portfolio that is 54% VTI, 36% VXUS, 7% BND, and 3% BNDX, it would seem very similar if not completely identical to the Target Date Fund 2045, at that point in time. Of course, Vanguard shifts the proportions over time for you, whether it suits your needs or not, whereas you would need to do the same yourself and could tailor the balance to suit your individual needs.

But that's only the half of it. Let's look more closely at those expense ratios—the fees you pay to Vanguard. For our replication of their Target Date Fund 2045 with ETFs, the corresponding expense ratio is

$$54\% \times 0.04 + 36\% \times 0.11 + 7\% \times 0.05 + 3\% \times 0.12 = 0.0683$$

so the Target Date Fund 2045 has an expense ratio that is 0.0917% greater than the ETF replication. Now this may not look like much, but let's see. If the average annual rate of return on the investment is 8%, dividends and interest reinvested—about average for these investments over time—let's see what that 0.0917% greater expense ratio amounts to after 30 years (around retirement time), assuming it remained the same as the fund ages.

We can use the Appendix formula (A.2) to add up the yearly losses, giving a general formula for the total loss. For an annual loss L and annual rate of return on investment r, after n years, the total loss is $L(1 + r)\frac{(1+r)^n - 1}{r}$. So, for an investment of $100,000, with $L = \$100,000 \times 0.0917\%$, $r = 8\%$ and $n = 30$ years, the loss of investing in the Target Date Fund, over the cost of the equivalent ETF replication, is $11,219. That's over 11% of the original investment—a lot to pay to have Vanguard do for you what you easily could do better on your own.

5

When to Exchange Equity for Fixed Income Investments

Equity is exchanged for fixed income investments (and cash) at propitious times and only to cover anticipated expenses. Each exchange occurs within an allocated time span, upon a trigger condition, as described in Chap. 4. Too short a span risks missing a trigger and thus a loss from needing to sell depressed equity. Too long a span risks holding fixed income investments longer than needed, leading to a shortfall in portfolio appreciation (since equity appreciates faster than fixed income investments).

The more cautious investor who may be tempted to prepare to convert equity to fixed income investments far in advance of when needed in order to greatly reduce the likelihood of needing to sell depressed equity should keep in mind the ultimate goal: to limit the likelihood of portfolio failure (outliving savings). Holding fixed income investments for a long time before they are needed displaces equity holdings and thus reduces growth; inadequate growth also can lead to portfolio failure.

The central goal of this chapter is to show how to calculate the optimal length of the time span to allocate for the exchange.

There are many times prior to retirement when the level of fixed income investment holdings might need to change, for example, prior to buying a home, paying college tuition, and the appearance of a new family member. In retirement, savings may need to replace salary to pay expenses, requiring a major increase in fixed income investment holdings. Such times of increased spending needs mostly can be predicted in advance. Chapter 4 described how to calculate how much to hold in fixed income investments. What remains is to decide when to make the exchange from equity.

© The Author(s), under exclusive license to Springer Nature Switzerland AG 2022
R. P. Kurshan, *Investment Industry Claims Debunked*,
https://doi.org/10.1007/978-3-030-76709-9_5

Søren Kierkegaard 1840

So, how long before an increased need for funds should one be willing to make the exchange? No one can really know for sure, but looking back in time is informative. As Søren Kierkegaard has written, "Life is lived forwards, but understood backwards." While there is no guarantee that the patterns of the past will hold in the future, short of a crystal ball, past performance is all we have to go on. Even financial models that make predictions based on concepts of market behavior nonetheless test, tune, and adjust those models on past experience. There is no economic model that is guaranteed to predict accurately the length of time required for an economic recovery.

The investment industry consistently warns that past performance does not predict future performance, but then blithely bases predictions and recommendations for the future on past performance—it's that or nothing.

model presented here is data-independent

The driving concepts presented here for determining the optimal replenishment schedule for fixed income investments are given in Sect. 5.4. These concepts define a model that is data-independent, so not tied to assumptions about the future.

setting model parameters

To use the model to compute the optimal length of the time span to allocate for the exchange of equity to fixed income investments, values must be assigned to model parameters. To assign these values, some assumptions about the future are required. The required assumptions can come from anywhere.

5 Exchanging Equity for Fixed Income 119

The parameter settings used here are based on historical market behavior over the past 65 years, but could be changed to reflect other expectations.

Reiterating from Sect. 4.2, *the calculation of the optimal time span length presented here illustrates a concept; I do not claim that the general market behavior of the past half-century will necessarily continue into the next (although my best guess is that it will). The reader is invited to substitute any other assumptions about future market behavior (and get a different answer).*

the prime investment question

We already decided that our savings should be invested quite simply, mostly in lowest-fee broadly diversified stock and bond index funds and cash. What then remained at the heart of financial planning was to decide how much of our savings should be invested in each. We argued that this too is very simply decided: hold just enough bonds and cash to cover near-term expenses that are to be paid from savings, replenished at propitious times by selling stocks. What finally remains is to determine the replenishment schedule.

Take a moment to reflect on this. Many investors consider the prime investment question to be what to invest in. We dispatched that question in Chap. 2, giving the simple answer just cited. With that answer, the central investment question shifted to: in what proportions? This question, which has led to a misguided investment industry torment (Sect. 4.7), was found after all to have a ready, natural answer as well. But, we can't simply replenish bonds and cash when depleted: that could necessitate selling depressed stocks, the avoidance of which is the whole point of holding bonds and cash in the first place. Thus, the transition from stocks to bonds and cash needs some flexibility, so that it can occur at propitious times, in advance of when the funds are needed.

> *The prime investment question thus is not what to invest in, not even in what proportion to hold stocks and bonds, but how far in advance to prepare to shift funds from stocks to bonds and cash to cover expenses that are to be paid from savings.*

5.1 Historic Lengths of Market Downturns

In 2015, the investment firm Morgan Stanley analyzed 43 "bear markets," defined by a 20% or more decline from peak to trough.[1] Over the last 50 years, they found that the S&P 500 took a bit over a year on average to recover, with a mean peak to trough decline of 28%. The *longest* decline for the S&P 500 was the bursting of the "dot-com bubble" on March 24, 2000, lasting until September 10, 2002: 643 business days. The decline in value was 40%, the third worst after the 451 day drop of 48% that began on January 11, 1973. The worst decline was 56% that began with the 2006–2007 bursting of the sub-prime mortgage real estate bubble and the ensuing banking fiasco, but the decline lasted "only" 370 business days. This is for the U.S. market. Japan experienced a "lost decade" that skewed their mean bear market to 568 business days.

However, this is only half the story. After the decline, time to full recovery is the other half. For the S&P 500, the report only states that after a decline of 11% (not even a "bear market"), on average it recovers 18% over the following year. As $.89 \times 1.18 = 1.05$, this constitutes a full recovery. But what about the bear markets?

The Wall Street Journal[2] reported (see Fig. 5.1) that the longest recovery was for the second biggest decline of 48% that began on January 11, 1973. Although the decline ended after 451 business days, it took almost 12 years for the Dow Jones Industrial Average to recover back to the level at the start of the decline.[3] However, this was an extreme outlier. It occurred under conditions of skyrocketing double-digit inflation that are considered unlikely to recur now, on account of financial "dampers" that have been put in place since then. The next-worst crash-through-recovery period since 1950 began with the bursting of the dot-com bubble in 2000 and lasted 8 years, according to The Wall Street Journal report, while most others recovered in under 2 years, giving an historical average time from crash to recovery of 3.1 years: Fig. 5.1. (This figure shows longer recovery times than the years, on average, reported by Morgan Stanley, for the S&P 500.) Using daily market data from Yahoo! Finance, I found that for the S&P 500, dividends reinvested, the recoveries were shorter: Fig. 5.2.

---

[1] bloomberg.com/news/articles/2016-01-26/morgan-stanley-analyzed-43-bear-markets-and-here-s-what-it-found = tinyurl.com/uuq58ay.

[2] Mark Hulbert, "Not Every Bear Market Will Stick Around," March 7, 2016.

[3] By contrast, the S&P 500, dividends reinvested, recovered in 3 1/2 years.

5 Exchanging Equity for Fixed Income   121

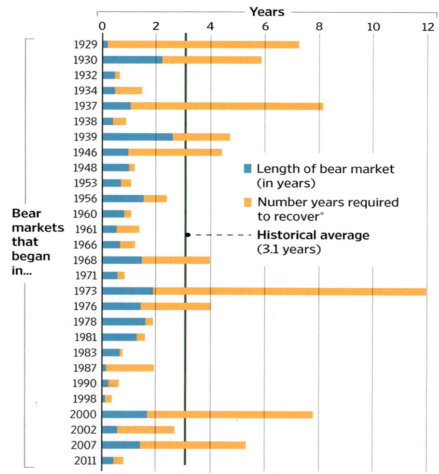

Fig. 5.1 Bear market recovery times.

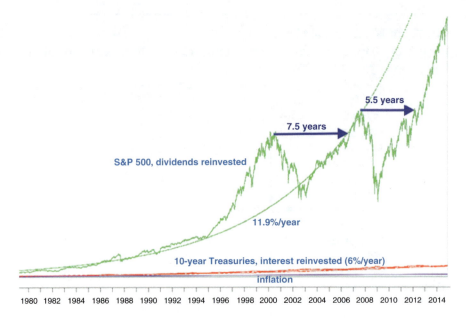

Fig. 5.2 Worst bears since 1980, dividends reinvested.

Since 1950, there were only three severe stock market depressions that, including their recovery times, lasted over 4 years (1973, 2000, and 2007). Kindleberger gives a classic account, now updated,[4] of market crashes.

5.2 Times Between Market All-Time Highs

There have been a few very long periods during which stock prices remained depressed (Fig. 5.1). However, on average, in the period 1950–2015, the S&P 500 experienced an all-time high once a month.[5] Although this average might be deceptive, since highs tend to proliferate during periods of market expansion, all-time highs of the S&P 500 are fairly common.

If we consider growth with dividends reinvested (as we should), then since 1950, the longest stretch between all-time highs of the S&P 500 has never been more than 7.5 years (cf. Fig. 5.2). Without reinvesting dividends, there have been only 21 stretches of time that lasted 100 trading days or more (Fig. 5.3).

---

[4] Aliber and Kindleberger (2015).
[5] marottaonmoney.com/how-frequently-do-new-sp-500-highs-stick/.

5 Exchanging Equity for Fixed Income   123

NEW	VALUE	DAYS BEFORE	PREVIOUS HIGH
5/29/90	360.65	100	1/3/90
6/26/52	24.75	107	1/22/52
8/18/93	456.99	110	3/11/93
7/29/92	423.02	135	1/15/92
11/1/61	68.73	137	4/17/61
4/29/68	98.61	146	9/25/67
2/12/91	370.54	146	7/16/90
2/13/95	482.86	260	1/31/94
7/11/16	2143.16	286	5/20/15
3/11/54	26.69	296	1/5/53
4/28/67	94.77	305	2/9/66
1/21/85	175.45	323	10/10/83
1/27/61	61.24	374	8/3/59
8/30/63	72.71	432	12/12/61
7/26/89	338.05	484	8/25/87
11/3/82	142.88	488	11/26/80
9/24/58	49.78	539	8/2/56
3/6/72	109.4	818	12/2/68
4/10/13	1589.07	1381	10/11/07
7/13/07	1555.1	1833	3/24/00
7/17/80	121.84	1897	1/11/73

Fig. 5.3 Longest stretches between S&P 500 all-time highs. Values are the new daily highs; dividends are *not* reinvested; "days before" are trading days from the previous high to the new high; data is from Yahoo! Finance.

There have been only nine stretches of time since 1950 that the period between milestones for 90% of a new all-time high exceeded 100 trading days, and only six that lasted more than a year (Fig. 5.4). The longest lasted 6 years, the next longest 5 years and 10 months, the third longest 3 years and 10 months, and the fourth longest 1 1/2 years. For milestones within 20% of the previous all-time high, there were only five periods that exceeded 100 trading days and only three lasting over a year: the longest lasted a bit over 4 years and the next longest 2 1/4 years (Fig. 5.5).

We seek to avoid the loss of selling stock in a depressed market by waiting for a recovery to sell. There are many possible measures of "recovery." Impersonal measures refer only to market parameters. Personal measures include the cost bases of one's portfolio assets (the costs at which they were purchased).

90% OF NEW HIGH	VALUE	TRADING DAYS BEFORE	PREVIOUS 90% OF NEW HIGH
1/16/67	85.28	119	7/25/66
1/14/63	65.5	171	5/8/62
6/12/58	44.75	184	9/18/57
10/7/82	128.96	283	8/24/81
2/9/71	98.5	313	11/12/69
4/18/89	306.25	379	10/15/87
3/27/12	1419.15	969	5/21/08
8/21/79	109.68	1465	10/31/73
11/15/06	1401.35	1509	11/10/00

Fig. 5.4 Longest stretches between 90% of previous all-time highs. Details as in Fig. 5.3. Each milestone is higher than 90% of the previous all-time high. Only two stretches (of 6 years) exceeded 4 years.

80% OF NEW HIGH	VALUE	TRADING DAYS BEFORE	PREVIOUS 80% OF NEW HIGH
10/6/70	87.75	121	4/15/70
4/25/78	97.91	157	9/8/77
1/14/76	97.47	454	3/27/74
12/29/10	1262.6	572	9/19/08
7/28/05	1245.15	1034	6/13/01

Fig. 5.5 Longest stretches between 80% of previous highs. Details as in Fig. 5.3. Each milestone is higher than 80% of the previous all-time high.

pre-retirement trigger condition

Since in any case there is considerable latitude among such definitions, I propose a very simple trigger condition for the exchange of equity for fixed income investments (assuming the equity tracks the S&P 500): when the S&P 500 is within 10% of its last all-time high value. Historically, this milestone comes around frequently. Since 1950, the two longest periods between such triggers (Fig. 5.4) were 6 years (1973–1979 and 2000–2006), the next longest was 4 years (2008–2012), then 1 1/2 years (1987–1989), then 1 1/3 years (1969–1971), and all the rest, a year or less.

It is hard to argue that one reasonable trigger condition is better than another, given all the uncertainties and inability to predict the future. If you have a trigger condition that you prefer, then by all means use that. For the sequel, pre-retirement, I'll use the trigger condition that the S&P 500 is within 10% of its all-time high value. Note that this trigger condition can be caught automatically by a limit sale (Sect. 2.7.1). For that reason, I use daily high values rather than closing highs.

If you prefer a different trigger condition, then modify the optimal length transfer window calculations based on it (Sects. 5.3 and 5.4) accordingly.

retirement trigger condition
For retirement portfolio longevity, it is explained in Sect. 11.2 that for the historical market data since 1950, exchanging equity for fixed income investments once the S&P 500 hit 85% of its previous all-time high value was optimal.

5.3 Shortfall Exchanging Stocks for Bonds

Between 1950 and 2015, the S&P 500 experienced an average annual growth rate, with dividends reinvested, of around 11%[6] (cf. Fig. 5.2). During the same period, 10-year Treasuries experienced an average annual growth rate, with coupons reinvested, of 6%[7] (Fig. 5.6). That's a 5% difference. During sub-periods between 1950 and 2015, these rates varied, but over longer sub-periods, these could be taken as "representative." For the sake of choosing numbers, we'll use these numbers in our model, to compute the shortfall of holding bonds in place of stocks. Small variations in these numbers make little difference to the outcomes. After n years, the investment shortfall factor is $1.11^n - 1.06^n$ (*not* $1.05^n - 1$). If you have preferred numbers, then please use them in the model, instead.[8]

We need to weigh this shortfall against the expected loss of waiting too long to exchange stocks for bonds and cash, and then finding that we need to sell stocks during an economic downturn. Selling in a downturn could result, possibly, in losing 30–40% or more in value. The *average* bear was a 28% decline (Sect. 5.1). On the other hand, if we conservatively exchanged stocks for bonds, (say) 5 years before we needed to spend the money, this results in a shortfall of 35%. So: wait too long to transition, and we could lose a lot; be too cautious, transitioning too soon, we experience a big shortfall (also losing a lot).

---

[6] https://dqydj.com/sp-500-return-calculator/.

[7] https://dqydj.com/treasury-return-calculator/.

[8] Some have suggested that in the future, bond growth may exceed equity growth. However, a company could not sustain interest on its bonds at a higher rate than the rate of growth of the company. On the other hand, there are scenarios in which equity growth could come much closer to the interest rates on fixed income investments. One extreme example could be if COVID-19 decimated the earth's population, depressing consumer demand and thus equity growth.

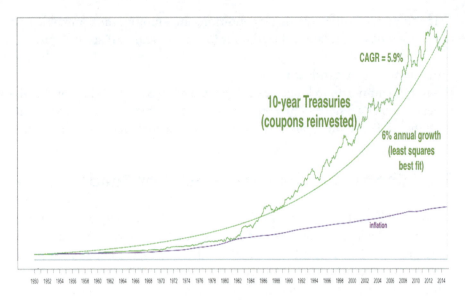

Fig. 5.6 Ten-year Treasuries 1950–2015, coupons reinvested.

5.4 Optimal Transition Window Length

In this section I present means to calculate the optimal length of the transition window. In the window, one waits for a trigger condition (see end of Sect. 5.2), signaling that it's safe to exchange equity for fixed income investments. The fixed income investments are to be used in a forthcoming year to cover an anticipated expense (Sects. 4.2 and 4.3). When the trigger condition is satisfied, one converts the required amount of equity to fixed income investments: see Fig. 5.7. This locks in a good value for the equity, thus avoiding the potential unrecoverable loss from needing to sell depressed equity.

As explained in the previous section, we seek to make the transition from equity to fixed income investments as late as is reasonable before needing the funds for expenses. This is in order to preserve the better average growth of equity. On the other hand, it is unreasonable to delay a transition so long that we miss the trigger and thus at the end of the window hold unexchanged equity that needs to be sold at a depressed price.

Hence, we seek to find the time span t before the anticipated expense that optimizes the tradeoff between the expected shortfall from holding fixed income investments from the time of a trigger until the end of t, on the one hand, and the expected loss incurred from needing to sell depressed equity in case no trigger materializes within the time span t, on the other hand.

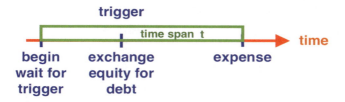

Fig. 5.7 Waiting for trigger, starting t years before expense.

As t increases, the expected shortfall from holding fixed income investments (Sect. 5.3) increases, while the expected loss from selling equity decreases, since increasing t allows more time for a market recovery (and the appearance of the trigger condition). The span length t is optimal when the sum of the expected shortfall and the expected equity loss is minimal.

I calculated this tradeoff based on the assumption that historical market data between 1950 and 2015 can reasonably be taken as a predictor of future market behavior, in terms of volatility and persistence of recessions. If you have what you consider to be a better predictor,[9] then you can use your preferred data instead, in the functions used to compute the tradeoff. While the function parameter settings are guided by expected market behavior, the functions themselves are independent of any assumptions about the future.

The span length t is optimized through four functions of t: $P(t)$, which defines the probability that within the span, the trigger condition is satisfied; $w(t)$, which defines the expected wait within the span until the trigger is satisfied, given that it is; $B(t)$, which defines the expected shortfall from holding fixed income investments from the time of a trigger until the end of the span (when it is spent); and $S(t)$, which defines the expected loss from needing to sell depressed equity in case no trigger materializes within the span. Both B and S are mediated by P and expressed as a fraction (percent/100) of the value transferred.

We seek to find the value of t that minimizes $B(t) + S(t)$, the expected *cost* of transferring equity to fixed income investments. (This cost reduces savings.)

Pre-retirement, we've decided (Sect. 5.2) on the trigger condition that the S&P 500 is within 10% of its last historical all-time high (counting only the first time, if any, within the window). With this assumption, the optimal transition span length t is around 2 years (see below).

---

[9] A better predictor of volatility and persistence of recessions may result from running tens of thousands of market simulations using a commercial market simulator such as Fidelity's. I have no access to such data. However, the resulting tradeoff difference may be slight, as there already is considerable slack in the resulting recommendations coming from other uncertainties.

computing the optimal window length *t*

This subsection describes the methodology used to compute the optimal value of *t* and may be skipped by readers uninterested in the computations used. The computations were made with a small program written in the R programming language, with comments explaining all formulas. It is available from the author upon request. In the program, all parameters may be adjusted to suit one's personal expectations of the future (not necessarily based on historical market performance), thus producing different results.

The shape of $P(t)$ is reflected in Fig. 5.8. Using market data for the years 1950–2015,[10] and a trigger condition that is an S&P 500 price that is 90% of its previous all-time high value,[11] the trigger condition is satisfied in 61% of trading days. However, triggers are not evenly ("uniformly") distributed over time, so it would be incorrect to conclude that on a "typical" day, there is a 61% chance of a trigger. Also, since we seek to avoid the potentially calamitous result of needing to sell depressed equity to cover expenses, using the expected (i.e., average) behavior to define P would obscure the "long tail" of the distribution of recession lengths that could materialize with much less than average probability, but nonetheless be very damaging.

Therefore, I partitioned the 65 years of data into 79 periods[12] (each thus slightly shorter than a year that, typically, contains 252 trading days). For each

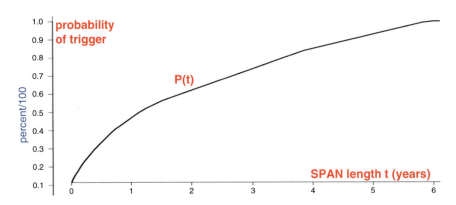

Fig. 5.8 Probability of the pre-retirement trigger condition occurring in a span of length *t*.

---

[10] finance.yahoo.com/quote/%5EGSPC/history?period1=-631123200&period2= 1499324400&interval= 1d&filter=history&frequency=1d = tinyurl.com/vo6sqwb.

[11] Since sales of an S&P 500 index ETF may be accomplished in a limit sale (Sect. 2.7.1), I used the daily high value.

[12] The choice of 79 allows equal integer-length periods that cover the data set.

5 Exchanging Equity for Fixed Income   129

day of each period, I calculated whether there was a trigger within a span of length t that started on that day. If there was, let's say that day "has a trigger for t." For the period, I defined $P(t)$ to be the fraction of days in the period that have a trigger for t.

For shorter values of t, periods reflect the economic condition of their time and mostly have either very high or very low trigger probability, reflecting growth periods and recessionary periods, respectively.

I then sorted the 79 periods according to their trigger probabilities. To be conservative, in order to emphasize the tail of the distribution (having few triggers), I defined $P(t)$ globally to be the average of the bottom 40% of the period probabilities. This accentuates the periods with longer distances to triggers—the periods we worry about. (Below 40%, the probabilities drop sharply, reflecting inadequate representations of the better periods.)

With this definition, the probability $P(0)$ of a trigger on a particular day came down from 61% to 12%, giving a more cautious view of the prospect of a trigger. Nonetheless, by a week short of 6 years, every day in the data had a trigger for t, so $P(t) = 1$ for all $t \geq 6$ years.

With t the time in trading days, $YR = 252$ denoting the number of trading days in a year; s and b the assumed growth rates of stocks and bonds, respectively; and K an "expansion" factor, defined below, for triggers that happen at the very start of the span and thus may reflect a price above the trigger condition. The equation for B (the expected shortfall for bonds) is

$$B(t) = P(0)K \left((1+s)^{t/YR} - (1+b)^{t/YR}\right) +$$

$$(P(t) - P(0)) \left((1+s)^{(w(t))/YR}\right) \left((1+s)^{(t-w(t))/YR} - (1+b)^{(t-w(t))/YR}\right)$$

as plotted in Fig. 5.9.

For s and b, I used the assumptions of Sect. 5.3. $K > 1$ is the average equity value increase factor of those increases that exceed the 90% trigger level. At the beginning of a time span, the equity value may exceed the trigger level (that's the only time that it can affect the calculation of B, as otherwise, the equity value rises to the trigger value, and thus the trigger value is the value used). With our parameters, $K = 108\%$.

I might have let $w(t)$ be the average of the times $\leq t$ to reach a trigger from some day (i.e., the sum of distances $\leq t$ from some day to a trigger—distances measured in days—divided by the number of days from which a trigger is reached in $\leq t$ days). However, this definition doesn't take into account the tail of the distribution where triggers are fewer and farther between. The technique

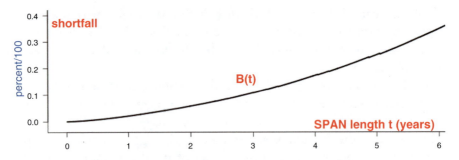

Fig. 5.9 Expected shortfall from holding fixed income investments instead of equity. As a function of the transfer span length t, mediated by P (Fig. 5.8).

used to compensate P for the tail of the distribution doesn't quite work for w, because the denominators—the numbers of days from which a trigger is reached in $\leq t$ days—differ from period to period. Therefore, the average of the period averages do not equal the original average. Nonetheless, taking the average in the 40% of periods with worst period numerators—the biggest sums of distances—gives a result that is close to acceptable, in that as the 40% is increased to 100%, the result approaches the original (unbiased) average. I use this to determine the value of $w(t)$. As with P, using less than 40% of the worst period numerators causes the expected times to increase sharply (see below), reflecting inadequate representation of the better periods. In the discussion below, let q be the parameter that defines the proportion of worst periods used for the definitions of P and w. So in the foregoing, $q = 40\%$, and $q = 100\%$ gives the unbiased functions. As we will see, the difference in B for $q = 40\%$ and $q = 100\%$ is small, so the distortion in computing w is not troublesome.

To compute S (the expected shortfall for stocks), we need to know the expected drop in equity value from its previous all-time high, in case there is no trigger condition within the time span. As with P and w, the expected (average) value hides the tail of a distribution with very unlikely but damaging drops. Thus, analogous to the bias used for P and w, instead of using the average drop, to be conservative, I used the mean value L of the 5% lowest ratios $h/0.9A$ for daily high value h and previous all-time high A. With that, the expected drop is $L - 1 = -33\%$. (The biggest drop down from the trigger value was -51%. The mean of all drop down from the trigger value is -13%. If the trigger condition is set at 100% of the all-time high, a condition that occurs only 7.5% of the time, then the biggest drop is -56%[13] and $L - 1 = -40\%$. The mean of all drops from the previous all-time high value is then -11%.[14])

Since selling equity at the trigger price is considered to result in $0 loss, the expected loss $S(t)$ in equity value from the transfer is the expected loss (as a percent) from needing to sell equity at the end of the span, in case of no trigger. Thus, for a span of length t,

$$S(t) = (1 - P(t))(1 + s)^{(t/YR)}(1 - (1 + P(0)(K - 1))L)$$

where the multiplier of L is the expected starting value of equity, $P(0)K + (1 - P(0))1$, and the value drop is multiplied by -1 to be represented as a positive amount. This is shown in Fig. 5.10.

Hence, the expected cost under the described conditions of the transfer of equity to fixed income investments within a window of length t is $B(t) + S(t)$ (Fig. 5.11).

Mathematically, there are some problems with this analysis, mostly related to the actual distributions of triggers and equity value drops. However, the uncertainties in the predictive value of the data don't support a very exacting, theoretically correct formulation. So, let's just keep it simple.

the answer(s)

With these assumptions, the transfer cost $B(t) + S(t)$ attains its minimum for a time span window of $t = 1.5$ years (Fig. 5.11). This is the optimal window length under our assumptions. With the unbiased $w(t)$, the results

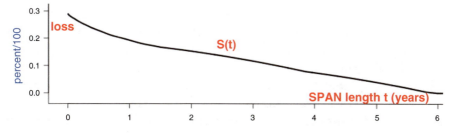

Fig. 5.10 Expected loss from needing to sell equity in a span of length t.

---

[13] You thought that starting from a value that is 10% higher should give a drop that is 10% greater: -61%? Drops are multiplicative. If D_y is the biggest dropdown from a trigger condition that is $y \times$ the all-time high, then $D_y = h/yA - 1$, where h is the lowest daily high value and A is the previous all-time high. So, $D_1 - D_{.9} = -(1/9)(h/A) = -(1/9)(D_1 + 1) = -.05$ (rounded).

[14] With a higher trigger condition, more small drops get included in the mean.

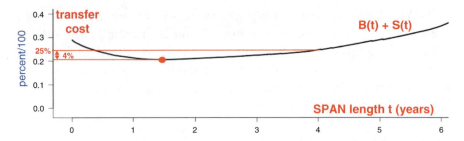

Fig. 5.11 Transfer cost for a span of length t. Minimized (for given assumptions) at t = 1.5 years. The difference in cost for extending the span to 4 years is 4%, or 1% per year.

are essentially unchanged, showing that for $q > 40\%$, the model is robust with regard to the definition of w.

The expected cost of the transfer is 21% of the amount transferred (cf. Fig. 5.11), reducing savings by that amount, and the expected transfer loss (defined by S) is 17% of the amount transferred. Thus, on average, only 83% of the equity earmarked for transfer can be expected to be applied to expenses. This requires the equity earmarked for transfer to be augmented by 20%. Thus, 120% of the amount needed should be earmarked for the forthcoming expense; if a trigger condition materializes as expected, then the extra 20% of equity is retained, and only the amount needed for the expense is transferred to fixed income investments. (The extra 20% is earmarked to cover an unlikely event in the tail of the distribution.) With a trigger condition, the most likely outcome, the actual cost reduces to $B(1.5) = 3\%$.

The expected loss (=cost) of equity sold directly for expenses (no attempted transfer to fixed income investments) is 29% of the value of the equity (almost twice as much), leaving only 71% of the equity value to apply to expenses. This is the loss that we seek to avoid through the planned transfer of equity to fixed income investments.

Decreasing q from 40% to $q = 30\%$ increases the optimal window size sharply, to 3.7 years. The expected transfer cost increases to 24%, and the expected transfer loss decreases to 12%, while the expected cost of equity sold directly for expenses surges to 32%. With $q = 100\%$ (no bias toward worse periods), the optimal window size is only 4 months, and the transfer cost reduces to only 10%—still less than the 12% expected cost of a direct sale of equity. While this may seem appealing, it is a dangerous gamble, ignoring the destructive distribution tail.

As explained in Sect. 4.3, we may choose to lengthen the window in case the unlikely need to sell depressed equity could spell difficulty. Increasing the

5 Exchanging Equity for Fixed Income — 133

window to $t = 4$ years adds an expected cost of 4% over the optimal, as shown in Fig. 5.11, while increasing the chance to get a trigger by 2/3. Even with this premium, the 25% total cost is still better than the expected direct transfer cost (29%), while the expected *loss* decreases to 10% (cf. Fig. 5.10), so less equity needs to be earmarked for the transfer.

If we changed the trigger condition to 100% (so, wait for the next all-time high), then with $q = 40\%$, the optimal exchange window is $t = 3.4$ years. The transfer cost for this span is more: 31% (because we have reset the definition of "no loss" to 100% of the last all-time high value). However, the expected direct transfer cost is twice as much: 60%. If we also used the mean of all the period trigger probabilities instead of the worst 40%, to compute P and w, by setting $q = 100\%$, then the optimal window reduces to 1.7 years (cf. Fig. 5.1, with different assumptions and different reference data), and the transfer cost reduces to 18%—less than a third of the 63% expected cost for a direct transfer of equity to cover the expense.

So, there's a short range of optimal window lengths, depending on your perspective, between 4 months and 4 years. To me, the most useful answer is 2 years (rounding up the 1.5 year optimum), with 4 years for more critical pre-retirement expenditures like school tuition or home purchase, in the case that covering a loss from an unusually sustained and severe market downturn would present difficulties. Keep in mind that when dealing with probabilities, the goal is to be "approximately right most of the time".[15]

Ironically, the longer the market is depressed, the better (to a point), as that decreases the time that fixed income investments are held before they are spent.

If there's no trigger condition within the window and the need for the funds by the end of that span were only for a possibility that did not materialize, then of course you should wait longer either for the market to recover, or for the funds actually to be needed.

5.4.1 Catching the Trigger Condition

Find the last all-time high value of your equity. This can be done quickly on the internet: searching for it by its ticker symbol gives a graph of its past performance. By selecting the maximum view, you can see what was the last all-time high value. If your equity is an ETF or actual shares of stock, you can set up a limit sale as described in Sect. 2.7.1. Set the sale price at 90% of the last all-time high value, and you don't need to watch it after that. You'll get an

---

[15] Anonymous.

Fig. 5.12 Yields of 10-year Treasury Notes 1961–2019. Price is inversely proportional to yield. The shaded bars delineate recessionary periods.

email when it sells. When it does, transfer the funds to bonds if the expense is still far off—say, more than a year in the future. Otherwise, retain the sale proceeds in cash, which can be stored in a savings bank or money market fund. As a practical matter, limit sales need to be renewed periodically (often, every 2 months).

5.4.2 Decreasing Expense Allocation

What if your allocation to fixed income investments is deemed too great? Perhaps the amount budgeted for an anticipated expense decreases. Then the excess value in fixed income investments should be transferred back to equity. While bond values have some volatility, unlike equity, whose average value inexorably rises over time, bond prices are driven inversely by interest rates that may rise over one quarter of a century and then fall over the next[16]—Fig. 5.12. There is no way to anticipate a "propitious" time to sell bonds. Delaying the transfer of bonds back to equity by seeking to predict when the value of bonds will be "up" has been shown to be generally unprofitable (Sect. 1.8.1).

---

[16] For a historical account of interest rates, see Homer and Sylla (2005).

Therefore, any excess value in fixed income investments should be transferred to equity when identified.

Such exchanges should not be done rashly, though: consider first if there are other looming expense requirements that require the reverse transfer. Capricious transfers back and forth can incur unnecessary costs as market values change, and especially in terms of tax consequences from realized gains (taxable capital gains realized upon a sale), whereas fixed income investments earmarked for one expense can be freely transferred to another.

6

Calculating Spending

However one manages finances, financial planning starts with understanding spending needs and priorities. In this chapter I give a very simple way to estimate spending needs—essential for knowing how much of savings to hold in stable assets (like bonds and cash). As already discussed, in order to avoid the possibility of needing to draw down depressed stocks, expenses need to be covered by stable assets. It's worth repeating, though, that outside of covering expenses, in order to optimize savings growth, remaining assets should be invested in equity.

If you already are maxed out with non-discretionary spending, leaving nothing for discretionary spending, much less savings, then your planning is simpler! But it's still worth reviewing that non-discretionary spending, since there always are ways to shift expenses, like seeking less expensive sources for food or moving to more economical housing (especially if you rent). There's a time-honored rule of thumb that housing costs (rents, maintenance, common charges, mortgage payments) should not exceed a quarter of your gross income.

You may discover that you have significant expenses that you have pushed "under the radar." How much are you secretly spending on that daily Lotto habit? Dinners out? Nightclubs? Alcohol? Pot? Should they really be characterized as "non-discretionary"? Look, no one will jump out from this book to point a finger; the choice is yours. But it's good to be fully aware of your expenditures, simply to prioritize, not just for today, but the future, on into retirement. If Lotto is more important to you than a vacation, so be it. But it should be an informed choice, not something that just happens, because the money has been spent and there is nothing left for the vacation.

© The Author(s), under exclusive license to Springer Nature Switzerland AG 2022
R. P. Kurshan, *Investment Industry Claims Debunked*,
https://doi.org/10.1007/978-3-030-76709-9_6

In the next section, I discuss how to calculate what you are spending. It's actually not as hard as it may sound. If the result doesn't allow for sufficient discretionary spending or retirement savings at the level wished for, it can be life-changing to go through the list of current expenses, then add to the list desired (but unfunded) expenses, put them all in a priority order, and ask yourself two questions: are the current expenses all more important than those left unfunded? If not, are there places where current expenses can be reduced? On the one hand, this sounds like such simple and evident advice; on the other hand, we all are creatures of habit, unaccustomed to giving much thought to financial planning. If you have more money than you ever will need, then continue to live the life—you don't need any planning. For everyone else, a little financial thinking can be life-changing.

Since spending priorities are likely to change over time, it is advantageous to periodically reconsider your spending along these lines, say, every couple of years, or when you do your taxes.

There are life transitions across which spending may change dramatically. On the brink of retirement, future expenses need to be estimated with an eye to future as well as to past spending. Such an estimate is likely to be wrong, but after a couple of years into retirement, the simple calculation of spending presented here should once again prove reasonably accurate.

6.1 Calculating Spending Needs

So, how do we calculate our living expenses? First of all, ditch that little notebook in which you record every expense for a year. It won't work. First of all, you'd need to be super-human to keep it up to date. And even if you did, there would be so much data there that analyzing it would be prone to errors.

But there's a really simple way to compute your expenses over a year that works for most people.

How do you pay your bills? Nowadays, the simplest way to pay recurring bills like rents, mortgages, utilities, insurance, and possibly credit card charges is to sign up for Automated Clearing House (ACH) payments—"auto-pay." You authorize the payee to automatically debit your checking account for the required amounts or amounts that you authorize. That way, you never risk forgetting to pay a bill and be responsible for the consequences (late charges, lowered credit ratings, etc.) You still get monthly statements, and if anything is amiss, correcting it is typically handled with a simple phone call.

6 Calculating Spending 139

If auto-pay doesn't appeal to you, then you probably pay your bills by check or one-time bank transfers. Either way, they all go through your checking account.

The easiest case is when you have a single checking account and I'll assume this is the case. If you have more than one, just do the same for each one.

What about cash payments? If the cash comes from your bank's ATM, then cash payments are also visible in your bank statements—often most conveniently viewed online. You can quickly add up the annual totals for each ACH payee, getting the exact costs. Any expenses that you pay by check are also visible in your bank statements (or in your checkbook ledger, if that is easier to read). Don't bother with one-off or small payments. They'll come out as "miscellaneous." However, expenses like weekly piano lessons (paid by check or cash) are worth listing as a specified expense item, especially if they're recurring charges of the same amount, so easy to calculate (say, $X \times 52$).

Most credit cards give an annual summary in terms of the expense category, like travel, entertainment, dining, etc. The categorization is often inaccurate, but it gives a quick and simple means to get annual totals for important categories.

What about income? If you are a salaried employee and have your salary automatically deposited into your bank account, you can quickly add up all those deposits. "Income" here is net taxes and pre-tax deductions. Likewise for other sources of income that go through your bank: freelance income, annuity payments, Social Security, tax refunds, royalties, honorariums, etc. (Although you may not consider a tax refund to be "income," for the purpose of computing your expenses—and for the IRS, for state taxes—it is.) Likewise, money that you transfer from savings to your checking account also counts as "income" for the purpose of computing expenses. (For computing expenses, don't think in IRS terms, think in terms of "income" = money that "comes in" to your checking account.)

Conversely, money that goes from checking to savings counts, for these purposes, as a *deduction* from income. What happens in savings stays in savings: for these purposes, ignore savings income that's reinvested in savings, and ignore expenses associated with savings. Money paid to manage investments (especially, real estate investments, but also investment fees of any kind) gets charged as a deduction from "savings": it is a deduction from savings appreciation, not an "expense," because without the investment you wouldn't have the cost. Do not count reinvested investment income in this calculation. Money earned by your investments that is reinvested, although taxable, does not enter into the expense calculation, so you can restrict your accounting to your checking account.

140   **R. P. Kurshan**

Likewise, if part of your salary is automatically invested somewhere, it doesn't count as income for this calculation. Nor does the part of your salary that is deducted for tax withholding. The only relevant part of your salary is the part that gets deposited into your checking account. If it doesn't come through your checking account, it's irrelevant for this calculation.

Your annual tax bill (or refund) *is* treated as an expense (or income). This introduces an error, because part of your tax is on the growth of your investments. Although you can try to separate this out, it likely would be quite complicated to get it right. Instead, just treat your entire tax as an expense, and understand that it is overstated. Except for the very wealthy, the error mostly won't make much difference, and since it leads to an overstatement of your actual non-investment expenses, the result is conservative. If you want a more precise result, you can estimate the amount of your tax bill on investments and deduct that from your stated tax expense.

In the end, you are doing something very simple: note what was in your checking account on January 1, add to it all income that came through your checking account, from that sum, subtract whatever you sent from your checking account to savings (including investment expenses) and what remained at the end of the year. To put living expenses in a formula:

$$expenses = starting\ balance + income - investments - ending\ balance$$

The only people this advice won't help directly are those who, for whatever reason, are mostly cash-based. They receive cash income and pay bills from the same cash supply, avoiding banks or any other institution that would keep your income and spending records for you. Such people need to figure it out for themselves but can rely on the same technique. Even in this case, an estimate may be more accurate than trying to keep an accurate ledger. Just add up an estimate of your expenses and compare this with what was in your pocket (or under your mattress) a year earlier, plus what you took in during the year, minus what is there now. If they're roughly the same, your estimate is probably reasonable. If not, think what expenses you forgot and redo.

So, now we have established an easy way to calculate total annual expenses. If you have a single checking account through which all expenses flow, you can complete this calculation in under an hour. (That's about what it takes me.)

But for financial planning, we need to break down those expenses into three categories.

6.2 Recurring Non-discretionary Expenses

First, we'll break off living expenses that are expected to continue for a number of years, are recurring throughout the year, and are non-discretionary.

All calculations need to be reviewed periodically—even annually, if you are up to it. Therefore, recurring expenses like tuition for 4 years of college should be counted now as a recurring expense. When that expense stops, we need to recalculate everything.

Examples of recurring non-discretionary living expenses:

- Rents, mortgages, condo common charge, coop maintenance charge
- Groceries
- Eating out (the part that is considered non-discretionary, like work lunches)
- School (tuitions and related expenses)
- Household (an estimate of average recurring costs for household goods)
- Clothing (a good part of which may be considered discretionary)
- Utilities (electricity, gas, tv, telephone)
- Housekeeping, laundry
- Baby-sitters, nanny
- Car costs (maintenance, garage, gas)
- Travel (commuting to work, unreimbursed business travel)
- Healthcare (insurance premiums not already deducted from income, co-payments, out-of-pocket)
- Insurance (investment real estate excluded)
- "Can't do without" extra-curricular activities (piano lessons, tennis court fees, gym)
- Taxes (income and *home* real estate paid from checking, *not* sales or value-added taxes that can be considered included in a price)
- Miscellaneous (can be estimated from how much cash you withdraw from the ATM)

Exclude any expenses associated with investments such as real estate management costs for an investment property. As already stated, these are part of the cost of the investment and figure into the investment's net return.

Taxes exclude tax deductions from income—count only what you pay from your checking account.

Estimate the annual amount of each recurring non-discretionary living expense. In some cases, you can see the exact numbers on your monthly checking account statements. This could be the case for rents, utilities, healthcare, and the like.

For others, look at your credit card statements. The annual credit card summary can be very helpful here. For groceries, look at your bills for a "typical" week and multiply by 52, unless it's spelled out on your credit card summary. You pay for groceries with cash? Think about using your credit card! Nowadays, we live in a "cashless" society, and even very small charges can be paid by credit card (or other digital device). It makes the financial accounting much easier, and you can eliminate the need to carry loose change.

There's no point in trying to make these estimates very precise. For one thing, they are mostly variable. Whatever discrepancy there is falls into the "miscellaneous" category. This category should be relatively small, and it's probably not worth the effort to partition it into discretionary and non-discretionary expenses. Just let it be. So our calculation of miscellaneous expenses looks like this:

$$\text{miscellaneous} = \text{total} - \text{itemized} - \text{one-time}$$

where *total* expenses are the *expenses* that you calculated in the previous Sect. 6.1, *itemized* expenses are the recurring non-discretionary living expenses itemized above plus the recurring discretionary living expenses itemized in the following Sect. 6.3, and *one-time* living expenses are as calculated in Sect. 6.4. Just categorize all miscellaneous expenses with non-discretionary expenses (to keep the calculation simple).

When estimating taxes, remember that *income* was defined to be what you receive after taxes are deducted, so "taxes" is just the amount that you paid additionally at tax time, plus any amounts that you paid in estimated taxes. If you get a refund, then the "taxes" are negative, so count here as income— provided the refund doesn't go to savings. The amount is shown on your last tax return, and shows up as a checking account deposit.

Don't forget real estate taxes on your home (that are not included in another category, like a condo common charge). Treat state and local income taxes in the same manner. *Exclude* sales or value-added taxes, which are folded into the cost of the item or service.

Once past the age of 70 1/2 or, starting in 2020, age 72 if you did not reach 70 1/2 yet, taxes must be paid on RMDs (required minimum distributions from an IRA—Sect. 13.1). This is easy to overlook, as RMDs are distributions of your own savings and thus do not feel like income. The distribution amounts can be quite significant, and thus the associated taxes as well. The taxes on these distributions are part of your income taxes.

6.3 Recurring Discretionary Expenses

This list gives "slack" that you can draw from if the financial going gets rough. It includes all expenses that you can skip for a year (or more) and then reinstate once you can again afford them. Examples:

- Dining out
- Clubs (night-, golf-)
- Vacations
- Luxury travel (flying first class when you can go coach)
- Entertainment (theater, concert subscriptions, museum memberships, sport admissions, unmentionable expenses)
- Luxury clothing, jewelry
- Knick knacks and other discretionary "consumerism"
- Spas, massages (although some may consider these non-discretionary)
- Gambling (I'd list this under "entertainment," but serious gamblers might disagree.)
- Alcohol, tobacco, other recreational drugs (if you're an addict, include instead under non-discretionary)
- Contributions
- Gifts
- Funds set aside for heirs[1]

It can be useful to further break down each of these categories, if you need to put some on hold. For example, no theater series this year, but we won't give up our Madison Square Garden box seats. If you take both winter and summer vacations, list those separately, so that if you need to cut back only a little, you have a finer view of the options. If you go heli-skiing as part of your ski vacation, you might keep the vacation, just ditch the heli- (and go back-country: even more fun, keeps you in good physical shape and saves a bundle).

---

[1] Instead of allocating a specific annual amount to be set aside for heirs, many instead just seek to maximize portfolio longevity. That way, whenever one dies, the amount remaining is as large as possible, subject to spending choices.

6.4 One-Time Expenses

Looking at the list of your annual expenses, pick out any major expenses that you consider "one-time." Examples:

- House down-payment
- Car, boat purchase
- Home renovation
- Non-recurring charge for an unreimbursed major health need
- Major contribution to help a child, grandchild, friend
- Legal fee (major fine, lawyer costs)
- Major one-time political or social contribution

These one-time expenses are used only as an offset to the checking account ending balance, in order to compute the *miscellaneous* expenses in Sect. 6.2.

6.5 Tallying the Expenses

Add up all the itemized living expense estimates:

$$\text{itemized expense estimates} =$$

$$\text{recurring non-discretionary} + \text{recurring discretionary} + \text{one-time}$$

How does this number compare with the *expenses* number you got from your checking account in Sect. 6.1? If they are more or less the same, then make them equal by adjusting the "miscellaneous" category in recurring non-discretionary expenses. Otherwise, try to figure out what you've missed.

This exercise ends up with two very useful numbers: *recurring non-discretionary expenses* and *recurring discretionary expenses*. These two numbers can be used to decide how to decrease spending, if necessary, as well as for retirement budgeting. Keeping spending from exceeding means simply through periodic adjustments to *recurring discretionary expenses* can be a fairly benign and simple way to guard against financial failure. Towards the end of our career, we can use these numbers to estimate if we have saved enough to retire (Chap. 10), and later, in retirement, we can use them to predict the extent to which our retirement spending is sustainable (Sect. 11.6).

If C is the annual after-tax amount available from savings to spend on expenses in retirement, then the maximum annual level of *discretionary* spending supported in retirement is

$$\text{discretionary spending} \leq \text{income} + C - \text{non-discretionary expenses}$$

7

Insurance Mediates Risk

My father taught me something about insurance that in retrospect is fairly obvious but still might escape notice. Insurance can be one of two things. The first is protection against a catastrophic loss. The second is a bet against an insurance company. While the first can be prudent, the second is for suckers.

If you buy dental insurance without benefit from an employer subsidy, then you are betting the insurance company that your yearly bills will exceed the premium you pay. Even if you have "insider" information that you will be needing five root canals in the coming year, be sure to read the fine print of your policy. Will those root canals be considered the consequence of a pre-existing condition that's not covered? Is the potential payout capped so that you never can get much more than your premium? You can pretty much assume that a bet against an insurance company is a losing bet. After all, they are in business to get more money from you than they pay to you, and they have an excellent track record of winning that wager.

7.1 Protection from Catastrophic Loss

Nonetheless, some insurance does provide a vital function. It protects against a catastrophic loss. Take a simplest example: your home. If your home burns down, you may not have the funds to recover. It may render you homeless. So you buy fire insurance to protect against this. The insurance company has calculated (very well, thank you) the probability that your home will burn and their loss in case it does. Multiply these two and add some hefty fees to pay for

© The Author(s), under exclusive license to Springer Nature Switzerland AG 2022 **147**
R. P. Kurshan, *Investment Industry Claims Debunked*,
https://doi.org/10.1007/978-3-030-76709-9_7

the CEO's airplane, all the company salaries and other expenses, and give the stockholders a nice profit, and you get your premium.

As a business proposition, it's a disaster for you: don't buy a house and wait for it to burn down, to get rich. But that's not why you bought the fire insurance. You don't care if it's not "cost-effective"; you care that you are protected from a catastrophic loss. In the unlikely event that your house burns down, the insurance company pays to rebuild it, and the disaster won't render you homeless. Thankfully, on account of the economy of scale, you likely can buy fire insurance at a somewhat nominal cost that requires little hesitation— less than the cost of a few dinners out, perhaps.

But how much are you willing to pay to protect against another catastrophic loss? What about flood insurance? If you live by the ocean, the cost of flood insurance could be enormous. How about insurance for loss from war? Most policies exclude this, but if you are willing to pay enough, you can be covered for everything, including loss from a comet strike that wipes out all life on earth.

Indeed, insurance can be carried to absurd proportions, especially by the ultra-wealthy. Afraid of a nuclear holocaust? If you're wealthy enough, you can buy a decommissioned missile silo to hide in, in case of a nuclear attack.[1] You can even purchase one with "concierge" service: you fly your private jet into an airport within 100 miles, and they'll pick you up and whisk you to your silo.

This one is actually quite funny. So, let's try to imagine the scenario: you've paid $100 million for your very own lavishly provisioned silo, complete with servants' quarters, 1000 bottles of your favorite wines, and a self-sustaining solar-powered ecosystem to provide a continuous supply of fruits and vegetables. And lo, the unthinkable actually happens. You call your trusty pilot just in time before the total disruption of all communications by an electromagnetic pulse from the attack. Your pilot, ever loyal, forsakes his wife, children, and grandchildren, responding to the call of duty. Also just in time, you called your concierge, who despite the general panic, keeps to his word and starts the 100-mile drive to pick you up. Of course, he could just put your call on hold (with appropriate music) and invite his own family into your lavishly appointed silo, but honor-bound, he too forsakes his family and meets your jet in a Humvee with champagne for the 100-mile drive to your silo. Once there, you thank him profusely with a $100 tip (well, that's all you had in your wallet, and anyway, what good is money now?).

---

[1]wsj.com/articles/for-sale-renovated-luxury-condo-can-survive-nuclear-attack-1415575922
tinyurl.com/yagu3ld3.

7 Insurance Mediates Risk 149

Comfortably settled into your silo, you start to think about all your family and friends left behind, by now probably turned into cinders. But you're alive and safe! As time goes on, boredom with all those tv reruns begins to gnaw. You'd love to venture outside, but the radiation levels are too high. So you savor the cozy silo life and consolation that thanks to your wealth, you are one of the lucky survivors. And, you're so beloved by your servants that they don't dream of revolting, kicking you out, and taking your place. You look fondly at photos of your wife, children, and grandchildren, for whom there simply was no time to round up. You try hard not to think about what became of them.

Sometimes, even if you're very rich, it's useful to think things through, not just spend money.

If your house is worth $2 million and that is much more than you could ever afford if you needed to replace it, an insurance policy covering loss in case of war, with a premium of $100,000/year is also probably more than you can afford. How about $10,000/year just for flood insurance? You may reasonably decide to take your chances, since the prospect of paying such a large premium also cuts into your style of life—not as much as losing your home, but it can hurt a lot, too.

You may reason this way: if I bought flood insurance, I'd need to forgo my annual family vacation (having spent the money on the insurance). If I didn't buy insurance and lost my home, I couldn't afford to rebuild so I'd need to rent what would be a less desirable place. That would suck, but the chances of the loss are small. Forgoing the annual family vacation would lessen family ties and thus significantly decrease my overall sense of enjoyment of life. This loss would be a certainty, whereas losing my house to a flood, only a possibility. I'll forgo the insurance and take my chances.

If the premium is affordable,[2] then insurance against a catastrophic loss is a great investment, whose value is measured in terms of the protection it provides, not the expectation that you get back more than you pay. But: not every premium is affordable. For all those cases, you are left with the risk. It's human nature that pretty soon you stop worrying about it. But, that does not mean that it's not still there.

In the same way, an investor might choose an investment with higher volatility if it can provide a chance to live a retirement with a certain level of expenditures, even though, in so doing, the chances of a catastrophic failure

---

[2]I like to measure the impact of such expenses in terms of "dinners out." If you dine out once a week and your annual premium is paid for by forgoing 1 month's dining out, then the comfort alone that the insurance provides may seem comparable to the pleasure provided by those dinners, not to mention the protection it provides.

150   R. P. Kurshan

(meaning that the savings will not last the retirement) also increase—as long as those chances are not too high and there is an acceptable fallback in case savings run out.

7.2   Making Insurance Cost-Effective

If you do buy insurance, raising your deductible can significantly reduce your premium as well as reduce the component of the insurance that's a (bad) bet against the insurance company. The premiums you save will be greater than the decrease in coverage from an expected loss, and you can afford that first $1000 if there is a loss. (The insurance company also gives you a significant break with a $1000 deductible, because it saves them from the bureaucracy of petty claims.)

Also, add-ons can be unnecessarily costly. You have $10,000 in jewelry? If you're afraid of it being stolen, how about just putting it in a home safe or hiding it in your sock drawer? Is insuring it really worth the extra premium? If you do lose it, how catastrophic is that? Although losing that diamond ring might be sad, would it be life-changing? If so, would getting compensated for the loss provide a cure? (It won't bring the ring back.) For sure, insuring it is not cost-effective.

7.3   Longevity Insurance

There's another type of insurance that one may consider: insurance against living "too long" (defined as out-living savings). This type of insurance generally is called a "fixed rate deferred annuity" (Sect. 2.10.2). It pays a periodic stipend (generally each month) in case one "lives too long"—that is, with payouts beginning after a deferral period, e.g., past 85 years of age. Annuities come in many flavors, discussed in Sect. 2.10 and Appendix A.9. An *immediate* annuity starts paying a (typically monthly) stipend as soon as one pays the premium, and it continues to pay until death. With both immediate and deferred annuities, one pays a one-time premium. In this sense, they are like an investment: "invest" the premium, and anticipate a dividend in the form of the stipend. However, they differ from an investment in that the premium can never be retrieved. In this sense they are like insurance and, indeed, are sold by insurance companies.

The deferred annuity appears more like insurance if one thinks in terms of longevity insurance: die early, you won't run out of money; live longer than expected, the annuity pays for this "loss." Like long-term care insurance (Sect. 7.5.2), a deferred annuity is significantly back-loaded, and thus the risk of insurer failure is a salient—if hard to calculate—factor.

7.4 Life Insurance

If the insurance companies weren't afraid of frightening away customers, they would have called life insurance "death insurance," because that is what it insures against. You die, they pay. But it's more pleasant to imagine ensuring "life" (which, of course, no insurance can possibly do) than insuring for the "d word," which we fear even to contemplate.

7.4.1 Term Life Insurance

If you have children or even only a significant other, *term* life insurance can be especially cost-efficient when purchased (or received free as a benefit) from one's employer, getting discounted group rates. It can provide your loved ones with a financial offset to the possibly catastrophic financial loss to them of your income, were you to die. Even if you are young and healthy, it's a good idea to consider how they would manage in case of your untimely death, and figure what amount of life insurance makes sense. Sometimes, coverage for 1–2 years of salary is provided for free by one's employer. If not, or to supplement that, discounted group life insurance is available through many professional groups. How much life insurance should you carry? That depends on how much savings you have and to what extent those left behind can be provided for by themselves or others. If your spouse has a sufficient income to provide for the family left behind, even if the style of living may need to be compromised as a result of the loss of your income, paying for more life insurance may not be worthwhile. If the loss of your income would not be financially catastrophic, consider the risk of its loss (amount of loss times its probability—if you can estimate that) versus the loss resulting from paying yearly premiums.

Given the possibility that both providers can die together, at least one should carry term life insurance to protect children, if any.

Although both spouses may work, the possibility that one could lose employment or choose to stop working should be considered, especially in early middle age, when acquiring life insurance for the first time may no longer be possible. Once acquired, as long as one pays the premiums, the insurance cannot be canceled. Although back-loaded, the premiums are generally low enough when one is younger and most needs this type of insurance. As one ages, savings generally increase, children become self-sufficient and the need for life insurance decreases.

7.4.2 Whole Life Insurance

There's another type of life insurance called "whole" life insurance. This is a combination of term life insurance and an investment sold in a package that's generally so complicated (its intention, it seems) that its value is hard to discern. Generally, these "products" represent an unconscionable effort by insurance companies to gull the gullible—sadly, most commonly those who can least afford to have their savings compromised: the elderly and/or the financially unsophisticated. Although often hard to untangle their actual terms, one can see the intent from afar, and discretion (more bluntly: run fast in the other direction) is good guidance. As a general principle, one can easily understand that the more hands between your money and its investment, the less is left for you. While term life insurance requires an insurance company to spread the risk in order to provide an affordable product, the same cannot be said for investing—why would you want to use an insurance company to invest for you? Combining the two seems only a means to hide a cost-ineffective part behind a cost-effective part.

7.4.3 Write Your Will!

Speaking of life insurance, there's another type of insurance related to death that can be very inexpensive—even free—that can save your loved ones from lengthy and costly delays in receiving the benefits of your estate in case of your death: it's called a "will." Young people commonly defer writing a will because death seems so remote. But most calamities covered by insurance are remote. You carry liability insurance for your car? You should also write a will! Although lawyers can charge a thousand dollars to write a will, simple wills can be written at no cost using forms available on the internet. A lawyer can provide more sophisticated estate planning such as a bypass trust that can provide tax protection to heirs.

7.5 Health-Related Insurance in the United States

Unlike the rest of the industrialized world, health insurance in the United States is piecemeal, extremely expensive and difficult to manage.

7.5.1 Medical Insurance

Medical insurance in the United States has become very complicated, making its analysis essentially imponderable. Since any reasonable medical insurance does cover very high expenses, one generally wants the best medical insurance that is affordable. With higher premiums comes access to better doctors. On the other hand, one can lower premiums by allowing higher deductibles. Unless you know that you will have claims just above the lower deductibles, and know that they actually will be covered (something that may require considerable detective work), higher deductibles are generally a way to save money on average. However, some insurance companies don't let you pick and choose: to get higher deductibles, you need to also accept lower-quality doctors. (Doctors, of course, don't come with quality grades around their necks. But the doctors that agree to be part of an HMO or otherwise assigned to a patient pool tend to be doctors that cannot make it on their own, and there's a reasonable presumption that the reason for that is doctor quality. There always are exceptions to every such surmise.)

a strange reason to take $0 deductible
With medical insurance, though, there's a strange reason that you may want to pay more for coverage by taking a $0 deductible option. It is fairly common for a health insurance company initially to deny the full coverage to which a patient actually is entitled. Whether a result of intention or accident, it can take hours of phone calls and letters, and months of time, even dodging bill collectors for illegitimate bills, before billing problems are finally cleared. Many people just give up (which some believe is what the insurance company hopes for). If you have insurance that pays for everything—like Medicare "Medigap" F—then you (generally) avoid these problems.

the charge is more for the same thing if you're uninsured
Worse, the healthcare insurance system is rigged so that if you have insurance, your total hospital or doctor bill is less than if you had no insurance. Thus,

154 R. P. Kurshan

if you have a high deductible and thus must pay 100% of some bill, that bill generally is less than if you had no insurance. The reason for this is that insurance companies have agreements with the healthcare providers about how much they can charge for particular procedures, and you benefit from these agreements even if you need to pay the entire bill. This feature alone can make health insurance cost-effective. (One might hope for regulation that would outlaw this unfair practice and standardize costs across carriers the way they are standardized with Medicare.)

7.5.2 Long-Term Care Insurance

In the United States, coverage for a long-term disability that requires housing in an extended care facility or nursing home typically is not covered by medical insurance beyond a short period of time. To cover this expense, which can over time deplete all one's savings and more, there is "long-term care" insurance. This can be quite expensive—several thousand dollars annually, depending on age, and thus requires some careful thinking about its cost-effectiveness.

Past a certain age, or once pre-existing conditions set in, it may no longer be possible to obtain. Premiums rise over time, and there's generally no cap on allowed increases, although normally state insurance authorities must approve increases. Nonetheless, there are sad stories of people who have carried coverage for years in order to maintain their insurability later in life when they otherwise may no longer be insurable, only to find that as a result of an enormous increase in premium, they no longer can afford to carry the coverage. The money paid so far was not exactly "thrown away": it paid for coverage that although not needed, might have been needed. However, while the premiums were affordable, the likelihood of needing the coverage was low, and once the insurance becomes more important, the premiums can become unaffordable.

This type of coverage differs from other insurance coverage in an important aspect: its protection is significantly back-loaded. When you buy home fire insurance, your chance of collecting may be remote, but the premium is low. It seems worthwhile to pay an almost negligible premium for protection against an event that while highly unlikely, would be catastrophic were it to occur. When you buy health insurance, your premium may be high, but you also have a relatively high chance of at least partial reimbursement in the current year (through medical service received) and you are protected against a catastrophic loss in the current year.

7 Insurance Mediates Risk   155

However, when you buy long-term care insurance, for many years you pay relatively high premiums with a very low expectation of collecting in the given year. The reason you pay these high premiums for many years is to protect against a not insignificant expectation that at some point in the far future you will need long-term care whose uninsured cost would be prohibitive. You pay the premiums now, although you are young and healthy, because if you wait until you are old or infirm, you will be uninsurable. Thus, you suffer high premiums now to protect against uninsurability in the future. (As long as you continue to pay your premiums, you cannot be denied continued coverage.) So the premiums are high and the expected payback is far-term or back-loaded.

This distinction of a significant back-load has three salient factors. First, it entails delayed "gratification," something many have difficulty embracing. When we pay a lot, we like our value *now*; it requires a level of sophistication and maturity to embrace the delay. However, it is not all psychology. There also is the possibility that after paying high premiums for many years in order to assure continued insurability, the premiums become unaffordable. Finally, there is the possibility, however remote, that after paying high premiums for many years to assure continued insurability, the insurer goes bankrupt or otherwise is forced by regulators to shut down, with the result that you suddenly are denied future coverage after all. Even if you already are in a nursing home with your costs covered, the demise of your insurer can result in termination or reduction of your coverage. When this happens, other insurers pick up some of the losses (in amounts that differ from state to state), but the coverage usually is significantly reduced. Once your coverage ends, you can be expelled from your nursing home and end up on Medicaid, the last resort medical insurance for those in poverty. (Of course, the same can happen under ordinary circumstances if you exhaust the amount of coverage that your policy promises and you have no further resources.)

When an insurer is in trouble, it commonly is acquired by another insurer in a manner that is largely transparent to its clients, especially for big, national insurers, which thus rarely fail outright. However outright failures do occur. In 2017, a reasonably large national insurer, Penn Treaty of Allentown, Pa., liquidated, leaving tens of thousands of clients high and dry.[3] When such a default happens, policies typically are canceled, and existing claims are significantly capped to half or less of what was owed. Counter-party failure is a real albeit very small risk. However, this risk could increase (or decrease) with changes

---

[3] nytimes.com/2017/04/01/business/policyholders-in-limbo-after-rare-failure-of-insurer.html=tinyurl.com/ybdzmjgt.

156   R. P. Kurshan

in the economic or political climate. This makes it very hard—probably impossible—to determine objectively the value of significantly back-loaded insurance such as long-term care.

Long-term care ratings and rates are discussed in Sect. 16.5.

7.5.3 Disability Insurance

Finally, in the United States, there's disability insurance: insuring your paycheck against your possible disability. If you live in California, Hawaii, New Jersey, New York, Rhode Island, or the Commonwealth of Puerto Rico, short-term disability coverage is provided to workers either by the state or by employers (in some cases, with a small mandatory employee contribution). In other states, many employers pay some or all of the cost. Short-term coverage usually lasts for 60–180 days and covers 80% of income. There is also long-term coverage available. It provides less coverage—typically, 60% of income—but for a longer period, even for the rest of your life. It may also be provided by some employers, typically with some employee contribution. There are overlapping coverages through state workers' compensation that only covers work injuries, and through Social Security, which sets a restrictive definition of "disabled," usually requiring that you are unable to hold any job, not just the job you had. Since one's salary is usually the most valuable monetary asset one has, losing the ability to work can be catastrophic, and insuring it makes sense.

7.6   Summary

In summary: insure against catastrophic losses, as long as the premiums are affordable. "Affordable" generally means that its cost doesn't measurably depreciate your quality of life; if it does, then you need to guess where the tradeoff boundary lies: paying a premium of $X necessitates giving up some benefit that costs $X. If you can't afford both, which do you want more? Flood insurance or that family ski vacation? One protects and gives peace of mind, but may never be needed; the other gives immediate gratification.

Lower your premiums by opting for high deductibles, except for U.S. medical insurance, where $0 deductible frees one from the hassle of fighting with the insurance provider (mostly).

Shun insurance that's only a bet against the insurance company, since that is a bet you are expected to lose. When the premiums are not subsidized, losing bets generally include dental insurance, pet insurance, and virtually always include insurance against a loss that you can afford to cover with your savings. If you are tempted to insure that diamond wedding ring on account of its sentimental value, keep in mind that the insurance cannot return the ring, only some part of its value (which may be less than what you paid for it).

Finally, ponder the risk of premium increases or insurer failure for significant back-loaded insurance such as long-term care or longevity insurance.

8

Fraud Deterrence

All your financial ducks lined up in a row? Perfect investment strategy? (Well, ok, there is no such thing.) But the greatest financial management system can be wrecked if someone pilfers your savings. And the nicest day can be wrecked if someone assumes your identity and is able to obtain credit under your name, for which you then become responsible until you succeed to extricate yourself from under the mess. That can take a long time, cause great aggravation and consternation, and put your good credit rating in jeopardy, making it hard or impossible to get the credit that *you* need.

Heard it all, but what to do? The answer is surprisingly simple for U.S. investors. Freeze your credit reports at the three major credit rating agencies.

8.1   In the United States, Freeze Your Credit Reports!

With your credit reports frozen, someone impersonating you, even with all your numbers and secrets, still can't succeed to get credit in your name. Even *you* can't without a single secret "pin" number given to you when you first order a freeze (and as of this writing, these secret numbers have not—so far—been stolen).[1] When you need to apply for credit, you use that secret number to unfreeze a chosen account for 1 day (or another period of time), just long

---

[1]Update: Alas, recently all three of the main credit reporting agencies, Equifax, Experian, and Transunion, have implemented bypasses to providing the pin, based on a quiz about personal facts (like a previous address or town where you were born) that is known to be insecure since all such data is accessible in

---

© The Author(s), under exclusive license to Springer Nature Switzerland AG 2022   **159**
R. P. Kurshan, *Investment Industry Claims Debunked*,
https://doi.org/10.1007/978-3-030-76709-9_8

enough for your credit provider to check your credit. This can be done online in about 5 min. You order a temporary unfreeze and the re-freeze happens automatically.

For security, it would make sense for a credit reporting agency to notify you immediately through an alternate channel if your account has been unfrozen. Astonishingly, this simple security mechanism has not been applied uniformly by the agencies. In some cases, there is no notification. In others, notification comes by U.S. Postal Service, a month later. Without adequate government regulation, we can only hope that recent notorious security lapses will lead to this simple security measure becoming routine.

The nominal costs previously associated with freezing and unfreezing that varied from state to state have been canceled by a May 2018 federal law,[2] so now both freezing and unfreezing are free. This came about as a result of legislation following the 2017 Equifax fiasco in which "sensitive information for 143 million American consumers, including Social Security numbers and driver's license numbers" was said to have been compromised,[3] causing the federal government to finally step up and offer some uniform protections. Many suggest that not only should freezing and unfreezing credit reports be free, but freezing also should be the default (after all, we never asked for these reports to be maintained—they're maintained as a service to banks that want to make credit approval an easier and less costly task for themselves).

One more bugaboo: after its fiasco, Equifax has offered a "free for life" credit *lock*. Did you catch a difference? "Lock" vs. "freeze"? The "lock" can take longer, may cost money, and lacks the regulatory protections of the "freeze." What else does it lack? Caveat emptor.

Ron Lieber of The New York Times has posted very specific suggestions for dealing with the Equifax breach.[4,5]

Why isn't freezing the default? Why, perhaps, have you never even heard of freezing? Of course, you can guess: the credit agencies want to be able to sell your data to credit peddlers (that's how they make their money), and if your account is frozen, they can't do that.[6] The credit reporting agencies fought (and

---

the public domain, sometimes even via just a simple search engine. Hopefully, this will soon change. Meanwhile, freezing still provides a simple, worthwhile additional impediment to stealing your identity.

[2] congress.gov/bill/115th-congress/senate-bill/2155.

[3] https://nytimes.com/2017/09/07/business/equifax-cyberattack.html.

[4] nytimes.com/2017/09/08/your-money/identity-theft/equifaxs-instructions-are-confusing-heres-what-to-do-now.html = tinyurl.com/y7ksqbtm.

[5] nytimes.com/interactive/2017/your-money/equifax-data-breach-credit.html.

[6] nytimes.com/2017/09/08/business/equifax.html.

Ron Lieber

lost) the battle to disallow credit report freezes altogether and, with the new law, have lost the battle to charge a fee. But freezing is not a feature they'd like to be widely known or widely used. I find it remarkable that the ubiquitous news articles, posts, blogs, and letters from financial institutions that advise how to keep your accounts secure virtually never mention the credit report freeze, while they bloviate about strong passwords, two-factor authentication, periodic password changes, and on and on. Why no mention of credit report freezes? The only reason I can imagine is that it's not in their financial interest, in particular, not wanting to antagonize their financial supporters/advertisers.

Ron Lieber has been on a single-handed crusade since at least 2009 to get people to use this simple and most effective security tool.[7] Here are the links to freeze your credit reports at the three major[8] credit reporting agencies:

- freeze.transunion.com/sf/securityFreeze/landingPage.jsp
- experian.com/freeze/center.html
- equifax.com/personal/credit-report-services/credit-freeze/

and you can get an annual credit report for free from:

- www.annualcreditreport.com/index.action

---

[7] nytimes.com/2011/05/07/your-money/identity-theft/07money.html.
[8] There are two more credit reporting agencies, Innovis and PRBC, but these are the three that most lenders rely on and thus need to be frozen in order to neutralize the financial danger of identity theft.

as recommended by Ron Lieber as well. Beware of fraudulent look-alike names (examples below) that seek to sell you this free service. (Oiy, the financial industry is a snake pit, thanks to lax government regulation.)

Although a frozen credit report cannot be used to apply for a line of credit (the most important protection), it still can be accessed by certain agencies and organizations, including:[9]

- Companies that provide access to your credit report or credit score or monitor your credit report
- Federal, state, and local government agencies and courts
- Companies using the information in connection with the underwriting of insurance, or for employment, tenant, or background screening purposes
- Companies that have a current account or relationship with you and collection agencies acting on behalf of those whom you owe
- Companies that authenticate a consumer's identity for purposes other than granting credit or for investigating or preventing actual or potential fraud

And, if you want to stop receiving those pre-approved offers of credit or insurance, you must explicitly opt out. They make it difficult to do this permanently (they'll only let you do it for 5 years online).

You still need to be vigilant in case your identity already has been stolen: do check your monthly credit card and bank statements. Invariably, from time to time, you'll find some unrecognizable charge that comes from a service you never knew you signed up for, but did by clicking on some link you didn't read carefully. Sometimes these are small ongoing monthly charges that the vendor hopes you won't notice. These charges usually can be canceled, sometimes even retroactively (in case you only noticed after some months).

8.2 Strong Passwords?

"Strong passwords" has become a mantra—but sometimes I get the feeling that this push is just a way for institutions to displace blame for their lax security onto their clients and customers. What would a thief prefer: to pick on a single client, running through a billion password combinations until succeeding to break into that one account or just use readily available online

---

[9] help.equifax.com/s/article/Who-can-view-my-credit-report-if-I-have-a-security-freeze-or-credit-report-lock = tinyurl.com/ycs9tsrr.

hacking tools to hack into a bank or other institution and in one fell swoop, gain access to *all* accounts? The negligence is much more on the shoulders of the institutions that, to save money, have not bothered to institute adequate security. I hope that federal investigators look into allegations that Equifax was lax in responding to a known security weakness.[10,11] I don't mean to suggest that you shouldn't bother with strong passwords, though. You should. If nothing else, it prevents your kids from hacking into your bank account by entering your birthday.

8.3   Frequently Change Passwords?

Another annoying "security" practice is enforcing the "best practice" that requires frequent password changes. Intuitively this may make sense as enhancing security. However, frequent password changes can actually weaken your security, for the simple reason that when forced to change passwords frequently, people understandably follow some easy-to-remember pattern for the changes, like appending the date to an unchanging prefix. Hackers test for this, and research indicates that they are able to guess a majority of passwords created to fulfill mandatory frequent changes.[12]

You don't need an app to circumvent this problem. Just keep a small file on your computer and phone that contains all your critical passwords. Generate these passwords by imitating the monkey writing Shakespeare's plays: just hit a bunch of random keys, including the top row of numbers and characters, some letters capitalized, and put it in your file. The file should contain lines of the form *institution: password*. When you need to enter a password, you do a *copy* from the file and a *paste* to where you need to enter the password.[13] No need to remember these passwords. If you're paranoid, the file may be encrypted with a simple, unchanging password, although your devices themselves should already be well-secured.

---

[10] usatoday.com/story/money/2017/09/14/equifax-identity-theft-hackers-apache-struts/665100001/   = tinyurl.com/y7t54ywy.

[11] For a hair-raising account of how Equifax (inadvertently) enabled identity thieves, see: krebsonsecurity.com/2013/10/experian-sold-consumer-data-to-id-theft-service/.

[12] ftc.gov/news-events/blogs/techftc/2016/03/time-rethink-mandatory-password-changes   = tinyurl.com/h7dtmwl.

[13] A very few institutions require that you actually type in your password, a particularly counterproductive "best practice," because it inhibits the use of strong passwords. For the very few that do, you need to copy manually.

8.4 Two-Factor Authentication?

So-called two-factor authentication has become an increasingly popular security enhancement urged or sometimes required, especially by financial institutions, but also by one of the biggest phone and computer companies.

You initiate a login, enter your password, get sent a one-time key (a short number) to your cell phone or email address, and then enter that number online to complete the login process. This makes it harder for someone to access your account by impersonating you. That is, unless they can guess your password and have your phone—or a device that the telephone company thinks is your phone: a much higher hurdle to jump.

The main downside to this is the annoyance factor, which can be prohibitive. What if you're out of the country, the key is sent only to your phone and don't have phone access? (Apple doesn't allow key transmission by email.)

Is it worth it? An alternative, which often is practiced in addition to two-factor authentication, is to send an email confirming any transaction (or, sometimes, any transaction over a threshold amount). This provides a sort of after-the-fact two-factor authentication. It's a very good idea to set up such notifications, and it's so simple and unobtrusive that I'm surprised it's not a universal practice.

As for two-factor login authentication itself, it's unclear to what extent this actually prevents cybercrime (on top of all the other security measures) and to what extent it's a Maginot Line that may actually decrease security by lulling institutional officials into a false sense of security that deters putting in place more robust security measures.

In fact, it's been known for a few years that it's pathetically simple to hack two-factor authentication.[14] Here's how it works. The thief sends you an email purporting to be from your bank, with the message that there is a critical problem with your account and you should login to see a secure message. They conveniently include a link to log in. However, the link leads to a web site page that looks identical to the login page of your bank but in fact is controlled by the thief. If you happen to check the web address, it also looks plausible—instead of Bank.com, perhaps it shows MYBank.com. Once you enter your password on the fake login page, the thief takes it and logs in to your actual bank account. But, wait: two-factor authentication—he can't. Instead, he gets a request to enter the code number that was just sent to your phone. The thief sends the same request to you, to enter the code sent to your phone. This

---

[14] nytimes.com/2019/01/27/opinion/2fa-cyberattacks-security.html.

looks normal to you, because you expect two-factor authentication. You enter the number sent to your phone in answer to the thief's request, and the thief then enters it in the request from your actual bank. Now the thief is in your account, the bank thinks the thief is you, and the thief can do anything you can do inside your account. To complete the process, the thief sends you an apology that due to technical problems, your login can not be completed, and you should please try back in an hour.[15]

There's a strong cautionary moral to this story. *Never* click on a link in an email that leads to a web site that asks for sensitive information (like a password). (If the link is an invitation to see wedding pictures, it won't require that you enter identifying information, so it's probably ok to click on it. If a web site asks for your email address, likely the worst that can happen is spam.) When you get an email urging you to login to your bank or other sensitive location, again *don't click on an offered link*. Instead, you should keep bookmarks in your browser, address book, etc. for all the sensitive sites you need to log in to. Use *that* link to log in to your bank, etc. This practice protects you from this attack.

8.5 In the United States, IRS Identity Protection

An increasingly common scam is a form of identity theft wherein the thief gains access to your W2 information and files a fraudulent tax return as you, claiming a refund. While in the end, the IRS generally restores the situation in your favor, it can take a lot of paperwork and long waits.[16] To protect against this, the IRS now offers an "identity protection pin",[17] a secret number that must be filed with your tax return, without which the return is not accepted.

As of 2020, this is offered only in 19 states and Washington, DC. To be eligible, you must have filed a federal return in the previous year as a resident of Arizona, California, Colorado, Connecticut, Delaware, District of Columbia, Florida, Georgia, Illinois, Maryland, Michigan, Nevada, New Jersey, New Mexico, New York, North Carolina, Pennsylvania, Rhode Island,

---

[15] This simple exploit purportedly was used to infiltrate the security firm FireEye in the context of the SolarWinds attack, called the most damaging hack of U.S. intelligence assets in history. FireEye caught the intrusion and alerted the intelligence community. See politico.com/news/2020/12/16/russian-hackers-fireeye-cyberattack-447226.

[16] taxpayeradvocate.irs.gov/get-help/lost-or-stolen-refund.

[17] irs.gov/identity-theft-fraud-scams/get-an-identity-protection-pin.

166   R. P. Kurshan

Texas, or Washington. But the IRS states that they plan to expand the program nationwide.

8.6   Sadly, You're on Your Own

Unfortunately, it is more and more urgent for computer and phone users to set up their own security defenses, since if the individual doesn't do this, there's no one out there that generally will be doing it for you. The threats are various:

- Emails with fraudulent offers
- Emails with attachments or even just *links* that, when opened or double-clicked, can compromise your computer or phone
- Silent intrusions into your computer, during which your data can be stolen or your computer can be used to victimize other computers (often, in your name)
- Intrusions that can freeze your own access to your own data unless you pay a ransom (ransomware)

The best generally available defenses against these threats are mostly simple, routine, and transparent to the user once implemented and reasonably effective, although research has shown them to be more often ignored than implemented. Here they are:

1. *Back up your data! Back up your data! Back up your data!* There are a number of programs that perform periodic—even hourly—back-ups to an external hard drive or the cloud. Redundancy is king.

   If you lose your financial data, you may be unable to verify that you have not been the victim of financial theft from your online accounts.

   Back-ups to an external disk drive are useful in case your computer disk crashes, you accidentally delete a needed file, or you simply wish to check an earlier version of a report you are writing.

   However, if your computer is attacked by ransomware, it may also freeze your access to an attached external hard drive. Therefore, it's useful to have an additional external hard drive that you back up to and then physically disconnect from your computer. Such back-ups can be performed less frequently, say, after you complete a vital report or have downloaded some important documents. These back-ups can be performed by special-purpose "cloning" software—for the Mac, my favorite is *Carbon Copy Cloner*.[18]

But what about physical theft? What about fire? A thief can steal (or incidentally destroy) your external hard drives along with your computer. A fire can destroy both. Therefore, good insurance is to cycle your external hard drives, say every month, to a remote location—your trusted relative's home or a bank safe deposit box. That way, the worst case is to lose a month's worth of data.

Some practitioners advocate using a "cloud-based" subscription service to back up to.[19] This saves the trips to the off-site location and guards against unlikely joint disasters (both your home and your relative's home are destroyed in the same earthquake) that irrevocably destroy all your data. It also may make it reasonable to perform off-site back-ups more frequently. However, you need to trust the cloud server that they won't go out of business or otherwise become inaccessible. And reliable cloud servers generally aren't free.

In fact, I use *all* of the above. Redundancy is king.

2. Turn on your computer and/or router firewall, if available (it's just a click on an option); it hinders unauthorized access to your computer; turn on whole disk encryption (if you have it), especially on your laptop, to render your data unreadable if someone steals your laptop while you are traveling.

3. Install antivirus software—often free, for example, *Sophos* for Macs and *Avast* for PCs; while mainly post-threat (not protecting against previously undiscovered viruses), it does guard against proliferations of known threats; it may be redundant, if you immediately install all security updates for all your software, but generally doesn't hurt (if you install a free version).

4. Be careful before you open an unexpected email attachment, even from a friend—if in doubt, call and ask what it is that the sender sent; the attachment could contain a virus sent by someone impersonating your friend.

5. As already explained, don't click on a link in an email that leads to a web page that requires sensitive information, like a password for your bank account—instead, navigate to the page using a link stored with your bookmarks or contacts.

6. Although I haven't heard of this being a problem, when I get a pop-up advising me to "click here" to download the latest security update for one

---

[18] https://bombich.com.

[19] One popular service is backblaze.com.

of my applications or my computer, instead, I go to the trusted source via my bookmarks, and update from there.

7. Avoid logging in to any password-protected account from a unsecured public Wi-Fi, even to your email server, as any password you entered can be easily be snooped.

8. Be wary of look-alike web addresses that lead you to a different place than the one you intended.[20] It can involve as simple a deception as replacing the web address suffix ".org" with ".com," or using a Cyrillic character similar to a Roman character.[21] The only web site that provides a free annual credit report under explicit federal government direction, *annualcreditreport.com*, has many look-alikes, such as "freecreditreport.com," and "creditreport.com" (both acquired by none other than our old friend Equifax!), which offer for-pay financial services (along with a free credit report).

9. Check your financial statements monthly for any unrecognized activity; sometimes, fraudulent access begins with a tiny charge, to see if you notice, before it escalates.

10. Use passwords that are at least too hard for your kids to guess.

11. With all the computer intrusions making the news, it has become increasingly popular to cover your computer camera with a small bit of tape (I use an easily removed tiny disk cut with a paper hole-punch from the sticky portion of a Post-It note)—it's been documented how easy it is for a hacker to spy on you by using your computer camera; if you want to hold a video session, just peel off the cover.

12. If you have a spare old computer, consider dedicating it to secure financial logins (no web surfing, no email)—that way, it separates more sensitive financial transactions from actions more likely to compromise computer security. This has been recommended by Fidelity Brokerage Services.[22] It may be a little impractical but can be workable in some circumstances. You can use a USB "thumb drive" to transfer files from the secure computer to your regular computer.

---

[20] en.wikipedia.org/wiki/Spoofed_URL = tinyurl.com/yc9fwgzq.

[21] en.wikipedia.org/wiki/IDN_homograph_attack = tinyurl.com/d87ttcc.

[22] fidelity.com/viewpoints/wealth-management/target-for-cybercrime.

8.7 And Then There's Robocalls...

Finally, one must mention those infuriating telephone robocalls and outright scams. Why hasn't the government intervened? It's said that "Phone companies can stop robocalls. They're just not doing it."[23] Why not? "Conflict of interest. All of these robocalls represent billable minutes." Yet another result of lax government regulation.

The scams range from the laughable (who hasn't received at least one call or email from the Nigerian prince who wants your help to launder his ill-found $13,000,000?) to the atrocious. The worst of the worst are scams that threaten to turn off your electricity or withhold information about a fabricated car accident involving your kid, unless you give a credit card number or some personal identifying information. Elders have been taken in and wiped out.[24]

8.8 In the End...

Without adequate government regulation, we are left just to wring our hands, or, with an astronomically wasteful dis-economy of scale, each become our own IT specialist security guard.

---

[23] latimes.com/business/lazarus/la-fi-lazarus-fcc-robocalls-20160729-snap-story.html= tinyurl.com/yc93-uvbx.

[24] ncoa.org/economic-security/money-management/scams-security/top-10-scams-targeting-seniors/= tinyurl.com/pt6ddog, cnbc.com/2017/08/25/elder-financial-fraud-is-36-billion-and-growing.html=tinyurl.com/yagel9ds.

9

General Investment Issues

This chapter covers several general investment issues, most importantly, *mind your fees!* (They may look small, but they compound over time and can really add up.) Likewise, discretionary expenditures from an equity fund that is depressed in value can be more costly than you may imagine. There is value to having a mortgage, even if you think you don't need one or even want one. The cost of bonds often moves inversely with that of stocks. Etc.

9.1 Make a Budget

If you are young, you probably will ignore this advice, and that's probably fine. Getting overly obsessed with money is unhealthy, and if you have strong employment prospects for many future years, a "budget" can be reduced to these two guidelines:

1. Don't spend more than you earn (excluding mortgages and student loans,[1] but *including* credit card debt—it's ridiculously expensive, can lower your credit rating, and contributes undeservedly to banks.[2])
2. Guard against overly expensive housing that can "break your bank"—a common credible rule of thumb is to pay in rents or condo common charges

---

[1] Be very careful with student loans: diligent research to find safe loans can save you from bankruptcy or a life of indentured servitude to a callous scavenger that has bought your debt.

[2] Just keep the banks' sticky fingers out of your wallet! You'd turn away a pick-pocket; banks are the same, except they've arranged the laws to make their usury legal.

© The Author(s), under exclusive license to Springer Nature Switzerland AG 2022 **171**
R. P. Kurshan, *Investment Industry Claims Debunked*,
https://doi.org/10.1007/978-3-030-76709-9_9

172　R. P. Kurshan

or home maintenance costs plus mortgage payments no more than 25% of your gross salary or income.

These simple budget rules may be enough until you approach retirement. If you want to buy a car or a house or a boat, you should "save" for it. That may mean purposefully forgoing some discretionary spending and, instead, socking away funds to grow large enough for the purchase. The best "sock" can be equity (in an index fund), if you are flexible about when you make your purchase. Since on average equity appreciates faster than a fixed income investment, it's the better bet, but you may need to wait out a market depression. Otherwise, if timing is an issue, see Sect. 4.4.

Another common form of "budgeting" is simply to accumulate unspent income, and then one day say "hey, we have enough money—let's buy a boat!" This is ok, as long as you give a little thought to other possibilities, like college tuition or buying a house for a growing family. Prioritize and spend on what's most important. If, after consideration, it's a daily Lotto habit, so be it.

When young and carefree, a real budget can be most useful to the types who will never bother to make one: profligates. For them, the most useful part of making a budget could be a forced confrontation with spending. (Are you sure that you want to spend half your income on nightclubs and jewelry? Did you realize that you spend as much eating out as you spend on housing?)

As you approach retirement, however, it's essential for eventual retirement planning to know how much you regularly spend, what spending is discretionary, and what is non-discretionary.

How to do this was covered in Chap. 6.

9.2　Fees

The Vanguard study discussed in Sect. 1.6.2 made the case for low fees being the single most significant factor for predicting how well a mutual fund (or ETF) will perform. They found that "a fund's expense ratio [reflecting all embedded fees] was the most reliable predictor of its future performance, with low-cost funds delivering above-average performance in all of the periods examined." They cited a study by Christopher B. Philips and Francis M. Kinniry Jr. that showed that "using a fund's Morningstar rating as a guide to future performance was less reliable than using the fund's expense ratio" (cf. Sect. 2.6.1).

As Morningstar[3] explains, the *expense ratio* of a fund or ETF is the annual fee, as a percent of holding, charged to shareholders. "It expresses the percentage of assets deducted each fiscal year for fund expenses, including 12b-1[4] fees, management fees, administrative fees, operating costs, and all other asset-based costs incurred by the fund."

Significantly diminished fund growth can result from elevated fees. This is conveyed vividly in Figs. 9.1 and 9.2 from the U.S. Security and Exchange Commission's Office of Investor Education and Advocacy. Using fee spreads that are less than those in expense ratios commonly found in the marketplace, Fig. 9.1 shows how, in a portfolio that grows smoothly at a compounding interest rate of 4%, an increase of a fee from 0.25% to 1%—only 0.75% more—results in a loss after 20 years of 14%. The fee dollar amount of course grows along with the growth of the portfolio value and thus deducts an increasing amount from the portfolio, which hence grows at a reduced rate. Figure 9.2 shows the impact of a 1% fee on the same portfolio. The bottom sector shows the growth of the portfolio net the 1% fee. The middle sector is the increasing dollar amount paid in fees. And the top sector is the additional dollar amount that would have accrued had one been able to avoid paying the

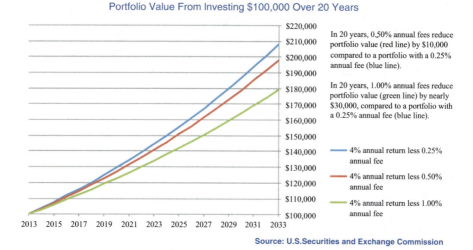

Fig. 9.1 Growing loss from fee differentials over 20 years.

---

[3]https://morningstar.com/InvGlossary/expense_ratio.aspx.
[4]Distribution fees, capped by the SEC.

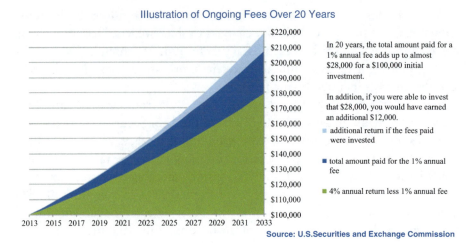

Fig. 9.2 Impact of a 1% fee over 20 years.

fees and instead invested the saved amount. After 20 years, the cost of a 1% fee is an 18% loss in portfolio value.

Think about it. A standard for financial advisors is to charge a 2% annual fee on the value of the portfolio that they manage (whether it goes up or down, of course). By contrast, the Vanguard expense ratio for their S&P 500 index fund, at this writing, is 0.04%—yes, four hundredths of one percent: only 2% of the 2% that the financial advisors take. The financial advisors, by taking 2% of portfolio value, are taking 50 times more *each year*. After 20 years, that's a staggering 48% difference. And the financial advisor is expected to do *worse* with your portfolio than what you can get simply by investing in the market as a whole (Sect. 1.5). (A few do better, but one cannot predict which.)

9.3 Let's Buy a Boat

Before we start drawing down our savings, we want them to grow as large as possible. For an undrawn portfolio, the best growth is afforded by equities. If you want to buy a boat, say, an expense that you can defer as long as necessary, it's a discretionary expense. If it fits within your budget, you can afford it. However, if you decide to buy it by selling some equity when the market is depressed, then its effective cost becomes more than buying the same boat when the market is "up."

If the market dropped 20%, then you need to sell 25% more of your equity $(1/(1 - .2) - 1)$ to pay for the boat than you would have needed before the drop. But that's not all. If you didn't lose that 25%, it would compound over the years. So the loss is significant. If equity appreciates at 10%/year (dividends reinvested), then 15 years later, the amount lost would grow to more than the cost of the boat. This is money you would have had in savings, had you not bought the boat when the market was depressed. Being a discretionary expense, you had the option to avoid that loss by deferring the purchase until the equity market recovered.

9.4 Pay Off a Mortgage Early? Pay All Cash?

One's final mortgage payment is a traditional cause for celebration. The note gets burned in the fireplace, while the whole family cheers. If one has the resources, it is tempting to advance the celebration by paying off a mortgage early.

But is that a good idea?

The same question applies to someone who thinks to pay "all cash" for housing, avoiding a mortgage altogether. In addition to the emotional benefit, being an all-cash buyer can provide an incentive to a seller who prefers not to have a sale contingent on the buyer obtaining a mortgage. The all-cash buyer thus can expect preferential treatment, perhaps in terms of a lower price or preference in case of competitive bidding.

That same preferential treatment should obtain, however, as long as the buyer does not require a mortgage contingency in the sales contract (whether or not the buyer eventually gets a mortgage). Is it thus, after all, a good idea to avoid taking out a mortgage if one can afford not to?

First, ask yourself the simple, obvious question: how is the money invested that you might use to pay off your mortgage, or add to a down-payment in order to buy without a mortgage? If it's in the stock market, growing on average 11%/year, does it really make sense to use those funds to pay off or avoid a 4% (say) mortgage? Nominally, you'd be losing 5%/year, and the difference compounds. But that's not all. You may get a tax write-off for the interest you pay on the mortgage. Moreover, an investment in equity appreciates through capital gains, which get taxed only when the equity is sold. If you sell the equity now to pay off or avoid a mortgage, then you pay tax on any capital gains now as well. This earlier taxation of gains creates a loss that continues into the future (loss of appreciation of the tax amount).

If you sell a home with a mortgage, you pay off the mortgage from the sale price, so there's no concern there about needing to pay off a mortgage with possibly depressed invested funds.

When you hold a mortgage, you have the bank as a partner to share the risk of the investment. Sure, you have fire insurance. What about flood insurance? Not in a flood zone? Are you over three miles from water? If not, the insurance companies consider you to be at some risk of flooding, even if it never happened before. None of the above? How about an earthquake? If you're not in an active earthquake zone, it's unlikely that you carry earthquake coverage. But an earthquake can happen just about anywhere. An act of war? It's very unlikely that your home will be destroyed by an act of war or terrorism, but if it was, you're probably not covered. Do you live in New York or Los Angeles or Boston or San Francisco or Chicago (or some other prominent urban area)? If so, there's a risk that a terrorist will set off a "dirty bomb." While the destruction would be limited, there could be hard-to-remediate radioactive contamination for blocks around. If your apartment was in the contamination zone, its value would drop to zero. Depending on your financial condition, your housing options could be limited (Fig. 9.3).

"I never thought I'd have to move back in with my parents."

Fig. 9.3 One fallback alternative. The New Yorker ©Condé Nast.

9   General Investment Issues   177

If you own something, there's always some risk of an uncovered loss. If you sought to carry extra insurance for every conceivable loss, your premiums would be astronomical. A much more reasonable form of insurance coverage is to share the risk with a bank through a mortgage.

If your mortgaged property is destroyed, that won't free you from your debt obligation. But it gives you leverage against the bank. Their option to foreclose is no longer viable for them. Hence, you should be able to negotiate terms with them through which you and the bank both share the loss.

Possibly the most important and over-riding consideration, however, is this: In paying off or avoiding a mortgage, one is trading a relatively liquid asset—the funds used for the payoff or purchase—for an illiquid asset, namely, increased equity in a home. If suddenly you needed that money for an unforeseen emergency or other event, you *may* be able to get a home equity loan (with possibly a higher interest rate than on the mortgage you paid off) or even a new mortgage (but, at what rate, and how quickly?). Or, maybe not. If you are retired, you may not be able to refinance your home at all. In some cases, the only sure way to get the needed funds is to sell your home. Selling a home involves losses in fees and taxes, especially capital gains taxes that are not adjusted for inflation (applying to higher priced homes). So, even in theory, you may not be able to recoup the money you used to pay off your mortgage.

In summary, there are three reasons to have and keep a mortgage: the saved funds likely can be advantageously invested; risk of loss is shared with the bank; and liquidity risk is avoided. Paying off or avoiding a mortgage, at least to some extent, is a one-way street. And, it is not one to travel down motivated only by emotions.

9.5   Is Dollar Cost Averaging a Good Idea?

Prior to retirement, when an employee invests a fixed portion of each paycheck in equity, say, inside a 401(k), the fact that a fixed periodic investment buys "more shares" when "the market is down" (although fewer when "the market is up") has widely been described as beneficial in that it smooths to the average share price. This is in contrast to the (theoretical, but not actual) alternative of investing the accumulating investments all at once, thus risking doing so in an up-market and ending with fewer shares. This benefit is widely termed "dollar cost averaging."

Note that this is not a strategy, but a consolation. There is no alternative. The money is invested when earned, irrespective of the state of the market.

178   R. P. Kurshan

In fact, this dollar cost averaging confers an additional often overlooked benefit. As shown in Sect. 11.1.2, volatility in the investment portfolio increases the effective rate of growth of periodic investments.

A second version of "dollar cost averaging" is an intuitive strategy with plenty of proponents in the investment industry.[5] It stipulates that if you receive a large lump sum contribution to your savings—from an inheritance, say, or from rolling over an IRA—then you should not invest it all at once. Instead, break it up into pieces and invest the pieces over time, in order to achieve the "dollar cost averaging" effect just described.

This differs from the first version in that in this version there is discretion: one can invest it all at once when acquired or bit by bit over time.

In this second version, there are two downsides to investing in increments. While one holds the funds in cash, they earn less than if invested; and although the market may be "up," it can continue to rise, and then one misses out on this increase in value. By waiting, you can end up investing when the market is higher than when the funds were acquired.

So which is better? Investing in pieces, hoping that dollar cost averaging saves you from paying too much per share? Or investing all at once, accruing better (average) returns from the start?

Vanguard has done some research on this question.[6,7] Their answer is that investing all at once outperformed dollar cost averaging two thirds of the time.

They studied the effects of spreading out the investment in equal monthly investments over 6, 12, 18, 24, 30, or 36 months. The results were compared after various investment holding periods ranging from 1 to 30 years. For each chosen holding period length, they used the historical record for every holding period of the given length between 1926 and 2012, separately for various balances of stocks and bonds from 100–0% to 0–100%, separately for each of three countries: the United States, the United Kingdom, and Australia. For each chosen balance, the portfolio was rebalanced monthly.

Their results were essentially the same for each country. Moreover, they found that investing all at once was better on average for every holding period studied: 1–30 years. As the holding period increased, so did the benefit of having invested all at once. In the United States, for 10-year holding periods,

---

[5] e.g., Malkiel (2015).

[6] personal.vanguard.com/pdf/ISGDCA.pdf While this link is now dead (it is very annoying how Vanguard moves studies around or simply deletes them), a copy can be found here: docplayer.net/3803492-Dollar-cost-averaging-just-means-taking-risk-later.html.

[7] money.com/why-dollar-cost-averaging-is-a-lousy-retirement-investing-strategy/.

investing all at once was better than dollar cost averaging over the first 3 years, in 90% of the 10-year periods between 1926 and 2012.

For the optimal balance of 60% stocks, 40% bonds, and a 10-year holding period, investing all at once led to an average 2.3% higher end value than dollar cost averaging over the first 12 months. Finally, they showed that even after adjusting for risk using the Sharpe ratio (Sect. 3.3), investing all at once still provided better returns on the average.

9.6   Don't Buy a Dividend or Coupon

If you are preparing to buy a share of stock or of an ETF or mutual fund, using funds that are not tax-advantaged, and the timing is not critical, it may be worth checking when its next dividend is due. If you buy shortly before the dividend issues, then you'll owe taxes on the dividend. If you delay the purchase until after the issue, then you not only avoid the taxes, but you pay less per share (by the amount of the dividend, which the market factors into the share price). Delaying the investment significantly can result in missing out on appreciation in the interim. However, if it's a matter of days, it may well be worth waiting.

Likewise, if you bought a bond just before a coupon is redeemable, the coupon value, like all outstanding coupons, is part of the price of the bond (Appendix A.4). When a coupon is redeemed, you normally pay tax on the resulting interest. Thus, if you had a choice between buying a bond just before or just after a coupon became redeemable, the latter choice avoids the tax, and the bond is cheaper by the amount of the coupon.

There is no reverse rule that applies to selling equity. Since a long-term capital gain (Sect. 12.7) or long-term capital gain distribution are generally taxed at the same rate, if you sell just prior to a distribution, the price reflects the anticipated distribution, and your long-term capital gain increases by that amount, whereas if you sell just after the distribution, your capital gain is less by the amount of the distribution (which you received and gets taxed). So it's the same either way.

However, if you sell a bond before a coupon issues, the increased sale price is likely taxed at the lower capital gains rate, while if you sell after the coupon issues, you pay ordinary income tax on the coupon. So it's better to sell just before the coupon issues.

9.7 Stocks and Bonds Often Move Inversely

Often the bond market moves in the opposite direction from the stock market, as investors protectively move funds from stocks to bonds when stock values are falling and, conversely, to participate in a rising stock market. In fact, only three times—4% of the years between 1928 and 2013—did both the S&P 500 and 10-year Treasury notes fall in the same year: 1931, 1941, and 1969.[8] In all of these cases, the drops in stocks: -43.84%, -12.77%, and -8.24%, respectively, were significantly greater than the corresponding drops in bonds, namely, -2.56%, -2.02%, and -5.01%. The same author looked at quarterly declines in the Barclays Aggregate Bond Index since 1976, again compared to the S&P 500, and found that in only 14 quarterly periods—9% of all—they both fell together. (In fact, on a yearly basis, these two indices never fell together during the same year.)

Therefore, if one is inclined to move funds in response to changing stock prices, when stock values are falling, there not only may be a loss from the sale of the stocks but also an increase in the price of the bonds, compounding the loss. And the same double loss may incur when moving funds from bonds to stocks to chase rising stock prices.

9.8 Rebalancing

The investment industry points out that whatever proportions of a portfolio are chosen for stocks, bonds, cash, and domestic and foreign holdings, these proportions drift unless the portfolio is "rebalanced." Allowing such a drift is equivalent to choosing a different—*a priori* unknown—"balance" (ratio) (Chap. 4). Thus, it generally is recommended to rebalance a portfolio annually to restore the originally chosen balance. This is accomplished by selling what there's too much of in order to buy what there's too little of.

However, this advice is misguided. It's not a static balance that one should seek to maintain, but a dynamically adjusting amount to be held in stable, liquid assets (fixed income investments and cash) to cover expenses, as explained in Chap. 4. This amount adjusts over time, with changing expenses and market conditions.

---

[8]Ben Carlson, September 14, 2014: awealthofcommonsense.com/2014/09/often-stocks-bonds-decline-time/ = tinyurl.com/wgrlvcj.

9 General Investment Issues 181

Moreover, to maintain some given balance as the investment industry recommends can require a forced sale of depressed equity (Chap. 4). This would lead to an unrecoverable loss of the depressed equity value (a loss that compounds over the lifetime of the portfolio).

Any rebalancing comes with a cost. Equity sales may entail a capital gains tax. There also may be fees for both sells and buys, or at least bid/ask spreads (the difference between the selling and buying price). Since small imbalances, if left alone, may correct themselves, even if one sought to follow the investment industry advice to rebalance, one shouldn't rebalance on some regular schedule as they advise, but only when really needed. And, certainly not at times when doing so entails selling depressed equity.

In taxable accounts, to ensure that the lower long-term capital gains tax applies, it is beneficial if any rebalancing that involves the sale of equity occurs *no less* than a year and a day from the purchase date. There are likely equities with different buy-dates in the same fund or ETF holding. It's best to use a first-in-first-out protocol for selling, in order to avoid selling shares purchased more recently than a year ago. Recent purchases may result from automatically reinvested dividends and not be immediately evident to the holder, who may feel that the fund "hasn't been touched for years."

10

Can I Afford to Retire?

If you have some control over your retirement date, before you cut the cord, you should check if you have enough savings on which to retire. If you have no control over your retirement date, this check can tell you the expected level of spending possible in retirement. *Expected* is a very significant and operable adjective: it says that this or more is possible in 50% of the modeled futures. For the other 50%, less is available. Therefore, this check should be considered a feasibility check only, not the basis of a spending plan. Chapter 11 gives an investing/spending plan based on the "shock absorber" described in Sect. 4.2, tailored for retirement. That plan dampens the volatility of investments used to cover expenses, hence limiting *degradation* (Sect. 11.1.1), which decreases the effective growth rate of a periodically drawn-down volatile investment. This considerably increases the likelihood that a feasible level of spending determined by the check given here can be realized.

How to check? First, use the guidelines in Chap. 6 to establish annual income and expenses. Exclude from savings any amounts that have been earmarked for special purposes, such as schooling (Sects. 4.3 and 14.1) or a home renovation (Sect. 4.4). What remains is the *retirement expenses fund* to be used for living expenses.

Set P to the present value of the retirement expenses fund, set n to the number of years more that you think you will live,[1] and set r to the expected

---

[1] Just make a guess, or else check longevity tables or a longevity calculator (see Appendix A.9.1—**longevity tables**) to see how long you or the last to die of you and your significant other are expected to live. Then adjust for the health of you both.

© The Author(s), under exclusive license to Springer Nature Switzerland AG 2022   **183**
R. P. Kurshan, *Investment Industry Claims Debunked*,
https://doi.org/10.1007/978-3-030-76709-9_10

184 R. P. Kurshan

annual *real* (i.e., inflation-adjusted) rate of return from P over the course of those n years, as explained next.

One can find the nominal expected growth rate of an investment from its web page. It generally gives the average annual rate of return for various periods, like the last year, the last 5 years, and so on. For each investment in the retirement expenses fund, pick a growth rate that looks "representative," taking into account recent economic conditions. For investments with respective current values P_1, P_2, ...and growth rates r_1, r_2, ..., the value of the fund after n years is $Q = P_1(1 + r_1)^n + P_2(1 + r_2)^n + \ldots$. The fund's *compound annual growth rate* (CAGR) over the n years is $r_0 = (Q/P)^{\frac{1}{n}} - 1$. This is the growth rate such that $Q = P(1 + r_0)^n$.

To get the "real" rate, one needs to adjust the nominal rate r_0 for inflation. One way to do this is to use the average inflation over the past decade. The U.S. Bureau of Labor Statistics provides an online inflation calculator[2] that uses the CPI-U measure of inflation. Enter last month as the ending date, a decade ago last month as the starting date, and \$1 as the amount. The calculator gives the amount that one needs to pay today to get the value of that \$1 then. Say it's \$1.18. Then the annual average rate of inflation for the past decade is $I = 1.18^{\frac{1}{10}} - 1 = 1.67\%$ (as above).

Some people think, incorrectly, that the real annual average rate of return is the difference between the nominal rate r_0 and the rate of inflation I, namely, $r_0 - I$. The reason that's incorrect is that as a rate, the real rate r is related multiplicatively, not additively to the nominal rate r_0 (a rate compounds multiplicatively, not additively). Applying the rate of inflation to the real rate gives the nominal rate, $(1 + r)(1 + I) = 1 + r_0$, or

$$r = \frac{1 + r_0}{1 + I} - 1 \qquad (10.1)$$

explicitly. Many economists define returns in terms of logarithms. Taking *ln* of both sides of the previous equation does turn the ratio into a difference: $ln(1 + r) = ln(1 + r_0) - ln(1 + I)$.

For an estimate[3] of the annual income C available from the retirement expenses fund with value P, solve the mortgage formula (A.7) for C:

---

[2] https://bls.gov/data/inflation_calculator.htm=tinyurl.com/y3xbqdem.

[3] Moshe Milevsky Milevsky (2012) gives a continuous time version of (10.2): instead of discrete time in terms of n, his formula is correct at every instant of time t (and he solves for t). However, that formula is harder to derive (he doesn't), and the difference is unlikely to be relevant here. Moreover, for $r < 10\%$, the two are almost identical.

$$C = P \frac{r(1+r)^n}{(1+r)^n - 1} \tag{10.2}$$

Let's see what can happen if we fail to adjust for degradation. The year is 1973. Wearing a wizard hat, we correctly predict that the average rate of inflation between 1973 and 2003 (30 years later—our desired term for the investment) will be 4.96%. We also correctly predict that our investment of a half-half mix of S&P 500 and 10-year Treasuries (a common investment industry recommendation) produces an annual average return in those 30 years of 9.9% (dividends and interest reinvested). This produces a 4.7% real rate of return ($= 1.099/1.0496 - 1$, by (10.1)). We decide to draw down our savings annually by just 0.05% more, 4.75%, adjusted annually for inflation.

Using (10.2) with $n = 30$ and $C = 4.75\% \times P$, we find that the required interest rate r is a mere 2.45%. This is the real growth rate required of our savings, to support the 4.75% drawdowns for 30 years.

Hurray! we say, because our 4.7% expected real rate of return is almost twice that, and using (10.2) again, with $r = 4.7\%$, we find that our savings will last 100 years.

Imagine our dismay when after 27 1/2 years, we find all our money gone. Time to move in with our children for the last 2 1/2 years. What happened???

The source of our mistake was a failure to account for degradation. For our balanced fund, degradation was 1.9%/year (mostly due to a 5.5%/year degradation from the S&P 500—c.f. Sect. 11.1.2). Had we adjusted the expected rate of return of our investment for degradation, we would have found that the expected longevity of our portfolio was not 100 years, but less than 33 years (using $r_0 = 9.9\% - 1.9\%$). This leaves little room for a margin of error. Remember *expected*, discussed at the start of this section?

Where do the errors come from? Well, for example, we applied the *average* rate of inflation uniformly to the term of the investment. In the last decade of the retirement, it was only 2.4%, while in the first, it was 8.7%. Coming at the beginning of retirement, this was particularly damaging. (Far from yielding a 4.7% real rate of return, during this decade our investment produced a measly 1.1%.) Thus, after allowing for 1.9% degradation, the 33-year expected longevity should have been considered too close for comfort, and the resulting longevity of 5.5 years less (27.5 years) should have come as no great surprise.

The lessons here are as follows: (1) allow for degradation (see Sect. 11.1) when regularly drawing down a volatile asset, and (2) increase the term n by, maybe, 20% over what you think you need, to allow for the variability of the estimate.

R. P. Kurshan

But even with these insights, we still cannot rely too heavily on this estimate, as in reality, we miss one essential ingredient: the wizard hat. Over 25–30 years (typical for a retirement), we cannot expect to be able to predict inflation or expected market growth rates with any accuracy at all.

Thus, this calculation is only a "back-of-the-envelope" estimate, not a guarantee. If we use the "shock absorber" plan of Sect. 4.2 as tailored for retirement in Sect. 11.2, we can significantly reduce the effect of degradation, by reducing regular drawdowns of volatile assets.

So, this calculation is better at telling you that you *cannot* afford to retire, than reassuring you that you can. If C plus income (Social Security, pensions, etc.) is less than your non-discretionary expenses, you're in trouble: P is likely insufficient to support your retirement as planned. In this case, either continue to work or find some other way to grow P (Sect. 11.7).

If the calculations don't rule out the feasibility of an n-year retirement with the chosen drawdown C, it would be reassuring to get some confirmations. A way to do this is to use a retirement calculator (Sect. 3.5, footnotes 22, 23). These give professional probability estimates of how long one can expect P to last, given C, n, and a selected balance of stocks, bonds, and cash. If instead of maintaining a static balance as they presume, one follows the "shock absorber" plan, their answers can be considered underestimates. In this case, the retirement expenses fund is likely to last somewhere between their estimates and the (10.2) estimate with 0.5–1% allocated to degradation (see Sect. 11.2), and the calculated term n diminished by, maybe, 15%.

11

Investments After Retirement

In retirement, a major concern is to not outlive one's savings.

During early working years, a primary financial focus may be just to enjoy spending surplus earnings. Later, for many families, the focus shifts to balancing income against a seemingly endless stream of expenses: children's schooling, housing, home renovations, piano lessons, family outings, cars, and on and on.

But eventually the family grows up, the nest empties, and old expenses disappear. Then the focus may shift to "wealth": increasing savings.

Finally, in retirement, the financial objective needs to shift again: to how best to cover from savings those expenses that exceed income (Social Security, pensions, annuities, etc.). As economics Nobel laureate Robert Merton has said regarding retirement wealth management, we need to "shift the mind-set and metrics from asset value to income".[1] This necessary shift can be overlooked when thinking about retirement. It means that in retirement we need to manage finances, not with the goal of increasing savings, but with the goal of maintaining a drawdown stream from savings to cover expenses for as long as we live. As we see next, these two goals are very different. To maximize savings longevity, we need to sacrifice some asset growth. This is in order to cover expenses with a stable source of funds, in order to reduce the risk of needing to sell depressed equity (Chap. 4). Thus, the manner in which savings are drawn down to pay expenses is a crucial factor to successfully manage retirement savings.

---

[1]Merton (2014).

© The Author(s), under exclusive license to Springer Nature Switzerland AG 2022
R. P. Kurshan, *Investment Industry Claims Debunked*,
https://doi.org/10.1007/978-3-030-76709-9_11

187

188   R. P. Kurshan

To support the required drawdown flow through some sacrifice of asset, growth is not an oxymoron. As emphasized many times in the foregoing chapters, the loss from selling depressed equity can be profound, not only in terms of its immediate drop in value but also in terms of the lost opportunity for the depressed equity, once sold, to restore its value at a later time and continue to grow inside the portfolio. These losses can far outweigh the growth shortfall incurred when more volatile equity is exchanged for more stable fixed income investments. Chapter 4 explained how higher-growth equity can be exchanged at propitious times for lower-growth fixed income investments to provide a stable source of funds to cover expenses. This is tailored to a retirement expenses fund (Chap. 10) in Sect. 11.2, where it is shown how through sacrificing some growth, drawn-down savings can be made to last longer.

In addition to the potential loss from selling depressed equity, there is a *degradation* of effective equity growth rate, if it is regularly drawn down for expenses (even if it is never depressed). Equity volatility causes regular drawdowns to, in effect, lower the undrawn equity growth rate. This surprising and often overlooked effect is explained in detail next.

11.1 Regularly Drawn Volatile Savings

Two versions of "dollar cost averaging" were described in Sect. 9.5. In the first version, salary invested periodically distributes across time the purchase of investment shares. This avoids the possibility that all purchases occur at an unusually high price when the market is "up" beyond its mean. Purchases in an "up" market eventually are balanced by purchases in a "down" market when the shares are cheap.

Thus, the prices of shares average out to the mean, so on average one pays the average price. In fact, as shown in Sect. 11.1.1, it's even better: volatility in the investment portfolio increases the effective growth rate of periodic contributions.

In retirement, by contrast, if an equity portfolio is subject to regular withdrawals (say, for living expenses), the same effect that enhances the growth of a volatile portfolio subject to periodic investments, degrades the growth of a volatile portfolio subject to periodic withdrawals (Sects. 11.1.1 and 11.1.2).

This detrimental effect of regular withdrawals from volatile savings has been observed empirically, and was aptly named "reverse dollar cost averaging".[2]

Like regular 401(k) deposits, regular withdrawals cannot be timed to the performance of the portfolio (such as waiting until the market value of the portfolio is "up" to make the withdrawal). When a withdrawal aligns with a market downturn, the withdrawal constitutes a larger portion of the portfolio's average value than it does during a market upturn. While one might imagine that the two opposite effects balance each other, this in fact is not the case, as explained next.

11.1.1 Degradation

Imagine $1 million invested in a savings bank that gives $I = 6\%$ interest, compounded annually. Its growth is shown by the smooth curve v_n in Fig. 11.1. If instead of investing the money in a savings bank, the money is invested in a stock that appreciates at the same *average* rate (6%), but in successive years, decreases in value by 75% or increases in value by 75% compared to its average, in alternation, the resulting value of the portfolio is shown by the sawtooth

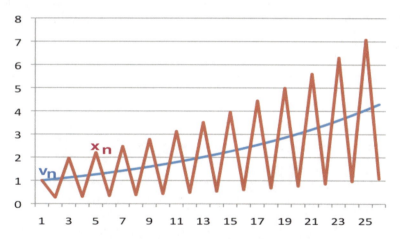

Fig. 11.1 Portfolio growth. The value of a stock that appreciates at an annual rate of $I = 6\%$ while fluctuating 75% in successive years is shown by x_n. Investing the same value with the same appreciation rate in a savings bank is given by the smooth v_n, a regression curve for x_n. The horizontal axis measures years and the vertical axis relative value.

---

[2] analyzenow.com/Articles/Investments/Investment%20Articles/ ReverseDollarCostAvg1-1-01.pdf = tinyurl.com/yb5l5jzh.

x_n in Fig. 11.1. In this context, v_n is a "regression" curve for x_n, showing the average value of x_n. After the 25th year, the value of the stock never goes below its initial value and, in its peaks, reaches above $7 million. Although the stock value fluctuates, its *average* value is always the same as that of the savings bank investment v_n.

Now, suppose we draw down these two investments by withdrawing from each one $40,000/year (a withdrawal rate of $w = 4\%$ per year of the initial investment). The savings bank investment v_n continues to grow nonetheless, because the 4% withdrawal rate is less than the 6% savings bank interest rate: $w < I$ (and, moreover, I compounds). However, the stock portfolio value goes to $0 in the 18th year, as seen in Fig. 11.2. This is because periodic drawdowns of a fluctuating investment degrade its effective growth rate, in this case, lowering it below the 4% drawdown rate.

The big take-away from this is that **one cannot expect a regularly drawn-down volatile portfolio to sustain its average growth rate minus its draw-down rate**.

Furthermore, a less volatile portfolio with a lower average growth rate can outlast a more volatile portfolio with a higher average growth rate. An example of this is shown in Fig. 11.3. The degradation is still visible (notice how the mean value of x_n slowly sinks below v_n). But the lesser degradation is not enough to prevent the portfolio from increasing in value despite the drawdowns.

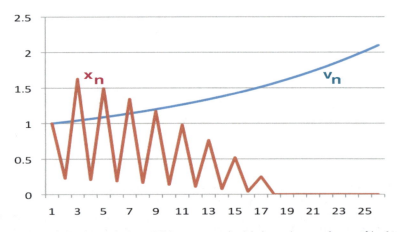

Fig. 11.2 Portfolio degradation. With an annual withdrawal rate of $w = 4\%$ of initial savings, and underlying annual growth rate of $I = 6\%$, v_n shows continued savings growth despite the drawdowns, because $w < I$. However, with the same rates, in the fluctuating portfolio, the resulting degradation causes the portfolio value to go to $0 in the 18th year.

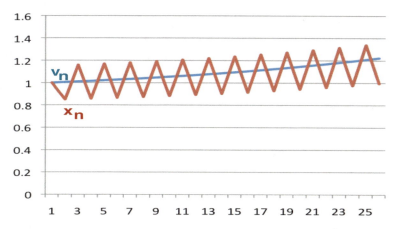

Fig. 11.3 Less degradation with less volatility. With the same annual withdrawal rate of $w = 4\%$ as in Fig. 11.2, but a lower underlying annual growth rate of $I = 4.5\%$, and lower fluctuation of 15%, the fluctuating portfolio nonetheless increases its value over time, despite the annual drawdowns, on account of its lesser degradation—an example of *less is more*.

If one's goal is to maintain a drawdown rate of w for as long as possible, then in this example, the lower-growth, lower-volatility portfolio accomplishes this in perpetuity, whereas the higher growth portfolio with higher volatility lasts only 17 years on account of its greater degradation (a consequence of its greater volatility).

By stripping out all the random variations of a real market investment, the essential effect of degradation stands out in the examples illustrated in Figs. 11.1, 11.2, and 11.3.

The general point is that while an undrawn volatile investment oscillates about its mean, whose value grows at the average growth rate of the investment, when the same investment is regularly drawn down, periodic withdrawals have the effect of decreasing its mean growth rate below its undrawn mean growth rate minus the withdrawal rate. If the investment were in a savings bank that gave interest at a rate I, it would be as if when the savings were regularly drawn down, the bank lowered its interest rate to a rate $I' < I$ (although since a savings account experiences no volatility, it also is not subject to degradation). The diminished rate (I' in this savings bank example) is termed the *imputed* (mean) growth rate of the regularly drawn investment, and the difference $I - I'$ is the degradation.

In an actual market investment, the imputed growth rate can get distorted and obscured by market forces and the order of market fluctuations (often

192 R. P. Kurshan

called the "sequence of returns"). However, typically, these distortions cancel one another, and the degradation is readily apparent.

In some cases of a sustained rising market at the start of retirement, the imputed rate can be higher than the mean growth rate of the undrawn portfolio. This would result in a negative degradation—an enhancement of the mean growth rate. While this can happen, it's atypical.

11.1.2 The Math of Degradation

The mathematical cause of degradation, illustrated in Figs. 11.2 and 11.3, is simple to understand. Consider two consecutive withdrawals W from a portfolio. Suppose the portfolio value at the time of the first withdrawal is an amount d above the portfolio's mean value m, and then in the following withdrawal, the value of the portfolio has fallen to d below its mean value (on account of market fluctuations). The first withdrawal is a smaller fraction $W/(m+d)$ of the then value of the portfolio than the second withdrawal, which is the larger fraction $W/(m-d)$ of the value of the portfolio at that time. The average of the two fractions is

$$\frac{1}{2}\left(\frac{W}{m+d} + \frac{W}{m-d}\right) = \frac{mW}{m^2 - d^2} \ .$$

On the other hand, had the portfolio not fluctuated, then each withdrawal (so the average of the two) is the fraction W/m of the portfolio value. Since for all d with $0 < d < m$,

$$\frac{mW}{m^2 - d^2} > \frac{W}{m}, \tag{11.1}$$

the two consecutive withdrawals from the fluctuating portfolio do not balance each other with respect to the portfolio mean value, and in fact, the average withdrawal degrades the portfolio by the rate difference

$$\frac{mW}{m^2 - d^2} - \frac{W}{m} = \frac{Wd^2}{m(m^2 - d^2)} > 0 \tag{11.2}$$

compared with the same withdrawal from the non-fluctuating portfolio.[3]

---

[3]If the fluctuation is modeled instead as a geometric rate (dm, m/d), a similar—although typically smaller—degradation occurs. (The relationship between the two degradations depends on whether, for $d > 1$, $m < d(d^2 + 1)/(d - 1)$, in which case the geometric degradation is smaller.) In fact, although use

By the same argument, if instead of withdrawing W, one added W to the portfolio each time, then the same (11.1) constitutes a dual effect that is an *enhancement* of the portfolio by the rate difference (11.2). This is a beneficial effect of dollar cost averaging (beyond its stabilizing effect).

This simple observation provides a mathematical explanation for the beneficial effect of dollar cost averaging and the degrading effect of reverse dollar cost averaging. In particular, a volatile investment is "risky" not simply because its value may be depressed when needed, but because on average, volatility by itself lowers expected returns from a periodically drawn-down unstabilized portfolio.

In general, the extent of degradation with reverse dollar cost averaging (or benefit with respect to dollar cost averaging) depends on the rates of market growth, portfolio drawdown (or, respectively, deposits), and market volatility, but market fluctuations are, in ranges of interest, significantly destructive for periodic withdrawals (and would be correspondingly beneficial for periodic deposits).

The imputed growth rate r of investments in a periodically drawn-down portfolio can be measured: it is the growth rate r that, when diminished by the given inflation-adjusted withdrawal rate, gives a statistically good fit[4] to the values over the time of the actual drawn-down portfolio. Just as the mean value of an undrawn investment determines a smooth (exponential regression) curve about which the actual value of the investment oscillates, the imputed growth rate determines a smooth curve about which the drawn-down investment oscillates (cf. the lower smooth curve in Fig. 11.5). The degradation is the difference between the nominal growth rate for the undrawn investment and the imputed growth rate of the same investment when drawn down.

For an investment in the S&P 500 (i.e., an index fund that tracks it), its degradation when periodically drawn down can be as much as 6% (for the 30-year period that began in 1969, when drawn down annually at 4.75% of the initial investment, adjusted thereafter for inflation).

Degradation is a function of the drawdown rate and market conditions. Typical S&P 500 degradation rates for a 4.5–4.75% drawdown are in the range 0.5–5%. For a 4% drawdown, degradation typically is less, around 0–3.5%. Although a 2% degradation may not seem a lot, like fees (Sect. 9.2), its effect

---

of an arithmetic rate is more widespread, geometric appears to offer a better model. See, e.g., Peters and Gell-Mann (2016).

[4] A least squares best fit to the actual drawn-down portfolio values by a function determined by the given withdrawal rate and the constant growth rate r.

194   R. P. Kurshan

compounds and over time can make a significant difference to the longevity of a retirement portfolio.

The lesser volatility of 10-year Treasury notes keeps their degradation rate well under 1%.

11.1.3 Market Example of Degradation

Let's revisit the case of a retirement that began in 1973 (cf. Fig. 4.2). Suppose that instead of stabilizing the funds to be used for forthcoming expenses as proposed in Chap. 4, we followed the standard investment industry advice described there. Recall that they recommend to achieve portfolio stability by maintaining some chosen balance of equity and fixed income investments. Suppose our portfolio consisted of an index fund that tracked the S&P 500 (for growth) and 10-year Treasury notes (for stability). Imagine that we magically had the foresight to create a portfolio with the optimal balance of these two components, and maintained that balance throughout the retirement period by rebalancing, with dividends and interest reinvested. With an inflation-adjusted annual withdrawal rate that initially was 4.5% of the investment, the optimal balance, when averaged over all retirement periods that began in the years between 1950 and 1985 (allowing for a 30-year retirement period), was 68% Treasuries and 32% S&P 500. With this balance, the average of the respective portfolio longevities was greatest for the given withdrawal rate (among portfolios that achieved stability through maintaining a balance). For the retirement period that began in 1973, this portfolio lasted 32 1/2 years, not bad, considering the terrible first 2 years. (In Chap. 10 we saw that for the larger withdrawal rate of 4.75% and a sub-optimal 50/50 balance, the portfolio lasted 27.5 years.)

If the portfolio had been left undrawn, it would have appreciated at an average rate of 9.5% per year (0.4% less than for the 50/50 portfolio described in Sect. 4.7). This is shown in Fig. 11.4, where the smooth curve shows the mean growth and the fluctuating curve is the daily values of the portfolio. However, when drawn down, its degradation is evident in Fig. 11.5, showing an imputed growth rate of only 8.9% (0.6% less—the lower smooth curve). The portfolio value over time is the jagged curve, and the mean drawn-down value of the portfolio, had its imputed growth rate remained the same as its 9.5% undrawn growth rate, is the top curve. Thus, had there been no degradation, the portfolio value would have fluctuated around the upper smooth curve and would have lasted another 2 1/2 years, or 7.7% longer. Thus, the 0.6% degradation had a significant destructive effect.

11 Investments After Retirement 195

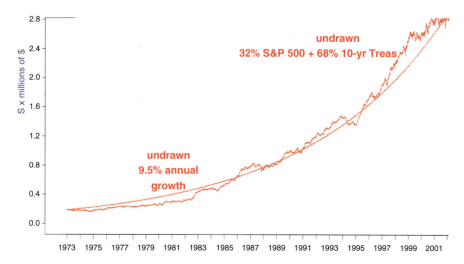

Fig. 11.4 Undrawn investment. A 1973 investment that maintained a balance of 32% in S&P 500 and 68% in 10-year Treasuries, dividends and interest reinvested, grew on average 9.5%/year, shown by smooth line.

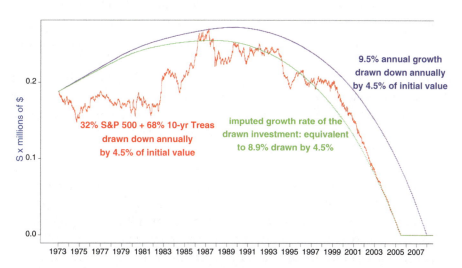

Fig. 11.5 Drawn investment. With the same conditions as in Fig. 11.4, but drawn down at an initial annual rate of 4.5%, thereafter adjusted for inflation, its imputed growth rate (lower smooth curve) is 0.6% less than the mean growth rate of the undrawn investment less the inflation-adjusted withdrawal rate, shown as the upper smooth curve.

11.1.4 Degradation Seen with a Commercial Market Forecaster

For another illustration of degradation, consider the following. A well-established financial tool, the Fidelity Brokerage Services *Retirement Income Planner* can be used to illustrate degradation on commercial market forecast data. This online tool is generally available (through a guest sign-in). It provides a lot of user-defined parameters, is very well documented, and is very useful for retirement financial planning.

The tool uses historical financial market data from 1926 to the present, and Monte Carlo simulations based on Fidelity's model of market behavior, to predict the outcome of an investment. It is given in terms of a user-defined balance among "stocks," "bonds," and "short-term," a user-defined inflation-adjusted withdrawal rate and a user-selected length of retirement. A range of final values of the portfolio ("at least $\cdots$") is calculated for four confidence levels: with probability 90%, 75%, 50%, and 25%. A detailed description of the tool assumptions and calculations is given in a 28-page white paper.[5] "Stocks" are represented by the S&P 500 index, "bonds" by U.S. Intermediate Term Government Bonds, and "short-term" by 30-day U.S. Treasury bills. Historical growth rates for the various asset classes are based on performance numbers provided by Ibbotson Associates in the Stocks, Bonds, Bills, and Inflation (SBBI) 2001 Yearbook (annually updated by Roger G. Ibbotson and Rex A. Sinquefield). Annual growth rates assume the reinvestment of interest income and dividends, no transaction costs, no management or servicing fees, and an annual inflation rate of 2.5%, as stated in the white paper.

The Fidelity Retirement Income Planner is used here to calculate the expected degradation due to drawdowns of a volatile retirement savings portfolio. The degradation is given relative to a theoretical performance measured by drawing down at the same rate a non-fluctuating portfolio whose fixed rate of growth is the average rate of growth of the undrawn fluctuating portfolio.

For this demonstration, the length of the retirement period was set to 25 years, and in order to demonstrate degradation in a generally increasing portfolio, the annual drawdown rate was set low, to 2.5% of an initial investment (of $1M—but, the results are independent of this amount). The chosen investment was 100% stocks. In order to avoid tax offsets of the investment, the investment was designated as a Roth IRA.

---

[5] Search for rip_methodology.pdf; the location changes, and the new version of this documentation, with a different name, is less informative.

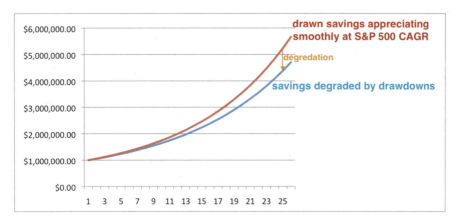

Fig. 11.6 Portfolio degradation in Monte Carlo simulations. The degradation in value due to periodic drawdowns in the face of volatility is the difference between the two curves.

The tool was set in order to perform simulations in two ways. In the first way, *Scenario A*, withdrawals ("expenses") were set at $1 per year (the tool disallows $0, but $1 is close enough to $0), in order to compute the expected undrawn growth rate. In the second way, *Scenario B*, the portfolio was drawn down in the first year at the rate of 2.5% of the portfolio's initial value, thereafter adjusted for inflation, so the actual withdrawal rate increased each year, both with inflation and as a proportion of the decreasing portfolio value.

In Scenario A, the Fidelity calculator computed an expected compound annual growth rate [CAGR] of 9.5%,[6] in keeping with many published historical rates for the S&P 500 having the start date of 1928. In scenario B, had there been no degradation, then the drawn-down portfolio would grow at this nominal growth rate less the drawdown rate, or at 9.5% − 2.5% = 7% annually, shown as the top curve in Fig. 11.6.

For Scenario B, the expected end value V calculated by the Fidelity calculator with 50% confidence was used to calculate the non-volatile growth rate of a investment subject to the same 2.5% inflation-adjusted annual drawdown rate that produced the end value V after 25 years. That rate was 8.87%. This is the imputed growth rate of the drawn-down portfolio, the lower curve in Fig. 11.6 (cf. Fig. 11.5). The lower withdrawal rate for the 100% S&P 500 fund resulted in the same degradation as a higher rate for the less volatile 32–68% balance.

---

[6]This is obtained by dividing the 50% confidence level end value by the initial investment and raising that to the power 1/25, for the 25-year investment period.

The difference in growth rates for Scenarios A and B is the degradation caused by the Scenario B periodic withdrawals of the Scenario A volatile investment. In this case the degradation was $9.5\% - 8.87\% = 0.63\%$, fairly low because the withdrawal rate was so low. (We saw in Sect. 11.1.2 that for a 4.75% withdrawal rate, the degradation could be as high as 6%.)

The 0.63% degradation degraded the value of the portfolio by 17% over 25 years.

11.2 Retirement Portfolio Shock Absorber

In this section I explain how to maintain a retirement expenses fund to support the "shock absorber" strategy (Chap. 4), tailored to retirement. As in pre-retirement, this strategy is based on sacrificing some growth for stability while seeking to hold no more fixed income investments and cash than necessary to support spending. Here, it addresses the consequence of a large equity downturn near the start of retirement (when it is most damaging). The retirement strategy reduces this sacrifice over time, as it becomes less beneficial.

For this strategy, retirement begins with enough cash to cover the first 6 years of retirement expenses beyond retirement income. Call this the *retirement cash buffer*.

In order to populate the retirement cash buffer, Sect. 4.6.3 explained the value of a (long, say) 10-year pre-retirement preparation window. With the start of this window, 10 years before retirement, the imminent retiree waits for the trigger condition that the S&P 500 is within 90% of its previous all-time high value. Upon a trigger, the imminent retiree transfers enough equity to fixed income investments (and here, cash is best, as retirement nears) to cover expenses that are projected to be paid from savings in the first 6 years of retirement.

The reason for the long window is on account of the catastrophic effect on retirement savings of needing to support the first years of retirement by selling depressed equity. Such a loss creates a lost earning opportunity that compounds through the rest of retirement (cf. Fig. 4.2).

Starting retirement with the first 6 years of expenses covered by cash gave the longest average retirement expenses fund longevity on the historical data. All 25- and 30-year retirement periods starting in each respective year between 1950 and 1985–1995 (with the last period ending in 2015) were analyzed.

If you have a better way to decide with how much in fixed income investments/cash to start retirement, then by all means use that. There is no way to know for sure that the historical trends will continue into the future.

11 Investments After Retirement

Once retirement begins, the retiree uses the cash buffer to cover retirement expenses (to the extent that it is adequate). On the historical data, although an intermediate-term bond fund had better average growth than cash (held in a money market fund or savings bank), the bonds exhibited enough volatility to render the overall performance of cash superior for covering expenses, in terms of the expected longevity of the retirement expenses fund. Therefore, it appears more advantageous for this buffer to be held as cash.

In retirement, maintain the cash buffer as follows. Replenish it, up to a chosen level (initially, 6 years' worth of expenses if we use the historical guide), by transferring the required amount of equity to cash each time there is a trigger condition. In retirement, for the 1950–2015 data, a trigger that was 85% of the then current S&P 500 all-time high value was optimal, in terms of expected longevity of the retirement expenses fund. Expenses are covered by the cash buffer as long as it is adequate (otherwise, from equity).

Finally, seeking to maintain the size of the cash buffer at a level that covers the next 6 years of expenses, successively, throughout retirement was found to be inefficient. The 6 years is important at the start of retirement, when a loss from selling depressed equity compounds throughout retirement. However, as retirement progresses, the greater average growth of equity was found, over time, to outweigh the potential loss from needing to sell depressed equity. Thus, it is better to reduce the amount held in cash (allowing for greater holding of equity). So, if $v(t)$ is the (inflation-adjusted) value of cash needed to support retirement expenses for the 6 years following t, where t measures years of retirement, then for an N year retirement period, a better target level for the cash buffer in year t is

$$\max\left\{\left(\frac{N-t}{N}\right)^{\frac{t}{N}}, \frac{1}{6}\right\} v(t) \tag{11.3}$$

(thus, never less than 1 year's worth of expenses). Figure 11.7 plots the multiplier of $v(t)$ in (11.3) for $N = 30$.

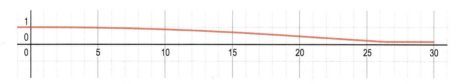

Fig. 11.7 Reduction of the retirement cash buffer over time.

For a 30-year retirement period, after the 26th year, the cash buffer looks only 1 year ahead ((11.3) reduces to $v(t)/6$). In the example given in Fig. 4.3, the cash buffer ran out in the last half of retirement. In other retirement start years, it was maintained through the end.

Nonetheless, despite the degradation and potential for loss associated with a potentially higher level of equity toward the end of retirement, its short hold period rendered these less destructive, on average, than the shortfall that would have resulted from converting more funds to fixed income investments. This is an empirical observation for all 25- and 30-year retirement periods that began in 1950 and ended in 2015.

When applied to historical market data for the period 1950–2015, retirement savings managed with this "shock absorber" strategy outlasted—or, in just a few worst cases, merely matched—*every* maintained balance of S&P 500 and 10-year Treasuries, as well as any such balance that changed linearly over time (increasing or decreasing the ratio), as described in Sect. 4.1.[7] The balance-based methods, as the reader by now well knows, are the strong recommendations of the investment industry (Sect. 4.7). For the retirement that began in 1973, the comparison is shown in Fig. 4.3.

It is fairly stunning that a retirement expenses fund managed in this manner outlasted every balanced portfolio, but the reason is clear: following the investment industry recommendation to maintain a balance of stocks and bonds forces the degradation of the periodically drawn-down portfolio as well as a shortfall from holding more in fixed income investments than necessary to cover expenses. A portfolio managed in a manner that seeks to maintain just enough cash to cover expenses tends to avoid the shortfall and degradation. (Once the cash buffer runs out, it becomes necessary to sell depressed equity and suffer the degradation of a periodically drawn-down volatile investment. But its benefit is front-loaded, where its effect is most significant.)

In practice, the size of the cash buffer should be adjusted to reflect changes in expenses. The decision of when to sell equity (at 85% of its previous all-time high value) can be set up and automated as a limit sale (Sect. 2.7.1). With all the uncertainties in the applicability of the historical data to the future, it should be adequate to roughly estimate the value of (11.3).

---

[7] The data set uses values for the S&P 500 (dividends reinvested) and cash earning interest at the Federal Funds Rate, often considered to be an adequate proxy for a (top) savings bank interest rate. The interest generated by the cash also is reinvested. Expenses are drawn monthly, and the cash buffer is replenished to the chosen level each time there is a trigger (so, at most once a month).

The numbers "85%" for the threshold trigger and "6 years" for the size of the initial cash buffer were determined empirically on historical market data. Looking forward in time, the optimal values for these numbers can well change. Therefore, they should be considered *guidelines* (of a concept), not hard and fast numerical rules. How their values might change in the future can only be a matter of speculation.

Once past the age of 70 1/2, or, starting in 2020, age 72 if you did not reach 70 1/2 yet, enough of the cash buffer should be held inside a traditional IRA to cover RMDs ("required minimum distributions"). This is so they need not be drawn from depressed equity: see Sect. 13.1. The IRA cash is not in addition to the cash to be drawn for expenses, but simply a part of it; it's the holding of the cash inside a traditional IRA (in anticipation of an RMD) that's pertinent.

Milevsky and Posner[8] present a way to counter the destructive consequences of needing to sell depressed equity, based on put and call options,[9] derived from a strategy called "portfolio insurance".[10] It is unclear which strategy performs better, the one presented here or one based on puts and calls. Both effectively reduce portfolio volatility, sacrificing some portfolio growth; but the one given here is certainly simpler to understand and to implement. Moreover, their strategy only avoids isolated needs to sell depressed equity, not the general degradation accompanying periodic drawdowns of equity in retirement. Its analysis is beyond the scope of this book.

summary
Begin retirement by holding enough cash to support 6 years of retirement expenses (that exceed retirement income): the *retirement cash buffer*. To the extent possible, draw retirement expenses from this buffer. Replenish the buffer up to the level determined by (11.3) by transferring equity to cash each time that the S&P 500 is within 85% of its previous all-time high. This strategy significantly outperformed the investment industry recommendations, on historical data in the period 1950–2015.

---

[8] Milevsky and Posner (2014).
[9] See Malkiel (2015) for an explanation of these.
[10] Leland (1980).

William Bengen 1996

11.3 Retirement Discretionary Spending

The considerations of Sects. 4.6.1 and 4.6.2 apply once you've retired. Is it more important to front-load expenditures while you are younger and may be able to enjoy that Himalayan trek, or to back-load in anticipation of increasing healthcare costs, or a plan to contribute to the upbringing of grandchildren? While thinking can't necessarily create money where there is none, it can help prioritize what you have.

11.4 The 4% Rule

No guideline for retirement savings is more widely cited than the so-called 4% safe withdrawal rule promulgated by William Bengen.[11] This very popular and widely promoted guideline states that in a 30-year retirement, you will not outlive your savings if you limit your annual drawdowns to 4% of your initial savings value, thereafter adjusted for inflation.

The rule was extended in the so-called Trinity Study,[12] with many follow-ons. Subsequently the number "4" has been revised many times, recently upgraded to a "4.5% rule" and then downgraded to a "3% rule," but never mind.

It is predicated on an investment of savings half in stocks, half in bonds, with this balance maintained through annual rebalancing, and is based on an analysis of almost a century of historical market data. Both this "safe"

---

[11] Bengen (1994). He credits Bierwirth (1994) for the inspiration.
[12] Cooley, Hubbard, and Walz (1998).

withdrawal rate and best asset allocation balance are said to depend on the length of the retirement period—the longer the period, the smaller the safe withdrawal rate, and the higher the proportion of stocks for the best results.

These results later were extended by Bengen who refined his recommendation, stating that the best outcome for a 30-year retirement period was given by holding 70% in stocks. In fact, in Table 4.1, the 4% rule for $N = 30$ shows that every balance between 30% bonds and 70% stocks to 70% bonds and 30% stocks fulfills the promise of the 4% rule by lasting the full 30 years.

FIRECalc,[13] updated periodically, is an interesting retirement calculator that was inspired by research that followed Bengen's idea to base retirement portfolio analysis on historical market data, in particular, the Trinity Study. It allows one to vary the portfolio investment components and balances, as well as the historical period used, and has provisions for income as well. Unfortunately, it is poorly documented, and some of its results appear anomalous.

Other studies have shown that reordering the same monetary events can have dramatic effects on the safe withdrawal rate, reducing it to less than 2% (for an early "down" market) or increasing it to over 20% (for an early "up" market). As we have already observed (Fig. 4.2), a market downturn at the start of retirement can compound the loss throughout the retirement period with severe consequences, if depressed stocks are sold to cover expenses. The converse naturally happens with a market upturn at the start of retirement.

11.4.1 Is the Rule Reliable? Useful?

In fact, none of the "4% rule" variations is grounded in theory, and all go counter to serious economic analysis. Their most basic flaw is to extrapolate into the future, without theoretical justification, an artifact of historical market performance.

This is the fundamental difference between the "4% rule" and model-based theories. For example, the "shock absorber" strategy is a model-based theory that works for any parameter values. While a proposed *implementation* is based on historical data (the times between market all-time highs, and average market growth rate differences between stocks and bonds), it can be implemented using any other values for these, based on any economic insights or other data (cf. Sect. 5.4, footnote 9). Changing the parameter values naturally alters the resulting numerical recommendations, but they all are based on the same theory (model). Performance comparisons between the

---

[13] Sholar (2018).

shock absorber strategy and standard investment industry recommendations based on the historical data are just examples.

Absent any theoretical justification, a particular behavior found in 100 years of data is not considered to have sufficient statistical significance to predict that it will continue, That's why financial market performance tools run many thousands of simulations when they seek to predict future behavior.

Scott, Sharpe, and Watson[14] give a nice summary of the history and "universal popularity"[15] of the 4% rule. They point out flaws and theoretical inefficiencies in the class of such financial "safe withdrawal rules" that stipulate conditions by which a retiree can "safely" draw down some inflation-adjusted fixed annual percentage of initial savings. They attach particular disapprobation to the idea that retirement spending should be supported by drawing down volatile assets. In their words, "Supporting a constant spending plan using a volatile investment policy is fundamentally flawed."

First, they take issue with recommendations based only on extrapolations of the historical record, since the historical record comprises too few scenarios to be robust with respect to estimation error. Instead, they recommend stochastic models based on the salient values, variances, and correlations observed in the historical record, which can be run in arbitrary multitude to overcome this limitation. (Although, these still would be based on extrapolation into the future of the historical record.)

More saliently, they show that this class of rules leads to spending plans that are unnecessarily risky with regard to failure rate, are unnecessarily wasteful with regard to the amount used to fund the spending policy, and are unnecessarily inefficient in accruing unspent surpluses when the market outperforms expectations.

11.4.2 Some Famous Economists Weigh in

The second author in the above study is the Nobel laureate William F. Sharpe, of the "Sharpe Ratio" (Sect. 3.3), a renowned expert on financial planning, cited a number of times throughout this book.

In the above study, they argue that the only guaranteed "safe withdrawal rate" is the one supported by a ladder (Sect. 2.3.3) of risk-free zero-coupon bonds that adjust for inflation. Another prominent economist, Nobel laureate

---

[14] Scott et al. (2009).

[15] They cite support for the rule from preeminent financial institutions, including Schwab, T. Rowe Price, Vanguard, and AARP.

11 Investments After Retirement 205

Robert Merton, likewise has argued that the retiree should invest *all* savings "*risk-free*": in TIPS—U.S. Government bonds that adjust for inflation.[16]

In fact, there are some basic flaws in these recommendations, traceable to unrealistic assumptions. Also, these recommendations exceed most investment industry recommendations to hold *some* bonds and *some* stocks.

Unlike financial industry studies, which may be founded on faulty or non-existent analysis, the flaws in the recommendations of economists normally derive not from faulty analysis but faulty assumptions.[17] Economists build models within which they draw conclusions, especially concerning optimizations. Their conclusions may fail to reflect reality, but only insofar as their models fail to reflect reality—which, unfortunately, is often inescapable.[18]

Economists concede that their models cannot accurately predict at a fine level of granularity, but insist that their models are valuable for identifying general trends. But, if I'm an investor, should I take into account the possibility of economic disasters like the 2008 financial meltdown? This was warned about by a (very) few (and ignored by everyone else), but its coming was not predicted by any economic theory, just—if at all—by empirical observations of colliding circumstances. As an individual seeking to manage my personal finances, I need guidelines that can adjust to such unpredictable disasters, such as the guidelines of Chap. 4 and Sect. 11.2, not a theory that seems ok on sunny days.

To be fair, the focus of Scott et al. (2009) is to critique as inefficient and unreliable the "4% rule". If we *assume* that what one wants is a fixed inflation-adjusted income for 30 years, then TIPS is a candidate that conceptually avoids the inefficiencies of the "4% rule." The focus of Merton (2014) is to promote a switch in retirement from wealth generation to income emulation. Their arguments are based on the idea that in retirement, it is inefficient to subject investments to risk, as then one needs to underspend in order to compensate for volatility. They argue that the retirement income stream should emulate the reliable (??) income stream during employment.

So perhaps these recommendations were not meant to be actual financial guidelines, but rhetorical positions meant to illustrate a theoretical point.

---

[16]Merton (2014).

[17]This is not to say that there has not been some highly influential economics that eventually was proved wrong as a result of faulty analysis. There has, e.g., nytimes.com/2013/04/19/opinion/krugman-the-excel-depression.html.

[18]For a strident (but not completely accurate) take-down of economics by a world-renowned professor of economics—who was one of the very few to predict the 2008 economic meltdown—see Keen (2011).

If one takes these recommendations literally, though, the most evident problem is that "risk-free" is an imaginary concept not to be found in real life: risk is inescapable (Chap. 3). During employment, there is a considerable risk of losing one's job (and hence one's "reliable" income stream). They assume that a ladder of TIPS can pay out the amount required each year. However, it is unlikely that TIPS are available for each year of a retirement, as required. Moreover, TIPS are not even zero-coupon. Both of these points generate inefficiencies in the ladder (Sect. 2.3.3). (Although U.S. Treasury I-Bonds are both zero-coupon and inflation-protected, their purchase is limited to $10,000 per year per Social Security number, and this limitation makes them generally insufficient for such a ladder.) The term of TIPS is capped at 30 years, so if the retirement is longer, there is considerable risk in rolling them over to extend the term. (To be risk-free, the plan also must assume that one dies with certainty within the 30-year maximum term of TIPS.) They assume a risk-free rate of 2%, whereas in 2019, TIPS returned around 0.6%, supporting an annual return of a bit less than 3.7% of the investment, and by 2020, the return on TIPS was *negative*. And even the promise of TIPS to adjust for "inflation" is risky: for example, the inflation index used under-represents average costs of the elderly,[19] whose healthcare costs push their actual inflation rate above the rate used in TIPS. The TIPS inflation-adjusted rate also may be subject to future reduction by redefining the inflation index (a political decision). An additional complication is that the inflation adjustments are considered "income" by the IRS, thus reducing their benefit. Moreover, "risk-free" (U.S. Treasury) bonds are a worse investment than negligibly risky highly rated corporate bonds (Sect. 3.2).

These are some technical flaws in their arguments. But there are five overarching problems with their model that basically render it useless for real life. They assume:

- That long before retirement one can predict one's spending needs
- That those spending needs are constant in real dollars throughout retirement
- That TIPS are not depressed at retirement, when the ladder is established
- That it *never* is necessary to invade the TIPS ladder for unforeseen expenses (health emergency, grandchildren, · · ·)

---

[19] Huang and Milevsky (2011).

11 Investments After Retirement 207

- And perhaps most damningly, that the meager TIPS return is all one should seek in retirement—that one should never take a little risk to enjoy a significantly better return.

I think that most people would consider these assumptions to be absurdities.

Regarding the last assumption, we take risks in everything we do (cf. Chap. 3), and as just noted, the TIPS strategy also is not risk-free (except in a very narrow, theoretical sense). Therefore, one should be educated to evaluate risks and prepare for their various outcomes, not seek the impossible: to avoid all risks.

To say that one should adjust one's living standard in order to be able to live off the meager income produced by TIPS (if even possible) is to misunderstand human nature, priorities, and flexibility. People can/do/must cope with changing circumstances throughout life, and to say that we should scale our living to the least level of risk possible is condescending. Most people undoubtedly seek to maintain a desired standard of living with the understanding that if later in life, finances take a beating, it may be necessary to cut back. I think few people would be inclined to cut back now, in order to relax with the support of a "risk-free" income stream if led to understand that with the "risk-free" course, there still are many risks: unanticipated emergencies, changes in the law, changes in taxation, changes in where one lives, and so on, and the risks associated with these costs are greater when one has fewer savings to fall back on. (Merton does allow that if the risk-free stream is inadequate to provide the required income, the alternative is to trade off some risk for a growth opportunity, and then keep your fingers crossed. Not terribly reassuring, and seemingly in complete contradiction to the concept of the "risk-free" stream. This apparently is based on the idea of the "risk-reward" tradeoff discussed in Sect. 3.7.3.)

Of all these risks, the greatest undoubtedly is liquidity risk (Sect. 3.8). This is the risk that you unexpectedly need to draw from your "risk-free" investment, thus destroying its risk-free structure. Since it's impossible to predict future needs accurately, the chances of needing to do this are very high.

Waring and Siegel (2015) circumvent the liquidity risk and the need to project future expenditures (but they reintroduce price risk) with a "virtual annuity" that pays out at the TIPS rate, adjusted annually. This is based on the assumption that the current TIPS rate reflects the current value of capital projected into the future. However, can one not say this about any bond or index rate? And they are all somewhat different!

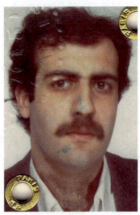

Nassim Taleb 1980

Notwithstanding all of this, it has been argued that all such models fail to adequately represent low probability catastrophic events.[20]

Experience has shown that these models, while mathematically appealing, are not very useful in reality; although often right, they fail to account for devastating low probability events or even common behaviors that are not accurately captured by the models' simplifying statistical assumptions. Thus, while mathematically precise, these models can end up being dangerously misleading.[21]

Better than seek to define away risk is to study means to manage it. That has been the main subject of this book, with the proposed means presented in Chap. 4 and Sect. 11.2.

11.5 Will Your Taxes Decrease in Retirement?

While it often is written that one's taxes decrease significantly in retirement, the decrease may be less than one imagines, especially for the U.S. investor, on account of Social Security benefits, pensions, RMDs (Sect. 13.1), and capital gains on investments.

For some, taxes actually increase, as mortgages are paid off, resulting in the loss of those interest deductions; real estate holding are sold, resulting in the loss of depreciation deductions; and other deductions such as the home office

---

[20]Taleb (2007).

[21]See Mandelbrot and Taleb (2005) for a bracingly strident popular press view on this, prescient about the catastrophic 2008 crash that followed their article by 2 years.

11 Investments After Retirement 209

deduction for a freelance worker are eliminated. (At the same time, expenses may increase with increased leisure time that leads to more travel, children to help with housing expenses, grandchildren to help with schooling, and so on.)

11.6 Most Important: Monitor Your Spending

After retirement, finance management is both easier and harder. It's easier because there are fewer moving parts. No more salary, probably no more childcare, school costs, and so on. It's harder because now your financial future depends essentially on what you so far have saved, and you need to shepherd that to last your lifetime.

The fundamental idea is: monitor/adjust. Monitor how you are doing; adjust so it lasts.

The once New York City mayor Ed Koch famously used to ask the press and everyone else "So, how am I doing?". That's what you need to ask yourself, say, once a year, after you have paid your taxes. Use the method described in Chap. 6 to determine your non-discretionary and discretionary spending in the previous calendar year. Then, use formula (10.2) of Chap. 10 to determine your projected annual income C from your presently remaining retirement expenses fund P, for the remaining number of years n that you want to be able to support your retirement. Don't forget to include an appropriate offset for degradation. If you had any unbudgeted one-time expenses or restored a depleted emergency fund (Sect. 4.5) in the previous year, then P gets reduced accordingly, perhaps below the previous year's projection. If the market is depressed, or investment growth rates have diminished, this too reduces C.

This is the "monitor" part. So, how did you do? If your C plus *income* (Social Security, pensions, investment income, and the like) covers all your anticipated non-discretionary and discretionary spending for the coming year, then the answer is "You're doing great!".

Even if your retirement cash buffer has become depleted on account of an unexpectedly long market depression, the possible need to sell depressed equity for expenses was factored into the calculations for supporting the shock absorber. As long as your calculated C covers your expenses, you're doing fine. Sell the depressed equity to cover your expenses (and don't worry about it).

Otherwise, then what? You have a choice. You can either ignore the warning and spend beyond your C plus income, in effect, borrowing from the future. Or, you can curtail your spending to bring your total spending in line with C. Or, you can augment your savings (e.g., Sects. 11.7.1 and 11.7.2) enough to support C. Or, finally, you can find a way to decrease your retirement period (Sect. 11.7.3).

Ignoring the warning (borrowing from the future) can make sense if you believe that C is reduced on account of temporary market conditions, if spending beyond C does not require selling depressed equity, and if you believe that the market will rebound soon enough to pay yourself back.

If the shock absorber (Sect. 4.2) is working properly, then there's a good chance that you hold sufficient funds in the retirement cash buffer to cover expenses beyond C. Why cancel that traditional annual family ski vacation just because the market is a little depressed. No need to become obsessive or dogmatic. The market will rebound. When it does, you will replenish the retirement cash buffer, paying back what you borrowed and likely restore your required C.

11.7 If Savings Becomes Insufficient

Perhaps your newly calculated C is inadequate to cover expenses because P was depleted by an unbudgeted one-time expense. If your retirement cash buffer can cover the difference, then you can borrow from the future. But how will you pay yourself back? Moreover, reducing the retirement cash buffer can affect future years, where it may be inadequate in an equity depression to cover expenses. That's a significant risk.

What if your newly calculated C is insufficient to cover expenses and your retirement cash buffer fund is insufficient to make up the difference? Then, if you decide nonetheless to borrow from the future, what you borrow (and spend) now is equity, which you must pay back to yourself later, *with interest—* you will have lost both the principal and its expected growth. It is much worse if the equity is depressed: a dollar spent from depressed equity is more than a dollar times its long-term expected growth rate (Sect. 9.3).

In all these cases, it may be appropriate to curtail spending to a level that allows all expenses to be covered by the newly calculated C. If you can do this, then even if covering expenses requires selling depressed equity, you're ok, as above (Sect. 11.6). Of course, discretionary spending would be curtailed first.

Curtailing expenses may be as simple as spreading a discretionary expense over some years. For example, perhaps you think that rather than curtail the ski vacation in the coming year, you will curtail two or more such vacations in the following decade, when you may be too old to ski anyway, and your family will have dispersed. Then you will pay back the current loan from the future simply by cancelling the expense in some years to come. This can be a reasonable decision especially if the market is not depressed and therefore an equity loan from the future does not incur an excessive interest rate.

Whether you decide to borrow from the future, with the expectation of being able to pay back the loan with sufficient interest to restore the original C, or decide to reduce spending, is mostly a matter of personal disposition.

Say you are concerned about what other unanticipated expenses may loom over the horizon as your health deteriorates or grandchildren come into being. Then reducing expenses sufficiently to support expenses with the calculated C can be a reasonable course.

There's the "eat, drink and be merry, for tomorrow I may be dead" personality and the more Calvinesque personality that agrees to take rewards only when the money is there. I see equal merit in both. Maybe hedge your bets: sometimes, this way, sometimes that. Cf. Sects. 4.6.1 and 4.6.2. But repeated borrowing from the future soon enough may result in an unrecoverable loss.

There are other (perhaps more disruptive) ways to restore C. You can increase savings. Do you have a country house? Would selling it enable you to return to your desired level of discretionary spending? Would its loss be worth it? No more beach house, but back on track with the family vacations. Or, would the loss of the house be too regretful as a first remediation?

In the end, you have three options: reduce spending, increase savings, or reduce your retirement period.

The first is eminently practical, but needs to be done with care if you seek to maintain your style of living to the greatest extent possible. Revisit your expenses, make a priority order, and think what you might do without. Perhaps the sacrifice will only be temporary. Start with discretionary spending. That weekly massage seems essential, but it's pretty costly and maybe it can be suspended for a bit.

The second option can be achieved by selling some property, including possibly your home, or getting a job (Sects. 11.7.2 and 11.7.1).

The third seems draconian if it involves defenestration, but there are other alternatives: Sect. 11.7.3.

The need to make such choices is always unsettling. However, no one can predict the future. When conditions change, the constructive course is to deal with it.

First rule: don't panic! Conditions could improve, putting you back on track. The equity market could "take off," increasing P beyond expectations and restoring C to the original level. The equity market does this from time to time. That's why you shouldn't be too quick to adopt an irreversible remedy like selling your home.

For now, the first step is to determine how bad your situation has become. An insufficient C can be viewed in a few ways. One way is that it is just a temporary situation, and borrowing from the future doesn't seem unreasonable. Another is that some expenses should be trimmed. Perhaps you decide that you can maintain your previous spending for a few years. Then, if market conditions improve, you are back on track. Otherwise, you could move to a less expensive community (Sect. 11.7.2). While market conditions are impossible to predict, if you think they could improve shortly, that would give you an opportunity to defer an irreversible decision for a while. You may have a few fallback options. You could move sooner to a less expensive but attractive environment. Or, delay the move with the hope of a market recovery. If that fails to materialize, then move later to an even less expensive, but less attractive environment.

11.7.1 Earning Money in Retirement

If you find that your retirement is underfunded, or you simply become bored, one solution is to get a job. While it may not be possible to resume working at the job you retired from, there are other possibilities besides becoming a check-out clerk at Walmart.

The standard retirement job for professionals is to become a consultant in the same field that you previously worked in. This may require using your network of professional contacts to find a place interested to employ you. The competitors of your previous employment may be good places to look.

Were you an academic? How about adjunct professor?

If you are so inclined, you may be able to create salable art. You may be able to write a salable book :-).

Do you have a great voice? How about doing voiceovers? These can be as simple as corporate training videos and audio-books.

Do you know a foreign language? How about document translation or becoming an interpreter?

Do you have a green thumb? How about horticulture (gardening, landscaping)?

Then there's starting a small business. It can be as simple as dog-walking, but with success, branch out into other services, including pet care and house-sitting.

11 Investments After Retirement 213

There's Task Rabbit,[22] exemplifying the new "gig" economy, that pairs an individual's abilities with consumer demand, mostly from those seeking freelance labor for everyday tasks.

Some agencies specialize in retirement job listings.[23,24,25]

How about Craig's List?[26]

If you are adept with tools, a "handyman" (not gender-specific) is always in great demand.

There's tour-guiding, event-planning, travel agent, real-estate agent, and tax preparation.

There's elder or child care-giving, medical assistant, baby-sitting, and tutoring.

How about becoming a camp counselor or park ranger?

There are office jobs like bank teller and hotel concierge where the employer may value age, experience, and responsibility.

Of course, there's driving a taxi, now made more open through services like Lyft and Uber. Also, security guard.

While foster care is not meant to be an income-producing undertaking, for some it is.

Finally, there's volunteer work. While not directly providing income, it can provide connections leading to employment.

11.7.2 Move to Less Expensive Housing

The canonical way to reduce spending is to move into a smaller home or to a less expensive community. If you are a homeowner, this typically is irreversible, as once you move and spend some of the assets gained from the move, you may not have the resources to move back. As we age, such moves are more stressful and less likely. So, in all likelihood, selling your home and moving to a less expensive home elsewhere is effectively irreversible. If you rent, it can be easier to move back and forth, but again, as we age, moves become more stressful and less likely.

If you think to "down-size" your home (sell your home, buy a less expensive home and add the difference to savings), don't forget to consider all the fees

---

[22] taskrabbit.com.

[23] retirementjobs.com.

[24] retirementliving.com/retirement-jobs.

[25] https://snagajob.com/.

[26] thebalancecareers.com/how-to-find-and-apply-for-jobs-on-craigslist-2060943.

214   R. P. Kurshan

and taxes involved. At the same time, you can reduce expenses by moving to a less expensive town, moving in with your children or moving back with your parents (Fig. 9.3).

But, you don't need to move right away. You can calculate by when you need to make the move. The money that is expected to be saved from such a move can allow you to delay the move. Let's see how that works.

First, let's calculate how long your current spending C will last. (You also can adjust C to represent changes in expenses—up or down.) Use the mortgage formula (10.2) from Chap. 10. Set r to be the imputed real average annual growth rate of the portfolio, as in Chap. 10. Solve for the largest x such that $y \geq 0$ for

$$y = P - C \frac{(1+r)^x - 1}{r(1+r)^x} . \tag{11.4}$$

This x is the number of years that the amount P remaining in the retirement expenses fund is expected to last, given spending C.

One way to calculate this is to use an online calculator such as the free graphing calculator *desmos.com/calculator*. Let's try an example. Say you have $P = \$1$ million left in your retirement savings portfolio, your portfolio's imputed real average annual growth rate is $r = 2\%$ (accounting for inflation and degradation). Suppose $C = \$50,000$ (per year), representing non-discretionary expenses and some discretionary expenses, net income. Using these numbers, enter (11.4) into the Desmos calculator, as shown in Fig. 11.8. You can change the scale of the y axis by clicking on the "Graph Settings" icon in the upper right-hand corner (not shown in Fig. 11.8). With the chosen setting, we see that the portfolio goes to $\$0$ in 26 years. (Click on the zero-crossing to see the exact value of x, as shown.)

It should be kept in mind that this is only the *expected* (average) number of years left in the portfolio. The actual number can be more or less, on account of the variance of market prices.

According to the Vanguard retirement calculator (Sect. 3.5, footnote 22), this portfolio, invested in 70% equities and 30% cash, lasts 26 years with 80% likelihood—i.e., much better than average—while it lasts 20 years with 90% likelihood. This doesn't reflect the advantage of using the "shock absorber" schedule of Sect. 11.2. With that schedule the actual percentages should be better. It also suggests that the imputed rate $r = 2\%$ used in (11.4) is fairly conservative.

Since the input numbers (C and r) can change over time, the calculation should be repeated periodically, especially as the end date gets near.

11 Investments After Retirement

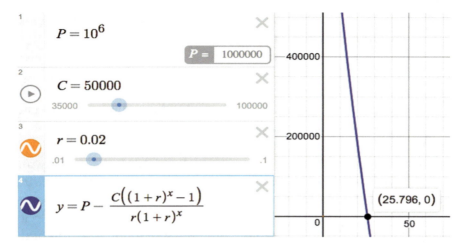

Fig. 11.8 Computing portfolio longevity with Desmos calculator. See how changing expenditures C and expected rate of return r change the longevity of a retirement expenses fund with $1 million remaining.

It can be informative to compute x for varying levels of discretionary spending, by adjusting C. This is easy to do in the Desmos calculator by implementing C with a "slider" as shown in Fig. 11.8. At one extreme, C accounts for all non-discretionary and discretionary expenditures beyond income and, at the other extreme, only non-discretionary expenditures beyond income. In between, C can account for all non-discretionary expenditures plus a few discretionary expenditures. By prioritizing discretionary expenditures and playing with various levels for C that reflect supporting fewer or greater discretionary expenditures, one can see the effect on x. Likewise, using a slider for r, one can see the implications of varying rates of return.

Since the demise of the portfolio is over two decades away, a lot can change in the interim. "Watchful waiting" may be better for now than a more drastic, irreversible option like selling your home. Eventually, moving to a community where living is less expensive (and in which you thus can manage with a smaller C) can restore the required longevity to your portfolio.

How should you compute the time when you actually need to make that change? If you wait until the end, your portfolio will be depleted, so the move may not help, unless selling your home alone provides an adequate portfolio for the then remaining retirement.

Suppose that by selling your home, you net H after paying off a mortgage, fees, and taxes and buying a home in your new community. If you rent, set

$H = 0$. If the time that you actually sell your home is far in the future, then periodically revisit the value chosen for H, and adjust it accordingly.

The question is under current conditions, when should you make the move so that the funds then remaining in your portfolio are adequate to fund your then remaining retirement.

With current rate of spending C, let n be the number of years until your retirement expenses fund goes to $0. (In the above example, $n = 25.796$ years.)

Suppose that you sell your home, move to a less expensive community, and realize a gain of H (as above) to your retirement expenses fund. At the same time, in the less expensive community, your expenses after income decrease from C to $C_2 \leq C$. If you currently rent, use $H = 0$, and if then you decide to *buy* a home, set $\$H$ to the *negative* number equal to the gross cost of the new home, including all fees and associated expenses.

Let's suppose that you can do this now or later, with the same H. Let $x < n$ be the number of years from now until when you make the move, and let P be the current amount in your retirement expenses fund. Then x must be chosen such that for

$$y = P - C\frac{(1+r)^x - 1}{r(1+r)^x} + H - C_2\frac{(1+r)^{n-x} - 1}{r(1+r)^{n-x}} \tag{11.5}$$

$y \geq 0$. Again, one can enter this equation into the Desmos calculator to compute the biggest possible value of $x < n$ for which $y \geq 0$. (Even if $y > 0$ for values of $x > n$, this is not an option, because you cannot start spending the profit H before you sell your home! It just means that you can wait until your portfolio hits $\$0$. However, doing that would be very risky if H is not assured at the moment you need it.)

Waiting until the biggest $x < n$ for which $y \geq 0$ allows you to maintain the spending supported by C as long as possible, then sell the home (if you have one), and move to a less expensive community where the required annual drawdown from the retirement expenses fund is reduced to C_2. Again, though, waiting until the bitter end is risky if the value H is not assured to be available at that moment. Once you find the biggest x for which $y \geq 0$, better back off by a few years to allow for selling and the possibility that you get less than H. If you rent, then $H = 0$ and you can wait until x.

In the worst case, this can be repeated. Sell the home; move to a somewhat less expensive community. If things get bad again, move to an adorable hut in the middle of the woods.

Finally, there may be an option to take a roommate or move in with the kids. You can explore these successive options through iterations of (11.5).

Since conditions constantly change, the calculations—especially (11.5)—should be updated from time to time, making any necessary adjustments.

11.7.3 Decreasing the Retirement Period

There are a variety of ways to decrease the retirement period. None is particularly benign, but it may be worth making them clear.

If you have the option to move in with your kids (say), as a dependent, and they will take care of you (as you once took care of them[27]), then your expenses could be substantially reduced.

While this may not be a palatable solution for many, in some societies it is a fully accepted tradition and the norm. If this is an option, then it provides a fallback in case you outlive your savings. Armed with this option, you can invest more aggressively with the hope of increasing your savings, while resting assured that if the riskier investments failed, you still have a place to sleep. Pursuing such an option should only be done with eyes wide open and adequate discussions with your kids (or whoever provides you with the fallback option).

Logically, there is another way way to decrease a retirement period. It is socially condemned and possibly illegal, so I will say no more about how to do it. However, undoubtedly there are some who strongly favor front-loading retirement satisfaction (Sect. 4.6.1), willing to pay the ultimate price if things do not work out financially.

In actuality, this consideration is probably just a mind game. If push comes to shove, there are many alternatives short of the one implied here. Indeed, in the United States, there is a social safety net that helps the utterly destitute. There are many people who would not entertain this as an option, and yet if it came to that—well, there are all types of people with an amazing range of backgrounds and prior wealth who inhabit the bottom rung of society. The risk of ending there should be considered by those who, in retirement, have continually borrowed from the future (see above). Refusing to entertain the possibility does not prevent it from happening.

---

[27] In this case, you can hope that you were a good, caring parent!

For the U.S. Investor

12

Pre-retirement Investment

This chapter reviews U.S. tax-advantaged accounts (like a 401(k) or IRA). Tax-advantaged investment accounts are mainly of two types, "tax-deferred" and "tax-exempt."

Tax-deferred accounts are built mostly with pre-tax funds (commonly, invested from a portion of salary which is then not taxed). All activity within the accounts (exchanges, receipt, and reinvestment of dividends and interest) remains untaxed. Ordinary income taxes become due on all amounts withdrawn, and usually withdrawals are restricted to retirement. Examples include the 401(k)—while employed—and the traditional IRA (Sects. 12.1 and 12.3).

Tax-exempt accounts are built with after-tax funds, for which gains, interest, dividends, and withdrawals are not taxed. The main examples are the Roth 401(k) and Roth IRA.

There's also a lesser-used hybrid called a nondeductible IRA, which is funded with after-tax funds, but then gains and interest are tax-deferred until withdrawal (at which time they are taxed as ordinary income). This is useful when limits for a traditional IRA have been reached, and it thus is no longer an option.

A 403(k) is very similar to a 401(k), except it is restricted to nonprofit organizations and government employers. Most statements about 401(k)s apply also to 403(k)s. Other tax-deferred accounts include certain types of annuities, partnerships, and a variety of specialized plans.

Other tax-exempt accounts besides the Roths include tax-free municipal bonds (Sect. 2.3.1), certain annuities, certain types of partnerships, and certain

---

© The Author(s), under exclusive license to Springer Nature Switzerland AG 2022
R. P. Kurshan, *Investment Industry Claims Debunked*,
https://doi.org/10.1007/978-3-030-76709-9_12

specialized types of investments like a "municipal investment trust" that invests solely in tax-free municipal securities and delivers a monthly tax-free premium to the holder.

In the sequel, I'll describe issues pertaining to the 401(k) and the traditional IRA as representatives of tax-deferred plans, and the Roth 401(k) and IRA as representatives of tax-exempt plans. These descriptions mostly apply to the others as well.

12.1 Traditional 401(k) Plans

During employment, most employers with more than 100 employees (and some with fewer employees) make available to their employees a "defined contribution" savings account that conforms with the U.S. Internal Revenue Service (IRS) regulation 401(k), established in 1978. This regulation allows employees to contribute a certain amount of their salary to the savings account, and the amount contributed is deducted from the employee's stated wage income as it appears on the W-2 form used to report taxable wages.

Moreover, it allows employers to contribute a tax-deferred amount as well, for example, to match $0.50 of every $1 that the employee contributes, up to, say, an employee contribution of 6% of income. Thus, an employee who contributes 6% of income to the savings account can, under this arrangement, receive 9% of income to that account (6% from the employee and another 3% from the employer).

There are a number of varieties of 401(k) plans, each with somewhat different rules. However, they all are subject to caps on allowed contributions. Those over age 50 are generally allowed to exceed these caps by a "catchup" amount.

Contributed amounts that exceed the allowed caps are taxed (as ordinary income) and should be withdrawn from the plan, or else they are taxed again when distributed (so taxed twice). *Unfortunately, your employer and plan manager may not adequately warn about such excesses, and it is incumbent on the employee to assure that excess contributions do not remain in the plan and thus get taxed twice.* You have until April 15 of the following year to notify your plan manager to refund to you any excess. Such a payment is adjusted for any gains or losses.

The amounts invested in the 401(k) account generally are managed by a financial manager selected by the employer. Typically, the financial manager invests the proceeds in financial market funds, and the employee is given some limited discretion over which funds and in what proportion. Unfortunately,

12 Pre-retirement Investment 223

regulation of these financial managers has been lax. In some cases, the managers select investments that benefit themselves—and in some cases the employer as well—at the expense of the employee. It therefore is incumbent upon the employee to select investments with the least fees possible, among those that conform to the employee's investment goals.

The disadvantages of investing in higher priced funds were discussed in Chap. 2, and the corrosive effect of fees was examined in Sect. 9.2. Typically, the funds with lowest fees are index funds, which are exactly what you should want (Sect. 2.6): an S&P 500 or Total Stock Market index fund for equities and an intermediate bond index fund for fixed income investments. Hopefully, your 401(k) offers these. If not, complain!

The intent is that the 401(k) proceeds are to be used for retirement, and there are significant monetary penalties for withdrawing any portion before retirement age, except in case of certified "hardships" (see Sect. 12.4). Once funds are withdrawn from the account, unless they are "rolled over" into an IRA (see Sect. 12.3), taxes must be paid at the rate of ordinary income tax on the total amount withdrawn, as already stated.

For many people, the 401(k) is the only savings available in retirement. If you're young and retirement sounds like science fiction, believe me there are only three possibilities: you die young, you work past retirement age until you die, or you retire. Although you may plan on the second, circumstances (if not desire) can put you in the third. If you are planning on dying young, chances are you're not reading this book. So, for everyone reading this, max out your 401(k)! …to the extent that you can afford. That extra few percent of your salary is unlikely to be make-or-break now—just imagine that your salary is that few percent less. You'd probably still keep your job. But that few percent will build and compound and give you a more sustainable retirement.

If you are self-employed or do not benefit from a 401(k) plan, as long as you have income, you are entitled to open an IRA (Sect. 12.3), which works the same in concept as a 401(k), except is subject to different rules and limits (and enjoys no employer contribution). But the arguments for utilizing this opportunity to the maximum extent possible are the same.

12.2 Roth 401(k)

The Roth 401(k) was established in 2006 as an alternative to a traditional 401(k). The Roth receives *after-tax* salary but then allows tax-free appreciation, tax-free exchanges (sells and buys within the account), and tax-free withdrawals—this last allowance subject to restrictions that generally are all removed after retirement age. "Tax-free" applies not only to federal but generally state and local taxes as well.

A Roth 401(k) is subject to the same limits as a traditional 401(k). As with a traditional 401(k), employer contributions (if any) are made to a *traditional* 401(k), *not* to the Roth 401(k).

Surprisingly, a Roth 401(k) requires minimum distributions (RMDs) starting when the holder reaches age 70 1/2, or, starting in 2020, age 72 if you did not reach 70 1/2 yet. However, this requirement can be avoided by rolling the Roth 401(k) over to a Roth IRA (see Sects. 12.5 and 12.11).

12.3 IRAs

IRA stands for "Individual Retirement Arrangement," as defined by the IRS. It can be used either to *defer* income tax on contributions of income to the IRA and on their earnings in the IRA, or to *avoid* taxes on earnings (including capital gains) generated in the IRA—but not both together. In all IRAs, there is no tax on sells and buys within the IRA. The IRS has a very good and generally readable summary of the regulations that apply to IRAs.[1]

A "traditional" IRA is invested with pre-tax dollars and defers income tax on contributions and their earnings (as with a traditional 401(k)). A "Roth" IRA is invested with after-tax dollars and avoids taxes on the IRA's earnings (as with a Roth 401(k)).

A third less-used type of IRA, called a "nondeductible" IRA, has the worst features of the other two: it neither defers income tax on contributions nor avoids tax on earnings; its only benefit is to defer taxes on earnings until they are withdrawn, at which time they are taxed as ordinary income (as in a traditional IRA). This type of IRA is used when the other two are unavailable on account of income limits.

There is a fourth type of IRA designated "SIMPLE"—an acronym for Savings Incentive Match Plan for Employees of Small Employers. The SIMPLE IRA is for small employers and the self-employed, and differs from the traditional IRA mostly in technicalities, mainly contribution limits (higher for SIMPLE), age restrictions, employer contributions, and early withdrawal penalties. It defers income tax on contributions like a traditional IRA.

One can have more than one type of IRA at the same time.

---

[1] https://irs.gov/pub/irs-pdf/p590a.pdf.

The traditional IRA generally is funded with pre-tax earned income (or a rollover of a 401(k) or other traditional IRA), whereas a Roth IRA is funded with after-tax earned income or a rollover of an IRA or 401(k) on which ordinary income taxes are paid at the time of the rollover. ("Rollover" simply means conversion from one type to another.) Except for rollovers, the amount of (earned) income that can be contributed to any IRA is subject to an annual cap that increases after you become 50 years old (you then can contribute an additional $1000—so-called "catchup" contributions). Income from investments does not count as "earned" income.

All IRAs are subject to contribution limits: in 2019, to no more than $6000, or $7000 if you're age 50 or older (but never more than your income). A traditional IRA is subject to an income cap that depends on whether or not you are covered by a workplace retirement plan. For example, for 2019 not-covered joint filers, contributions to a traditional IRA are fully tax-deductible. For joint filers, one of whom has a workplace plan, with a modified adjusted gross income (MAGI—see Sect. 12.7) under $193,000, the full deduction is allowed (and is partially allowed for a MAGI up to $196,000). Joint filers both of whom are covered at work, with a MAGI over $123,000, cannot take any IRA deductions (and those with a MAGI over $103,000 can take only a partial deduction).[2] A Roth IRA is subject to income caps that are the same as the tax-deductibility caps for joint (or married, separate) not-covered traditional IRA filers, but oddly, for single filers, the two have been different. The contribution limits apply to each individual separately and can be split between different IRA types, say between a traditional and a Roth IRA, but you cannot contribute the total amount allowed to each separately.

Violating the income cap for a Roth IRA brings severe penalties: 6% per year of the disallowed amount, plus a 10% early withdrawal penalty, in order to correct, after the year in which the mistake was made.

Contributions to a nondeductible IRA are not capped by income. Although it may seem reasonable to contribute after-tax money to a nondeductible IRA if it is invested with income-producing securities such as bonds, thus deferring tax on the income, such a decision can be fraught. You must file a special form IRS 8606 in order to avoid paying taxes again on your after-tax contributions when you withdraw them, and even then, the IRS rules are convoluted, and if you have other IRAs funded with pre-tax contributions, the result can be paying tax twice on some part of your after-tax contributions. Additionally, of course, your after-tax contributions are subject to the same

---

[2] irs.gov/retirement-plans/ira-deduction-limits.

withdrawal restrictions that apply to an IRA generally, so unless you pay an early withdrawal penalty or have a permitted ("hardship") early withdrawal (Sect. 12.4), you tie up your money until age 59 1/2.

you can borrow short-term from your IRA
It isn't presented as such, but the IRS publication 590-A states that once in any 12-month period, you can roll over money from one traditional IRA to another—including to itself—tax- and penalty-free. You have 60 days to complete the rollover. This is effectively a 60-day tax-free loan. You can withdraw the funds, use them for some short-term purpose, and then return them to the IRA. However, if you miss the 60-day limit, then you must pay taxes due (and early withdrawal penalties, if any), and can no longer return the funds to the IRA, unless you receive a waiver, given only under extraordinary circumstances "in the event of a casualty, disaster, or other event beyond your reasonable control."

12.4 401(k)/IRA Regulations Worth Knowing

The IRS imposes a 10% early withdrawal penalty on withdrawals from a 401(k) or IRA plan taken before age 59 1/2. However, exceptions are allowed in case of "hardships," which include medical expenses, the purchase of a primary residence, college tuition for you and your dependents, and a few other categories of expenses. The penalty is also waived in case of a qualifying disability or if you are ordered by a court to give up the money (as in a child-care or divorce settlement).

Once you reach the age of 70 1/2, or, starting in 2020, age 72 if you did not reach 70 1/2 yet, you are *required* to take distributions from any tax-deferred plan according to a schedule provided by the IRS that takes into account your age and the amount in the plan. These *required minimum distributions* (RMDs—Sect. 13.1) have a very stiff penalty if they are not met: as much as 50% of the required distribution not taken! *Be careful!*

As already noted (Sect. 12.2), while a Roth 401(k) also has RMDs, these can be avoided by rolling the Roth 401(k) over to a Roth IRA (see Sects. 12.5 and 12.11). This requirement may be surprising, as people generally think of a Roth as having no requirements once the holder has retired.

However, if you are still working, you normally are exempt from the RMD requirement *for a 401(k) plan from your present employer only*, until April 1 of the year after you retire. For this, you need to have been employed for the entire year, and the plan needs to allow the deferral. Even if your last day of work is December 31, that current year is considered the "year you retire," and the RMD for that last working year is due by the following April 1. It is calculated based on the amount in your 401(k) on December 31 of the year *before* you retired—the previous year. The RMD based on the year that you retired is due by December 31 of the following year. Therefore, in the December 31 retirement example, you pay two RMDs in the following year: one based on the value of the 401(k) in the year before you retired, due by April 1 of that following year, and the second based on the value of the 401(k) at the end of the year in which you retired, due by December 31 of that same following year after your retirement. This is in addition to the RMDs due on other IRAs that you may own.

If you have other IRAs with RMD requirements, *you still must take these RMDs, even if you are earning income.*

Your first RMD can be deferred to April 1 of the year following the year in which it normally is due (useful in case you expect to be in a significantly lower tax bracket in the following year). However, if deferred, then two RMDs are required in that following year: the one for the previous (deferred) distribution and one for the current RMD (due by December 31). Except for a deferred RMD due by April 1 of the following year, an RMD is due by December 31 of the year in which it is due.

You can instruct your plan manager to withhold from the RMD some or all of your income taxes that will be due for the tax year (including state and local income taxes). This potentially avoids the need to pay estimated taxes throughout the year. RMDs are covered more generally in Sect. 13.1.

12.5 Roth IRA

A Roth IRA has no RMD, and therefore if you think your withdrawal rate required for paying your living expenses will be less than the mandated RMD rate, a Roth IRA has the benefit of allowing you to maintain the tax-free appreciation, while a traditional IRA does not. You can leave your assets in a Roth IRA for as long as you live.

Contributions to a Roth IRA have income restrictions, whereas to a traditional IRA do not. On the other hand, one can contribute earned income to a Roth IRA at any age, whereas one cannot contribute to a traditional IRA past age 70 1/2.

Both IRAs have caps on how much can be contributed in a single year. The cap for a traditional IRA increases when the income earner passes age 50.

228 R. P. Kurshan

The income restrictions for a Roth IRA can result in no contributions being allowed, if your taxable compensation is too high: in 2019, a MAGI (modified adjusted gross income—see Sect. 12.7) of over $203,000 for a couple filing jointly.

However, there's a loophole that lets you circumvent this restriction, called a "back-door Roth IRA." (Has anyone ever seen a loophole that applies to non-wealthy individuals?) The way it works is this. You contribute to a traditional IRA, which is not income-restricted, and then immediately thereafter roll that IRA over to a Roth IRA. Ah, so simple! You should do the rollover right away, before it earns income, to avoid any additional tax when you do the rollover.

Caps and limits apply to the total contributions, even if one has multiple IRAs. If you file a joint tax return, allowable contributions may be reduced by the contributions of a more highly compensated spouse to either type of IRA. This rule has the name "Kay Bailey Hutchison Spousal IRA Limit."

You cannot contribute more than allowed by applicable limits even if you under-contributed in previous years. If you *over-contribute*, you have until your taxes are due to correct the over-contribution (by withdrawing the excess). After that, you are subject to a 6% tax on the excess, for each year that the excess remains. You can eliminate an excess by withdrawing it—and paying ordinary income tax on the withdrawal, as with any IRA withdrawal—or by compensating for the excess in subsequent year(s) by under-contributing by amounts equal to the excess. However, not only are you then taxed 6% annually on the excess, but you are taxed *again* on the excess when you finally withdraw it.

What if by mistake you contribute more than allowed to a Roth IRA? You have a couple of choices: pay the penalty now, or wait to see if the IRS catches you. If they do, then you must pay the bigger penalty for all the years that have lapsed, and there is *no statute of limitations* on unreported over-payments to a Roth IRA. After 11 years, you've lost your entire contribution (and it doesn't stop there). Use IRS form 5329 to pay the penalties and withdraw the over-contribution. If the mistake is in the current tax year, you can correct it without penalties; for the previous tax year, you can avoid the 6% penalty by filing an amended return by October 15, following the instructions in form 5329. In form 5329, there also is a provision to request a waiver of penalties for an unintentional error.

If contributions are made to both Roth IRAs and traditional IRAs, your contribution limit for Roth IRAs is reduced by the amount of the contributions to the traditional IRAs.

The decision of which is more beneficial, a traditional or a Roth IRA, is addressed in Sects. 12.10 and 12.11. It devolves essentially to the return on the

12 Pre-retirement Investment 229

funds used to pay the income taxes due, in case of a Roth, and a prediction of one's retirement tax bracket. There are many online calculators available to help you with this (just search for "Roth calculator"), but they mostly don't consider all the relevant parameters (and cannot predict the future). Thus, they produce questionable and often unfounded results. If you pay taxes from your checking account and your investments generate a high rate of return, a Roth may be better. If you think that your tax bracket in retirement will be lower than now, then a traditional IRA may be better, because you defer paying taxes until the money is withdrawn. When estimating taxes in retirement, don't forget the ordinary income tax that you must pay on your RMDs (Sect. 13.1). Although you may imagine that you will be in a very low tax bracket once you retire, with only a bit of income from Social Security and investments, if you have significant savings in IRAs, then with the "income" from RMDs, your total income can come close to your pre-retirement income (see Sect. 11.5).

You have the option to roll any part of a traditional IRA over to a Roth IRA (see Sect. 12.11). To do this, you need to pay ordinary income tax on the amount of the rollover. If you decide to do this, you may want to roll over a limited amount in each of a succession of years, in order to avoid the amount of the rollover pushing you into a higher income tax bracket. Not only does a higher bracket entail paying income tax at a higher rate, but the higher income also can result in crossing the threshold that activates the 3.8% net investment income tax (Sect. 12.7). If you are on Medicare, this also can push your Medicare premium into a higher bracket in the following year, as well. (How much you pay for Medicare depends on your income in the previous year.)

A Roth IRA has a 5-year restriction regarding withdrawals of *earnings* within the IRA. There is no restriction on withdrawals of the base amounts contributed to the IRA. The restriction states that, with some exceptions, earnings withdrawn before the end of the 5-year limit are subject to taxes and a 10% penalty. For an IRA funded from income, the 5-year window starts on January 1 of the year that your first Roth IRA was funded. That same window applies to any other such Roth IRAs, present or future. For an IRA that results from a rollover of a traditional IRA, the 5-year window starts on January 1 of the year of the rollover. Each rollover has its own 5-year window. Thus, for a succession of rollovers, the sum of the rolled over amounts can be withdrawn at any time without penalty or taxes due; but all earnings on the respective rollovers must be held for their respective 5-year windows. Therefore, the accounting is easier if successive rollovers in different years are made to respectively distinct Roth IRAs, rather than all to the same Roth IRA.

12.6 Deferred Compensation

Some companies allow certain employees to defer part of their compensation. The deferred salary is kept by the company as a credit, usually including some guarantee of growth such as being pegged to the S&P 500. When the employee retires (or, sometimes, upon some other trigger condition), the deferred investment is transferred to the employee as a lump sum, at which time ordinary income tax must be paid on the total amount.

In some cases, under the terms of the plan, the employee is required to forfeit deferred benefits in case of employment terminated before the trigger condition. Such plans, known as "non-qualified deferred compensation" (NQDC) or 409(a) plans, are regulated by federal tax code.

For the employee, the plan provides a way to extend the allowed tax-deferred investments beyond the caps permitted by the IRS for defined contribution plans. For the employer, it's a way to show improved cash flow, as the liability is deferred to the future.

However, an NQDC plan presents significant risks for the employee. If the company goes bankrupt, the deferred compensation can be lost. For many employees, such plans should be considered putting too many eggs in one basket (see Sect. 17.2.4).

12.7 Federal Taxation

For the sequel, we need to look more closely at federal taxation.

The IRS form 1040 defines four levels of income. *Total* (or *gross*) *income* is the sum of wages, pension income, part of the Social Security benefit, investment income, IRA distributions, business income, royalties, alimony received, unemployment compensation, and the like. *Adjusted gross income* (AGI) is gross income minus "adjustments" such as educator expenses, IRA deductions, alimony paid, student loan interest, tuition, and fees. *Taxable income* is AGI minus the "standard" or itemized deductions and qualified business income. *Ordinary income* is taxable income minus long-term capital gains (see below) and qualified distributions.[3] It does not appear explicitly on the 1040 form, but only deep in the bowels of a worksheet where the tax is calculated, accounting for long-term capital gains and qualified distributions.

---

[3] A *qualified distribution* is a tax-free distribution allowed from a retirement plan such as a 401(k) or IRA.

As if all that weren't enough, there's a fifth anomalous level: the *modified AGI* (MAGI), which is computed by adding together the AGI and "certain amounts of income that are not taxable." Such "certain amounts" include the untaxed portion of the Social Security benefit, tax-exempt interest income (ha! gottcha!) such as any non-taxable interest payments from tax-exempt municipal bonds, as well as "interest from U.S. savings bonds used to pay higher education tuition and fees, earned income of U.S. citizens living abroad that was excluded from gross income, and income from sources within Guam, American Samoa, the Northern Mariana Islands, or Puerto Rico, not otherwise included in your AGI." (Is this material for a Tom Lehrer song?) The MAGI is used for many computations including defining IRA caps and computing other taxes such as the net investment income tax (below), the tax on Social Security benefits (Sect. 15.6), and additional income-related charges for Medicare (Sect. 16.3.3). For such an important number, I find it astonishing that I could find no instructions on the IRS web site to compute it precisely. The IRS and Social Security Administration compute it for you, using their seemingly secret internal formulas. This leaves you unable to check their computation, although ways to estimate one's MAGI can be found online.[4]

Federal tax on ordinary income is "progressive," in the sense that the tax rate increases across successive *tax brackets*—income ranges delineated by successively increasing *marginal tax rates*. So, if your ordinary income crosses a tax bracket, you pay more tax on the last dollar earned than on the first dollar earned. Your *effective tax rate* for ordinary income is the ratio of your ordinary income tax to your taxable ordinary income, and your *marginal* ordinary income tax rate is the rate paid on your last ordinary income dollar.[5]

The 2019 federal marginal tax rates for ordinary income[6] and the tax rates for long-term capital gains, based on taxable income, are given in Fig. 12.1.

For example, if you are single and your ordinary income is \$150,000, you pay ordinary income tax of 10% of the first \$9700 of that \$150,000, or \$970; plus 12% of the next \$29,775 (\$39,475 − \$9700), or \$3573; plus 22% of the next \$44,725 (\$84,200 − \$39,475), or \$9,839.50; plus 24% of the last

---

[4] e.g., https://money.howstuffworks.com/personal-finance/personal-income-taxes/how-to-calculate-modified-adjusted-gross-income.htm=tinyurl.com/y6ytwwb9.

[5] There is another tax rate worth contemplating: your "actual" tax rate, being the ratio of your total tax to your *gross* income. This tax rate can be very low, especially for those of considerable wealth, who can use myriad deductions and tax "loopholes" through which tax on income is circumvented.

[6] Although tax tables usually are said to be based on *taxable* income, since the progressive ordinary income tax rates apply only to ordinary income, it is more accurate to say that the tax tables are based on *ordinary* income.

Marginal Tax Rate	Single	Married, filing jointly	Married, filing separately	Head of household
10%	$9,700	$19,400	$9,700	$13,850
12%	$39,475	$78,950	$39,475	$52,850
22%	$84,200	$168,400	$84,200	$84,200
24%	$160,725	$321,450	$160,725	$160,700
32%	$204,100	$408,200	$204,100	$204,100
35%	$510,300	$612,350	$306,175	$510,300
37%	remainder	remainder	remainder	remainder
Long-Term Capital Gains Tax Rate				
0%	$39,375	$78,750	$39,375	$52,750
15%	$434,550	$488,850	$244,425	$461,700
20%	all greater	all greater	all greater	all greater

Fig. 12.1 2019 federal tax brackets. The marginal rates apply to ordinary income, and the gains rates apply to taxable income, through the respective amounts shown in the table.

$65,800 ($150,000 − $84,200), or $15,792; which amounts to a total tax of $30,174.50. The effective tax rate is 20.1%: $30,174.50/$150,000, while the marginal tax rate—the rate on the last $65,800 earned—is 24%.

Long-term capital gains refers to gains in the value of capital assets (like equity, fixed income investments, and real estate) held for over a year. The gains are taxed at a generally advantageous rate when the assets are sold. Gains over a shorter period are deemed *short-term* and are taxed at the ordinary income tax rate. (Although bond *interest* generally is taxed at the ordinary income rate, a bond that is sold for a profit over its acquisition price incurs a capital gain.)

Tax on long-term capital gains is also progressive, but only starting at the level of ordinary income. Thus, for example, referring to Fig. 12.1, if you are single, with ordinary income of $30,000 and long-term capital gains of $20,000, then you pay 0% tax on the first $9375 of the gains (the portion between your ordinary income and the 0% bracket limit) and 15% on the rest. Your $50,000 of taxable income puts you in the 15% long-term capital gains tax bracket, but you pay that 15% only on the amount on top of your ordinary income that exceeds the 0% bracket. In principle, one thus could pay respective parts of a long-term capital gain at each of the three possible rates.[7] If you are single, have a taxable long-term capital gain of $20,000, and your ordinary income is $150,000 (so, over $39,395, but no more than $434,550), then (referring to Fig. 12.1), your tax on the capital gain is simply 15% of that gain (so, in this case, not progressive—your ordinary income puts you in the 15% gains bracket and your gain keeps you there).

Analogous to the effective ordinary income tax rate, the *effective long-term capital gains tax rate* is the total long-term capital gains tax[8] divided by the total long-term capital gains. Thus, in the first example, this would be $(1 - \$9375/\$20,000) \times 15\% = 8\%$, while in the second, more typical example, the effective rate is simply the bracket rate.

For tax payers with long-term capital gains that fall in the 0% bracket, Michael Kitces[9] suggests "harvesting" the gains by "selling the investments that are up, and buying them back again immediately (without any wash sale rules to navigate!)," to get a step-up in basis "without any (Federal) tax liability!". He warns that this nonetheless generates income that could affect "certain deductions and tax credits, and the taxation of Social Security $\cdots$ and Roth conversions." It also could count as income on state tax returns.

By the new (2017) tax law, after 2018, the tax bracket income ranges are adjusted for inflation using the chained urban consumer price index (C-CPI-U), generally less than the CPI-U, the urban consumer price index that the IRS has used previously.

For those with higher incomes, there is a 3.8% "net investment income tax".[10] It applies to married couples who file jointly with a modified adjusted gross income (MAGI) of more than $250,000, to married couples who file separately with a MAGI over $125,000, and to single and head of household filers with a MAGI over $200,000. It attaches to investment income: capital gains, dividends, interest, royalties, IRA distributions, and rollovers to a Roth.

---

[7] The net investment income tax described below can inflate the rates by 3.8% for higher-income tax payers.

[8] Plus the applicable net investment income tax—see below.

[9] kitces.com/blog/understanding-the-mechanics-of-the-0-long-term-capital-gains-tax-rate-how-to-harvest-capital-gains-for-a-free-step-up-in-basis = tinyurl.com/s2vpz3j.

[10] This tax came about as a part of the 2010 Health Care and Education Reconciliation Act but took effect only in 2013, with the Affordable Healthcare legislation. It also is referred to as the "Unearned Income Medicare Contribution Tax" or "3.8% Medicare Surtax" (although it does not go to the Medicare Trust Fund). There is another unrelated 0.9% Medicare tax on earned income that also is called "the Medicare Surtax."

In addition, for individuals enrolled in Medicare parts B (medical insurance) or D (prescription drug coverage), there is a graduated income-based premium surcharge. This surcharge shows up as an "income-related monthly adjustment amount" or IRMAA that typically is deducted from Social Security payments. It generally is based on one's MAGI of 2 years before, so you have up to 2 years before you actually pay it. However, if you just retired from a highly paid job, now earning very little, you are smacked with a big IRMAA nonetheless. In 2020 (based on the 2018 MAGI), the thresholds were as follows. For married couples who file jointly with a MAGI over $174,000, the surcharge was a bit less than 0.4% of the premium for Medicare part B and 0.08% for Medicare part D. The successive MAGI thresholds for married couples filing jointly were $218,000, $272,000, $326,000, and $750,000. After the highest threshold, the surcharge was 0.56% for part B and 0.1% for part D—all down from 3 years earlier, despite the ever surging medical costs.[11]

12.8 Tax-Deferred vs. Ordinary Investment

Now, armed with a good understanding of federal taxation, let's return to tax-deferred investments. Remember: the price of deferring tax is to pay ordinary income tax on the total investment, when withdrawn, while after-tax equity investments are subject to the preferential capital gains tax rate. So, which is better, a tax-deferred or ordinary investment?

Mostly, *tax-deferred* is better: if your effective tax rate in retirement will be less than now; in many cases even when it won't; and in almost all cases if your employer matches 50% of your contribution. These are shown next.

let's do the calculation
Let's compare two options: Option A is an investment in a tax-deferred account, and Option B is the same investment in an ordinary (taxable, after-tax) account. Assume first that the investment grows over time, and let $R > 1$ be the appreciation factor over the investment period, so an investment of S yields SR at the end of the investment period, when cashed out, before subtracting taxes.

Consider first the case when the tax-deferred account gets no employer-matching contribution.

---

[11] For the complete schedule, see medicare.gov/Pubs/pdf/11579-Medicare-Costs.pdf, or, as the location keeps changing, search for "Medicare costs" or "Medicare Premiums: Rules For Higher-Income Beneficiaries."

12 Pre-retirement Investment   235

Let t_1 be the effective ordinary income tax rate under Option B (ordinary investment), at the time of the investment of after-tax dollars, and let t_2 be the effective ordinary income tax rate under Option A (tax-deferred), when the accrued funds are withdrawn some years later.

Assume that the investment is 100% in equities, thus getting a worse tax treatment in a tax-deferred account where ordinary income tax is levied upon withdrawal, than in an after-tax, taxed account, where long-term capital gains get preferential tax treatment. So this is the worst case for a tax-deferred account, compared with holdings that include some fixed income investments.

For an investment of S, with Option A, when sold, the after-tax net is $(1 - t_2)SR$—paying ordinary income tax on the entire investment (basis and appreciation). With Option B, one first pays tax on S and thus, after tax, invests only $(1 - t_1)S$.

Although with Option A, one pays tax at a higher rate at the end, in the meantime, the amount one otherwise would have paid in income tax with Option B appreciates along with the rest of the investment.

Under Option B, when the investment is redeemed, only long-term capital gains tax is due on the gains (since the investment was assumed to be all in equities), netting the basis (principal) $(1-t_1)S$ plus the after-tax gain. In total, for effective long-term capital gains tax rate t_3 at the time of withdrawal, this is

$$(1 - t_1)S + (1 - t_1)S(R - 1)(1 - t_3) \tag{12.1}$$

where, for simplicity, I'm ignoring reinvested dividends, which, if considered, increase the benefit of Option A over Option B.[12]

Thus, Option A (investing pre-tax dollars in a tax-deferred plan) wins over Option B (investing the same income, after tax, with no tax advantage) if and only if

$$(1 - t_2)SR > (1 - t_1)S + (1 - t_1)S(R - 1)(1 - t_3) \tag{12.2}$$

or, when $t_1 - t_2 + t_3(1 - t_1) > 0$

$$R > \frac{t_3(1 - t_1)}{t_1 - t_2 + t_3(1 - t_1)}$$

---

[12] If R included the effect of dividends reinvested at the Option B after-tax rate, then R understates the Option A appreciation rate (since Option A dividends are not taxed). Thus, the result would understate the benefit of Option A over Option B.

236   R. P. Kurshan

which is true when $t_2 \leq t_1$ (i.e., if the effective tax rate upon withdrawal is no more than the effective tax rate upon investment). Note that in the cases that Option A wins, for the reasons given above, it thus also wins for any mixed investment and for reinvested dividends.

If your employer matches 50% of your contribution (see Sect. 12.1), then the left-hand side of (12.2) gets multiplied by $b = 1.5$, expanding your pre-tax investment to Sb. Then Option A wins over Option B provided

$$R > \frac{t_3(1 - t_1)}{t_1 + b(1 - t_2) - 1 + t_3(1 - t_1)} \tag{12.3}$$

and this inequality holds whenever $t_2 \leq (2/3)t_1 + 1/3$.

examples
When $t_1 = 24\%$ and $t_2 = 32\%$, Option A still wins if the time to retirement is long enough (15 years, with the investment growing at 9%/year).

In fact, for many typical cases, Option A (the tax-deferred option) wins.

If $t_1 = t_2 = 24\%$, then after 20 years growing at an average annual rate of 9% (about average for the S&P 500), Option A gives at least a 14% greater expected after-tax savings over Option B.

For recent tax brackets, (12.3) holds for all marginal and thus for all effective income tax rates (for any $R > 1$), so with a 50% employer match, Option A (tax-deferred plan) always wins. Even adding local taxes of up to 8%, Option A still always wins.

With no employer match, if $t_2 > t_1 + t_3(1 - t_1)$, then Option B wins for any $R > 0$, so for $t_3 = 15\%$, if $t_1 = 10\%$ and $t_2 \geq 24\%$ or $t_1 = 22\%$ and $t_2 \geq 34\%$—both extreme examples—Option B wins. However, when young, deciding whether to invest in a 401(k), it might be hard, since by retirement, income will be so much higher. And thinking ahead to then, one might well reason: Well, if I become very rich, then having chosen disadvantageously when young to invest in a 401(k) probably won't matter to me. But if in retirement my income is less than now, then having invested in a 401(k) now will prove to have been the better choice. In this case, the better choice lengthens the period of time that savings will support retirement.

With a 50% employer match, after 20 years of 9% growth with $t_1 = t_2 = 24\%$, the tax-deferred account (Option A) leaves an expected after-tax balance that is 71% greater than the non-tax-deferred account. If the same contribution S continued over n years (normally, it increases each year), then the ratio of the two total after-tax account balances is

12 Pre-retirement Investment   237

$$\frac{b(1 - t_2)Q}{n(1 - t_1)t_3 + (1 - t_1)(1 - t_3)Q}$$

where here $n = 20$ and $Q = 1.09^n + 1.09^{n-1} + \cdots + 1.09 = 55.76$ by (A.2), so the total expected after-tax balance is 66% greater for the tax-deferred account than for the non-tax-deferred account. That's a quarter million after-tax dollars more for annual investments of \$10,000.

If instead of all equity, part or all is held in fixed income investments, then the tax-deferred plan is even more advantageous, since for after-tax investments, ordinary income tax on the fixed income investment interest is due every year, instead of only at the end. (Consider the fixed income investments separately: the same tax rate applies either way, but with Option A, the accrued interest is allowed to appreciate before taxes are paid.)

What if the investment suffers a loss ($R < 1$)? Then ordinary income tax is still due on the cashed out amount with Option A, but with Option B, there is a long-term capital loss. If one had other capital gains, then the long-term capital loss can be used (or carried over to subsequent years) to offset these gains, and thus the loss can be considered to have a cash value of $(1 - t_1)S(1 - R)t_3$, based on the long-term capital gains tax rate t_3 on the amount of the loss. Therefore, for the case that $R < 1$, the cash-out value of Option B is

$$(1 - t_1)SR + (1 - t_1)S(1 - R)t_3 = (1 - t_1)S + (1 - t_1)S(R - 1)(1 - t_3)$$

where the right-hand side is the same as (12.1) for $R > 1$. (When $R < 1$, the negative term $(1 - t_1)(R - 1)(1 - t_3)$ has the effect of discounting the loss by the amount of the tax credit for the long-term capital loss.) Thus, the expressions (12.2) and (12.3) (in case of the employer supplement) give the conditions for Option A to win over Option B.

In case of the employer supplement, (12.3) holds for all $R > 0.8$ and for $R > 0.486$ if $t_1 \geq 22\%$.

The largest drop of the stock market over a sustained period was during the Great Depression, when between September, 1929, and May, 1932, it dropped to less than 20% of what it had been (and took 26 years to recover back to where it had been, adjusted for inflation). As it was recovering, by May, 1942, it had dropped again to 39.5% of what it had been in February, 1937. The next biggest drop over a sustained period was during the 1973–1974 recession, where in September, 1974, it had dropped to 45% of what it had been in December, 1972 (and took 14 years to recover). After that, in the recent 2009 Great Recession, the market dropped to 51% of what it had been (and recovered back to where it had been, adjusted for inflation, in 6 years).

238   R. P. Kurshan

There was a comparable drop when the dot-com bubble burst in 2001 (but took 14 years to recover)—all figures adjusted for inflation. Other drops were substantially less.

Since you probably don't plan on investing to lose, the cases for $R < 1$ may not be particularly useful for planning, but may be reassuring with regard to a decision to invest in a 401(k). The worst cases are singular points in time, over relatively short investment periods—if you withdrew the funds a little sooner or a little later, or invested over a longer period, the effective R would be much greater. So, for the most part, even when $R < 0$, Option A (investing in a tax-deferred plan) wins.

Incidentally, if $R = 1$, then with no employer supplement, Option A wins if and only if $t_2 < t_1$, and with the employer supplement, Option A still wins no matter the effective tax rates, as can be seen directly from (12.3).

The same calculations govern the decision whether to invest in a traditional IRA while employed, except an IRA is subject to more severe contribution limits as described in Sect. 12.3 and has no employer supplement.

12.9 Roth vs. Ordinary Investment

What about a Roth 401(k) defined contribution plan, or a Roth IRA, two primary examples of tax-exempt accounts, into which after-tax income is invested? Between these and a non-tax-advantaged investment, the Roths win, as long as the investments experience positive average growth.

let's do the calculation
Let's go through the same Option A/B exercise with these to determine the benefit of investing in a Roth. With Option A, you invest after-tax dollars in a Roth 401(k) or Roth IRA. Assume first that the investments experience positive average growth with long-term appreciation factor $R > 1$. Clearly, Option A is better than Option B, which behaves the same, but with its gains and income taxed, ultimately or periodically (in the case of bonds or other interest-producing investments).

When $R = 1$, there is no tax consequence so the options are equivalent.

If $R < 1$, then the non-Roth (Option B) produces a long-term capital loss for stocks (which has value if you use it or carry it over to future years, to offset long-term capital gains). The Roth has no such benefit.[13] Therefore, if

---

[13] If you have a loss on *all* your IRAs of the same type (Roth or traditional) combined, then you can realize a capital loss by withdrawing all assets from all IRAs of that type.

12 Pre-retirement Investment 239

you plan on investing stocks in a losing manner, it is better not to put them in a Roth. Moreover, with a Roth, you lose the tax benefit of "realizing" losses even if over the long term, your investment gains. Some investors like to reap the tax benefits of realizing losses by selling temporarily depressed stocks and replacing them with others, even though later, the ultimate gain is bigger. This can be an advantage if you are in a higher tax bracket when you realize your losses than later when you realize an associated gain.

If you have only bonds in your Roth, then even if their price decreases ($R < 1$), you pay no tax on the dividends, unlike with an ordinary investment. However, you still can take a capital loss with an ordinary investment (but not with a Roth). The winner in this case depends on which is greater, the taxes on interest or the capital loss.

12.10 Traditional 401(k) or IRA vs. Roth

Finally, let's compare the relative benefit of investing in a traditional 401(k) or IRA, with that of the corresponding Roth. The "traditional" investments are pre-tax, but taxed as ordinary income when withdrawn. The Roth investments are post-tax, and no further taxes are due. The allowed contribution limit is the same for each, and neither is subject to salary caps.

Which option wins is more nuanced than in the cases discussed in the previous sections. The two most influential factors for determining whether it is more beneficial to invest in a Roth or in a traditional tax-advantaged account are (1) the relationship between the growth rate of the tax-advantaged investment and that of the funds used to pay the taxes, in case of a Roth investment; and (2) the relationship between the effective tax rates at the beginning and end of the investment term (usually, retirement).

The more influential is (1): if the tax-advantaged investment has the better growth rate, then a Roth wins, for a broad range of effective tax rates (2). This better growth is the case if the tax-advantaged account holds equities (contravening conventional investment industry advice—Sect. 12.12), while the taxes are paid from your checking account.

If the expected rate of return of the tax-advantaged account is significantly lower than that of the funds from which taxes are paid, then it is unlikely that a Roth is advantageous. (So, don't hold bonds in your Roth while paying your taxes by selling equity.)

When both the tax-advantaged account and ordinary savings have the same expected rate of growth, the Roth potentially can still be more beneficial than a traditional 401(k) or IRA in the early years of employment when earnings are substantially lower than those expected during retirement (when income can include investment returns, Social Security, a pension, and RMDs). However, as soon as one starts to earn "serious money," it is more likely that a traditional 401(k) or IRA is a better deal than a Roth.

Both options have the opportunity for an employer bonus. With both options, that bonus is pre-tax, invested in a traditional 401(k) (taxed as ordinary income when withdrawn), so the effect on both options is identical, and for the purposes of our comparison, we thus can ignore it.

Investing in a Roth increases your effective tax rate over what it would have been with a pre-tax investment into a 401(k). (You pay ordinary income tax on the Roth investment.) This can push your income across the next tax bracket. It is possible that an advantage conferred by a Roth 401(k) is limited to a level of contributions that do not do this. In this case, consider allocating to the Roth only a smaller portion that keeps your tax bracket unchanged, with the rest going to a traditional tax-deferred account.

let's do the calculation

Let Option A be to invest S pre-tax dollars in a traditional 401(k) or IRA and Option B be to invest S after-tax dollars in a Roth. Since the same investment amount S is allowed for a traditional 401(k) or IRA and a Roth, for Option B, we must account separately for the taxes paid on S.

As before, let $R > 1$ be the appreciation factor of an investment S over the investment period (typically, until retirement), but where now we can assume that pre-tax dividends and interest have been reinvested. Let t_1 be the current effective tax rate with Option B (Roth) (higher than with Option A, since in Option B, the after-tax investment S is part of ordinary income). Finally, let t_2 be the effective tax rate at the end of the investment period that applies to the traditional 401(k) or IRA when its funds are withdrawn. Assume that the income taxes due on S are paid from non-tax-advantaged funds that are invested with appreciation factor $R' > 1$, after-tax interest and dividends reinvested, over the same investment period. Then the overall expected value of Option B at the end of the investment period, after taxes are deducted, is

$$SR - t_1 S - t_1 S(R' - 1)(1 - t_3)$$

where the last term accounts for the lost opportunity cost of paying the taxes $t_1 S$ at the time of the investment, and t_3 is the effective capital gains tax rate[14] if the taxes are paid from equity, else $t_3 = 0$.

---

[14]The nominal rate adjusted slightly downward to account for the dividends in R'.

12 Pre-retirement Investment 241

A necessary and sufficient condition for Option B (Roth) to be better than Option A (traditional) thus is

$$SR(1 - t_2) < SR - t_1 S - t_1 S(R' - 1)(1 - t_3)$$

or, equivalently, when $t_2 > 0$,

$$R > \frac{t_1}{t_2} \left((1 - t_3)R' + t_3 \right) \tag{12.4}$$

examples
If R and R' are based on annual growth rates that are $\leq 4\%$ and $\geq 7\%$, respectively, and retirement is 8 or more years away, then (12.4) fails for $t_1 \geq t_2 > 0$, so Option A (traditional) wins. These growth rate bounds are typical of the case in which the tax-advantaged accounts contain fixed income investments, while the tax on the Roth is paid by selling after-tax equities. This combination (fixed income investments in tax-advantaged, equities in non-tax-advantaged) is (mostly wrongly) recommended by the investment industry (see Sect. 12.12). Later in one's career, one can expect the effective tax rate t_1, while working, to be greater than the t_2 rate, when retired. So, if one follows the investment industry recommendations, then a traditional tax-deferred investment would be expected to fare better than a Roth.

Early in one's career, with a relatively low salary, one might expect that if $t_1 \leq t_2$, then Option B (Roth) wins. However, for $R \leq R'$, there is only a relatively narrow set of conditions for this outcome. One is that current salary falls in one of the two lowest tax brackets, while by retirement, at most 28 years away, the effective tax rate at least doubles, while R and R' are based on annual growth rates of $\geq 4\%$ and $\leq 7\%$, respectively. Another is that $R' = R$ (and $t_1 \leq t_2$), so (12.4) holds.

The reader can check for other particular conditions by plotting (12.4) with the *desmos.com/calculator/*, using sliders to adjust the parameters.

What about $R > R'$? This case can arise if, contrary to investment industry advice (Sect. 12.12), the 401(k) or IRA is invested with equity, and fixed income investments are held in an ordinary (non-tax-advantaged) account and used to pay the tax on the Roth investment. (Then R' is the appreciation factor of the fixed income investments, so $t_3 = 0$.) In this case, if $t_1 \leq t_2$, then (12.4) is satisfied, and thus Option B (Roth) wins. In fact, since $t_3 = 0$, Option B wins as long as $R/R' > t_1/t_2$. Thus, for example, in 2019 (Fig. 12.1), if the equity grew annually at $\geq 7\%$, the fixed income investments at $\leq 4\%$,

242   R. P. Kurshan

with retirement at least 20 years away and effective retirement income tax rate $t_2 \geq 22\%$, Option B (Roth) wins.

When $R < 1$ (the investment lost value), then under differing circumstances, either the traditional or the Roth may do better. Since for stocks, in this case, the Roth always does worse than a taxed investment (Sect. 12.9), the traditional does better than the Roth in the cases that it does better than an investment with no tax advantage (Sect. 12.8).

12.11   Rollovers

"Rollover" simply means conversion from one tax-advantaged fund to another tax-advantaged fund.

You can roll a 401(k) over to a traditional IRA, without fees or tax consequences.[15] You should do this when you leave the company that supports the 401(k), as the alternative of withdrawing the funds has severe tax consequences: you must pay ordinary income tax on the entire amount, and, if under age 59 1/2, you must pay an additional 10% early withdrawal penalty.

You also can roll a 401(k) or a traditional IRA—or any part of it—over to a Roth IRA after paying ordinary income tax on the total amount of the rollover (without incurring any transaction fees). Is this profitable? There are many in the investment industry who say it is, unequivocally. The correct answer is "it depends": on essentially the same criteria as for investing in a Roth in the first place (Sect. 12.10). If the tax-deferred account to be rolled over has a greater growth rate than the fund from which taxes on the rollover are paid, then it generally is profitable, otherwise mostly not.

Before retirement, we use the "Option A/Option B" calculation of Sect. 12.10 to determine whether it's favorable to roll a traditional 401(k) or IRA over to a Roth IRA. After retirement, the considerations are very different, but the answer, perhaps unexpectedly, is largely the same (Sect. 13.2).

other considerations
Forget those apps that tell you which is better for you—they mostly don't consider all the relevant parameters and therefore produce questionable or unfounded results.

---

[15] If you are over the age of 70 1/2, or, starting in 2020, age 72 if you did not reach 70 1/2 yet, you must pay any RMDs due on the amount rolled over.

If you are rolling over to a Roth during a period of lower income, be sure that you can afford to pay the tax on the rollover. Since a rollover to a Roth IRA counts as ordinary income, making a rollover to a Roth IRA can push you into a higher tax bracket. To avoid this, you can roll a 401(k) over to a traditional IRA and then make partial rollovers from that IRA to a Roth IRA in successive years, with the partial rollovers calibrated to keep you in the same tax bracket.

A rollover to a Roth also can push you over eligibility thresholds for college aid and other benefits aimed at lower-income individuals.

And don't forget the effect of state taxes on a rollover to a Roth. If you are planning to move to a state with a lower tax rate, you may benefit by deferring the rollover until after you have moved, and conversely.

There are some states that reduce or even eliminate state taxes on retirement income. In such a state, a rollover to a Roth can be less attractive, as the state taxes on distributions from a traditional IRA are reduced (or eliminated)—although federal tax remains.

Finally, there are two extra taxes that IRA distributions and rollovers can trigger. For higher-income taxpayers, there is the 3.8% "net investment income tax" and the graduated tax adding to Medicare premiums for individuals enrolled in Medicare parts B or D. See Sect. 12.7. To accurately calculate the potential benefit and optimal size of a rollover, these taxes need to be taken into account.

For company stock in a 401(k), there are special tax-advantaged "net unrealized appreciation" (NUA) rules that generally are more advantageous than rolling the stock into a Roth IRA.[16]

It is essential that a rollover follows strict IRS rules, or it risks losing its beneficial tax status. If you want to perform a rollover, unless you are very confident of the required steps, it's best to have it done by the recipient financial institution. They can assure that it's performed according to IRS rules and that the tax benefit is maintained.

---

[16]irs.gov/taxtopics/tc412.

12.12 Bonds Go in an IRA, Equity Doesn't?

Mostly wrong! Although that's the traditional investment industry strategy,[17] calculations show that for typical cases, it can be better to hold fixed income investments in ordinary (taxed, after-tax[18]) savings and put equities in a tax-advantaged account (i.e., an IRA). That is demonstrated in this section.

Equity invested in a tax-deferred account stands to lose more to taxes, because any capital gain in a tax-deferred account, when withdrawn, is taxed at the ordinary income tax rate. A capital gain in an investment held for over a year in an ordinary account is taxed at the generally lower long-term capital gains tax rate (see Sect. 12.7). Moreover, mostly,[19] no benefit accrues from a capital loss inside a tax-deferred account. In an ordinary account, a capital loss can be used to offset capital gains, for tax purposes, and unused losses can be carried over to subsequent years.

Fixed income investment income (interest) is taxed as ordinary income either way, but in a tax-deferred account, that tax is deferred until withdrawal.

For these reasons, the investment industry commonly recommends to hold fixed income investments (e.g., bonds) in a 401(k) or IRA,[20] in order to defer taxes on its interest, and equity in an ordinary account, to obtain the tax benefits of capital gains and losses.

Let's test this investment industry strategy. We find it's mostly incorrect, especially when we include the opportunity to roll a traditional IRA over to a Roth. For a broad range of parameters, deferring tax on dividends is more valuable than the capital gains tax rate advantage.

let's do the calculation

I plotted[21] the tradeoffs, shown in Fig. 12.2. Define the following parameters:

- E: expected equity growth rate
- d: expected equity dividend yield

---

[17] E.g., vanguard.com/pdf/ISGIRA11.pdf [now moved or deleted, but see mention in personal.vanguard.com/pdf/goals-based-retirement-spending.pdf], fidelity.com/viewpoints/investing-ideas/asset-allocation-lower-taxes.

[18] Note that a Roth account is an *untaxed* after-tax account.

[19] See footnote 13, Sect. 12.9.

[20] An exception is tax-free municipal bonds and the like. One pays extra for the tax-free feature (through accepting a lower interest rate), an advantage that is squandered if they are placed in a tax-advantaged account.

[21] Desmos.com/calculator/plot.

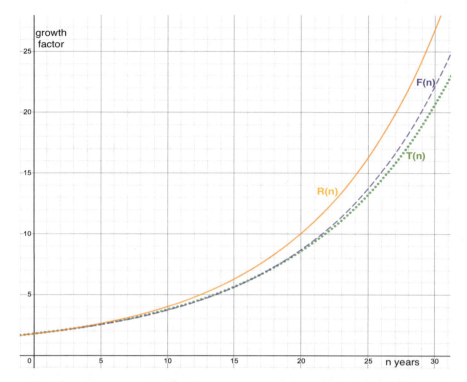

Fig. 12.2 Investment strategy growth factors. *T(n)* is for the *traditional* investment industry strategy of putting fixed income investments in a traditional IRA and equity in ordinary savings; *F(n) flips* this, putting equity in the IRA and fixed income investments in ordinary savings; *R(n)* is for *flip and roll*, using the *flip* strategy with a rollover of the IRA to a Roth, with taxes paid from the fixed income investments.

- i: expected fixed income investment interest rate
- t_1: effective tax rate during investment
- t_2: effective tax rate at end of investment period (in retirement)
- t_3: effective capital gains tax rate at end of investment period

Assume that equal amounts are invested in an IRA and in ordinary (not tax-advantaged) savings. I compute the growth factor over a period of n years for three different investment strategies: the *traditional* investment industry strategy of fixed income investments in a traditional IRA, equity in ordinary savings, producing growth factor $T(n)$; *flipping* that strategy, putting equity in a traditional IRA, fixed income investments in ordinary savings, producing growth factor $F(n)$; and *flip and roll*, putting equity in a traditional IRA, rolled

246   R. P. Kurshan

over to a Roth IRA, fixed income investments in ordinary savings, with taxes on the rollover paid from the fixed income investments, producing growth factor $R(n)$.[22]

example

Figure 12.2 shows the relations among the growth factors for $E = 7.6\%$, the average S&P 500 growth between 1950 and 2015, $d = 3.4\%$, the average dividend in the same period,[23] $i = 4.97\%$, the average interest in the same period for 10-year Treasury notes,[24] $t_1 = 24\%$, $t_2 = 22\%$, and $t_3 = 15\%$. For the chosen parameter values, the ratio $R(n)/T(n)$ for $n = 10, 15, 20, 25, 30, 35$ is quite significant: 106%, 111%, 117%, 123%, 130%, and 137%, respectively. The reason for this "unexpected" behavior is that after 19 years, the value of equity in the IRA exceeds the value of equity in ordinary savings, despite its better tax treatment in ordinary savings, on account of the extra growth afforded by the untaxed dividends. After 30 years, it exceeds by over 10%. After 22 years, the value of fixed income investments in the IRA exceeds the value of fixed income investments held in ordinary savings, but by 30 years, it exceeds by only 1%. The relationships between T, F, and R remain unchanged for typical ranges of E, d, and i, as well as for $t_1 \geq 20\%$ and $t_2 \leq 29\%$. It is very illuminating to copy the function definitions from footnote 22 into the *desmos.com/calculator/plot* calculator, provide sliders for the parameters, and see how the relationships between $T(n)$, $F(n)$, and $R(n)$ change as the parameters change: the graphs move, but as a unit, maintaining their value relationships in the main interesting ranges of the parameters.

On the other hand, for $t_1 \leq 24\%$, $t_2 > 35\%$, and $12 \leq n \leq 35$, we have $F(n) < T(n)(<< R(n))$ for this extreme case. Still, R is best.

---

[22] For the sum $U(n)$ of the after-tax reinvested dividends that accumulate and grow in equity held n years in ordinary savings, computed using the Appendix formula (A.2), for $a = (1 + E)(1 + d(1 - t_1))$, we find that $U(n) = (1 + E)d(1 - t_1)\left(\frac{a^n - 1}{a - 1}\right)$; we then get $T(n) = (1+i)^n(1-t_2)+1+(a^n - 1)(1 - t_3)+ U(n)t_3$, where the fourth term of $T(n)$ adds back the capital gains tax applied to the dividends in the third term; for $A = (1 + E)(1 + d)$, we get $F(n) = A^n(1 - t_2) + (1 + i(1 - t_1))^n$, and $R(n) = A^n + (1-t_1)(1+i(1-t_1))^n$ where the $(1-t_1)$ factor of the second term of $R(n)$ accounts for the ordinary income tax paid from fixed income investments on the rollover.

[23] For S&P 500 dividend yields over time, see multpl.com/s-p-500-dividend-yield/.

[24] cf. Figure 5.12, Sect. 5.4.2.

summary

For typical parameter values, the traditional investment industry advice to put fixed income investments in an IRA and equity in ordinary savings leads to a growth rate that's inferior to doing the opposite. One obtains the best growth by far by doing the opposite and rolling the traditional IRA over to a Roth. Deferring tax on dividends mostly is more valuable than the capital gains tax rate advantage. Over a period of $n = 20$ years or less, there is little difference between the outcome of the traditional advice and its opposite.

12.13 "Swap" Tax-Advantaged and Ordinary

If you hold both equity and fixed income investments in both tax-advantaged and ordinary accounts, you can effectively exchange some of one in one account with an equal value of the other in the other account, for example, by selling equity in the tax-advantaged account and using the proceeds to buy fixed income investments in the tax-advantaged account, while performing a reciprocal trade in the ordinary account (selling the same value of fixed income investments there to buy equity). This effectively moves equity from the tax-advantaged account to the ordinary account and an equal value of fixed income investments in the opposite direction. (Of course, you cannot do an exchange directly—only virtually, as just explained.)

Some care is required in making this type of virtual exchange in order to avoid violating IRS Code 1091 regarding a "wash sale." A wash sale occurs when a security is sold at a loss and is also bought, within a window from 30 days prior, to 30 days after the sale. The wash is regulated in order to prevent gaining the tax benefit of a loss without materially changing the portfolio. It applies not only to swapping out and back the identical security but also to a "substantially identical" security. In case of a wash sale, the capital loss from the sale is not tax-deductible. If such a loss is small, forgoing its capital loss tax deduction may be worthwhile, to avoid the uncertainty of the price 31 days hence.

12.14 Actively Traded Equities Go in an IRA?

When stocks are actively traded, short-term capital gains (over less than a year) are taxed as ordinary income, and thus with regard to where to hold them, behave like bonds, generating periodic short-term gains (you hope!) taxed as ordinary income.

For this reason the common advice is to hold actively traded stocks in a tax-advantaged account. Presumably, the actively traded equities have better growth rate than equities held long term, else why bother? In this case, the above calculations support the common advice. However, the premise that active trading can be expected to outperform the long-term growth of the S&P 500 is mostly a myth—see Sect. 1.6.1.

13

Tax-Advantaged Savings in Retirement

If you have tax-deferred savings like an IRA, that's great. If you have a Roth IRA, you already have paid taxes on the initial investment, and no further taxes are ever due on its gains, dividends, interest, and, after 5 years, their withdrawals. (The amount invested can be withdrawn at any time.) If you have a traditional IRA, then you pay no taxes until you withdraw from it, but in retirement, there are required minimum distributions (RMDs): annual amounts that you are required to withdraw and pay taxes on the amount withdrawn (Sect. 13.1).

Since IRA income is tax-deferred, you not only defer paying taxes on that income, but the income itself produces income, including on the amount that was saved by deferring taxes. For this reason the investment industry advises to keep as much as is allowed in your tax-deferred accounts, spending after-tax savings first, except for the required annual RMDs. Once your after-tax savings is exhausted, you then draw from your tax-deferred savings, and then finally, from your tax-exempt accounts.

In fact, this is not the best strategy. Moreover, there are inherent contradictions in this advice. The investment industry advises placing fixed income investments like bonds in tax-advantaged accounts (Sect. 12.12), in order to defer taxes on its interest, and yet mostly fixed income investments should be used to pay for expenses: for the 40% of the time that the equity markets are depressed or recovering (Sect. 5.4). They also advise to keep equity in non-tax-advantaged accounts (to take advantage of the lower capital gains tax). But if these accounts are drawn down first, then for the same 40% of the time, depressed equities are sold for expenses, leading to a degradation of savings.

© The Author(s), under exclusive license to Springer Nature Switzerland AG 2022 **249**
R. P. Kurshan, *Investment Industry Claims Debunked*,
https://doi.org/10.1007/978-3-030-76709-9_13

250 R. P. Kurshan

A better withdrawal policy is presented in Sect. 13.4, including the "flip and roll" strategy from Sect. 12.12 that places equity in an IRA that is rolled over to a Roth. As explained in Sect. 13.4, once sufficient fixed-income investments have been allocated to the retirement expenses fund for near-term expenses, of the remaining investments in the retirement expenses fund, those with the least growth rate should be drawn down first, irrespective of whether they are tax-advantaged.

13.1 RMD

Once you turn 70 1/2 or, under the 2019 SECURE Act, starting in 2020, age 72 if you did not reach 70 1/2 yet, federal tax law requires that each year, you take a "required minimum distribution" (RMD) from your tax-deferred savings. The required amount is based on the total savings in all your tax-deferred accounts at the end of the preceding year, and that amount can be taken from any one or more of those accounts—all that matters is that the total required amount is taken. It can be taken any time during the year. The later in the year that it is taken, the longer the amount can grow tax-deferred. The amount taken is taxed as ordinary income (at "tax time": April 15 of the following year).

The resulting taxes can be surprising and unwelcome: you feel that your income is low—which by all outward measures it may well be—but when you look at your 1040 tax return, your recorded income can be high, increased by the RMD. In fact, that increase might even push you into a higher tax bracket than without it.

Payment of the first RMD may be deferred until April 1 of the year following the year that the age of 70 1/2 was attained (or, starting in 2020, age 72 if you did not reach 70 1/2 yet). See Sect. 12.4 for the details. However, doing so requires the payment of two RMDs in a single year: one by April 1 and one by December 31. This double RMD also can push you into a higher tax bracket, so whether or not the deferral is a good idea requires some calculation.

There is one possible exception to the RMD. If you have been working throughout an entire year and have not retired by December 31 of that year (meaning that you are still working for at least part of the following year— even just a day is enough), a 401(k) associated with that employment may be exempt from the RMD calculation, provided some other technical conditions are met. See Sects. 12.1 and 12.3.

The RMD is a percent of the total value of all your tax-deferred investments. The percent generally increases year by year and is a function of the age

13 Tax-Advantaged Savings in Retirement 251

Table III (Uniform Lifetime)

Age	Distribution Period	Age	Distribution Period	Age	Distribution Period	Age	Distribution Period
70	27.4	82	17.1	94	9.1	106	4.2
71	26.5	83	16.3	95	8.6	107	3.9
72	25.6	84	15.5	96	8.1	108	3.7
73	24.7	85	14.8	97	7.6	109	3.4
74	23.8	86	14.1	98	7.1	110	3.1
75	22.9	87	13.4	99	6.7	111	2.9
76	22.0	88	12.7	100	6.3	112	2.6
77	21.2	89	12.0	101	5.9	113	2.4
78	20.3	90	11.4	102	5.5	114	2.1
79	19.5	91	10.8	103	5.2	115 and over	1.9
80	18.7	92	10.2	104	4.9		
81	17.9	93	9.6	105	4.5		

Fig. 13.1 IRS RMD table—spouse ≤10 years younger. The RMD percent of IRA value is the reciprocal of the distribution period.

difference between you and your spouse. The RMD for the beneficiary of a traditional IRA, with a spouse that is less than or equal to 10 years younger than you or is not the sole beneficiary of your IRA, can be extracted from the IRS table[1] in Fig. 13.1. With typical clarity, the IRS provides not the number you need, but its inverse. Find your age, say 73, and the corresponding "distribution period" (how long they allow that you may live), in this case 24.7 years; the percent of your tax-deferred accounts that must be distributed (the RMD) is the inverse of the distribution period, in this case, 1/24.7 = 4.05% (rounded to two decimal places). The percentages range from approximately 3.65% at age 70, 5.35% at age 80, 8.77% at age 90, 15.87% at age 100, 32.26% at age 110, and 52.63% at age 115 and beyond. You see: the IRS graciously doesn't increase your distribution percent after you pass age 115 (by then, your IRA balance won't be more than a few dollars[2]).

Since RMDs from several traditional IRAs can all be satisfied from one or more of the IRAs, you may be able to avoid selling investments disadvantageously. If one IRA is invested with shares of a stock that presently is depressed in value and thus you do not want to sell it to satisfy its RMD, then you can satisfy its RMD from another traditional IRA (together with that IRA's RMD).

Withholding from the RMD some or all income taxes due for the tax year (including state and local income taxes) potentially avoids the need to pay estimated taxes throughout the year. This can be a very handy way to pay taxes

---

[1] irs.gov/pub/irs-tege/uniform_rmd_wksht.pdf = tinyurl.com/ycd6qhj3.

[2] The effect of RMDs per Fig. 13.1 leaves 64% at age 80, 31% by 90, 8% by 100, 0.6% by 110, and 0.038% at 115, after which each RMD reduces the tiny bit left by half.

252   R. P. Kurshan

and defer their payment until December 31. More RMD details are available from the IRS.[3]

prevent RMDs from forcing a loss
What if you must take your RMD by selling stocks whose value is depressed? Won't that result in the very sort of loss we're trying to avoid? Not necessarily.

Let's say that your RMD is $25,000. On the very same day—in fact, the same minute, if possible—that you take your $25,000 RMD, buy $25,000 worth of what you sold to take your RMD, using the proceeds of the RMD. What you buy, of course, no longer has its income tax-deferred. But other than that, you generally are back to where you started, in terms of the investments in your portfolio.

There is a very small cost due to any management fees (hopefully, none) and the ask-bid spread (you get less when you sell than what you need to pay when you buy back the same shares).

13.2 Roll over a Traditional IRA to a Roth?

This question was addressed for the case of before retirement in Sect. 12.11. The answer after retirement is largely the same, although many conditions and even the question itself change after retirement.

Post-retirement, if one is regularly drawing down investments for living expenses, the question no longer is which option (rollover or no rollover) results in a higher balance at term, but which option confers greater longevity to one's retirement expenses fund as it is drawn down (hence, which supports a longer retirement).

The answer in this case also turns out to be simple and concords with the inequality (12.4), with $t_1 = t_2$. In retirement, assuming a constant effective tax rate, it generally is better to roll a traditional IRA over to a Roth if and only if the IRA has a greater expected growth rate than the funds from which the taxes on the rollover are to be paid. It is always better to pay these taxes from a non-tax-advantaged account. It is assumed that interest and dividends are reinvested—after tax for the non-tax-advantaged account. The expected growth rate of the funds from which taxes on the rollover are paid

---

[3] irs.gov/retirement-plans/retirement-plans-faqs-regarding-required-minimum-distributions = tinyurl. com/gr7dhap.

is before subtraction for capital gains tax, if any. While the answer is simple, the calculations that confirm it[4] take several pages and are beyond the scope of this book.

As in pre-retirement, the "flip and roll" option described in Sect. 12.12 is by far the most advantageous of the various decisions of what investments to place where and whether to roll over to a Roth: flipping the common advice, invest equities in the IRA, and roll it over to a Roth, paying the taxes on the rollover from lesser-growth fixed-income investments. However, it's mostly prudent to do this in sufficiently small annual increments that the additional "income" from the rollover to the Roth doesn't cause a tax bracket to be crossed.

13.3 What to Keep Where

A mix of fixed income investments and equity can be kept in traditional IRAs: just enough fixed income investments (including cash) for drawing down the RMDs, the rest equity, which can be rolled over to a Roth (at once or over time). See Sect. 12.12. Enough fixed-income investments should be kept outside the IRAs to cover expenses (beyond income and RMDs), according to the schedule described in Sect. 11.2. These fixed income investments can be kept as cash in a money market fund or savings bank. Automatic monthly transfers of the cash to one's checking account can be very handy.

If the amount held in fixed income investments is high, say, enough to cover a number of years of expenses, then some may be held in an intermediate bond fund. The bond fund can be converted to cash as needed, in order to hold at least 1 year's worth of fixed income investments as cash (including what's needed in the IRA for the next RMD). All the rest should be held in equity (to be transferred to fixed income investments per Sect. 11.2).

13.4 What Account to Draw First

Say your retirement expenses fund (Sect. 4.6) is held in one or more traditional and Roth IRAs and non-tax-advantaged funds. In what order should you draw them? One at a time? A little from each?

---

[4]Kurshan (2019).

254 R. P. Kurshan

The almost universal advice from the investment industry[5] is to draw down non-tax-advantaged funds first, then traditional IRAs, and finally Roth IRAs, in order to preserve as long as possible the tax advantage of the IRAs and the better tax advantage of the Roths. Sounds right?

Well, it's seems plausible, but it's wrong. One major investment house advises drawing them down in equal proportions,[6] also suboptimal.

The drawdown order that maximizes the expected longevity of the retirement expenses fund is to draw down the investments with the worst growth rate[7] first (Kurshan, *ibid*). This is mostly automatic with the drawdown schedule of Sect. 11.2, when all drawdowns come from fixed income investments.

---

[5] E.g. docplayer.net/13734564-Spending-from-a-portfolio-implications-of-withdrawal-order-for-taxable-investors.html = tinyurl.com/y9ouzr75.

[6] fidelity.com/viewpoints/retirement/tax-savvy-withdrawals.

[7] The growth rates are calculated as in Sect. 13.2: with interest and dividends reinvested, after-tax in non-tax-advantaged accounts, excluding capital gains tax, if any.

14

Tax Relief for Education and Gifts

The U.S. Government allows tax relief for funds used for education and charitable contributions to qualified recipients.

14.1 529 Education Fund

This section describes a way to save taxes in the United States on funds to be used for education.

A *Section 529 plan* is a "Qualified Tuition Program" under the Internal Revenue Code. It permits a type of fund similar to a Roth IRA that allows after-tax investments to grow without incurring federal income tax on gains, and without incurring federal income tax on withdrawals, but only when the funds are used for qualified educational expenses. As of 2018, it can cover accredited K-12, college, and vocational school expenses including tuition, mandatory fees, and for post-secondary school education, computers, printers, often room and board, and more (for which qualifying annual distributions are unlimited). For K-12, distributions are limited to $10,000 per year. Attendance at some foreign schools is also covered.

All 529 plan accounts must be "sponsored" by a state or educational institution that sets up the account and manages it. Many states confer advantages with regard to state tax and some even give matching grants.

© The Author(s), under exclusive license to Springer Nature Switzerland AG 2022 **255**
R. P. Kurshan, *Investment Industry Claims Debunked*,
https://doi.org/10.1007/978-3-030-76709-9_14

256   R. P. Kurshan

There also is a version that allows one to lock in tuition costs at the current price, at a particular college, or list of colleges, but generally cannot be used elsewhere and may have time limitations. Some states, but not the federal government, guarantee such funds, which are dependent on the financial health of the granting institution and thus, like an annuity (Sect. 2.10), are subject to counterparty risk.

The alternative 529 "savings" plan has no limitation on when or where the funds may be spent for qualifying expenses. The savings plans also are not guaranteed by the federal government, with the exception of funds invested in savings bank-type products that are guaranteed by the FDIC. States do not guarantee the savings plans, although there could (hypothetically) be legislative redress for losses due to malfeasance of the sponsoring state's plan manager. However, losses, if any, are the expected result of market underperformance, for which there is no guaranteed cushion.

Contributions to a 529 plan are subject to the annual gift tax limitation of \$15,000 per person (as of 2019, so \$30,000 for a couple) tax free, and may be front-loaded for up to 5 years' worth of contributions, meaning that each person may contribute up to \$75,000 tax free (so \$150,000 per couple), but then may not contribute again for 5 years. The benefit of front-loading is significant, in that it allows the larger contribution to grow tax free for longer. In addition, one's children also may contribute tax free, up to the per-person annual limit.

Up to \$15,000 of funds in a 529 plan may be transferred annually to a 529 ABLE plan, which supports individuals with disabilities (and has its own rules).

Drawing down a 529 plan should be done with care to limit exposure to taxes, penalties, and bureaucracy. It's often best done by transferring funds to the beneficiary. This way, if for some reason the distribution exceeds the qualified expenses, the beneficiary (not the account holder) is taxed (at the beneficiary's tax rate), although if taxes are then due on account of the distribution exceeding qualified expenses, the entire excess is taxed as income (not just the gains on the original contribution to the fund). If the account holder pays the school directly, then the account holder's tax return must include an IRS 1099-Q form, and to avoid taxes and penalties, the account holder must provide appropriate proof that the distribution is qualifying. On the other hand, if funds are transferred directly from the fund to the school, this can alert the school to a source of funding that may cause the school to reduce financial aid. When done right, distributions from a 529 plan are free of federal and most state taxes.

14 Tax Relief for Education and Gifts 257

Since a plan surplus cannot be used for non-qualified expenses without paying a penalty, care should be taken in planning. Compute the expected qualified expenses, the expected growth of contributions before they are distributed, and tailor contributions accordingly, so that the end result leaves no surplus. However, in the worst case, a surplus can be transferred to a new beneficiary that is a relative.

Non-qualified distributions from the plan are subject to taxes plus a 10% penalty, on fund income. The penalty may be waived in some cases that result from a change in circumstances that cause a part of a distribution to become non-qualifying (like a reduction in tuition caused by receiving a scholarship).

A 529 distribution cannot be used for an expense that is claimed as a tax credit, such as the "lifetime learning credit" and the "American opportunity tax credit."

Investments opportunities in a 529 plan are limited to managed funds, under the auspices of an investment company or, in some cases, the state. (The ostensible justification is to ensure that investments reduce risk and volatility.) The available choices vary by state.[1] Investment fees reduce the value of the fund to varying degrees and should be evaluated. In addition to the underlying investment fees, these can include advisor fees, fund manager fees, and even fund maintenance charges. A 529 account holder needs to evaluate these fees and determine whether they provide cost-effective value (which they often *do not*). A prudent choice often is the plan with the lowest fees. The Financial Industry Regulatory Authority (FINRA) has a calculator that helps compute plan costs for one or two alternatives together.[2]

Any person can contribute to a 529 plan (although it must have a single owner). A plan can have only one beneficiary at a time, although the beneficiary can be changed to a relative of the current beneficiary any number of times. A person can own multiple 529 plans, and an individual may receive distributions from multiple plans, within limits set by each state. The 529 account holder and beneficiary maybe the same person. States limit the maximum total amount that may be received by one beneficiary, mostly in excess of $200,000.

Most states allow some deduction for contributions to 529 plans and allow annual tax-free rollovers to another 529 plan, although many states with income taxes assess charges for transferring a plan to another state.

---

[1] plans.collegesavings.org/planComparisonState.aspx.
[2] tools.finra.org/529_calculator/main = tinyurl.com/r63rdld.

There are other tax-advantaged education savings plans, including Education Savings Bonds (eligible U.S. Treasury series EE and I savings bonds) and the Coverdell Education Savings Account, which is more restrictive than a 529 plan, limiting the amount of annual contributions and restricting income level. A 529 plan is generally more flexible than these. Other alternatives include Uniform Gifts to Minors Act (UGMA) accounts and Uniform Transfers to Minors Act (UTMA) accounts, which allow some gains to be taxed at the minor beneficiary's presumably lower tax bracket, as well as distributions for any expenses for the benefit of the minor.

14.2 Charitable Contributions

Before the 2018 U.S. tax "reform" bill passed, one could get a tax offset by itemizing qualified charitable contributions on one's tax return. There were limits (up to 50% of adjusted gross income, although an excess could be carried over to subsequent years). And there were record-keeping requirements: single contributions with cash value greater than $250 required written documentation. Goods contributed to charitable organizations also were deductible, with more stringent record-keeping requirements for goods whose value exceeded $500. In some cases an appraisal was required.

However, with the new 2018 tax code, many taxpayers no longer are able to itemize deductions. If you are on the edge of being able to itemize, one strategy is "bunching": contribute 2 or more years' worth of contributions in a single year (and then forgo contributions in the subsequent years).

For those over age 70 1/2 with a traditional IRA, "qualified charitable distributions" provide a mechanism to subtract donations up to a total of $100,000 from ordinary income, even if taking the standard deduction. This requires some additional paperwork, as the contributions must come directly from the IRA account. The IRA account holder may put limitations on such contributions—for example, presently, Vanguard requires each contribution to be at least $250. Other IRA account holders that offer check-writing privileges from the account have no such limitation. As with other tax-deductible charitable contributions, the recipient must be a 501(c)(3) charity.

There are many other ways to contribute, including charitable trusts,[3] charitable remainder trusts,[4,5,6] and through estate planning: leaving contributions in your will. These can be very complex and apply mainly to the wealthy.

For more details, consult the IRS code.[7,8]

---

[3] irs.gov/charities-non-profits/private-foundations/charitable-trusts.

[4] gpo.gov/fdsys/granule/USCODE-2011-title26/USCODE-2011-title26-subtitleA-chap1-subchapJ-partI-subpartC-sec664 = tinyurl.com/y84l93c7.

[5] https://irs.gov/pub/irs-drop/rr-08-41.pdf.

[6] en.wikipedia.org/wiki/Charitable_remainder_unitrust = tinyurl.com/m6ql6ff.

[7] irs.gov/charities-non-profits/charitable-organizations/charitable-contribution-deductions=tinyurl.com/zx6thch.

[8] https://irs.gov/pub/irs-pdf/p1771.pdf.

15

Optimizing Social Security

People who have worked at least 10 years during which they paid the Social Security payroll tax (mandatory for most employees) are eligible to receive Social Security benefits in retirement. This includes some non-U.S. citizens and excludes certain public (federal, state, and local) workers, who are covered under other retirement plans. Since 1991, Social Security became mandatory for most state and local employees not covered by an equivalent public pension plan. However, those who receive a public pension earned from employment exempt from the Social Security payroll tax and who also are eligible to receive Social Security benefits will see the latter reduced accordingly. According to the Social Security Administration, in 2018, 96% of American workers are covered by Social Security.

The spouses—and in some cases, ex-spouses—of people eligible to receive Social Security benefits are themselves eligible to receive benefits additional to those received by their spouses.

Even if one lives abroad, in most cases, one is eligible to receive Social Security payments.

The Social Security code is in continual flux, and for the latest details, one is best served by consulting the Social Security Administration web site *sss.gov*. Nonetheless, there are a few general principles worth noting (although perhaps not a book's worth) in order to optimize Social Security benefits.

© The Author(s), under exclusive license to Springer Nature Switzerland AG 2022
R. P. Kurshan, *Investment Industry Claims Debunked*,
https://doi.org/10.1007/978-3-030-76709-9_15

15.1 Deciding When to Start

Optimizing Social Security payments before retirement is the same as after, except that if still working past the age at which one is first eligible for the benefits, it may be more advantageous to defer them, thus augmenting future benefits by 6% and later 8% per deferred year.

Taking benefits for investment, before needed for expenses, may not result in a big advantage and puts at risk the level of support available in old age. It also can easily result in a loss if the early benefits are invested in risky assets, while without such risk, the growth of invested benefits may not match the 6–8% annual advantage of deferring them.

15.2 Deferring Benefits

One can begin to receive Social Security benefits as early as age 62 (under the present law, although this may be increased by those of our politicians eager to shift funds away from the elderly). However, beginning benefits early results in a reduced monthly payment for the rest of one's life. The longer that one defers receiving Social Security benefits, the greater the monthly benefit. If one defers receiving Social Security benefits, the monthly benefit grows by around 6–8% per year deferred, up to the age 70.

Some have proposed an analogy: to imagine your Social Security benefit as an investment—of your deferred benefits—that grows until you begin to draw on it. The 8% growth is a very nice rate, comparable to an investment in the stock market, but without the volatility of an actual investment in stocks. This analogy is inaccurate, as you never get the deferred stipends. An annuity (Sect. 2.10.2) is a more accurate analogy, where the "premium" is the value of the deferred stipends.

If you defer until the maximum benefit at age 70 (after which there is no further benefit in deferring), then the break-even age is around the early 80s—the age at which the government expects you to die, calculated from the age the deferrals end.[1] If you live longer, then deferring ends up giving you more; if you die sooner, then you will have received less than if you started receiving benefits sooner (but in this case you won't be around to care). If you think you are certain to die before you reach 80, and start receiving Social Security benefits as soon as you can, you will have more money to spend or leave to

---

[1]ssa.gov/oact/STATS/table4c6.html.

your heirs. Otherwise, defer the payments as long as you can (until age 70) in order to increase the payments as much as possible.

There are situations in which it's clearly better *not* to defer payments: one is if you need the payments for living expenses; another is if you have a magical no-risk way to invest the benefits so that they grow at a rate that is significantly greater than the rate of inflation—say, 3–6% over inflation (a rate that needs to be calculated for your specific situation).

For the latter case, it's not enough merely to *expect* to earn at least that rate (meaning that you have a 50% chance of doing so)—you should have a very high probability of doing so, or else the anticipated benefit has a good chance of not materializing. Taking benefits early in order to invest them is typically risky, and should not be considered if eventually you will rely on those benefits or view them as a safety net in old age. When factoring in risk, the proper comparison is to take benefits early and invest them in TIPS (Sect. 2.3.1). However, compared against the 6% to 8% guaranteed growth from deferring benefits, together with COLAs (Sect. 15.7), investing benefits in TIPS (with a much lower rate of return) is not a good strategy. Investing the benefits in a bond or CD can be worthwhile if you plan to die early and need the money for your funeral.

If the monthly benefit is not needed for expenses, then deferring benefits and letting them grow can be viewed as a low-cost insurance policy against destitution in old age.

If you take Social Security benefits early, before the full retirement age, and your earnings are above some low limit, there is an additional penalty if you also are still working (including self-employment). It is as much as 50% of the amount earned over the limit and is subtracted from your Social Security benefit until you reach the age of full retirement. A nice summary of the issues and tradeoffs can be found in a Fidelity report.[2]

15.3 Reversing a Benefit Election

If you elect to receive benefits and then change your mind in the first year thereafter, you can pay back the benefits that you received, and the system is reset, as if you never elected to take the benefits.[3] This can be useful if, for example, you lose your job and are uncertain about finding another, so you

---

[2] fidelity.com/viewpoints/retirement/social-security-and-working.

[3] ssa.gov/planners/retire/withdrawal.html.

264   R. P. Kurshan

elect to receive benefits, but then find a new job within the year and thus can afford to defer the benefits.

15.4 Divorcee Benefit

Divorcees can claim Social Security benefits based on an ex-spouse's earnings provided there has been at least 10 years of marriage, unless the divorcee remarries.[4]

15.5 Goodbye to "File and Suspend"

There used to be a great Social Security loophole that allowed one spouse who reached retirement age to "file and suspend" Social Security benefits, with the result that the second spouse could begin to collect benefits based on those of the first spouse, while the first spouse delayed taking benefits until a later age (when the level of benefits would be greater, growing at the rate of 8% for each year suspended)—sort of having your cake and eating it too. In 2016, this opportunity was eliminated. (Most loopholes in the federal code are meant only for the wealthy—who need them least, but seem most determined to defend and extend them. There remains no end to off-shore tax havens, hedge fund tax credits, and "corporate welfare" entitlement loopholes that are politically untouchable.)

At the time of this writing, in order for the second spouse to receive the spousal benefit, the first spouse must actually begin to receive benefits (thus forfeiting the opportunity to defer payments and thus receive greater payments later). Thus now, in order for the first spouse to defer payments, the second spouse must forfeit spousal payments until the first spouse begins to receive payments. The new law also eliminated the possibility for the second spouse to defer benefits while receiving spousal benefits and, then at a later age, switch to the level of benefit entitled to the second spouse based on the deferral. Now, once the second spouse begins to receive a benefit, it can't be switched. So the second spouse can only receive the higher of the spousal benefit or the benefit to which the second spouse is entitled at the time the second spouse's benefits begin. This represents a very significant reduction from what the previous rules allowed, while also illustrating yet another example of how the government

---

[4]https://ssa.gov/planners/retire/divspouse.html.

has shifted its support away from lower-income citizens (who depend quite significantly on Social Security) and middle-income earners. All the while, the government never ceases to strengthen its largesse for the wealthy and businesses—the most recent example being the new 2018 tax law.

15.6 How Much Social Security Benefit Is Taxed?

From 0% up to 85% of your Social Security benefits are subject to federal ordinary income tax. In addition, some states also tax Social Security benefits to some extent, although more than half do not.[5] The federal tax depends on your MAGI (modified adjusted gross income—Sect. 12.7). The higher your MAGI, the more of your Social Security benefit is taxed (up to 85%).

15.7 COLAs

In theory, Social Security benefits keep up with inflation ("cost of living") although in practice, political pressures have kept the annual Social Security cost of living adjustment (COLA) below the level of inflation, while the elderly face a cost of living increase rate that is in fact *higher* than inflation,[6] largely due to ever rising healthcare costs.

15.8 Is Social Security Going Broke?

There is much discussion of Social Security "going broke." However, such claims may be alarmist and political, with various motivations. One motive comes from politicians who seek to undermine confidence in Social Security with the aim of eliminating it. Another comes from defenders of Social Security who seek to muster opposition to those who seek to kill it. That doesn't leave much room for calming influences.

The reality is this: as of 2017, if nothing is done to bolster the Social Security retirement trust fund, it will be unable to pay the full benefits due, starting in 2035.[7] However, from then until around 2090, payroll tax receipts alone

---

[5] https://taxfoundation.org/monday-map-state-income-taxes-social-security-benefits.
[6] Huang and Milevsky (2011).
[7] https://ssa.gov/oact/tr/2017/tr2017.pdf.

are expected to be adequate to fund over 75% of required Social Security payments. Eliminating Social Security does not appear to be a serious option, and there are a number of solutions to the underfunding.

Many experts consider the default outcome of a 20–25% across the board reduction in Social Security benefits starting in 2035 to be politically suicidal and therefore unlikely.

One way or the other, the federal government could decide to bolster the trust fund (an option hated by some political segments). Payroll tax contributions could be increased by raising the annual income threshold subject to payroll tax (an option hated by some wealthier wage earners who thus would be required to pay more into the fund—presently, higher wage earners reach the threshold after a few months, while with a higher threshold, payroll taxes could be required throughout a greater part of the year).

Or, without adding to the fund, the retirement age could be increased, and/or some form of means testing could be implemented, meaning that the more wealthy would receive lower benefits.

Increasing the retirement age is a popular alternative, but this unfairly injures manual laborers and those with health issues who are physically incapable of working to a later age. It is popular among workers with less physically taxing jobs, who plan to work to a later retirement age anyway (and who likely need the benefit less than those whose benefits would be sacrificed).

Means testing, whereby those of greater means receive a lower benefit, while seemingly very fair and socially progressive, is despised by some. While they may need the benefit less, they feel entitled to it nonetheless, because they contributed into the fund while working and see the benefit as "my money." Of course all the money that one earns is "my money," and yet taxpayers are accustomed to contribute some of it to the federal Treasury, from which some of those funds go to support people in need. (Some people hate this too.)

Another way to bolster the fund would be to decrease benefits subtly, by disconnecting cost of living adjustments (COLAs) from the currently mandated CPI-W index (the Consumer Price Index for Urban Wage Earners and Clerical Workers), substituting an index that would result in lower COLAs. This would result in a "stealth" reduction in benefits that may be less visible to some voters and therefore more likely.

However, the anticipated depletion of trust fund assets is actually only part of the problem and perhaps the lesser part. The Social Security trust fund receives income from the payroll tax and pays Social Security benefits (less the tax received on benefits paid). In a given year, often income exceeds expenses. The surplus is credited to the trust fund in the form of non-marketable government obligations (something like Treasury bonds), which pay a "market rate" of interest that over the last four decades has averaged 2.8% a year. The government then takes this surplus and spends it on unrelated projects. The government does the same for the related Social Security Disability Insurance program. By the end of 2015, the combined government obligation for these two Social Security programs was $2.8 trillion (*ibid*). This is money that the government has borrowed from the Social Security trust funds and spent on other unrelated projects, in effect issuing IOUs for the money taken. Once Social Security benefits exceed Social Security payroll tax income, the government is obligated to start paying back this $2.8 trillion. It is important to note that this $2.8 trillion is *not* money that the government is being asked to contribute, in order to keep Social Security solvent. This is money that the government has *borrowed* from the Social Security trust funds and is *obligated* to return. The accounting system that has allowed this is called "pay-as-you-go."

To put the number in perspective, $2.8 trillion is 74% of the entire federal budget of $3.8 trillion for 2015, or 15% of the 2015 GDP—around $12,000 for every man, woman, and child in the United States.[8]

So, where will the money come from to pay off these government IOUs? Raising taxes, borrowing, cutting other spending, or increasing the deficit ("printing more money") are the four main possibilities.

A number of economists have questioned the probity of pay-as-you-go accounting, and the government knows better: for private pension providers, they require actual payments into a pension trust fund, and they closely monitor the fiscal state of the fund, pressuring providers to supplement funds that become underfunded (cf. Sect. 17.2.3). If the government applied the same rule to themselves, using the surpluses to buy back government debt (in effect, investing the surpluses in actual Treasury bonds) instead of spending it, there likely would be no incurable problem with Social Security.

Why doesn't the government follow its own rules? "Free" money!! They make the rules and thus they can get away with it. There are no fiscal watchdogs with adequate voice to shame the government into fiscal responsibility. And the temptation is too great, maybe even for voters: which would you prefer, another B-1 bomber, a man on the moon, or responsible accounting?

Actually, there was an intense debate on how to fund Social Security when the Social Security Act was passed into law as part of the New Deal, in 1935, with conservatives arguing (and prevailing) for pay-as-you-go.[9]

---

[8] https://nationalpriorities.org/budget-basics/federal-budget-101/spending/.
[9] ssa.gov/history/altm5.html.

16

Healthcare

Non-U.S. readers: check out this chapter to see how lucky you are. In the United States, little is more fraught in the realm of personal finance than healthcare. We all need it. Few can afford to pay for it at today's prices without outside help. The economies of scale that should be expected to bring down the costs are blocked by special interest groups determined to preserve their ever-growing revenue streams, over considerations of the public good.

Even when there is a big range of costs for the same services (e.g., an MRI) and thus an opportunity for marketplace competition, consumers don't know how to choose and often go to a much more expensive provider simply because that is the one recommended by their doctor (who often is ignorant of the cost differences).[1] There are many ways to overcome such market inefficiencies, but most require some sort of regulatory or organizational action.

When ever was there a stronger case for government marketplace intervention? As we all sadly know, most possible interventions are blocked by our own government, whose politicians owe their positions to the very organizations that they should be reining in for the public good.

In theory, we should be able to elect leaders willing to champion the public interest, but elections have become sham spectacles wherein voters are gulled into thinking they control their government, when the opposite is the reality. As we now know better than ever, the choices between candidates can be real and frighteningly significant. And yet, there's at best but a small influence

---

[1] nytimes.com/2018/07/30/upshot/shopping-for-health-care-simply-doesnt-work-so-what-might.html = tinyurl.com/y8knq289.

© The Author(s), under exclusive license to Springer Nature Switzerland AG 2022 **269**
R. P. Kurshan, *Investment Industry Claims Debunked*,
https://doi.org/10.1007/978-3-030-76709-9_16

270   R. P. Kurshan

that voters have when it comes to healthcare, perhaps their most significant economic issue. Although 60% of Americans support universal ("single payer") healthcare,[2] its attainment is out of reach. This is the sad commentary on what our governing system has become.

What is left to the individual consumers of healthcare is to navigate a complex maze of alternatives and choose the least worse ones. These paths are explored next.

16.1 Before Retirement

While employed, most Americans enjoy employer-provided healthcare benefits. Although this seems so normal that its logic is rarely questioned, its genesis was a fluke that derived from inflation fears.

Until the 1930s, the cost of a visit to the doctor or to the hospital largely was paid directly by the patient. Although there were isolated examples of employment-based healthcare coverage as early as the nineteenth century, these were few and far between. Some companies ran clinics to care for employees injured on the job, but these were mostly put in place to keep workers working. Sulfa drugs (1930s) and mass production of penicillin (1940s) helped increase public awareness of the potential of healthcare, while its increasingly broad availability made it no longer just the province of the wealthy. Increasing interest in healthcare led to the creation of Blue Cross as a nonprofit subscription service that provided free hospital care to members and also was championed by hospitals for getting their bills paid. (The nonprofit tax exempt status was essential for bootstrapping the service. It was granted "in the public interest.") Physician healthcare insurance developed more slowly (first under Blue Shield) due to physician fears that regulation would limit their fees. But, when doctors saw the popularity of Blue Cross, they came around and decided to make their own system before one was imposed upon them.

During World War II, the U.S. Government feared that with much of the labor force absent, competition for workers could lead to the sort of hyperinflation that helped push Germany to fascism. To prevent this, wage and price controls were implemented. To mollify labor group objections, including massive strike threats, the government agreed to exempt employer-paid health

---

[2] pewresearch.org/fact-tank/2017/06/23/public-support-for-single-payer-health-coverage-grows-driven-by-democrats/ = tinyurl.com/yxz6cduq.

insurance from wage controls and also from income tax. Employers immediately saw this as a valuable differentiating factor for attracting workers—if not through better wages, then with better healthcare—while workers saw it as a valuable benefit. Labor unions saw it as easier wedge than wages, and soon dental and vision care were added. By two decades later, employer-provided health insurance was ubiquitous.

Public employees (federal, state, and local) are covered by various government plans, and many of these carry over into retirement.

Only in the last few decades have employers begun to whittle away at these benefits, recoiling from exponentially increasing healthcare costs.

For the self-employed, there is the possibility of acquiring healthcare insurance on an individual basis, but these policies tend to be very expensive. The 2010 Affordable Healthcare Act ("Obamacare") provided some relief, especially for lower-income individuals, but this has increasingly been dismantled by the Trump administration. An alternative available to some is health insurance acquired through an association, generally based on membership in a professional organization.

Even if you are working, you normally should sign up for Medicare Part A (hospitalization) prior to your 65th birthday. The only exception is if you have not paid the Medicare payroll tax for a total of 10 years. In this case, you still can sign up for Part A but need to pay a monthly premium. If you decline to sign up for Part A or Parts A and B by your 65th birthday because you are still working and have "creditable" coverage through your work plan, you still may sign up within 8 months after you stop working (or lose your coverage). Also, your employer may require that you are enrolled in Medicare.

An individual can establish a Health Savings Account (HSA) to which pre-tax income may be contributed and which may be used to pay for a wide range of qualified medical expenses. However, amounts remaining in the account at the end of the year cannot be rolled over to the following year and are lost for the account holder. One is not allowed to contribute to an HSA after the date that one is eligible for Medicare or the date 6 months before one signs up for benefits from Medicare, Social Security, or the Railroad Retirement Board, whichever of these dates occurs first. If you do, there is a tax penalty.

For those recently separated from employment that had provided health insurance, the Consolidated Omnibus Budget Reconciliation Act (COBRA—don't you love the clever names our politicians dream up?) requires most group health insurance plans to temporarily extend coverage past the separation date, usually for an additional year and a half (up to 3 years). The insurance is paid for by the ex-employee, but at the preferred rate enjoyed by the employee. When the ex-employee also is eligible for Medicare, Medicare becomes the primary insurance, and the COBRA coverage assumes the role of "Medigap" coverage described in the next section. Rules and requirements are complex and require close attention in order to avoid losing out on available benefits.

16.2 After Retirement

After retirement, the options include possibly COBRA (for a limited time, usually, 1 1/2–3 years) and individual policies. But, the main option is Medicare (or Medicaid for the indigent) plus "Medigap," which is (government-regulated) private insurance that starts where Medicare stops and comes in a dozen or so varieties. Generally, COBRA is a (temporary) replacement for Medigap. There also are separate private insurance policies available for dental and vision care.

There are no widespread policies that completely cover hearing, which is odd, given the health significance and prevalence of hearing deficiency among the elderly. Many private policies (but not Medicare) do cover the cost of hearing aids to some extent. But, as of 2018, only Arkansas, New Hampshire, and Rhode Island mandate full insurance coverage in private policies for hearing aids for adults.[3] Perhaps the general thinking is the less the elderly hear, the better?

Many public employees have retirement plans that include healthcare that can be coordinated with Medicare (for augmented benefits).

But as of 2017, states have saved only about $31 billion, or 5%, toward their healthcare obligations. Unlike the private sector, public employee retiree health benefits are "pay-as-you-go" obligations (Sect. 15.8) of the employer, without funding requirements. Many economists see a funding crisis looming as a result of this underfunding, as an increasing portion of the population enters retirement.

The news for Medicare hospitalization insurance (Part A) is better, but there's still a problem: the government expects Part A to run out of money by 2029 without intervention.[4,5] (The other parts of Medicare, funded through beneficiary premiums and general subsidies, are not expected to be in financial trouble in the foreseeable future.) The shortfall causes and possible remedies

---

[3] healthyhearing.com/help/hearing-aids/insurance-financial-assistance.

[4] cms.gov/ReportsTrustFunds/downloads/tr2017.pdf.

[5] Since 1970, projected time to insolvency has varied from 2 years to 28 years: fas.org/sgp/crs/misc/RS20946.pdf (This Congressional Research Service report does not appear to be directly available from them online.)

for Part A are similar to those for the analogous problem for Social Security (Sect. 15.8). If the Medicare hospitalization fund ran dry, incoming revenues (from the Medicare payroll tax) would pay for only 88% of its expenses (*ibid*), resulting in a 12% cut in Medicare hospitalization benefits (calculated using current costs). This could be devastating to those without substantial savings.

If there were an increase in the Medicare payroll tax by 0.365% for each of employers and employees, from the 1.45% each pay currently (the self-employed must pay both halves), Medicare would be expected to stay solvent for the next 75 years.[6] Although this would constitute a 25% increase in the (very small) Medicare payroll tax, it is within 1.4% of the increase passed in 1981 under President Reagan. Nonetheless, even such a tiny increase, with a Republican historical precedent (the increase under President Reagan), at the time of this writing, it is considered infeasible in today's political climate (consistently blocked by the Republicans).

This increase could be reduced if Medicare were allowed to negotiate drug prices, something currently forbidden by Congress (under pressure from drug companies, which seek to maintain their revenues and have bought from both parties the political influence needed to maintain the status quo).

Although Medicare is funded using the same pay-as-you-go accounting used for Social Security, the government owes the Part A trust fund much less: "only" $205 billion at the end of 2015.[7]

16.3 Medicare

Medicare and Medicaid,[8] primary health insurance available after retirement, were instituted along with a wave of progressive "Great Society" social programs (the Civil Rights Act, Voting Rights Act, "Head Start," federal aid to education, the Housing and Urban Development Act, the Economic Opportunity Act to help rural families, the Clean Air Act, the Water Quality Act, the Endangered Species Preservation Act, the National Trails System Act, the Aircraft Noise Abatement Act, the Immigration and Nationality Act that abolished immigration quotas, the Economic Opportunity Act, the National Endowments for Arts and—separately—Humanities, the Corporation for

---

[6] https://fool.com/retirement/2016/09/10/5-must-know-facts-about-medicare.aspx.

[7] cms.gov/Research-Statistics-Data-and-Systems/Statistics-Trends-and-Reports/ReportsTrustFunds/ TrusteesReports.html = tinyurl.com/yaffp6g9.

[8] Medicaid provides healthcare coverage to low-income individuals, both before and after retirement. It is administered by the states.

Public Broadcasting, the High Speed Ground Transportation Act that led to the Metroliners between New York and Washington, the Cigarette Labeling and Advertising Act that led to the cancer warning labels, the Truth In Lending Act, the Wholesale Meat Act and more) during the L. B. Johnson administration (1963–1968)—all brought to us by the father of the Vietnam War.

Medicare is single-payer insurance available to all Americans age 65 and older. The government advises people to sign up for Medicare 3 months before their 65th birthday, although some Medicare offices say that's "too soon" and to call back just a few days (or even "48 hours") before your birthday. You have until 3 months after your birthday month to sign up. The 3 months before your birthday month through the 3 months after (7 months in all) is called your "initial enrollment period" (IEP). You sign up through the Social Security Administration (*ssa.gov*). Those already receiving Social Security benefits who live in the United States are enrolled automatically.

Signing up for Medicare requires a number of important considerations that can affect how much you need to pay for insurance premiums and the healthcare that you will receive. It can take some time and energy to go through the possibilities and choose the one that is best for your circumstances. Plan possibilities differ from state to state, so if you are planning to move, you need to take this in consideration as well. The government provides an informative web site to guide you through the choices.[9]

Medicare has four Parts:

- **Part A** for inpatient hospital care—there is no premium if either you or your spouse have paid Medicare payroll tax for 10 years (although if hospitalized, there may be deductibles that you need to pay).
- **Part B** for outpatient care and doctors' and others' medical services—for which there is a premium that usually is paid automatically as a deduction from Social Security payments.
- **Part C** "Advantage" plans offered by private insurers approved by Medicare, in lieu of the other parts, often at a reduced cost (but with less choice of provider—similar to HMO plans).
- **Part D** for prescription drugs.

---

[9] https://medicare.gov/people-like-me/new-to-medicare/getting-started-with-medicare.html=tinyurl.com/y7u6vxly.

In addition there is private (but government-regulated) "Medigap" (Supplementary) insurance that takes over where Part B stops paying.

Some states subsidize Medicare premiums, deductibles, drug costs, and co-pays for individuals with few financial resources (as defined by the federal poverty level).

16.3.1 Deadlines: Important!!

If you don't enroll in Parts A and B by your 65th birthday, or within 8 months of when you stop working with "creditable" health insurance coverage (insurance during retirement doesn't count), you may have to pay a late enrollment penalty that is a 10% premium increase for each year late, *for as long as you have that coverage.*[10,11] You also then may need to wait to enroll until the next general election period: January 1 to March 31.

For Part D, you have 63 days to sign up after employment coverage *or* COBRA ends. There is also a penalty for a late sign-up to Part D that changes from year to year.[12] You can change your Part D plan during the Medicare Open Enrollment Period, which may change slightly from year to year (check it online), but occurs toward the end of the year—in 2019, it was October 15 to December 7.

For Medigap plans, you have 6 months to sign up after employment coverage or COBRA ends. You need a letter from your employer certifying that your coverage was "creditable" (meaning that it met required Medicare standards) and a COBRA termination letter (if you had COBRA). As long as you meet this deadline, the Medigap carrier is not entitled to ask medical questions, and coverage is not conditioned on your health. However, if you miss the deadline, your insurability and/or costs may be conditioned on the results of a medical exam.[13]

Even if covered by other health insurance, when you turn 65, you should still sign up for Medicare Part A in most cases (as required by your other insurance). Your other insurance then becomes the secondary payer after Medicare.

---

[10] medicare.gov/your-medicare-costs/part-b-costs/part-b-late-enrollment-penalty.

[11] cms.gov/Outreach-and-Education/Find-Your-Provider-Type/Employers-and-Unions/FS3-Enroll-in-Part-A-and-B.pdf = tinyurl.com/y7ckmrrd.

[12] medicare.gov/part-d/costs/penalty/part-d-late-enrollment-penalty.html.

[13] medicare.gov/supplement-other-insurance/when-can-i-buy-medigap/when-can-i-buy-medigap.html = tinyurl.com/ycbvdj28.

16.3.2 Choices

When signing up for Medicare, there's a succession of choices to be made:

1. **Hospitalization** Do you want Medicare at all? Part A (hospitalization) usually has no premium, as above, but may require deductibles and co-pays, if used.
2. **Advantage** If you want Medicare, do you want an often less costly "Advantage" plan (Plan C above), but with less choice of doctors and hospitals? If so, you're done.
3. **Medical** Else, you probably want to sign up for Part B; its premium is generally deducted from your Social Security payment, and the cost is income-dependent and hard to compute (see Sect. 16.3.3 below).
4. **Rx** Parts A and B leave a lot of medical costs uncovered, including prescription drugs. Do you want to sign up for drug coverage? That's Part D, offered privately, and worth the effort of comparison shopping, because the prices for the same or similar coverage can vary considerably from one carrier to the next and from year to year.
5. **Medigap** Even with Parts A, B, and D, there still are uncovered costs. These can be covered with a private Medigap policy.[14]

In fact, with "Medigap" comes not one choice but 11: there are 10 different plans with different coverages, and the "cadillac" plan, "F," comes in two flavors, one high deductible. Again, comparison shopping is important as policy premiums among providers can vary significantly, although for a given plan the government-mandated coverage is the same.

Sadly, the Medigap "C" and "F" plans were eliminated for new enrollees in 2020, ostensibly to save Medicare money. Complain to your representatives in Congress.

An in-depth analysis of Medigap choices is provided by the U.S. Dept. of Health and Human Services.[15]

A detailed comparison of Medigap plans and carrier premium costs is available in some states. A good example is from New York State.[16] However, such detailed breakdowns of plans and carrier premium costs are hard to find.

---

[14] medicare.gov/supplement-other-insurance/compare-medigap/compare-medigap.html.

[15] medicare.gov/Pubs/pdf/02110-medicare-medigap-guide.pdf = tinyurl.com/ycvygm77.

[16] medicarerights.org/fliers/Medigaps/Whole-Medigap-Packet-(NY).pdf = tinyurl.com/yd9422gz.

A good place to seek help is from a State Health Insurance Assistance Program (SHIP) in your state.[17]

While at least in some cases, excellent up-to-date Medigap price information is available (like the New York State Whole Medigap packet just cited), Part D drug plan prices can be chaotic and almost unfathomable. The actual cost to you depends on what drugs you need, and this dependency varies from carrier to carrier and year to year. I was astonished to find that the coverage I signed up for, a best value at the time, became four times more expensive than another equivalent coverage, a few years later (that was more expensive when I first signed up).

A great source to compare Part D plans is provided by the government.[18] You can enter the drugs that you take and the pharmacies you use and find your actual annual costs under the various plans. Changing plans every year or two to the currently least expensive plan may be a worthwhile exercise. The prices can vary considerably. Drug prices are rising faster than inflation,[19] and the best plan one year may not be the best in the following year. Your local SHIP may be of some help here too.

You can change your insurer for Part D (drugs) during any annual open enrollment period. Your old plan then will end automatically.[20]

Astonishingly, you are *not* entitled to switch your Medigap coverage to another carrier, although it may be possible if you find a new carrier that is willing to accept you.[21] You always can cancel an existing Medigap policy, and if you can find a new provider to take you, you can switch at any time. However, the new provider may require a physical exam, so don't cancel the old policy before you have the new one assured.

16.3.3 IRMAAs

Just when you thought you've finally come to the end of the Medicare saga, a new goblin pokes up its head. There are hidden charges, called IRMAAs (income-related monthly adjustment amount)—Sect. 12.7. These

---

[17] shiptacenter.org/.

[18] Medicare.gov/plan-compare.

[19] Schondelmeyer and Purvis (2019).

[20] medicare.gov/drug-coverage-part-d/how-to-get-prescription-drug-coverage/how-to-switch-your-medicare-drug-plan = tinyurl.com/y897kp3o.

[21] medicare.gov/supplements-other-insurance/when-can-i-buy-medigap/switching-medigap-policies = tinyurl.com/ybs6lv4m.

charges are deducted from your monthly Social Security payments, along with any surcharge for a late enrollment penalty. If you have Plan D (drugs), there is a separate IRMAA for that.

The IRMAA, you may imagine, is related to your current income. Oh, no! It's related to your income from 2 years ago!

In 2018, with a 2016 MAGI between $214,000.01 and $267,000, for a married couple, filing jointly, your Part B monthly IRMAA would be $133.90 per month, and your Part D monthly IRMAA would be another $33.60.

16.4 Dental? Vision?

Private dental and (separately) vision care insurance are available outside of the Medicare system from private insurers. However, in my experience, the prices are high and the coverage limited. After all, it's fairly predictable what your typical annual expenses are for these coverages (you'll get your teeth cleaned, maybe a filling, and maybe new glasses). So you can bet that your premiums exceed your provider's charges for these services. While you may reason that you'll pay the premium just in case you might need that $15,000 bridge job, what you find when you dig through the fine print (or, at least what I found) is that your coverage is capped at such a low level that it's hard to construct a scenario where your coverage payout exceeds your annual premium. After all, as one can cancel and sign up for dental and vision insurance at any time, how could the insurance company make a profit if they significantly covered high-cost procedures? You could sign up for insurance if you anticipated a costly procedure, wait a year (often required to have held coverage for a major procedure), have the procedure, and then cancel the insurance. To protect against such gaming of the system, the insurance companies generally just cap their coverage to a level that is all but guaranteed to be less than the premium.

Without insurance, you may be able to negotiate with your provider to accept as payment what the insurance company reimburses. (Generally, "retail" charges are considerably higher than what the insurance company actually reimburses.)

16.5 Long-Term Care Ratings and Rates

Long-term care was discussed in Sect. 7.5.2. Most policies are "tax-qualified" for federal income taxes, which means that under the right conditions (now scant with the new tax law), you can deduct your premiums. Many states allow credits for premiums. And benefits, paying largely for nursing home or assisted living care, are not taxed as income.

The American Association for Long-Term Care Insurance provides a lot of good guidance, including typical premiums[22] and provider ratings.[23] The National Association of Insurance Commissioners also provides more in-depth periodic reports (generally, with a 2-year lag) on individual providers.[24] (You don't want to pay premiums for years only to find that your provider is no longer in business when you finally need the benefits that you paid for.)

For those indifferent to social norms, with a bent toward exploiting the system, an alternative to long-term care insurance is "Medicaid planning," the plain-vanilla term for the mini-industry of lawyers and others who help people arrange their financial lives so they don't spend every last dime on a nursing home.[25]

---

[22] aaltci.org/long-term-care-insurance-rates/.

[23] aaltci.org/long-term-care-insurance/learning-center/company-ratings.php.

[24] naic.org/prod_serv/LTC-LR-19.pdf = tinyurl.com/yaqhrrxl.

[25] nytimes.com/2017/07/21/your-money/estate-planning/the-ethics-of-adjusting-your-assets-to-qualify-for-medicaid.html = tinyurl.com/yd7m8832.

17

Pensions

For those lucky enough to have a pension, it is important for retirement planning to understand how reliable that pension is.

To assess reliability, some perspective is helpful. There is a very wide pension reliability spectrum, and where a pension sits in this spectrum depends, to a very large degree, on the "sector" and sub-sector of the employer providing the pension: private sector—single-employer or multi-employer; or public sector—federal, state, or local (definitions to follow).

The terms "pension plan" and "defined benefit plan" are synonymous, so "defined benefit pension plan" is redundant. "Defined benefit plan" is used more formally, while "pension" is ubiquitous in common usage.

The concept of *retirement* for ordinary workers began mostly with the 1935 advent of Social Security in President F. D. Roosevelt's New Deal. Before that, most workers worked for as long as they were able and, after that, were either supported by their family or else ended in a facility for the destitute run by charities or local governments. By the end of the Great Depression, these were overwhelmed and unable to meet demand.

In fact, though, the first private pension plan in the United States dates back to 60 years earlier, established by American Express in 1875. That plan was very restrictive, applying only to workers over 60 with 20 years of service and with approval by the Board of Directors. It paid 50% of the worker's average pay over the previous decade.[1] By the time of Social Security, there already were a

---

[1] Seburn (1991).

© The Author(s), under exclusive license to Springer Nature Switzerland AG 2022 **281**
R. P. Kurshan, *Investment Industry Claims Debunked*,
https://doi.org/10.1007/978-3-030-76709-9_17

282   R. P. Kurshan

few hundred U.S. company pension plans providing lifetime annuities to their qualified employees.

Some major U.S companies that established plans prior to 1930 were Standard Oil of New Jersey (1903); U.S. Steel Corp. (1911); General Electric Co. (1912); American Telephone and Telegraph Co. (1913); Goodyear Tire and Rubber Co., (1915); Bethlehem Steel Co. (1923); American Can Co. (1924); and Eastman Kodak Co. (1929).[2]

By 1975, most full-time workers for large companies and over 80% of all full-time U.S. workers had access to a pension plan, after a vesting period.[3] The vesting period is the amount of time an employee needs to be employed before qualifying for a pension—often 5 years of continuous full-time employment. After some designated retirement age, the employee receives a monthly stipend for the remainder of the life of that employee and, in most cases, the life of the employee's spouse (often with benefits reduced in case of employee death). In some cases, in order to participate, the employee has been required to contribute to the plan through payroll deductions. In most cases, the employer has funded the plan completely, and employee participation was automatic after a vesting period.

Pensions were highly valued by employees and companies alike, which viewed the pension as a way to promote employee loyalty and served to help retain valuable, highly trained employees.

Nowadays, though, fewer and fewer employers offer pensions to new employees, offering instead "defined contribution plans," most commonly 401(k)s.

These are much less costly for employers and correspondingly less valuable for employees. It's actually worse than this: they are less cost-efficient than pensions, for employers and employees taken together. The same money that an employer spends on a defined contribution plan can fund a pension plan of greater value to the employee (Chap. 18). However, employers have shifted away from this in order to avoid the financial risk associated with maintaining a pension plan—instead, shifting the risk to employees.

This shift away from pensions is in response to a number of factors. One is changing attitudes toward employees in relation to a company's objectives regarding growth and stock price. Another, perversely, is a reaction to toughened Labor Dept. regulations intended to protect employee pensions.

---

[2] ebri.org/docs/default-source/ebri-issue-brief/0101ib.pdf = tinyurl.com/ydx5dbca.

[3] https://census.gov/prod/2010pubs/p60-238.pdf.

For a good part of the twentieth century, employees were considered to be part of the "company family": valuable assets to be nurtured and rewarded. Employee retention was an important goal.

However, starting around the 1980s, this company attitude began to change. Employees began to be viewed as a resource, to be optimized: reduced or expanded as best suited immediate company financial objectives. This often reached counterproductive levels, where valuable, highly trained employees were terminated in across-the-board staff reductions intended to bolster near-term actuarial "profitability" as it appeared on balance sheets, thus bolstering the stock price. Then, a few years later, when the now "more profitable" company entered a period of expansion, it sought to hire staff to fill positions vacated only a few years earlier. This was something that proved difficult and costly, and in most cases the company was unsuccessful in restoring the previously discarded capabilities. Unsurprisingly, this did not lead to a more effective, more efficient company (quite the opposite). Nonetheless, it looked good on paper to investors, and bolstered the stock price. That became all that mattered.

In this vein, pensions came to be considered a drain on profitability. Maintaining the pension trust fund required diverting company funds to the trust in order to reduce the risk that the trust can become unable to meet its legal obligations. The idea developed to shift this risk to the employees: give them the funds earmarked for the pension trust fund, and let each employee manage the risk. This process was termed "de-risking" by the companies and "risk transfer" by others who sought to emphasize what was really happening.

The way funds were transferred to employees in lieu of a pension was mainly though a 401(k), which over time has largely supplanted pensions (although 401(k)s co-existed with pensions for a number of decades).

At the same time, acts of Congress that were intended to protect employee pensions had the perverse effect of accelerating the move away from pensions.

The 2006 Pension Protection Act increased funding requirements for defined benefit (pension) plans and strengthened their reporting and disclosure rules. At the same time, the 2006 accounting standard of the Financial Accounting Standards Board (FASB) changed to require private sector single-employer plan sponsors to recognize the funded status of their pension plans on their company balance sheet. In the case of an underfunded pension, this can add a large liability. Even for a fully funded pension fund, it can be a volatile entry that can skew the balance sheet with unpredictable and hard to control accounting results. The Bipartisan Budget Act of 2013 significantly increased employer Pension Benefit Guaranty Corporation (PBGC) premiums (mandated by the government to insure pensions against default) for single-

284   R. P. Kurshan

employer plans (Sect. 17.2.1). The Multi-employer Pension Reform Act did the
same for multi-employer pension plans (Sect. 17.2.2). Many companies sought
to run from these requirements by eliminating pensions.

As of 2019, just over 20% of American workers still participated in a pension
plan,[4] a quarter of the 1975 participation level. This 20% mostly are people
with plans initiated when pensions were popular with employers.

17.1 Workplace Sectors

The workplace is divided into two "sectors": private and public. The public
sector includes civilian wage earners paid by some government entity, divided
again into federal, state, and local. Teachers, police, and firefighters, for
example, are commonly local public sector workers. The private sector consists
of all other wage earners, excluding the military, which is considered separately.

The reason for these partitions is that regulations governing the administration and—most significantly—*protection* of pensions differ dramatically across
sectors and their subdivisions. This can and has made profound differences
in who can after all expect to receive the pension that they were promised.
In some cases, your sector can make the difference between getting your full
pension and getting little or nothing from your pension. This seems grossly
unfair, and it is. It is a consequence of political forces, union negotiations, and
the extent to which plan administrators conscientiously assume their long-
term fiduciary responsibility, or compromise that responsibility for political
or, in some cases, personal gain. This is very scary for those who depend on
or anticipate depending on their pensions in retirement. However, the news is
not all bleak, nor is the bleak news uniform. For many, there are at least partial
back-up protections; for others, protection depends ultimately on decisions of
the federal government—which, in turn, depend on which political party is
in control (a dependency that is also scary). This is discussed at length in this
section.

Among 116 million American private sector workers in 2007, only 19.4
million—17%—received, as a workplace benefit, enrollment in a pension
plan: see Fig. 17.1. In the public sector, on the other hand, state and local
pension plans covered 14.4 million people—almost three quarters of all those
workers (plus another 4.2 million inactive members): Fig. 17.2. Virtually all

---

[4] pensionrights.org/publications/statistic/how-many-american-workers-participate-workplace-
retirement-plans = tinyurl.com/wsxsdnz.

17 Pensions 285

	2007		2014	
PRIVATE SECTOR				
all workers	116M		118.5M	
with pension	19.4M	(17%)	14.5M	(12%)
# plans	49K		44.9K	
single-employer	14.8M	(13%)	10.5M	(9%)
# plans	47.5K		43.5K	
retired with pension	22.9M		23.2M	
single-employer	17.6M		17.2M	
total with pension	42.3M		37.7M	
pension assets	$2.65T		$2.99T	
single-employer	32.4M		27.7M	
pension assets	$2.16T		$2.48T	
funding (PBGC)	84%		82%	
multi-employer funding	56%		4%	
PUBLIC SECTOR				
all workers	23.5M		23.1M	
with pension	18.5M	(79%)	18.3M	(79%)
retired with pension	12.1M		15.6M	
total with pension	30.6M		33.9M	
pension assets	$4.1T		$4.6T	
TOTAL				
US population	301M		319M	(+6%)
all workers	139.5M		141.6M	
full-time	115.2M	(83%)	115M	(81%)
with pension	37.9M	(27%, 33%)	32.8M	(23%, 29%)
retired	31M		37.9M	
with pension	35M		38.8M	
total	170.5M		179.5M	
with pension	72.9M	(43%)	71.6M	(40%)
pension assets	$6.75T		$6.69T	

Fig. 17.1 U.S. pensions.

federal workers are considered to be "active" members of a pension plan, mostly because Social Security is considered part of that plan. (In some cases, especially in many state plans, employees do not participate in Social Security. Another exception applies to those who worked for Congress before 1986 and

286 R. P. Kurshan

```
PUBLIC SECTOR                         2007                      2014

STATE/LOCAL [U.S. Census Bureau and Federal Reserve data]
-----------------------------------------------------------------------------
    all workers               19.4M   FRED              19.1M   FRED
      full-time               13.8M   Wic2002           14.4M   SL14
      with pension            14.4M   (74%)+4.2M inact] 14.3M   (75%)
      # plans                 2547    3992:SLGP         2547
-----------------------------------------------------------------------------
    retired with pension*      7.5M                      9.6M   9.9M?SLPDa
-----------------------------------------------------------------------------
    total with pension*       21.9M                     23.9M
      pension assets          $3.1T   PA                $3.7T^^ S+L_P


FEDERAL
-----------------------------------------------------------------------------
    all workers                4.1M   TotG              4.0M    TotG
      civilian                 2.7M    "                2.7M     "
      uniformed military       1.4M    "                1.3M    AM14
    with pension               4.1M   PA                4M
      civilian                 2.7M                     2.7M    TotG
      uniformed military       1.4M                     1.3M
-----------------------------------------------------------------------------
    retired with pension*      4.6M                     6M
      civilian                 1.4M                     2.6M    OPM
      uniformed military       3.2M   Stat14            3.4M    Stat14
-----------------------------------------------------------------------------
    total with pension*        8.7M   PA                10M
      civilian                 4.1M                     5.3M
      uniformed military       4.6M                     4.7M
      pension assets          $.97T^  PA                .8T^    OPM


TOTAL
-----------------------------------------------------------------------------
    all workers               23.5M   FRED+Mil          23.1M   FRED+Mil
      with pension            18.5M                     18.3M
-----------------------------------------------------------------------------
    retired with pension      12.1M                     15.6M
-----------------------------------------------------------------------------
    total
      with pension            30.6M                     33.9M
      pension assets          $4.1T                     $4.6T

^  underfunded Pay-as-you-go funding (illegal for private) with $2.4T liability.
^^ underfunded by $.8T-$4T
```

Fig. 17.2 U.S. public sector pensions.

were covered by the Civil Service Retirement System.) For civilian federal
workers, there is a second pension plan that works like the typical private sector
pension plans, vesting after 5 years and paying on top of Social Security. They
also have a third component that is essentially a defined contribution plan.
The uniformed military have their own complex retirement plan (that unfairly
requires long service but then inefficiently encourages early retirement). All
together, 27% of all American workers—33% of the number of full-time
workers—were covered by a pension plan in 2007.

Seven years later, as America crept out of the Great Recession, the percent of
private sector workers covered by a pension plan had dropped to only 12% of all
workers; coverage in the public sector remained largely unchanged: Figs. 17.1,

and[5] 17.2. The *number* of private sector workers covered by a pension plan dropped 25%, despite a 6% increase in U.S. population. As full-time workers with a pension benefit left the workforce, they were replaced by full- and part-time workers with no pension benefit.

17.2 Private Sector Pensions

Private sector pension plans are divided between "single-employer" plans and "multi-employer" plans. In 2014 there were almost 45,000 private sector pension plans covering 14.5 million workers and another 23.2 million retirees (possibly working at another job) or their beneficiaries, for a total of 37.7 million participants, backed by pension trust funds with combined assets of almost $3 trillion—around 5% of the U.S. securities market. See Fig. 17.1. Of these private sector pension plans, almost 97% were single-employer plans that covered 72% of all private sector individuals with a pension plan.

17.2.1 Single-Employer Plans

Of the single-employer plans in 2014, 54% (22% of participants) were in services, 12% in finance (12% of participants), and 13% in manufacturing (41% of participants), accounting for 79% of the plans and 75% of the participants. There were 10.5 million active participants and 18.7 million receiving benefits—17.2 million excluding the beneficiaries of deceased plan participants or 29.2 million participants and beneficiaries overall.[6] The combined assets of the single-employer plans comprised 83% of private sector pension plan assets. That's 83% of assets covering 72% of the workers. There's a warning in that disparity: most single-employer plans have been adequately funded, maintaining a funding ratio *assets/liabilities* over the 80% that is considered by many to be adequate. Many multi-employer plans have not been adequately funded.

That single-employer plans cover roughly three quarters of individuals enrolled in a private sector pension plan is good news for that majority. These plans cover people that work (mostly, full-time) for a single company for a

---

[5]A worker may be retired and receiving a pension from one employer, while at the same time being a member of the workforce, working at another job. That explains why the total number of "retired workers" can be less than the total number of "retired with pension" workers in Fig. 17.1.
[6]Labor (2016a,b).

288 R. P. Kurshan

numbers of years—typically, at least 5 years, to become vested. The company puts aside funds in a trust to cover its pension liabilities: to provide pensions to its (vested) ex-workers once they reach retirement age. The amounts the company must set aside as well as the activities of the fund are tightly regulated by the federal government, under Title IV of the Employee Retirement Income Security Act (ERISA) of 1974. As a result, most of these trusts are adequately funded, and the pensions are considered largely safe.

This is not to say that a number haven't failed: they have, mainly when the company has gone bankrupt. Prominent examples include United Airlines ($7.4 billion pension liability), Delphi ($6.1 billion), Bethlehem Steel ($3.7 billion), US Airways ($2.8 billion), LTV Steel ($2.1 billion), and Delta Airlines ($1.6 billion), among others. Pan Am ($.8 billion—a decade earlier) and TWA ($.7 billion) were less. These are the biggest single-employer pension plans that failed on account of company bankruptcy between 1975 and 2011, the earliest on the list being PanAm (1991), next TWA (2001), and the rest between 2002 and 2005, until Delphi in 2009.[7] All told, between 1975 and 2014, 4640—10%—of the single-employer pension plans have failed, affecting 2.2 million vested participants with total claims of $48.8 billion. Most were in air transportation as just enumerated (29%) and smelting/refining (25%). Manufacturing and air transportation accounted for 87% of all failures in this period.[8]

In all of these cases, the pension liability was assumed by a federal government agency that insures private sector pensions: the Pension Benefit Guaranty Corporation (PBGC)—see Sect. 17.2.3.

The PBGC was created to cover failed pension funds and has done this consistently for the generally well-regulated single-employer plans. In FY 2013, the PBGC paid $5.4 billion to cover most of the retirement benefits of 851,000 retirees, and another 596,000 people will receive benefits from the PBGC when they reach retirement age.[9]

That's the good news.

---

[7] gao.gov/assets/590/587045.pdf = tinyurl.com/y9ctgcjv, Appendix I.

[8] pbgc.gov/documents/2014-data-tables-final.pdf = tinyurl.com/yavkdrsv, Table S-19.

[9] pbgc.gov/about-pbgc/who-we-are/retirement-matters/multiemployer-101-understanding-difference-between-single = tinyurl.com/y9ded7ua.

17.2.2 Multi-Employer Plans

For the remaining quarter of private sector workers with a pension who are enrolled in a multi-employer plan, the news is not altogether reassuring, as already noted. While some are solvent and on sound footing, too many are disastrously underfunded. Barring external intervention, a number are predicted to be bankrupt within a decade.

In 2007, the funding ratio *assets/liabilities* for single-employer plans was 84% (80% is considered adequate), while for multi-employer plans it was only 56%. Seven years later, in 2014, the average funding ratio of single-employer plans was maintained, at 82%, while for multi-employer plans it plummeted to a mere 4%, presaging insolvencies within the decade.

For this reason, multi-employer plans have raised considerable concern. It was never meant to be this way, although it shouldn't have been hard to see from the beginning that while single-employer plans were covered by sensible government regulations to ensure their sustainability, regulation of the multiple-employer plans was left largely to the fund administrators. This was putting the fox in charge of the chicken coop.

Multi-employer plans are union pension plans, whose terms are the result of collective bargaining. Their notorious under-regulation by the federal government has been more a result of political deals with unions than ideology.

About 10–15% of these, affecting 150–200 plans and covering 1.5 million workers, are poised to fail in the next decade.[10] Failure results in reducing pension benefits below the promised levels.

In the most extreme case that the PBGC multi-employer pension insurance fund is depleted and not bolstered by Congress, the result can all but eliminate steady pensions altogether, reducing them to whatever level can be funded by incoming premiums paid by existing workers. (But then, would existing workers agree to such a Ponzi-like scheme?)

Although the remaining multi-employer pension plans seem ok for now, that too can change as a result of their loose funding requirements that leave them open to mismanagement. The Department of Labor posts yearly lists of severely underfunded plans.[11]

How did this come about? There was a good originating idea that initiated these plans. It was that when workers—typically, in construction, trucking,

---

[10] pensionrights.org/publications/fact-sheet/facts-about-multiemployer-pension-plan-funding#HowWellFunded = tinyurl.com/yb643cza.

[11] dol.gov/agencies/ebsa/about-ebsa/our-activities/public-disclosure/critical-status-notices = tinyurl.com/y7ae26st.

290   **R. P. Kurshan**

and manufacturing[12]—change employers, as they do frequently, their pensions should follow them. Through collective bargaining, employers agree to contribute to the plans, thus pooling their contributions. That was a very advantageous scheme. Even if one employer went bankrupt, it had little effect on the plan, supported by all the other employers (who would be required to take up the slack, but the incremental liability would be small).

On account of this shared liability, the PBGC—which also covers multi-employer pension funds—required significantly lower insurance premiums than they did for single-employer accounts. This seemed like a win for everyone involved.

The potential for trouble began with the plan administration structure. Unions—seemingly sensibly—insisted on appointing half of the plan trustee positions, to ensure that union interests were adequately addressed. One consequence was that these plans—less regulated than the single-employer plans—to some extent can make up their own financing assumptions.

This was a disastrous consequence. In order to appear cost-efficient, overly optimistic fund appreciation rates as well as overly short member life expectancies were assumed, allowing underfunding of the pension trusts. Underfunding worked ok during robust markets but predictably moved pension trust funds to the brink of failure when markets became depressed. Moreover, when an entire industry was hit by a downturn and employers dropped out in droves, the remaining employers often were unable to pick up the slack.

As this happened, the underfunding became apparent. However, then increased funding requirements on the remaining employers began a death-spiral of failures. Even union-consent to raise employee contributions and decrease coverage was not always enough.

When an underfunded plan ceases to be able to pay its beneficiaries what was promised, in principle, the shortfall is covered by the PBGC. But wait: the PBGC is not a bottomless well either (Sect. 17.2.8). The PBGC fund for multi-employer plans is almost dry.

It has been said that the union trustees of troubled plans knew of their impending insolvency long before they began to fail.[13] Yet, some backed "reckless and even deceptive practices" while "allowing the financial status of their members' pension plans to continue to deteriorate, often while proclaiming the great promised benefits of those plans." The motive? To show union members the success and efficiency of their plans, thus, to win re-

---

[12] Also, retail trade workers; food, health, and other services workers; and others.
[13] Greszler (2015).

election and hopefully then to have moved on before disaster actually struck (*ibid*). Some union trustees may have counted on a worst-case federal bailout on the order of what was done in 2008 for the banks.

This is yet another a prime example of how letting an industry regulate itself can lead to disastrous consequences. Without a federal government bailout, already by 2015 both the pension plans of the Central State Teamsters and of the United Mine Workers looked destined to fail within 10–15 years or less, unless they implemented drastic cuts to their pensions. But a bailout is borne on the shoulders of the taxpayers and rewards bad behavior (as it did with the banks in 2008).

In 2016, the U.S. Treasury Dept. rejected a plan proposed by the Central State Teamsters that drastically cut their members' pensions. However, that reprieve may have been only technical. The reasons given for the rejection were that the proposed cuts were insufficient, not equitably distributed among retirees and inadequately explained.

Since 2015, there have been bills before Congress[14,15] to initiate bailouts for the Mine Workers. Given the proclivities of the Trump administration, taxpayer bailouts of such plans seemed likely, the alternative being a disastrous financial ending for key constituencies.

By 2019, the United Mine Workers pension plan was projected to run out of money in 2023. Hidden in the $1.4 trillion spending bill passed by Congress and signed by the President at the end of 2019 was the Bipartisan American Miners Act. That act indeed used taxpayer dollars to bail out the United Mine Workers pension plan.[16] Is this the first of many such federal bailouts?

There is an ironic cycle here. Those who supported the weakening of government, in particular, the weakening of government fiscal oversight, created conditions that, in the end, required the government to bail out failed businesses (first the banks, now union pension plans).

Moreover, as we shall see, the private sector multi-employer pension plans are not the only ones in trouble. Orders of magnitude bigger troubles lurk for state pension plans (teachers, firefighters, police, …). Could the Mine Workers and Teamsters be bailed out and not these others?

In the end, the ideologies that led to weakened government oversight may lead inadvertently to socialization of retirement benefits: in effect, expanding and strengthening Social Security, on the taxpayers' tab. That for sure would

---

[14] congress.gov/bill/114th-congress/senate-bill/1714.

[15] congress.gov/bill/114th-congress/house-bill/2403.

[16] nytimes.com/2019/12/24/business/coal-miner-pensions-bailout.html = tinyurl.com/w7rsmcm.

be more efficient than the piecemeal bailing out of failed pension plans. In fact this actually can be a good idea, given the sorry state of retirement today (Chap. 18). Is this what the "smaller government" folks had in mind? Unlikely, but it could be the consequence of their actions.

On the other hand, looking only at the 10–15% of multi-employer plans that are in trouble gives an overly pessimistic view. The vast majority are adequately funded. A 2014 report indicated that 85% of multi-employer plans have an actuarial certification as neither "critical" nor "endangered," up by 4% from the previous year. As such, they are not subject to rules of the Pension Protection Act of 2006 that can require curtailed pension payments.

A list of those that are in greatest trouble has been compiled by The Center for Retirement Research at Boston College.[17] It can be found at the Pension Rights Center,[18] which also provides a calculator (see Sect. 17.2.6) to determine how much a pension might be reduced.

17.2.3 The Pension Benefit Guaranty Corporation

The Department of Labor's Employee Benefits Security Administration[19] (EBSA) is the primary agency responsible for protecting private pension plan participants and beneficiaries from the abuse or theft of their pension assets, by enforcing ERISA (Sect. 17.2.1).

The Pension Benefit Guaranty Corporation (PBGC) was created under ERISA "to encourage the continuation and maintenance of private sector defined benefit [pension] plans, provide timely and uninterrupted payment of pension benefits, and keep pension insurance premiums at a minimum".[20]

It insures against default the retirement incomes of more than 40 million American workers and their beneficiaries, in nearly 45,000 private sector pension plans.

The PBGC is funded by insurance premiums collected from employers that sponsor insured pension plans. Under acts of Congress, these employers are obligated to pay these premiums as well as satisfy minimum funding standards and pay stiff penalty premiums if the funding standards are not met.

---

[17] crr.bc.edu/briefs/the-financial-status-of-private-sector-multiemployer-pension-plans/.

[18] pensionrights.org/publications/fact-sheet/multiemployer-pension-plans-projected-be-critical-and-declining-status = tinyurl.com/y9c53n66.

[19] dol.gov/agencies/ebsa/about-ebsa/about-us/history-of-ebsa-and-erisa = tinyurl.com/ycgct6mv.

[20] Unless otherwise indicated, much of the material in this section was taken directly from pbgc.gov, including possibly unquoted content.

The PBGC insurance coverage is divided between two separate programs, for single- and multi-employer plans, respectively.

In 2014, America's private sector pension and retirement savings system (including defined contribution plans like the 401(k)) covered almost 90 million individuals—including roughly 70% of those in full-time employment—in approximately 685,000 plans with assets totaling close to $8.3 trillion.[21] (This comprised 47% of the $17.6 trillion assets of private and public pension funds together, which by 2016 reached $18.6 trillion, 35% of the total U.S. securities markets.)

The maximum pension benefit guaranteed by PBGC is set by Congress and adjusted yearly. For a single-employer plan that terminated in 2020, the maximum guarantee for a 65-year-old retired worker who receives a pension without a survivor benefit is $5812.50 per month: see Fig. 17.3. If the retiree is 73, the amount increases to $14,461.50.[22]

Whatever the amount, it is set according to a PBGC table for the year in which PBGC benefits begin and doesn't change thereafter. In particular, there is no cost of living adjustment. If the amount the retiree was receiving at the time of failure was below the cap, then the PBGC continues to pay that amount for the life of the retiree; else, the PBGC pays the cap amount. Thus, the PBGC does not always pay the full amount for a defaulted pension. However, it has for 84% of the single-employer pensions it covered in 2006.

There are exceptions, and the details can be more complicated. The guarantee is lower for those who retire early or when there is a benefit for a survivor. The guarantee is increased for those who retire after age 65.

There are other PBGC coverage limitations that apply to special pension plan benefits that are conferred as a result of an "unpredictable contingent event"—mainly, a plant shut-down.

For multi-employer plans, the maximum guaranteed amounts are considerably less: under $13 thousand/year in 2013. In fact, though, for multi-employer plans, the PBGC does not actually take over the plan as it does in the single-employer case. Instead, it funds the pension plan according to its mandated formula. In the end, what an employee gets is mostly determined by the union of which the employee is a member, and this may be significantly less than what was promised.

---

[21] Labor (2016a).

[22] pbgc.gov/wr/benefits/guaranteed-benefits/your-guaranteed-pension.html = tinyurl.com/ydcspa8w.

PBGC Maximum Monthly Guarantees For 2020		
Age	2020 Straight-Life Annuity	2020 Joint And 50% Survivor Annuity*
75	$17,670.00	$15,903.00
74	$16,065.75	$14,459.18
73	$14,461.50	$13,015.35
72	$12,857.25	$11,571.53
71	$11,253.00	$10,127.70
70	$9,648.75	$8,683.88
69	$8,660.63	$7,794.57
68	$7,788.75	$7,009.88
67	$7,033.13	$6,329.82
66	$6,393.75	$5,754.38
65	$5,812.50	$5,231.25
64	$5,405.63	$4,865.07
63	$4,998.75	$4,498.88
62	$4,591.88	$4,132.69
61	$4,185.00	$3,766.50
60	$3,778.13	$3,400.32
59	$3,545.63	$3,191.07
58	$3,313.13	$2,981.82
57	$3,080.63	$2,772.57
56	$2,848.13	$2,563.32
55	$2,615.63	$2,354.07
54	$2,499.38	$2,249.44
53	$2,383.13	$2,144.82
52	$2,266.88	$2,040.19
51	$2,150.63	$1,935.57
50	$2,034.38	$1,830.94
49	$1,918.13	$1,726.32
48	$1,801.88	$1,621.69
47	$1,685.63	$1,517.07
46	$1,569.38	$1,412.44
45	$1,453.13	$1,307.82

* Above J&50% amounts apply only if both spouses are the same age. Different amounts apply if that is not the case.

Fig. 17.3 PBGC maximum monthly payments—2020.

Altogether, for 2014, the PBGC reports[23] paying "basic pension benefits earned by more than 41 million American workers and retirees in nearly 24,000 plans," while the number of pension plans paying premiums to the PBGC was 44,869, down from 48,982 in 2007.[24]

17.2.4 Uninsured Benefits

Some people, especially those considered to be part of "management," have an additional company contribution to their pension outside their defined benefit plan. These are not guaranteed by the PBGC and are likely to be lost entirely in case of company bankruptcy.

The same holds for deferred compensation (Sect. 12.6): compensation that is held by the company, not in a deferred benefit plan trust fund. The advantage of such deferred compensation is that it is tax-deferred. The risk is of putting too many eggs in one basket: if your company goes bankrupt, you may lose not only your job and pension but also money that you already have earned that is held by the company.

17.2.5 Single-Employer Pension Fund Termination

There are three ways a single-employer pension fund can be terminated. One is *standard termination*, when the plan provider proves that it has enough funds to pay all its obligations and then either purchases an annuity for its recipients that pays the stipends due or provides the recipient with an equivalent lump sum pension buyout. In some cases the recipient is given the choice between these two options.

If the plan is more than 60% funded but less than 80% funded, a plan with a lump sum option is allowed to pay out only 50% of the benefit as a lump sum. The rest must be paid as a lifetime monthly annuity. If the employer sponsoring the pension plan is in bankruptcy, then the plan is prohibited from paying lump sums unless the plan is at least 100% funded.

The other two termination types are *distress termination* and *involuntary termination*. In the first, the employer proves its pension fund is inadequate to meet all its obligations and that its only alternative is bankruptcy. In the second, the PBGC shows that the employer cannot meet its pension

---

[23] pbgc.gov/about/annual-reports/pbgc-annual-report-2014 = tinyurl.com/yb68gqtw.
[24] Labor (2016b).

296   **R. P. Kurshan**

obligations. In these types of terminations, the PBGC becomes the trustee of the pension fund and assumes its obligations subject to limits described in Sect. 17.2.3. For example, the 2002 United Airline bankruptcy spawned the largest pension plan default to date: $7.3 billion, according to the PBGC. The PBGC took over their pension plan in 2005 and paid 100% of pension obligations for 82% of the employees in their pension plan and, of the remaining 18%, paid 99% on average. However, of the $7.3 billion UAL pension fund obligation, the PBGC assumed only $6.6 billion. The difference represents the loss to the pension plan members as a result of the bankruptcy. This loss was borne mostly by the higher-paid employees: the pilots. They got caught in a Catch-22: while subject to mandatory retirement by age 60, the PBGC penalizes those who "retire early." As a result, some pilots received less than 30% of what they were promised, according to the Pension Research Council, citing a Newsday article. "Had the United Airlines pilots opted for lump sums [prior to the PBGC takeover] instead of monthly payments, they would have been a lot better off," they wrote.

As of 2014, 4640 single-employer pension plans have been taken over ("trusteed") by the PBGC. While plans come and go, some very large, some tiny, this is roughly 4% of all the plans covered by the PBGC since 1975. Of the 4%, 60% of the defaulted plans were in manufacturing (excluding "high-tech"). The largest number of single-employer plans taken over by the PBGC in a single year was 191 in 2009. In that year, the PBGC insured 27,797 plans,[25] so the percent of defaulted plans that year was less than 0.7% of all plans. Thus, on average, without taking the industry covered by a plan into account, the likelihood that one's single-employer plan will default is small.

On the other hand, in manufacturing (a category that excludes "high-tech" manufacturing as described below), 2782 plans defaulted between 1975 and 2014. This was a bit more than a third of the 7439 insured single-employer plans in manufacturing in 2007, the year before the 2008 economic crisis. Within manufacturing, the hardest hit industry was in primary metals (e.g., steel smelting). Primary metals accounted for over a quarter of the manufacturing claims between 1975 and 2014, affecting over three quarters of the number of primary metals plans insured in 2007.

The next hardest hit area was air transportation. Between 1975 and 2014, 63% of the number of those plans insured in 2007—68 plans—defaulted. (Note that this does not say that 63% of the 68 plans insured in 2007 defaulted. Most of the defaults occurred years earlier, and those plans were

---

[25] https://pbgc.gov/documents/2014-data-tables-final.pdf.

closed, while others were created. However, it does give an indication of the proportion of defaults.)

Thus, based only on the industry of a plan, one can observe that over a 40-year period, using 2007 as a baseline for the number of plans in each industry, the percent of plans that defaulted are as follows: 37% of the number of 2007 manufacturing plans, 77% of primary metals plans, and 63% of plans in air transportation.

On the other hand, the industry with the fewest defaults was the information industry. Its defaults in 1975–2014, amounted to only 9% of the plans insured in 2007. The information industry is a very broad category that includes industries that produce media (tv, movies, newspapers, books); information processing (legal, data processing, telephone, computer programming); manufacturing of information-processing devices like computers, telephones, and televisions; and other "high-tech" manufacturers that require significant research and development to produce their products. Again, using 2007 as a baseline causes this percentage to be overstated, since it excludes plans that closed. Given that only 4% of all plans across 1975–2014 defaulted and the information industry has the fewest defaults of all, the actual fraction of all defaults in the information industry across those years must be much less than 4%.

Yet, 4% is not zero. The recent bankruptcy of telecommunications giant Avaya is sobering. Its pension plan liability of $1.7 billion comprised 25% of its $6.3 billion debt,[26] and offloading this to the PBGC may have been a prime motive behind the bankruptcy. In this case, highly compensated retirees, who would get significantly less from the PBGC than what is owed to them, may regret not accepting an earlier pension buyout offer, although hindsight may distort the propriety of what foresight deemed correct in view of historically based expectations.[27]

What can one conclude from all this? I'd say that if you are a member of a single-employer pension plan in a resilient industry like the information industry that can redefine its directions based on changing economic conditions, the likelihood of default is extremely small—maybe 1% or less over decades. On the other hand, if you are a member of a plan in a single commoditized product industry like air transportation or steel smelting, then the industry is more fragile in the face of changing economic and technological conditions, and thus bankruptcy is a greater risk. In the worst cases, such as air transportation

---

[26] reuters.com/article/us-avaya-bankruptcy-idUSKBN1532JY.

[27] pbgc.gov/news/press/releases/pr17-11.

and primary metals, the risk of losing a part of one's pension as a result of the bankruptcy of the issuing company is significant. Even in these cases, once a pension is taken over by the PBGC, in most cases, the pensioner still receives 100% of the pension. However, someone who has taken early retirement or who receives a relatively high pension (such as management) may not receive from the PBGC the entire pension owed by the employer.

17.2.6 Multi-Employer Pension Fund Termination

The PBGC does not take over multi-employer pension plans as it does with insolvent single-employer plans. Instead, it makes loans to insolvent plans to enable them to continue to pay pensions. However, in the process, pensions are reduced to levels guaranteed by the PBGC, determined by a somewhat complex formulation.[28,29] The Pension Rights Center provides a calculator[30] to help with the calculation.

The Multi-employer Pension Reform Act of 2014 allows some plans that are projected to run out of money within 15–20 years to cut existing pensions to 110% of what is guaranteed by the PBGC. This regulation[31] is summarized by the Pension Rights Center, which provides another calculator[32] to determine what cutback is allowed for an individual.

Some multi-employer plans already are in immediate trouble. Retirees funded by the Iron Workers Local 17 fund of northeastern Ohio have lost up to half or more of their pensions, starting in 2017.[33]

More generally, the Multi-employer Pension Reform Act of 2014 allows certain underfunded multi-employer plans that are "critical and declining" to cut retiree pension benefits. As of February, 2016, at least ten plans have applied to cut retiree pension benefits under this act,[34] affecting 492,631 participants.

---

[28] https://pbgc.gov/about/factsheets/page/multi-facts.html.

[29] pbgc.gov/prac/multiemployer/multiemployer-benefit-guarantees.html.

[30] pensionrights.org/multiemployer-pension-guarantee-calculator.

[31] pensionrights.org/issues/legislation/summary-pension-cutback-provisions multiemployer-pension-reform-act-2014 = tinyurl.com/y7q56vz3.

[32] pensionrights.org/multiemployer-retiree-cutback-calculator.

[33] clevescene.com/scene-and-heard/archives/2017/01/05/local-ironworkers-facing-potential-pension-cuts-in-unprecedented-vote = tinyurl.com/ycfpohw3.

[34] pensionrights.org/publications/fact-sheet/pension-plans-have-applied-cut-benefits-under-multiemployer-pension-reform-a = tinyurl.com/ycushs85.

17.2.7 How to Find Out if Your Pension Plan is Underfunded

The most important consideration for evaluating the reliability of your pension is how well it is funded. The information you need is provided in an Annual Funding Notice that your pension provider is required by the Pension Protection Act of 2006 to send to you. You also may be able to find a copy online.

This law applies both to single- and multi-employer pension plans. The funding notice is required to provide a measure called the "funding target attainment percentage," which gives the percent that your pension is funded. It also is required to state the value of the plan's *assets* and *liabilities*, how those assets are invested, and how much the PBGC pays if it takes over the pension plan. The pension plan administrator is legally required to provide this information at any time, upon request.

Recently, Congress has relaxed pension funding requirements. As a result, the pension provider may be able to show that a pension is fully funded (or better), while the PBGC, which by law uses more stringent (and arguably, more realistic) funding standards, finds it is not. Ideally, they should be the same.

This disconnect is evidence of political meddling by companies that seek to lessen their revenue drain from pension fund funding obligations. There has been significant lobbying of Congress to reduce those obligations. However, many have argued that doing so presents a significantly increased risk. This risk is not only for the company, which is still responsible for their pension obligations and may be hit later with a devastating shortfall, but also for the taxpayer at large. In the end, the taxpayer may be called upon to bail out failed pension plans, either directly or indirectly through increased social support for people rendered indigent by their failed pensions. This risky and potentially devastating behavior is blithely termed "kicking the can down the road." It is a direct result of companies valuing their near-term balance sheets over the long-term effects, a consequence of CEO compensation that's heavily weighted towards near-term stock price.

The funding ratio $F = assets/liabilities$ is the single most important number to determine the health of a pension trust fund. *Assets* is the present cash value of the assets in the pension trust fund, and *liabilities* is an estimate of the amount the pension plan needs in order to pay its obligations, using certain actuarial and interest-rate assumptions. Its obligations are mostly to pay all future benefits promised under the plan. Key to computing F is the interest rates used to compute the expected earnings on the pension trust fund investments. These rates are based on current corporate bond yields, as published by the U.S. Department of Treasury, and then *adjusted* to fall within specified ranges of rates averaged over some period. Previously, the period was the prior 2 years, meaning that assumed appreciation of assets had to be realistic, given recent conditions. However, in 2012 and again in 2014 and 2015 for different cases, this 2-year period was extended to 25 years, under an act of Congress with the Orwellian name the "Moving Ahead for Progress in the 21st century Act" (MAP-21). It then was further extended by the "Highway and Transportation Funding Act of 2014" and again by the "Bipartisan Budget Act of 2015." Since interest rates were much higher over the past 25 years than over the past 2 years, this change had the effect of significantly decreasing the pension fund *liabilities* and thus increasing F—by over 15% in 2013, 23% in 2014, and about 21.1% in 2015. By thus increasing F, pension plans that otherwise would have been underfunded ($F < 100\%$), by dint of the Congressional magic wand, now became adequately funded, allowing companies to divert funds that otherwise would have been required to bolster their pension plans, to other priorities.

However, there is a flip side to this "kicking the can down the road," and not all companies adopted this relaxed definition of F. Companies have a certain time period in which to decide whether to utilize the relaxed MAP-21 definition or not but then must stick with whichever definition they choose. In their Annual Funding Notice, they must state which guideline they have chosen.

The flip side is that eventually, the company may need to add more to the pension plan trust fund as a liability underestimate confronts the *actual* liabilities. As this event nears, the result can adversely affect the rating of the company, especially if accompanied by weaker earnings.[35] Furthermore, the PBGC uses the pre-MAP-21 interest appreciation rate calculations for determining the premiums it charges single-employer companies and its own determination of whether a company is underfunded. A plan may be fully funded under the MAP-21 assumptions but underfunded under the assumptions PBGC is required to use. A company must pay a penalty insurance premium to the PBGC for being underfunded in the PBGC's view (as is reasonable, since being underfunded increases the PBGC's risk), and this penalty was recently tripled. So it may not be worth it for a company to use MAP-21 to reduce its funding requirements, and a company that can afford to

---

[35] https://benefitspro.com/2013/09/05/map-21-the-wrong-course-for-pension-plans.

fully fund its pension plan according to the more realistic standard may decide to continue to use that standard.

Even if your pension plan is fully funded, it can be degraded if your plan merges with an underfunded plan. When two companies merge, the result may be to combine a well-funded pension plan with a less well-funded one. Presently, there are efforts by the National Retiree Legislative Network[36] to require that PBGC and the Dept. of Labor approve such mergers and protect a well-funded plan for 5 years.

Moreover, actual unfunded liabilities are even greater than reported. Total liabilities are masked by the fact that the PBGC reports only unfunded liabilities that it expects to incur over the next 10 years. In other words, the liabilities of any plans that are expected to become insolvent in 11 years or more are excluded. In contrast, Social Security reports a 75-year unfunded liability.

In the end, though, the single-employer plans stand out as relatively secure, thanks to their strong regulation. The 10% in jeopardy have tended to be in sectors whose businesses have changed dramatically.

There's one more adverse possibility, though. Your pension obligation can be sold to an insurance company (Sect. 17.2.5). That insurance company then assumes full responsibility to pay your full pension, as an annuity. What if *it* went bankrupt? In this case, you no longer are covered by the PBGC. However, every state, the District of Columbia, and Puerto Rico have Insurance Guaranty Associations[37] that guarantee some of your loss. These are private, voluntary organizations run by the insurance companies. In effect, the insurance companies of a state chip in to protect the clients of one of their own in case of bankruptcy, in order to preserve the good name of the industry. Unfortunately, the coverage is significantly capped in terms of total payout, and you may end up with only a half a dozen years of pension after a bankruptcy.

summary

So, what are the chances that you can lose some or all of your pension? For multi-employer plans, it's sadly not insignificant. For private single-employer pension plans, in general, it's very low. Yet, who could imagine that Pan Am, the signature logo in the movie *2001: A Space Odyssey*, no longer would be with us by 2001? TWA? Eastern Airlines? Bethlehem Steel? All had

---

[36] nrln.org.

[37] nolhga.com/policyholderinfo/main.cfm = tinyurl.com/ybj2hf8o.

failed pension plans. In fact, the list of airlines that have sought bankruptcy protection under a Chapter 11 reorganization is long. However, pensions were affected in different ways. For example, before United Airlines sought Chapter 11 protection, it increased pension benefits by 40% for its 23,000 ground employees, passing the liability on to the PBGC. So far, most single-employer pension plans have strong long-term prospects.

There is a temptation to make a political observation: the pension plans under greatest stress are "blue collar" plans. Why is that? Do the political forces at play consider this group more expendable? It's a tempting conclusion, but the issue is more nuanced and multi-faceted. These groups tended to get their way through strong unions. It was easier for politicians to give in to their demands for independent control than insist on prudence. While the politicians bear the ultimate responsibility and thus blame, fiduciary neglect and corruption on the part of unions[38,39,40] played a dominant role.

A final word here. To a large extent, it's possible to predict the pension plans that are more likely to default, based on the industry. However, even with a default, much if not all of a pension is usually preserved. Like everything else in life, a pension has a risk. Overall, though, on the average, your pension is probably safe.

While the ultimate fallback to the PBGC for a failed pension may seem reassuring, it's a bit less than that, especially for more highly compensated employees. What might be worse, the PBGC itself is in trouble.

17.2.8 The PBGC Itself is in Trouble

Presently, the PBGC itself is underfunded. The following is a statement from the PBGC web site:

> Over the next decade or so, even before any new obligations are added, there is a substantial risk that, without significant change to the multi-employer plan system and PBGC's program, the multi-employer insurance program will become insolvent and not be able to pay financial assistance. PBGC has begun discussions with the Congress about approaches to reduce this risk.

---

[38] nytimes.com/1964/07/27/archives/hoffa-convicted-on-use-of-funds-faces-20-years-he-and-6-others-are.html = tinyurl.com/y8et2o2h.

[39] nytimes.com/2017/02/03/us/politics/andrew-puzder-labor-secretary.html.

[40] nytimes.com/2019/12/26/business/uaw-gary-jones-investigation.html.

thus, the fate of pensions lies with Congress

If the PBGC becomes insolvent, workers can lose PBGC protections and end up with nothing if their pension plan defaults. Moreover, risks of default in multi-employer plans are increasing, with potential unfunded liabilities reaching $42 billion.[41] However, this is just the tip of the iceberg: state and local pensions are underfunded by about $1 trillion (see Sect. 17.3). Could Congress bail out the truckers and coal miners and leave the teachers, police, and firefighters hanging out to dry? It is unclear if, when, and to what extent Congress will come to the rescue, putting the cost of their legislative regulatory oversight failures onto taxpayers.

17.2.9 Should You Take a Pension Buyout Offer?

Some employers have been offering a lump sum buyout of individual pensions. This means that the company offers the pensioner a one-time payment if the pensioner agrees to forgo all further pension payments.

Should you take it?

These companies are seeking to shed some of their pension liability, as explained in the introduction of this chapter.

Whether to accept a lump sum pension buyout is a fraught decision that can cause many sleepless nights. On the one hand, a pension is for the life of the holder, and frequently for the life of the holder's spouse or partner (although usually in a reduced amount). On the other hand, rarely is there a pension that is adjusted for inflation, so it becomes worth less and less over the years. And that lump sum can look pretty attractive. It's almost like getting all your pension for all the years to come, right now (assuming that you don't live past the age that you are expected to die, in an actuarial sense).

Certainly, if you have been diagnosed with a terminal disease and feel certain that you will die very soon, the buyout is a dream come true: it will allow you to splurge with exotic pleasures before you die, or leave a nice bonus to your beneficiaries.

Also, if you don't need your pension for living expenses and simply want to maximize your expected returns, then take the buyout.

What about everyone else? There's a quick answer and an answer that requires a computation. I'll give both.

---

[41]Greszler (2015).

Here's the quick answer. The company has projected its liability with regard to your pension assuming that you live the actuarially expected amount of time. You can find your number in actuarial tables.[42,43] You also can find the expected amount of time until the death of the second of you and your spouse.[44] Do you think you will live longer than that? If you think that's a reasonable possibility, if your company is not in a sector with a high risk of default (see preceding sections) and if you're not sure that you can produce better returns by investing the lump sum buyout than the very conservative assumptions that the government has forced the company to use in calculating the buyout offer (and you probably can't—see below), then no: stick with your pension.

Indeed, investing in ways that increase your expected return over the government-mandated conservative assumptions also increases your risk that you end up with much less. If you depend on your pension, then this is not a wise gamble.

Even if you are concerned that your pension provider will default, unless you have specific information to that effect, the general risk may be smaller than the risk of underperforming your pension with your investment of the lump sum buyout.

However, it's easy to be seduced into taking a buyout. For one, it may look like a windfall, and it's easy to forget that your pension serves a vital purpose. For another, the very low return rates on which the lump sum calculation is based seem easy to beat: just invest in an S&P 500 index fund, and instead of the government-mandated 2% rate of return on which the lump sum is based, you'll get an expected return of 9%. How can you go wrong?

Here's how. First, there's a fundamental question you should ask yourself: Why does my pension provider want to offer me a lump sum buyout? Ample reasons were given above that seem to have little to do with the pensioner. But that thinking is wrong. The essential reason has everything to do with the pensioner. The essential reason that your pension provider wants you to take a lump sum buyout is that if you accept, the provider's risk is reduced.

---

[42] ssa.gov/oact/STATS/table4c6.html.

[43] https://johnhancockinsurance.com/life-expectancy-calculator.html.

[44] Vanguard (2000); there are a number of tables out there, for example, another is pgcalc.com/pdf/twolife.pdf = tinyurl.com/yagkcyw5—and they give different results! They can differ by 4–5%. Why? Although they are all based on the same census data, they analyze the data differently. (Don't forget: these are predictions about the future, based on data from the past.) The Vanguard tool uses actuarial tables focused on retirement planning. The second table is calculated for insurance companies that may take a more "conservative" view of longevity. After all, in setting their premiums, they don't want to underestimate how long you are expected to live.

The risk the provider reduces is the risk of pension fund underperformance due to investment volatility. If uncorrected, this can lead to an inability to pay the pensions owed. To address this risk, the provider needs to adjust downward the expected trust fund growth rate, and then bolster the pension trust enough to ensure it can meet its obligations. If the lump sum is passed to you, then this requirement is passed on to you as well. You can't merely project potential lump sum payouts based on its average expected growth: Chap. 10. You must account for investment volatility just as the pension provider needed to when the funds were in the pension trust. The result is that the lump sum pays out less than an expectation based on expected growth, or lasts for less time when drawn down for expenses.

So the pension provider's risk that is shed when a pensioner accepts a lump sum doesn't simply evaporate! It is passed to the pensioner. Like a hot potato, along with the lump sum come all the risks of investing it. In the industry, this process is called "de-risking." The more honest term "risk transfer" makes it clear. The risk is not eliminated but simply transferred from the company to the employee.

The lump sum buyout recipient incurs much the same risks that the pension provider unloads and transfers: the risk of poor market performance and the risk of pensioner longevity (living longer than expected).

The pension provider can assume that you live your actuarially expected lifetime, because the assumption is averaged over all the pensioners. However, once the lump sum comes to you, you cannot safely assume that it will pay out more than it did as a pension, nor can you assume that it will last longer than your expected lifetime.

Thus, by taking the lump sum, on average, you gain nothing in payouts, while losing the opportunity to continue getting your pension past your expected lifetime.

Regarding the risk of pension plan default, this risk is mostly very small, as described in the foregoing sections. Moreover, even when a default occurs, as we have seen, it is not all or nothing: there are layers of protection that can preserve all or, in most cases, at least most of a defaulted pension.

Nonetheless, as we've seen, defaults do occur, and when they do, pensioners may come away with only a small fraction of their pension promises. This is especially true in the case of multi-employer pension plans. It behooves anyone given the opportunity to take a pension buyout to do a little online research regarding the long-term security of their particular pension plan. Again, though: it's important not to be spooked by general scares about pensions. Yes, there have been a few bad cases, and these are the ones you tend to read about. But no sooner than you stop driving because you read about a deadly car crash, should you abandon your pension without a very specific and well-thought-out reason. On average, you are better off keeping your pension.

One possible justification for accepting a buyout offer is liquidity. If you had a sudden urgent need for a lot of cash, you cannot get a cash advance from your pension, but you can liquidate part of your buyout. It's hard to weigh this advantage against the advantages of keeping a pension.

computing the value of a buyout offer

If you are still attracted to the possibility of accepting a pension lump sum buyout offer, it can be useful to compute its value in a few different ways. First, you can check the value of the offered lump sum using the government-mandated formula, based on (A.14) in Appendix A.11. The government rates are required to be included with the buyout offer.

Next, you can compute the periodic payouts of a bond ladder purchased with the buyout, as described in Appendix A.7. Set various terms (periods of time that you might live) and various yields, and see how the payouts compare with your pension. You can look up on the web various classes of bonds that may interest you and see what levels of yields for various terms are available presently. This provides an upper bound on what one can expect from a bond ladder, as in reality, it is unlikely to be able to purchase the required bonds for each ladder rung. Thus, there will be "holes" that reduce the payouts (Appendix A.7). (The "holes" are ladder rungs for which no bonds are available and which thus must be covered by earlier maturities, resulting in an overall lower yield.)

You are thus unlikely to be able to replicate the payouts of your pension with risk-free U.S. Treasury bonds, as the buyout lump sum is computed as an ideal. Moreover, the computation is based on three high-grade corporate yields (generally higher than for Treasuries, the bonds correspondingly riskier). If you actually built the ladder, the lower yields of Treasury bonds and ladder holes reduce your payouts. By accepting more risk, you can build a ladder of higher-yield riskier bonds that can reproduce or exceed your pension payout. But then, you need to ask yourself why you would want to replace a low-risk pension that lasts a lifetime (the only risk being its possible default), with higher-risk securities with a fixed term, after which you get nothing.

Finally, you can use the Fidelity Brokerage Services *Retirement Income Planner* calculator as described in Sect. 11.1.4 to find how long Fidelity estimates that the buyout lump sum is expected to last when drawn down at the pension payment rate, under various investment assumptions, for various confidence levels. The simpler Vanguard retirement simulator mentioned in Sect. 4.7 also gives such feedback.

17.3 Public Sector Pensions

In addition to private pensions, as of 2017 there was $3.8 trillion invested for state- and locally administered defined benefit public pensions, funding $4.1 trillion in pension obligations[45] according to the U.S. Census Bureau. This covered 88% of state and local government employees. The Pew Charitable Trusts estimates an even greater state pension funding shortfall of almost $1 trillion.[46] Other estimates go as high as $3 trillion.[47] (Variations in estimates of funding shortfalls derive from varying assumptions about how far into the future funding obligations should be calculated and the expected rate of appreciation of the invested funds.)

By another estimate, federal employee plans have asset levels that are only around 40% of their actuarial liabilities, and despite efforts to close this gap, their value in 2007 was $1 trillion compared with their benefit liability of $2.4 trillion.[48]

Public sector pension plans often are funded by mandated employee contributions, sometimes matched by the government authority and sometimes not. There are harrowing stories about how fully funded pension plans have been raided by politicians for partisan goals, leading to the plans' ultimate under-funding.[49]

Public pension liabilities for underfunded plans have contributed to municipality defaults and bankruptcies, with pension holders left, in a few cases, with little or no redress, getting a fraction of the pension that was promised.

There is a popular view that portrays public pension holders as having received too sweet a deal and therefore not to be pitied if they lose their

---

[45] data.census.gov/cedsci = tinyurl.com/y8lkhz2a.

[46] pewtrusts.org/en/research-and-analysis/issue-briefs/2015/07/the-state-pensions-funding-gap-challenges-persist = tinyurl.com/y77ey6fe.

[47] Greszler, *ibid.*

[48] Reinsdorf and Lenze (2009).

[49] dailyvoice.com/new-york/ramapo/police-fire/mt-olive-sgt-mike-pocquats-letter-to-the-police-unions/631566/ = tinyurl.com/yac76gsh.

Scott Walker 2017

pensions. This view ignores the fact that in many cases,[50,51] politicians bartered wage increases for pension increases. This was very handy for the politicians, as it allowed them avoid the cost of increased salaries, in exchange for a potentially empty promise to "make up for it" with large pensions later. Union leaders, who may have had the depth of view to be skeptical of such deals, often went along because it was an easy sell to the rank and file and made the leaders look good in the eyes of the union members. The rank and file believed what they were told and lacked insight into the serious risks afforded by little or no funding requirements for the pension plans. It was a win-win-win-lose deal: the municipalities won, the politicians won, and the union leaders won; only the workers lost, in agreeing to exchange increased wages today for increased pensions later, not understanding the considerable risks involved in accepting promises not backed by adequate funding requirements.

One of the most egregious examples occurred in Wisconsin. The Wisconsin pension and health plans are *100%* funded by workers through payroll deductions. This is the quintessential trade of wages now for pension later. However, the state, in large degree under its previous Republican Governor, Scott Walker, shifted these worker contributions to fund tax cuts that largely benefited the wealthy and corporations. Then, in language befitting George Orwell, Gov. Walker called upon these workers, whose deferred wages were misappropriated, to "pay their fair share" to compensate for the funding shortfall. What this actually meant was that Gov. Walker wanted workers to pay a still greater proportion of their wages into their pension plan, i.e., accept

---

[50]There are cases with other explanations. One of the most notorious is Vallejo, CA, where the police union has had a strangle-hold on the city politicians and, as a result, was able to extort outlandishly high compensation and pensions: Bauer (2020), footnote 51.

[51]sfchronicle.com/bayarea/otisrtaylorjr/article/Vallejo-police-chief-will-walk-away-with-a-13761301.php = tinyurl.com/y4ww4n6j.

17 Pensions 309

a larger deferral of compensation than was agreed upon. The immediate effect, of course, was simply to further reduce wages. Whether or not the reduction comes out the other end as increased pension payments may be informed by how well the state kept its earlier promise. In finance this arrangement is called "kiting" and is illegal: continually deferring payment of what is owed. Nonetheless, the political spin follows the "welfare queen" line, blaming the victims.

It is true that in some pension plans that include state contributions, the negotiated terms might be viewed as extravagant, promising early retirement and large benefits. However, with a very few exceptions (e.g., footnotes 50, 51), a deal is a deal. We don't know the negotiations and horse-trading that went into the deal. Moreover, there is evidence that the popular view of extravagant public pensions is largely political. One report finds "little basis for the conclusion that state and local employees are significantly overcompensated. On the contrary, pay is comparable at lower skill levels, and private sector employees are significantly better paid at higher skill levels".[52] It is hypocritical to point to public workers who "spike" their pensions by (legally) arranging for inflated last-year salaries (through a lot of overtime work, for example), while passively accepting the myriad tax loopholes used by the wealthy and virtually every company to "game the system" to their advantage. If the state's thinking for these extravagant promises was the expectation that they can be broken if necessary, it would represent an unbecoming cynicism for an entity that has an obligation to provide equitable treatment of its constituents. If there is blame to be assigned, it absolutely is not to the workers but to the politicians who agreed to the extravagant promises in furtherance of their political agendas. Of course, reality is never simple, and the arrows of cause and effect often appear circular. Voters sometimes elect politicians who harm them, voting against their self-interests, for a favored political party or on account of less important unrelated issues.

There is a view[53] that public pensions are in grave jeopardy since they are under-regulated and funded (and defaulted) at the whim of politicians. When the going gets tough, in this view, these politicians have no interest to throw money into ancient contractual obligations with no political payback. This is a very jaundiced view that sadly comes with some justification. But it is not the entire story. Indeed, public pension funds have *in some cases* been woefully underfunded, in good part for the reasons just given. Indeed, in a number

---

[52] huffpost.com/entry/government-pensions_b_4855776 = tinyurl.com/ya45qggj.
[53] huffpost.com/entry/pinching-pensions-to-keep_b_3820103 = tinyurl.com/yde4xjom.

310 **R. P. Kurshan**

of these cases, the politicians have sought to escape their contractual—and in some states, constitutional—pension obligations by abetting actions that lead to plan defaults. However, thankfully, it's not all up to the politicians. The courts generally have taken a dim view of failures to fulfill pension obligations. The result is that it's not very common—so far—for public sector pensioners to find their pensions unpaid or even under-paid—although it has certainly happened.

Heading the ledger of shame is Prichard, Alabama, where the city simply stopped all pension payments, ignoring various court orders. Eventually, some level of payment was restored as a result of court actions, but that level was as little as one third of the original pension obligation, following a byzantine formula. The city had experienced a population decline of approximately 50% over the past 50 years and filed for bankruptcy in 1999 after it was unable to pay approximately $3.9 million in delinquent bills.[54]

Detroit comes next, where public sector pensioners also saw a cut in their pensions. After much political wrangling to close a $1.88 billion pension plan funding gap,[55] pensions were cut by 4.5%, along with an end to cost of living increases and insurance.

Other municipalities in the news for underfunded pensions include Stockton and Vallejo, California, and Central Falls, Rhode Island. In the end, pensions were not cut in Stockton and Vallejo (although they could have been), but they were cut in Central Falls—up to 55%.

Municipal pension plans are contractual agreements—in some cases guaranteed by the state—upon which pensioners depend for living. Twenty-five percent of public sector workers are not eligible for Social Security, and their pensions are their only income in retirement. An unsettling aspect of these defaults and near-defaults is the lack of uniformity and clarity in the various court decisions. All this is very different from the highly regulated and federally insured private sector single-employer pension plans.

As scary as this is, it should be kept in perspective. The actual loss of pension payments has adversely affected only a minuscule number of individuals in the public pension system. As one example, New York State, with one of the largest public pension plans in the country, addressed its pension plan underfunding by increasing the retirement age and employee contributions and decreasing the promised payouts for new plan members, while keeping those promises

---

[54] blogs.reuters.com/muniland/2013/08/08/the-real-history-of-public-pensions-in-bankruptcy/ = tinyurl.com/ycueksny.

[55] https://reuters.com/article/us-detroit-bankruptcy-pensions-idUSKCN12322F.

for existing members intact. The retirement age increase was to age 63. The result left New York's pension plan fully funded by many accounts.

Since the 2008 financial melt-down, almost all states have made adjustments to their pension plans for new employees in order to compensate for underfunding. Most states now have enough funds in their pension plans for the next decade. Under the pay-as-you-go funding (Sect. 15.8) allowed for public sector pension plans (but not for private sector plans), pension plan funding is periodically adjusted—or not. A small number of public pensions remain notoriously underfunded, and their future is uncertain.

The real extent of underfunding of public pension plans is a numbers game, as already described. It depends on assumptions about expected appreciation of investments and time horizons. By one reckoning, projecting ahead for the lives of its members, a pension fund may be severely underfunded. By another reckoning, the same plan may be deemed fully funded for the next decade, and over time, funding will be adjusted as needed. The calculated degree of underfunding in 2015 is from $4.6 trillion down to a mere $300 billion (projected by the Census Bureau). Given the pay-as-you-go allowance for public sector pension plans, there is no good definition to say what is a right or wrong answer. (Whether it is right or wrong to allow public sector pension plans to be pay-as-you-go instead of fully funded by actuarial standards is a different question.) One de facto standard for public pension plans is to be fully funded for a decade. Depending on what point is to be made, one comes up with a model that shows pension funds to be woefully underfunded by 60%,[56] or merely by 7% (the Census Bureau projection).

But all this hardly matters, since it's obvious that there's a potential problem, even a potentially catastrophically serious problem. If you hold a public sector pension, what matters is not the generality but the condition of your particular pension fund. With over 2500 plans spanning 50 states, it's not possible to give reliable information about the health and funding level of a particular plan. As a pension holder, it behooves you to do a little research to see to what extent you can count on your pension, a necessary piece of knowledge for retirement planning. Put the name of your pension plan in your web browser, and see what turns up. As a general rule, no news is good news and bad news travels fast.

---

[56] huffpost.com/entry/the-real-pension-crisis_b_1694242 = tinyurl.com/y9ffvqjd.

18

The Looming Retirement Crisis

A landmark study[1] by the Pew Charitable Trusts looks at multiple factors pertaining to retirement funding. Their conclusion points to an inadequacy of savings and retirement income as a means for funding life in retirement. (Retirement income consists mainly of Social Security, but also income from pensions, annuities, and retirement jobs.) The inadequacy applies both to current and forthcoming retirees. They cite a 2015 study[2] from the Employee Benefit Research Institute that estimates that the current American workforce will face an aggregate retirement savings shortfall of $4.13 trillion. Put into more concrete terms, it is estimated that 30–40% of the "baby boomers" born between 1946 and 1964 "will not have enough income or savings at age 70 to replace 75% of their pre-retirement earnings, a common standard for judging income adequacy in retirement".[3] For older Americans of color, the problem is much worse.[4] The Center for Retirement Research[5] also shows that working-age American households will face a decline in standard of living upon entering retirement.

A 2015 report from the United States Government Accountability Office (GAO) concludes that 52% of American households whose primary wage

---

[1] pewtrusts.org/en/research-and-analysis/issue-briefs/2015/07/the-state-pensions-funding-gap-challenges-persist = tinyurl.com/y77ey6fe.

[2] ebri.org/docs/default-source/ebri-issue-brief/ebri_ib_410_feb15_rs-shrtfls.pdf = tinyurl.com/yadd4olb.

[3] Pew: urban.org/uploadedpdf/412490-boomers-retirement-income-prospects.pdf.

[4] Pew: demos.org/sites/default/files/publications/IASP Demos Senior of Color Brief September 2011.pdf = tinyurl.com/y7uhn7by.

[5] pewtrusts.org/en/research-and-analysis/reports/2016/06/how-states-are-working-to-address-the-retirement-savings-challenge = tinyurl.com/ybxlqoex.

© The Author(s), under exclusive license to Springer Nature Switzerland AG 2022
R. P. Kurshan, *Investment Industry Claims Debunked*,
https://doi.org/10.1007/978-3-030-76709-9_18

earner is over 55 years old have no "retirement" savings (e.g., a 401(k) or IRA), and of those, 56% also have no pension, and of those (29% of all), 41% do not own a home and have a net worth of $34,760, on average.[6] For households in which the retired primary wage earner is of age 75 and over, the picture is even bleaker, leaving most of them to depend mostly on Social Security.

It's been widely reported that our children are facing the prospect of poverty in retirement, to an extent not seen since the Great Depression. CNBC writes "The strain of this newly poor population on our social safety net will devastate local, state, and federal budgets for decades to come. It should come as no surprise that when polled, people consistently cite retirement security as their greatest economic concern."[7] Just google "retirement crisis" for 2.5 million hits.[8]

The CNBC article continues: "It may be tempting to blame saving rates, but the fact is that today's stagnant wages, rising health, rent, and childcare costs, and massive student loan debt serve as tremendous obstacles that inhibit Americans from building a strong retirement foundation."

A bigger question may be this. Why is it left to people who mostly have no financial background, to master a significantly complex matter—the subject of this book, after all—in order to provide for themselves a life out of poverty in their old age? And how did we let the venerable century-old tradition of a pension come to an end?

Since the New Deal and Social Security, it used to be that pensions were a normal part of the compensation that most full-time wage earners expected as a part of their compensation (Chap. 17). Today, many people retire on Social Security payments alone, which may not even be sufficient to lift them out of poverty.[9] Over 10% of those subsisting on Social Security alone remained in poverty even when economic circumstances were good.

At the time of this writing, fewer than a quarter of workers will have a pension from their current employers when they retire, down from a third over a decade ago. In the private sector (Sect. 17.2), it's less than 12%, and some of those pensions are in trouble and may pay their holders less upon retirement than they were promised (Sect. 17.2.5).

We know how this came about (Chap. 17). Starting in the Reagan years, employers began to view workers less as part of the corporate family, to

---

[6] https://gao.gov/assets/680/670153.pdf.

[7] cnbc.com/2016/03/15/americas-looming-retirement-savings-crisis-commentary.html.

[8] Don't be surprised to find contrarians among the 2.5 million: "No crisis: just look at all the RVs on the road!"; "Just sell your house!"; "Just get a job!".

[9] https://cbpp.org/sites/default/files/atoms/files/2-24-05socsec.pdf.

18 The Looming Retirement Crisis 315

be nurtured and retained for their expertise, and more as a resource to be optimized: fired and rehired as employee numbers affected the stock price. In this view, pensions became a drain on profitability and were replaced by defined contribution plans, mostly 401(k)s. This transferred the risk of investment from the company to the employee, as explained in that chapter. The replacement was billed as providing employees with "ownership" over their pensions, a theme very much in keeping with the attitudes of the time. Therefore, it was little noticed by employees that this was a massive transfer of cost and risk from employer to employee.

This was part of a greater movement of wealth transfer from workers to business owners that has fed a surge in social inequality. Over the last four decades, wages have remained stagnant and in many cases, in real dollars, decreased. While since 1980 "annual economic output of the United States has almost tripled, ⋯ the wealthy hoarded the fruits".[10]

The counterproductive nature of this transition from pensions is exposed by a study[11] reported by the National Institute on Retirement Security. That study shows that "the cost to deliver the same retirement income to a group of employees is 46% lower in a typical defined benefit plan than in a defined contribution plan." The reason is that defined benefit plans "need to only accumulate enough funds to provide benefits for the average life expectancy of the group." This reduces costs by 15% over what it takes for each worker to save for that worker's possible lifetime. The prudent worker needs to provide for the possibility of living longer than the actuarially expected lifetime, whereas the company can count on the average worker living exactly the average lifetime. Moreover, by pooling the assets targeted for all the workers, defined benefit plans are able to achieve an economy of scale of management costs. With pooled assets and staggered retirements, a smaller proportion of the funds need to be disbursed at any one time than for the individual retiree.

Thus, the study shows that for the same cost of capital, a defined benefit plan is twice as cost-effective as an equivalent defined contribution plan.

The study concludes that had there been no pensions in 2006, $7.3 billion in public assistance would have been paid to indigent retirees to compensate for the shortfall, increasing public assistance for the elderly by about 40%.

There is no dearth of constructive suggestions for bringing back pensions.[12]

---

[10] nytimes.com/2020/06/24/opinion/income-wealth-inequality-america.html.

[11] nirsonline.org/wp-content/uploads/2017/07/final_factsheet_by_the_numbers.pdf =
tinyurl.com/y7hf5esa.

[12] Ellis et al. (2014) and James and Ghilarducci (2016) are good places to start.

One suggestion to replace pensions is a Guaranteed Retirement Account (GRA).[13] Although this is an established option, experts have suggested many variations. In one version, it is a merit-based pension plan to which both employer and employee must contribute, managed by the Social Security Administration. Since plan management is disconnected from the employer, the pension plan is portable, continuing as an employee moves from one employer to another. Upon retirement, the pension stipend consists of a fraction of the last few annual salaries, determined by the total number of years of employment and adjusted annually for inflation. For example, the first year's pension might be a percentage equal to 1.5 times the total number of years worked, multiplied by the average of the last 5 years' salaries. Thus, for someone who has worked for 40 years, the salaries multiplier is 60%. This inflation-adjusted stipend continues for the life of pensioner and thereafter at a reduced rate (maybe, 50%) for the remaining life of the pensioner's spouse.

The economy of scale achieved by pooling all pension funds into a single trust fund reduces the cost significantly below the cost to each employer of managing a pension trust fund. Moreover, it relieves the employer of the risk and much of the cost of managing a pension trust. (Avoiding the risk of managing a pension trust fund was a principal motive for employers to flee from pensions.) Finally, it eliminates the trust fund insurance costs required by the PBGC (Sect. 17.2.3).

If the trust fund were operated according to responsible fiduciary norms (rather than pay-as-you-go), it would relieve the trust from the uncertainties and political pressures that plague Social Security (Sect. 15.8).

Employers still can offer defined contribution plans like a 401(k) as an employment benefit, with the goal of encouraging saving for retirement. With a pension of 60% of recent income plus Social Security and retirement savings, a pensioner might expect to be able to meet the goal stated at the start of this chapter to replace 75% of pre-retirement earnings.

Note that a merit-based GRA serves a different purpose from Social Security. The former provides a realistic merit-based pension for all workers. The latter provides a safety net for workers who may not have worked long enough to earn a meaningful pension. It can be reasonable to reduce or eliminate Social Security for individuals with adequate pension payouts.

---

[13] epi.org/research/guaranteed-retirement-accounts/, nextavenue.org/solution-americas-retirement-crisis/ are two somewhat different versions of the idea.

18 The Looming Retirement Crisis   317

A reversion to the defined benefit retirement system may in fact be inevitable: we are approaching a financial collapse of the ever-growing elderly demographic—a demographic that we all hope one day to enter.

Why do we not, as a society, naturally gravitate toward a solution that works best for society as a whole, while at the same time is best for each retiree? Sadly, in a political climate that has lurched toward decentralized government, we are left with the "prisoner's dilemma" paradox. The paradox is that there is a cooperative solution that's best for all, but without centralized government control to implement the optimally cost-effective solution, the end result is suboptimal for all.

The looming retirement crisis impacts your retirement. Write to your senators and representatives and tell them that you need a pension. Explain to them that a pension is the most financially efficient and fairest way by far for society to support retirement. Warn them that if the looming retirement crisis is not stemmed, the country as a whole is set up for a pervasive financial disaster of unparalleled proportions.

If you are young enough and you succeed, it will greatly enhance your retirement. Even if you are not young enough—perhaps you already are retired—it can help your children or grandchildren.

Some balk at any change that increases government control of finance (or anything else). Many of these same individuals also prefer to eliminate school taxes, or if this is unconstitutional—it is—then at least refund them through "vouchers." The reason for the wealthy is that they send their children to private schools and thus believe that they get no benefit from the school tax. Such anti-social egocentric short-sighted thinking can only last so long before the society it begets blows up.

How is that?

Investments in programs that primarily benefit the underprivileged still have value to those in the more privileged classes because they create societies with lower inequality and therefore less crime. For example, investing in after school programs for underprivileged kids takes those kids off the streets and therefore gives them fewer opportunities to engage in crimes of boredom (crimes that may very well impact the more privileged people). The result benefits everyone in society. That privileged kids already have such programs likely explains why fewer of them engage in such crimes.

The cost penalty for this short-sightedness keeps rising. Finally, even the most socially indifferent have begun to take notice. This already is happening now with a new Conservative initiative to decrease incarceration (long supported by Liberals). It wasn't its horrific unfairness that convinced the

318   R. P. Kurshan

Conservatives, but simply its absurd fiscal inefficiency. The same thinking eventually could create support for a universal merit-based pension.

This was a simple thought experiment about how "a rising tide lifts all ships." If we care for all our citizens, our own lives are also improved. Sometimes directly through reduced costs. Sometimes indirectly, simply though engendering a sympathetic society in which we all care for one another. A society whose by-ways are not awash with poverty improves all lives.

Meanwhile, we're on our own.

Appendix A

Some Simple Math

It turns out that the same simple formula—the "mortgage formula"—is used to price bonds; to compute the yield of a bond or bond ladder; to compute the value of a fixed rate annuity; to compute the value of a pension (in case you are offered a lump sum buyout); to compute how much to earmark in order to compensate for inflation with a fixed payout annuity or pension; to decide if solar panels are a good investment; and, naturally, to compute the monthly payments on a mortgage.

I also discuss here the general confusion around interest rate conversion from yearly to monthly. The resulting monthly rates, depending on how you compute them, are known as APR, APY, or IRR. They may represent an unexpected loss for mortgage recipients (and an unexpected gain for some bond buyers). I present some evidence that the confusion may extend to the financial community as well.

It is fairly straightforward to calculate the fair price of a bond, mid-term (I demonstrate how). However, there's widespread misinformation about this calculation. This puts the financial community in a further bad light.

A.1 Zero-Coupon Bonds

Imagine that you want to set aside some money so that your newborn gets $1000 on her tenth birthday. You found a savings bank that gives 1% interest, compounded annually, and want to figure what you need to deposit today, in order for it to grow to $1000 in 10 years. Let's call that amount D—you

© The Author(s), under exclusive license to Springer Nature Switzerland AG 2022
R. P. Kurshan, *Investment Industry Claims Debunked*,
https://doi.org/10.1007/978-3-030-76709-9

320   R. P. Kurshan

want to figure out the value of D so that if you deposit D dollars today, it will grow to $1000 by her tenth birthday. Well, if you put D dollars in the bank today, then in 1 year, it will grow to $D \times 1.01$ dollars—the D dollars, plus 1% interest. The year after, the $D \times 1.01$ dollars gets another 1% on top of that, so you have $D \times 1.01^2$ dollars altogether. By the tenth year, you'll have $D \times 1.01^{10}$ dollars, and that's what you want to be $1000. So, $D \times 1.01^{10} = \$1000$, or $D = \$1000/1.01^{10} = \$905.29$. That's what you need to invest today. It's also the "present value" of $1000 10 years off, to use a term of the trade,[1] as it gives a way to compute the present value of money to be received in the future (under an assumption of a prevailing rate of interest).

To state it formally, the *present value D* of a *principal P* that will be received at a *term* of n periods, with interest compounded at the rate r per period, is

$$D = \frac{P}{(1+r)^n} . \qquad (A.1)$$

When the investment is a bond, D is termed its *discount price, r* its *yield*, and P its *face value*.

A zero-coupon bond works this way. It produces no interest payments until it matures. At term (when it matures), it pays the principal (the face value of the bond), which includes the interest, since the bond was purchased at a discount. The way these bonds are marketed is that they show you how much you'll get at term (the bond's face value) and the yield (the interest rate produced by the bond). Its interest payments are figured into the "discount" price that you pay for the bond. To buy a 10-year $1000 zero-coupon bond with a yield of 1%, you should expect to pay $905.29 as above (plus any fees). When you get the $1000 after 10 years, you are receiving back your $905.29 purchase price plus $94.71 interest.

One significant drawback of zero-coupon bonds is that although the bond holder sees no income benefit before the bond is redeemed, the IRS considers that a zero-coupon bond produces annual interest at the virtual rate of return (yield) of the bond. This virtual interest, often termed "phantom income," is considered "income" by the IRS. Thus, if you bought a $1000 non-tax-exempt zero-coupon bond for $905.29, its taxable annual virtual ("phantom") interest is $1\% \times \$905.29 = \$9.05$ in the first year. In the second year, the earned interest is added to the base value, so the taxable virtual interest is $1\% \times (\$905.29 + \$9.05) = \$9.14$, and so on.

---

[1] And, the financial community likes, superfluously, to call the growth rate—here, 1%—the "discount rate," because the present value is "discounted" relative to the future value.

Appendix A   Some Simple Math   **321**

computing zero-coupon bond resale value
Typically, bonds can be sold on the open market before they reach term. In this case, the price takes into account any change in interest rates in the markets in general. When you want to sell your 1% yield bond, if someone can buy a similar bond that yields 2% and matures when yours does, then he won't buy your bond unless you lower its price to take into account the increased interest rate. If you have 5 years left before your bond matures, then by the same type of calculation, your bond is now worth $1000/1.02^5 = 905.73. That is only \$0.44 more than you paid for it. So, it's as if you invested \$905.29 for 5 years and earned only \$0.44 in interest. That's like earning interest at the rate r, where $905.29 \times (1 + r)^5 = 905.73$, so $r = (905.73/905.29)^{\frac{1}{5}} - 1 = 0.000097$—less than 0.01% per year (even your checking account does better than that). On the other hand, if interest rates went down to 0.5% in that 5 years (halving instead of doubling), you'd be able to sell your bond for $1000/1.005^5 = 975.37, for a profit of \$70.08, which is equivalent (calculating as before) to having earned $(975.37/905.29)^{\frac{1}{5}} - 1 = 1.5\%$ annually for 5 years—a 50% higher rate than you expected when you bought the bond. For the buyer of your bond, the nominal interest rate of 1% is no longer relevant. For the buyer, the yield of the bond becomes its effective rate of interest: $(1000/975.37)^{\frac{1}{5}} - 1 = 0.5\%$.

If you sold your bond and immediately reinvested the \$975.37 proceeds of the sale into another bond that matures in 5 years and yields 0.5%, after that second 5 years, you'd get $975.37 \times 1.005^5 = 1000, back where you started. Holding, or selling and reinvesting, is the same. But not really: if you sell, you have a taxable capital gain. And there are usually fees associated with any buy or sell transactions. Better just hold, unless you need the money.

A.2   Straight Bonds

A straight bond pays interest at regular intervals and pays its face value at maturity (Sect. 2.3.1). Suppose we have a 10-year straight bond with face value \$1000 and a yield of 1%, as before. For simplicity, assume it has a single annual coupon, a condition that we'll relax later (Appendix A.4.1). What should be its initial market value (its present value, the price at which it is first offered for sale)? I will assume throughout that the bond is sold at par, meaning that there is no discount or premium price as a result of market speculations about future interest rates or on account of the forces of supply and demand or inflation speculation (Sect. 2.3, Appendix A.4).

R. P. Kurshan

This bond looks a little more valuable than a zero-coupon bond, in that we don't need to wait until its maturity to get something back. We can spend (or reinvest) each coupon when we receive it. How should this financial advantage figure into its initial market value?

We can find the answer in the same way as for the zero-coupon bond, except in this case, we should imagine that we have 11 zero-coupon bonds, all with the same yield, but maturities generally 1 year apart. The face values of the first ten of these imaginary zero-coupon bonds is their coupon, while the face value of the last of these bonds is the face value of the actual bond. This mental trick breaks the problem of valuing the original bond into 11 simpler problems of a type that we've already solved.

How does this actually work?

For the actual bond, with a 1% yield and face value of $1000, each coupon has face value $1\% \times \$1000 = \$10$. So the first of our imaginary zero-coupon bonds has a term of 1 year and a face value $10. We've already seen how to compute its worth. Using the same idea as we used with the birthday present (Sect. A.1), it's $D_1 = \$10/1.01$, about $9.90 (as you might expect, we invested almost $10 at 1% interest for 1 year and made ten cents). How about the second coupon due after the second year? It's the same idea. We see that the present value (at the time that the bond is purchased) of the second coupon is $D_2 = \$10/1.01^2$ (about $9.80). And so on, except for the last of our imaginary zero-coupon bonds, which pays the principal of the actual bond (the amount invested) at the end of the tenth year. So its value is $D_{11} = \$1000/1.01^{10}$, a fraction less than $905.29. Adding up the values of all our imaginary zero-coupon bonds gives the initial market value of the actual bond: $D = D_1 + D_2 + \cdots + D_{10} + D_{11}$.

Adding these eleven numbers not only would be quite tedious, but error-prone as well. Let's not do it. Instead, let's find a way to get the sum through a single computation.

A.3 Geometric Series

Suppose n is a positive integer, and for some number $a \neq 1$ we want to find the value of

$$a + a^2 + a^3 + \cdots + a^n \, .$$

Euclid 300 BCE

(If $a = 1$, then the sum is obviously just n, but we'll need below to divide by $a - 1 \neq 0$.) Using one of the most famous[2] elementary tricks in algebra, we multiply this sum by $a - 1$. This gives

$$a^2 + a^3 + \cdots + a^n + a^{n+1}$$

$$-a - a^2 - a^3 \cdots - a^n.$$

Notice that all the "inside" terms cancel one another ($a^2 - a^2, \ldots, a^n - a^n$), leaving only $a^{n+1} - a$, so

$$(a + a^2 + a^3 + \cdots + a^n)(a - 1) = a^{n+1} - a$$

and dividing both sides of this equality by $a - 1$, we get

$$a + a^2 + a^3 + \cdots + a^n = \frac{a(a^n - 1)}{a - 1} \tag{A.2}$$

and equivalently, if $a \neq 0$ (or applying the trick to $1 + \cdots + a^{n-1}$)

$$1 + a + a^2 + a^3 + \cdots + a^{n-1} = \frac{a^n - 1}{a - 1}.$$

(Both forms are handy.) Voila! A simple "closed" form for the sum.

Now, let's put this in a form that's more convenient for our purposes. Let $a = 1/(1 + r)$, where $r > 0$ is an interest rate. Then, by (A.2), we have just shown that for any integer $n > 0$,

---

[2] It goes back at least to Euclid, 300 BCE.

324 R. P. Kurshan

$$\frac{1}{(1+r)} + \frac{1}{(1+r)^2} + \cdots + \frac{1}{(1+r)^n}$$

$$= \frac{\frac{1}{1+r}\left(\frac{1}{(1+r)^n} - 1\right)}{\frac{1}{1+r} - 1} = \frac{(1+r)^n - 1}{r(1+r)^n}$$

To summarize:

$$\frac{1}{1+r} + \frac{1}{(1+r)^2} + \cdots + \frac{1}{(1+r)^n} = \frac{(1+r)^n - 1}{r(1+r)^n} \tag{A.3}$$

A.4 Pricing Straight Bonds

Returning to our straight bond from Appendix A.2, we can apply the closed form (A.3) for a geometric series to get the market price or present value D of the bond. First note that each $D_i = \$10/1.01^i$ for $i \leq 10$. (We'll add on the anomalous D_{11} at the end.) By (A.3), with $r = .01$ and $n = 10$, factoring out the \$10 coupon value,

$$D_1 + \cdots + D_{10} = \$10\frac{1.01^{10} - 1}{.01(1.01^{10})} = \$94.71 .$$

That's the present value of all the coupons. The present value D_{11} of the principal is another $\$1000/1.01^{10} = \$905.29$ (look familiar?), so altogether, the present value D of our bond is \$1000—its face value! Are you surprised? That's because the earnings on the investment—its coupons—were drawn when they accrued. It's not surprising if you think of buying the bond as being the same as depositing \$1000 in a savings bank for 10 years at an interest rate of 1%, which interest you withdraw when it accrues. After 10 years, you withdraw your \$1000 principal. The fair cost of that investment was the \$1000 deposit, which you got back at the end (after having been rewarded by the annual interest payments).

We can easily prove that this is always the case.

For any bond term n and any annual interest rate r and any face value P, if the coupons pay annually, then the value C of each coupon is $C = rP$, and their combined present value, including the principal (paid at term), as

Appendix A Some Simple Math 325

we have just shown, is

$$\frac{rP}{1+r} + \frac{rP}{(1+r)^2} + \cdots + \frac{rP}{(1+r)^n} + \frac{P}{(1+r)^n} = rP\frac{(1+r)^n - 1}{r(1+r)^n} + \frac{P}{(1+r)^n}$$

$$= P\left(\frac{(1+r)^n - 1}{(1+r)^n} + \frac{1}{(1+r)^n}\right) = P.$$

Thus, in particular,

$$P = C\frac{(1+r)^n - 1}{r(1+r)^n} + \frac{P}{(1+r)^n} \qquad (A.4)$$

par, premium, and discount pricing
So indeed, the normal price for a newly issued straight bond that pays its
interest in annual coupons is the face ("par") value of the bond. The same
reasoning applies to any number of coupons per year (Appendix A.4.1).
However, there are reasons that a newly issued bond may not sell at its par
value. For example, suppose that between the time the coupon value was set
and the bond was issued, interest rates changed. Then the bond can sell at
a *premium* (above par) if the interest rates fell or at a *discount* (below par) if
the interest rates rose. Another reason for selling at a premium is that demand
exceeds supply. In troubled times many investors seek a "safe haven" in bonds
for their savings. Likewise, if the stock market is raging and many people are
selling bonds to "jump into the stock market," then demand can be slack,
causing bonds to sell at a discount.

There are other more complex reasons that the initial value of a bond may
be different from its par value. The above computation makes the simplifying
assumption that the value of each future dollar (received in a coupon or the
repayment of the principal) is the same as the value of a dollar today. Taking
inflation into account adjusts this assumption. For this reason, bonds can sell
at a discount if there is an expectation of inflation or at a premium if there is
an expectation of deflation. For a constant rate of inflation, r can be adjusted
to be the real rate, as in Chap. 10.

A.4.1 Coupons Issuing More Frequently than Annually

So far, I have looked mainly at the case that there is a single coupon that
issues at the end of each year. However, most bonds pay coupons twice or four

times a year (usually twice). They do this by dividing the bond's total annual interest paid by the number of coupons issued and assigning that value to each coupon. Thus, for a straight bond with face value of $1000 and a stated yield of "10%" with semiannual coupons, the value of each coupon is set to $50 (= (10% × $1000)/2). However, this pricing of the coupons is inconsistent with the stated yield. Two coupons per year of $50 each paid semi-annually are more valuable than one of $100 paid at the end of the year. You get the first interest payment 6 months sooner and thus can spend or reinvest it sooner. The actual yield, called the *annual percentage yield* (APY), is greater than the stated yield.

How much better is it to receive the bond's stated yield spread evenly throughout the year? Well, suppose a stated yield r were spread out into k equal and equally spaced coupons. If P is the bond's face value, then these coupons each have value $\frac{rP}{k}$, issuing k times a year. In each of the k (pre-coupon issuing) periods, the bond's actual yield (for the period) is the coupon value $\frac{rP}{k}$ divided by the principal P, or r/k. Thus, the bond's APY is $APY = (1 + \frac{r}{k})^k - 1$ (since $P(1 + APY) = P(1 + \frac{r}{k})^k$).

For the above example, $APY = (1 + \frac{.10}{2})^2 - 1 = 1.05^2 - 1 = 10.25\%$. So, the bond's actual yield, it's APY, is 0.25% more than its stated yield. Had the annual rate compounded quarterly, then the four quarterly coupons of $2.5\% \times P$ each create an actual annual yield (APY) of $1.025^4 - 1 = 10.38\%$.

In order for the stated yield r to be the actual yield ($r = APY$), the coupons would need to be reduced. If c_k is the correct coupon to give $r = APY$ for k annual coupons (evenly spaced) on a bond with face value P, then $c_k = P((1 + r)^{\frac{1}{k}} - 1)$. Hence, $c_2 = \$48.81$ and $c_4 = \$24.11$.

As it is, since the actual yield is greater than the stated yield ($APY > r$), bond buyers don't complain.

However, the situation is reversed when it's the consumer who's doing the borrowing.

A.4.2 Financiers' Interest Rate Confusion

The finance industry has created considerable confusion over interest rates. One can only wonder if it is the result of a disconnect between the accountants who do the computations, who surely understand the issue, and financiers who interact with the public. Do the financiers fail to understand the multiplicative nature of compounding? Thus, for example, we have *annual percentage* **rate**

(APR) that refers to a nominal—largely irrelevant—annual rate (10% in the bond example above) and the actual annual rate APY (*annual percentage yield*) that is greater than the APR when compounded more frequently than annually. When it arises in the form of *received* interest, it may come as a pleasant surprise, because you get more. When it arises on a credit card bill (with what in other places or times would be considered usurious interest rates exceeding 20%), expecting the advertised APR and then receiving a bill based (correctly, justified in the fine print) on the APY can be vexing.

When the finance industry states that a (nominal) annual interest rate APR is compounded k times a year, what they mean is that the rate APR/k is compounded k times a year, so the *actual* annual interest rate APY satisfies

$$APY = (1 + APR/k)^k - 1 \qquad (A.5)$$

so, for example, if $k = 12$ and $APR = 10\%$, then $APY = 10.47\%$. In the credit card case, if $APR = 20\%$, then $APY = 21.9\%$, almost 2% more.

In my opinion, all interest rates should be expressed in terms of APY, and any mention of APR should be eliminated, as it serves no purpose but to confuse the investor or borrower. (The periodic rate APR/k has a use to compute interest between periods, in case interest is compounded k times a year, and an investment or loan is made for less than a year. It can be given as, say, "the monthly rate" ($k = 12$), without mention of APR.)

An interest rate also may be compounded *continuously*. If the resulting APY is computed from a nominal APR, it is the limit of (A.5) as $k \to \infty$.

Leonhard Euler 1753

328 R. P. Kurshan

Using a little calculus, it is easy to show that for the famous *Euler number* $e = 2.71828\ldots$,

$$APY = e^{APR} - 1$$

so, for example, if $APR = 10\%$, $APY = 10.5\%$—only 0.03% higher than compounding monthly. In this case, the APR again is of no use. All anyone needs to know is the APY and that interest is compounded continuously. And, the interest rate for a fraction of a year t is simply $(1 + APY)^t - 1$.

On account of the confusion surrounding interest rates, in the last two decades, U.S. federal laws now require adequate clarification. As a result, I believe that also the financiers have come to better understand their products. However, I then can see no reason for the continued wide use of APR.

A.4.3 Calculating Bond Price Between Coupons

What should be the par price of a straight bond between coupon payments? Let's assume first that there's a single annual coupon.

If r is the bond's yield, then its daily yield r_d satisfies $1 + r = (1 + r_d)^{365}$ (in non-leap years), so $1 + r_d = (1 + r)^{\frac{1}{365}}$. Suppose there are m years and k days remaining to maturity. Let C be the coupon value, P the principal value, and D_0 the present value of the next coupon. Then (*cf.* the introduction of Appendix A.4) $C = D_0(1 + r_d)^k = D_0(1 + r)^{\frac{k}{365}}$, so $D_0 = C/(1 + r)^{\frac{k}{365}}$.

Likewise, let D_i, for $0 < i \le m$, be the present value of the m remaining coupons, after the next. Then

$$D_i = \frac{C}{(1 + r)^{\frac{k+365i}{365}}} = \frac{C}{(1 + r)^{\frac{k}{365}+i}} = \frac{C}{(1 + r)^{\frac{k}{365}}(1 + r)^i} = \frac{C}{(1 + r)^{\frac{k}{365}}}\frac{1}{(1 + r)^i}$$

Thus, the price (present value) D of the bond, applying (A.3), is

$$D = \frac{1}{(1 + r)^{\frac{k}{365}}}\left(C + C\frac{(1 + r)^m - 1}{r(1 + r)^m} + \frac{P}{(1 + r)^m}\right) \qquad (A.6)$$

Note that if $k = 0$, then D reduces to the right-hand side of (A.4), for $n = m$, plus the initial coupon C. If $k = 364$ (so the bond is priced the day after the previous coupon issued), then D is essentially the right-hand side of (A.4), for $n = m + 1$.

In case of multiple coupons per year, the price is calculated analogously (*cf.*, Appendix A.4.1).

Appendix A   Some Simple Math   329

financial misrepresentations of the price calculation

While the above computation is pretty straightforward, it has been widely misrepresented by financiers, who seemingly (and if so, astonishingly) misunderstand their own business. For example, the widely referenced *Investopedia*, an online finance encyclopedia, got this transaction wrong in three ways.[3] First, they overlooked the fact that the number of days until the next coupon affects not only the value of that coupon but all the rest, as well. Then, thinking that the only required adjustment is to prorate the next coupon value C, they suggested to do that by multiplying C by the fraction of the payment period that remains, an arithmetic correction where a geometric rate correction is needed. Finally, they add this superfluous (and improperly "prorated") amount to the cost of the bond,[4] although it is already included in the present value computation used to price the bond.

To use their formula, if the bond is bought on the day that a coupon issues, then the coupon must be free, because 0 days remain until the coupon issues. It's actually idiotic, because they present it as if there's a price for the bond (its "clean" price—"the price quoted in the newspapers") and then an additional amount that must be paid by the buyer to the seller "for the accrued interest since the last coupon," as if they were calculating the pro-rated refund of car insurance, cancelled mid-term. This is echoed by the esteemed *Wikipedia* (see "dirty bond price") and innumerable other *"here, we'll tell you how this works"* web sites (often illustrated with incorrect cartoons). Where did all this come from? I can't even imagine.

This misrepresentation seems to me to be so widespread within the OTC (over-the-counter) bond industry that I suspect it may be the reality, in a perverse fashion. OTC bond traders may determine the bond price correctly as above, but then in deference to some byzantine tradition, originating perhaps with early traders who misunderstood the arithmetic of their business, subtract the prorated amount and then add it back as a separate charge. Or, more ominously, the prorated charge may simply be added when the bond dealer can get away with it, with more gullible customers. Forbes has warned that OTC brokers have a bad reputation of taking advantage of their less knowledgeable clients (Sect. 2.3.1, **broker fees**, footnote 4), in a cited case, taking a 20% markup.

---

[3] partially fixed on Oct. 15, 2019.

[4] investopedia.com/university/advancedbond/advancedbond2.asp.

330   R. P. Kurshan

In fact, the entire OTC bond industry is shrouded in a cloud of arcana. For example, take the way bond prices are reported. A bond quote may be given as "97–182." What is this? To know, you must know the par (face) value of the bond. Let's say it's $1000. Then 97–182 = $975.70. Got it? No? The "97" means 97% of the par value. The "−182" means another $\frac{18}{32} + \frac{2}{8} \times \frac{1}{32} = 0.5703$ percent.[5]

If you buy a bond at par, compute its present value as in (A.6), and compare that to the price your dealer offers. The difference is the dealer's profit. For a bond bought at a discount or premium, there are other factors at play (see above) that are hard to evaluate. But you can compute the par price, multiply that by the stated discount or premium, and compare the result with the price your dealer is asking. Again, that difference is the dealer's profit.

A.4.4 Computing Yield, Given Price

In Appendix A.4.3, we computed the mid-term fair price D for a straight bond with face value P, yield r, and single annual coupon C (A.6).

Given a new value for D (resulting, say, from discount or premium pricing), its current annual yield can be computed as the value of r for which (A.6) holds. Although there is no nice closed-form solution for r, it can be approximated with any desired precision using a plotting calculator, as described in Appendix A.9.1, or manually through trial and error by plugging in different values for r to get the resulting expression close to D.

The yield computed as r above is also called "yield to maturity." And, in slightly different settings, it also is called the "internal rate of return" (IRR) and even the "discounted cash flow rate of return"—apparently one term is not enough. The ratio C/D of the annual bond coupon to the current price is called the "current yield," which neglects the return of principal at term. There is no apparent purpose for defining "current yield" and again may represent detritus along the path of financiers misunderstanding the arithmetic of their business; or, perhaps they just like naming stuff.

---

[5] cmegroup.com/education/files/understanding-treasury-futures.pdf = tinyurl.com/yccgrone.

Appendix A   Some Simple Math   **331**

A.5 Mortgages

A standard "amortizing" mortgage is a bond that you, the home owner, issues, backed by your home. Typically it is bought by a bank (that sets the interest rate they want to receive). As with a newly issued straight bond, the value of the mortgage is the principal P (the amount that the bank pays you for the bond, i.e., loans you for the mortgage), the coupons are the payments you make to the bank, and the term is the period until the principal must be returned. Unlike a straight bond, however, in a mortgage, the principal is returned together with the interest in the coupons, which issue monthly. While this may sound more complex than a straight bond, it actually gives a simpler and mathematically cleaner formulation, as the relation between the principal P and coupon payments C avoids the anomalous last summand required for a straight bond (A.4), in which all the principal is paid back at term. For a mortgage, we will see that the relationship is simply

$$C = P\frac{r(1+r)^n}{(1+r)^n - 1} \tag{A.7}$$

where r *should be* the *monthly* mortgage interest rate $r = (1+r_y)^{\frac{1}{12}} - 1$ derived from the advertised annual rate r_y, and n is the number of months in the mortgage term (number of years multiplied by 12). Note well the *should be*. Because generally it *isn't* ! What most banks do is to use the mathematically illegitimate *arithmetic* conversion, described above, of their advertised annual rate r_y to a monthly rate r given by $r = \frac{r_y}{12}$! When this type of conversion was done for bonds, it worked to our favor, but here, where it is *our* debt, it works against us. Did banks first do this because they didn't understand the correct conversion and then let it stand because the error was in their favor? Or, did they do this as an intentional deception?[6] Neither answer puts them in a good light. In the unreadable boiler-plate of your mortgage agreement, you find an inadequately explained statement that the actual annual interest rate you pay is the APY, which is greater than the brightly advertised APR r_y. The conversion from their "cheat" monthly rate $r = \frac{r_y}{12}$ to the actual annual rate (the APY) is given by $APY = (1+r)^{12} - 1$, by (A.5). Thus, for example, if they advertise "4%," you actually pay $(1 + \frac{.04}{12})^{12} - 1 = 4.07\%$. For a million dollar 30-year mortgage, that's \$14,808.80 more over the course of the mortgage.

---

[6]"APR and APY: Why Your Bank Hopes You Can't Tell The Difference": investopedia.com/articles/basics/04/102904.asp = tinyurl.com/ybo9qwt4 (but with a new title).

332　R. P. Kurshan

So, here's how you use (A.7). First, solve for r by taking the bank's advertised fake "annual percentage rate" (APR) r_y, and set $r = \frac{r_y}{12}$. Letting n be the term of the mortgage *in months*, (A.7) gives your monthly payments C, given the amount of the mortgage P (what the bank gives you).

Note that by (A.7), the monthly payments scale linearly in the amount of the mortgage. Thus, for a given interest rate r, if you want to double the mortgage, you just double the monthly payments.

justification of (A.7)

Like the fair price of a straight bond, at the start of a mortgage, the amount P that the bank pays for the mortgage is the sum of the present values of each successive payment C (which includes both interest and return of principal). By (A.1), the present value of the ith payment C is $C/(1+r)^i$ for $1 \le i \le n$, and their sum is

$$P = C \frac{(1+r)^n - 1}{r(1+r)^n} \tag{A.8}$$

by (A.3). Solving for C gives (A.7).

computing the portion of C that's interest

While the sum of the portion of each C that's a return of principal adds up to P, of course the sum of all payments to the bank $nC > P$. The portion of the ith payment C that is a return of principal is $C/(1+r)^{n-i-1}$ (the rest being interest), as shown next.

Let $p_1, p_2, \cdots, p_n$ be the respective portions of principal in successive payments C. For convenience, I reverse the order of the p_i's: p_1 is the last payment of principal, and p_n is the first. In the ith month from the end (i more payments required), the current payment consists of a return of principal p_i, with $C - p_i$ interest on the outstanding principal. The outstanding principal is

$$p_1 + p_2 + \cdots + p_i$$

(from the end, back, the last i principal payments). Thus, the final payment consists of the remaining principal plus interest on it, so

$$C = p_1 + r p_1 = (1+r)p_1$$

and hence

$$p_1 = \frac{C}{1+r}.$$

Appendix A   Some Simple Math   **333**

For $i > 1$,

$$C = (1+r)p_i + r(p_1 + \cdots + p_{i-1}) .$$ (A.9)

Using that, we can find the value p_2. From (A.9),

$$C = p_2 + rp_2 + rp_1 = (1+r)p_2 + \frac{rC}{1+r}$$

so

$$(1+r)p_2 = C\left(1 - \frac{r}{1+r}\right) = C\left(\frac{1+r-r}{1+r}\right) = \frac{C}{1+r}$$

so

$$p_2 = \frac{C}{(1+r)^2} .$$

Do you see the pattern? Let's suppose that we have shown that for some j, for all $i < j$,

$$p_i = \frac{C}{(1+r)^i}$$

(we already have shown this for $j = 3$, i.e., for $i = 1$ and $i = 2$). Then we can find the value of p_j as follows. By (A.9),

$$C = (1+r)p_j + r\left(\frac{C}{1+r} + \cdots + \frac{C}{(1+r)^{j-1}}\right)$$

so

$$p_j = \frac{C}{1+r}\left(1 - r\left(\frac{1}{1+r} + \cdots + \frac{1}{(1+r)^{j-1}}\right)\right)$$

and thus, by (A.3),

$$p_j = \frac{C}{1+r}\left(1 - r\frac{(1+r)^{j-1} - 1}{r(1+r)^{j-1}}\right) = \frac{C}{1+r}\left(1 - 1 + \frac{1}{(1+r)^{j-1}}\right) = \frac{C}{(1+r)^j} .$$

This gives a formulation (mathematical induction) for showing that

$$p_i = \frac{C}{(1+r)^i}$$ (A.10)

for all $i = 1, \cdots, n$.

334   R. P. Kurshan

If you want to count from the beginning instead, just use the index $n-i+1$ to find the ith value from the beginning: $C/(1+r)^{n-i+1}$.

Accordingly, from (A.3), when paid together with the ith mortgage payment, the **mortgage payoff amount** is

$$p_1 + \cdots + p_{n-i} = C\frac{(1+r)^{n-i}-1}{r(1+r)^{n-i}}$$

and

$$P = p_1 + p_2 + \cdots + p_n = C\frac{(1+r)^n-1}{r(1+r)^n}$$

giving another proof of (A.7).

You must have noticed that (A.10) looks just like the present value of the ith coupon, except time runs backward. One could say that it represents the "past value" of the coupon (the principal that was then forthcoming), looking back from term. These sometimes are called *cash inflow* values (in this case, from the perspective of the bank viewing its return of principal), dual to present value.

A.6   Drawing Down a Savings Bank Account

Let's say you want to estimate how long your savings P lasts if you invest it in a savings bank giving interest at a rate r, and you draw it down with regular withdrawals of value C. Or, given a term n and initial investment P, you wish to compute the required rate of return r needed to support periodic payments of size C. Or, given n, r, and either P or C, you wish to compute the other. It's all done with the mortgage formula (A.7), solving for the free variable. Solving for P or C is direct; solving for r or n is accomplished through successive guesses that bring the two sides of the equation ever closer or simply with a plotting calculator (Appendix A.9.1).

How to think of this: instead of the bank loaning you P, which you then pay back in periodic payments C, it's you that lends the bank P, which pays you interest plus periodic payments of size C until your account is empty.

Warning: as explained in Chap. 10, you cannot use this formula directly on a volatile investment, on account of degradation (Sect. 11.1).

Appendix A   Some Simple Math   **335**

A.7   Bond Ladders

Even if you don't intend to build a bond ladder (Sect. 2.3.3), knowing how to compute the cost or yield of a ladder can be useful as a means to evaluate a product like an annuity or a pension. A bond ladder provides a viable alternative to these, so if you can compute the value of a bond ladder, you can check whether an annuity is offered at a fair price (Appendix A.9) or a pension buyout offer is attractive (Appendix A.11). Likewise, if you have an annuity or pension that's not adjusted for inflation, you can compute the value of a bond ladder that determines how much of savings to earmark, to compensate it for inflation (Appendix A.10).

A.7.1   Building a Zero-Coupon Bond Ladder

If you are building a conceptual bond ladder only for evaluations as above, then a ladder of zero-coupon bonds is the simplest and most useful. Since this ladder is only conceptual, we can make two simplifying assumptions: that bonds are available for every ladder rung and that bonds can be bought to total to any desired principal value P.

The first assumption is unrealistic and is eliminated when we show how to construct an actual bond ladder for investment. For a conceptual ladder, we just need to keep in mind that the computed yield is slightly better than what is possible in practice.

The second assumption is not possible to realize because bonds are unavailable in fractional quantities. However, it is approximately true, since the bonds, usually available with $1000 face value, are bought in sufficient quantity that a resulting principal value P can be found that is proportionally close to the desired value.

Without assumptions, a given rung payout C can be realized for all rungs.

conceptual bond ladder, for evaluations
In this case, the ladder is constructed from possibly fictional bonds that mature after successive equally spaced periods (annually, monthly, or whatever other period is desired). For example, if the period is monthly, then the bonds in the first rung mature in 1 month, those of the second in 2 months, and so on. The yields of successive rungs generally can be expected to increase as short-term bonds give way to intermediate-term bonds. The cost P of such a ladder with n rungs with successive yields r_i $(1 \leq i \leq n)$ that pays out C per period, as above, is

$$P = \frac{C}{1+r_1} + \frac{C}{(1+r_2)^2} + \frac{C}{(1+r_3)^3} + \cdots + \frac{C}{(1+r_n)^n} \qquad \text{(A.11)}$$

(the principal and present value of the ladder). Indeed, by (A.1), the present value of each successive rung is $P_i = C/(1+r_i)$ for $1 \leq i \leq n$, and thus the present value of the ladder is $P = P_1 + P_2 + \cdots + P_n$. Of course, if we want to know the C that is supported by a given P, then solve (A.11) for C.

The yields r_i are chosen by selecting bonds whose risk is commensurate with the annuity, pension, or whatever we seek to evaluate. The appropriate yields can be found on the internet by looking at bond offerings that state their (risk) rating and term. Treasuries (bonds issued by the U.S. Government) have the lowest risk; next lowest are high-grade "investment grade" corporate bonds rated AAA, down through AA^- by Standard & Poor, or Aaa down through Baa3 by Moody.[7]

For initial rungs without bonds, use the interest rate given by a savings bank or money market fund. (In an actual ladder, you'd use cash for initial rungs with no available bonds.) For rungs thereafter, with no bonds that mature on the rung date, use the r_i for the last earlier rung for which bonds are available.

We seek the yield r of the ladder, for given P, C, and n, to make the required evaluation. Once we compute P (or C, given P), the r_i's no longer are relevant. By (A.3), we get (A.8). That's the mortgage formula! Indeed, you're loaning the bond issuer P and getting the return of interest and principal in n equal payments of amount C. To find the yield of the ladder, solve (A.8) for r.

actual bond ladder, for investment
If you start with a budget P, use the conceptual bond ladder calculation above to find the periodic payout C it supports, in concept. As explained above, while the payouts C will be maintained, it will be necessary to adjust the amounts stored in each rung. These adjustments will result in an adjustment of the principal P. The new value typically will be close to the original. If you start with the required payouts C, then accordingly, the resulting ladder principal P will be close to the value computed for a conceptual ladder with those payouts.

In order to build an actual ladder for investment that supports periodic payouts C, different values C_i are required for successive ladder rungs, to make up for "holes": rungs for which no bond is available with the required maturity date. Earlier rungs need to support the payouts required from subsequent holes.

---

[7] investopedia.com/terms/i/investmentgrade.asp.

Appendix A   Some Simple Math   **337**

Assign the yields r_i as for the conceptual bond ladder.

As with the conceptual ladder, use cash for the initial rungs for which no bonds are available. The cash invested in a rung is the present value of the cash needed for the rung.

Thereafter, if there are bonds for rung i, but there are no bonds available until k rungs after rung i or through the end of the ladder $k - 1$ rungs away ($n = i + k - 1$), then set $C_i = kC$, and for each missing rung j, set $C_j = 0$. The ith rung holds the value needed to support the payouts required for it and the following $k - 1$ "holes".

However, it may not be possible to buy exactly C_i dollars worth of bonds for each rung, since it is not possible to buy bonds in fractional quantities. We can deal with this by "juggling" the C_is, so that each is a realizable integer multiple of the available bond face value. For example, if $C_1 = C = \$10,400$ and the available bonds have face value $\$1000$, reset $C_1 = \$11,000$. Then we have an extra $\$600$ at the end of period $i = 1$. If $C_2 = \$31,200$ (because $C_3 = C_4 = 0$), reset $C_2 = \$32,000$. This leaves a total extra of $\$1400$. Therefore, if $C_5 = C = \$10,400$, we can reset it *down* to $C_5 = \$9000$, drawing on the extra, thus depleted. Continuing in this manner, the C_is all can be rendered realizable, and support the required periodic payouts of value C. (This juggling could be optimized with a computer program.)

The cost P of this ladder is given by the present value formula (A.1):

$$P = \frac{C_1}{1 + r_1} + \frac{C_2}{(1 + r_2)^2} + \frac{C_3}{(1 + r_3)^3} + \cdots + \frac{C_n}{(1 + r_n)^n} \qquad \text{(A.12)}$$

To compute the yield of the ladder, use P from (A.12), and solve the mortgage formula (A.8) for r.

If the r_i's are non-decreasing—the typical case—then this ladder costs more and thus has a lower yield than the conceptual ladder with the same C payouts and no holes, as each missing rung requires buying more bonds that mature earlier and thus are more costly.

As another practical matter, such ladders are generally limited to a maximum length of 30 years, generally the longest bond term available. A ladder may be extended beyond 30 years, by keeping the funds for the extension in reserve and extending the ladder year after year. The funds held in reserve can be added to successive ladder rungs.

A last practical matter to keep in mind: as already explained in Sect. 2.3.3, zero-coupon bonds have slightly lower yields than the straight bonds from which their coupons are stripped, and are subject to tax on "phantom" interest.

338   R. P. Kurshan

Therefore, in building a ladder for investment, straight bonds (bonds with coupons) are slightly preferable over zero-coupon bonds.

A.7.2 Building a General Bond Ladder

This is a bit like solving a jigsaw puzzle. Start by assembling the desired bonds that are available for various ladder rungs. This gives a good idea of the yields r_i that attach to the respective ladder rungs. If you start with a budget P for the ladder, compute C using a conceptual ladder of zero-coupon bonds (Appendix A.7.1). Hence, from here on, assume the periodic payout C and term n are known.

Begin by filling in the rungs of the ladder with the available bond principals that come to term on the rung date, starting from the last rung, working backward. Assign their coupons to respective preceding rungs. Use the techniques described for zero-coupon bonds to cover missing rings and to fill rung deficits. If holes or rung deficits remain, they can be filled with cash.

Once filled, the rungs will consist of bonds and cash with various yields, plus coupons. Adding up the bond principals and the cash gives the value P of the ladder. The ladder yield can be computed based on P, C, and n, using the mortgage formula.

A.8   Preferred Stock

Preferred stock behaves like a combination of common stock and a bond, in that it offers a dividend, often at a predetermined fixed rate. For most ordinary investors, it is recommended to *avoid* preferred stock, for many technical reasons having to do with an asymmetry between risk and benefit, although preferred stock can confer sizable tax advantages when held by corporations, their main buyers.[8]

Nonetheless, non-callable preferred stock with a fixed dividend provides an interesting example, in that it looks a lot like a straight bond with an infinite term. Since (A.4) computes the cost (present value) of a straight bond, what would be its cost if its term were infinite? The reason it can be infinite and still make sense is related to Zeno's Paradox: although there are an infinite number of positive summands whose sum is the cost, the successive values of the summands become very small very quickly. If we rewrite (A.4) as

---

[8]cbsnews.com/news/why-you-should-avoid-preferred-stocks/.

Appendix A   Some Simple Math   339

$$P = \frac{C}{r} - \frac{C}{r(1+r)^n} + \frac{P}{(1+r)^n}$$

and take its limit as $n \to \infty$, since the last two expressions go to 0, the present value of a share of preferred stock that gives a fixed dividend C that is a fraction r of its face value is simply C/r.

A.9 Annuities

It is easy to compute the present value of a fixed rate immediate or deferred annuity (Sect. 2.10.2). In fact, the formula is the same as the one we've been using for bonds and mortgages.

While an immediate annuity, one that pays a periodic stipend from the time of purchase until the death of the annuitant(s), is a special case of a deferred annuity—one that defers the first payment for a given amount of time—we start with an immediate annuity, because its analysis is simpler.

Although an immediate annuity might bring to mind preferred stock (Appendix A.8) since the payment of a fixed preferred stock dividend is not limited to a given term, preferred stock does have resale value and thus is the wrong model. Moreover, an annuity *does* have a limited term: the lifetime of the annuitant. Although this term may not be known to the annuitant when the annuity is purchased, it *is* known then by the insurance company that issues the annuity—on average, which is all that matters to them. As we shall see, the correct model for an annuity is a mortgage.

A.9.1 Computing the Value of an Immediate Annuity

A fixed rate immediate annuity sometimes is sold with optional bells and whistles, like life insurance, buyer's remorse rescission, or a stipend that tracks an index such as inflation or an increasing flat rate. All these extras may increase the cost of the annuity beyond the value of the components, or not, but adding them makes its analysis infeasible.

Without the extras, a fixed rate immediate annuity is a mortgage—that you give to the insurance company. Instead of the bank giving you a principal amount, secured by your home, you give the insurance company a premium, secured by their good name. Then they pay you back your money over time, together with some interest. Although the term is not explicit, it is assumed by the insurance company, as explained above.

340   **R. P. Kurshan**

For an annuity with survivor benefits, its "term" is determined by actuarial mortality tables used to determine the longevity of the second to die. Often, the stipends are reduced after the first dies, complicating the computation.

Although the buyer mostly doesn't know when she will die, she can easily find her expected mortality[9] or the expected last to die of her and her spouse.[10,11]

If you are healthier than most—exercise regularly, not obese, and don't smoke, for example—then your expected longevity is longer than the average; if you have a terminal illness, then it may be shorter. Research has shown a positive correlation between one's longevity and that of one's parents (especially, one's mother). Based on such considerations, pick what you think is a reasonable range of years for your longevity.

Don't be fooled by the nominal annuity rate of return: an annuity may state that it returns 6% of your premium, for life, but most of that 6% is the insurance company giving you back your own money. It's *not* the same as investing the premium in a bond and getting 6% interest, because with a bond, at term, you get your "premium" (the bond's face value) back (not to mention that you can sell a bond whenever you want, but you can never sell an annuity). With an annuity, the premium is gone. For a premium P and annual payout C, some insurance companies call C/P the "annual payout rate." While to a lay person this certainly sounds like a rate of return, if one bothers to read the fine print at the bottom of the page, there is a definition: "A percentage of the purchase payment, which includes both interest and return of principal, paid out each full year. The Annual Payout Rate is not an interest rate or a rate of return."

If you die after n payouts, the mortgage formula gives the resulting yield (rate of return) on your "investment" (the premium that you paid or are considering to pay). For the annuity premium P, stipend C, and number of payouts n, the yield is the value r given by the mortgage formula (A.8). One can find r by trial and error, guessing successive values, or directly using a plotting calculator (see below). If the payouts are monthly, don't forget to convert r to a yearly rate.

Having found r, you can compare it to the yield of a bond whose (risk) rating is comparable to that of the insurance company (insurance companies, like bonds, are rated in terms of risk of default: see Sects. 2.10.3 and 2.10.5).

---

[9] ssa.gov/oact/STATS/table4c6.html.

[10] Vanguard (2000) (Set the 'Time Frame' so that 'Either' is as close as you can get it to 50%—the 'Time Frame' value that gives the expected age of the last to die.)

[11] pgcalc.com/pdf/twolife.pdf = tinyurl.com/yagkcyw5.

Appendix A Some Simple Math **341**

The idea is that you can build a bond ladder of such bonds with similar yield (Sect. A.7.1).

Alternatively, start with the yield r that you can get from a bond whose rating is comparable to that of the insurance company that is offering the annuity. Yields for corporate bonds that are reasonable candidates for comparison can be found readily on the internet.[12,13,14] Then, solve the mortgage formula for n to see the equivalent "term" of the annuity. How does n compare to your expected longevity?

using a plotting calculator to find r or n

One can find r or n quickly and to high accuracy using a plotting calculator. Let's work out an example, using Desmos,[15] mentioned throughout this book. Say $P = 100,000$ and $C = \$8124$ annually (the quote with the highest payout that I found recently for an for an annuity for myself, with no survivor option). The "Annual Payout rate"—not given in this particular quote (good for you, Fidelity)—is $C/P = 8.1\%$

At the time that I got that annuity quote, comparable corporate bond yields were around 5%. Using the calculator, for $r = 0.05$, write in the box in the upper lefthand corner

$$y = 8124(0.05^{-1})(1 - (1.05)^{-n}) - 100000 \, .$$

This is the mortgage equation (A.8), slightly rewritten for convenience and introducing the variable y so that Desmos can plot a graph as a function of n, which it does instantly. The solution for n is where the graph crosses the x-axis ($y = 0$). Move your cursor to that point, and it instantly gives you the value of n: 19.588 years (Fig. A.1). That's my break-even point for this annuity: if I live more than 19.588 years more, I "beat the bank"; else I lose.

Let's say I decide that I don't want to bet on living more than 15 years from now. Let's see what yield just 15 years gives me. For this, use $n = 15$ and let r be the unknown:

$$y = 8124(r^{-1})(1 - (1+r)^{-15}) - 100000$$

---

[12] https://markets.on.nytimes.com/research/markets/bonds/bonds.asp.
[13] fred.stlouisfed.org/release?rid=427.
[14] fred.stlouisfed.org/series/BAA.
[15] desmos.com/calculator.

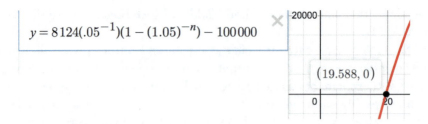

Fig. A.1 Desmos plot solution of mortgage formula.

Desmos gives the solution: 2.58%. If the annuity paid its stipend monthly at the rate of $\$8124/12 = \$677$ per month, the yield is slightly better: 2.75% (*cf.* Sect. A.4.1). Either way, if I only live another 15 years, the yield on this annuity doesn't look that great. The Social Security Period Life Table 2013[16] says I am expected to live only another 13.6 years. In that case, the yield is only 1.4% (1.49% if the payout is monthly). Yikes! I would have been better off putting my premium in a savings bank.

So, if I only live as long as I am "supposed" to, the annuity in this example seems like a bad bet. Indeed, that's how the insurance companies make their money. If you live significantly longer (and the insurance company survives at least as long as you do), an annuity can look reasonable. In my case, living to 93 was the break-even point for this particular annuity. To win, I'd need to live longer.

But how can one one predict? Healthy today, sick tomorrow.

Even if I feel very healthy today and expect to live long enough to "beat" the annuity, I'd still be carrying its liquidity risk (Sect. 3.8) and have no option if one day I sensed the company was headed for default.

longevity tables
A word about longevity tables. There are three principal sources: the Social Security Period Life Table 2013, the Society of Actuaries Retirement Participant 2000 Tables,[17,18] and the National Association of Insurance Commissioners Annuity 2000 Mortality Tables.[19,20] And guess what? They all give somewhat different answers (*cf.* Sect. 17.2.9). The Society of Actuaries' tables

---

[16] ssa.gov/oact/STATS/table4c6.html.
[17] Vanguard (2000).
[18] longevityillustrator.org/Profile.
[19] pgcalc.com/pdf/singlelife.pdf = tinyurl.com/y797aa4h.
[20] pgcalc.com/pdf/twolife.pdf = tinyurl.com/yagkcyw5.

are a refinement of the Government tables, the latter taking into account health, occupation, and other factors. But the Insurance tables are generic, like the Government tables. And *they* give different answers! The Social Security table tells me that I'm expected to live another 13.6 years, while the Insurance table gives me another 2 years and 4 months: 15.9 years. How can that be? Isn't it all just statistics? Why don't they give the same answers? The reason is that predicting longevity is just that: a prediction. The different tables may start with the same exact data, but the way they make their predictions based on that data can vary. It's also worth noting that while the Government needs the predictions to be as accurate as possible, because the results determine funding for Social Security and regulating private pension funding adequacy thresholds, the insurance companies lose only if they underestimate longevity. Based on this, you might expect that the insurance tables give a bit longer longevities. And indeed, that is the case. Perhaps there's sauce in the science.

adding a spouse or partner to an annuity

For an annuity with 100% survivorship—meaning that it continues to pay until the second of you and your spouse (or registered partner) dies—the yields are naturally worse, because the expected time until the second death is longer than until the first death (and the insurance company of course uses that to set the policy cost). In my case, adding my spouse reduced the annual payments to $C = \$6036$, three quarters of the payout for me alone. With Desmos, I quickly see the effects. The break-even point (as before) jumps to over 36 years—my wife and I would surely be dead by then. The effect on the yield is no less dramatic: for a 20-year term, the yield comes down from 5.1% to a mere 1.9%. Increasing the term to 30 years increases the yield only to 4.4%. We can use the mortality tables to see what is the insurance company's cost. In my case, according to the insurance longevity tables, the last to die is expected to be 24 years away (my spouse is female, so expected to live longer than me, and is 5 years my junior). For a term of 24 years, the yield is 3.2%—the same yield as for myself alone, living only another 15.9 years. This is as expected: the insurance company sets their target profit, and that defines the yield they give. Then, based on a term n equal to the expected longevity, they set the premium P in order that the annuity generates the target yield. If our average longevity is more closely predicted by the Government tables, then the insurance companies have set their premiums higher than needed, but since they all use the same tables, there's no worry about competition.

344   R. P. Kurshan

A.9.2 Computing the Value of a Deferred Annuity

A potentially attractive alternative to an immediate annuity is a (fixed rate) deferred annuity (Sect. 2.10.2). This type of annuity starts paying its stipend only after the end of a deferral period and thus should be correspondingly less expensive than an immediate annuity. It should be viewed as longevity insurance, providing a stipend in later years of retirement to insure against outliving one's savings.

The way to think of a deferred annuity is as a combination of a zero-coupon bond (Appendix A.1) and an immediate annuity (Appendix A.9.1). Say the premium for the deferred annuity is P and the deferral period is d years. First, you put the premium P into a zero-coupon bond that matures in d years. At the end of the deferral period, you use the bond to buy an ordinary immediate annuity. Assume that the two give the same yield (the bond can be chosen to give the same yield as the computed yield of the deferred annuity). Putting these two together gives

$$P(1+r)^d = C\frac{(1+r)^n - 1}{r(1+r)^n}$$

so

$$P = C\frac{(1+r)^n - 1}{r(1+r)^{n+d}} \tag{A.13}$$

Solve for r as above for various values of n. For each resulting yield r, check the (risk) rating of zero-coupon bonds with term d and yield r. Is it comparable to the rating of the insurance company? If the bond rating is lower, then the premium of the deferred annuity is overpriced for the computed yield, as the yield is then based on a bond yield only possible from a bond that is riskier than the annuity. Lower the yield until you can find a comparably rated bond for the given n that satisfies (A.13). That's the annuity yield for the given n.

I found a number of products. Ones from more highly rated companies naturally cost more. In fact, it wasn't easy to find the product I wanted. They were not generally available with 100% survivor benefit, for the deferral period I wanted, without unwanted extras (that raised the price). Among the ones that I did find, the one with highest annual payout gave \$18,054 per year (paid monthly), after a deferral of $d = 13$ years. However, it came with a one-time 2% commission. That effectively increased the premium by 2%.

I computed the yield for a term of another $n = 11$ years past the deferral period that ended at the last to die expected date. The monthly yield, given by

(A.13), was the r that satisfied

$$102000 = \frac{18054}{12} \frac{(1+r)^{11*12} - 1}{r(1+r)^{24*12}}.$$

Desmos gave the solution: $r = 0.3\%$, so the annual yield was $(1 + r)^{12} = 3.7\%$. This may seem disappointing as it's only 0.5% more than the 24-year immediate annuity (see above). The insurance company was giving me about the same yield for a deferred annuity as for an immediate annuity. The nominal benefit to the annuitant for waiting was an annual payout starting after the first 13 years, increased from \$6063 to \$18,054. But, I could just take the proceeds of a 13-year term zero-coupon bond bought at the price P of the deferred annuity premium and, after the 13 years, buy an immediate annuity, to the same effect. Compared with buying a deferred annuity, this would reduce liquidity risk, eliminate the counter-party risk that the insurance company would disappear before the end of the deferral period, and avoid the premium altogether, were we to die before the end of the deferral period. In short, we were barely rewarded for all these risks.

So in summary, the deferred annuities I found were not competitive with immediate annuities.

A.10 Inflation Compensation for Flat Payouts

In retirement savings management, inflation is an essential factor to consider. All expenses inflate with time, and the buying power of a fixed income stream (such as from a pension or annuity) diminishes.

Since we don't want to diminish our standard of living as our effective ("real") income decreases, the alternative is to earmark a portion of savings that will be drawn on to augment a fixed income stream so that it maintains its buying power. Then you can project budgets based on current costs and current income.

How to calculate the required size of the earmark is based on the present value formula (A.1).

Since we cannot foresee the future, in order to calculate what we need to earmark, we need to make an assumption about inflation. At the time of this writing, the industry standard prediction is 2.5% per year (although it is less at this moment). Let the inflation rate prediction be denoted by r. If your fixed income stream pays out C dollars per year, then after i years, if the stream is inflation-adjusted, the payout is $C(1 + r)^i$.

346   R. P. Kurshan

So, the inflation compensation earmark must "pay" $C(1+r)^i - C$ in year i to augment C to what it would have been if it adjusted for inflation. How much should be earmarked so that the inflation compensation lasts n years? (As with the annuity calculations, we can choose various values for n, depending on how long we think the fund should last, and see the results.)

Since we need the compensations yearly, while the undrawn earmark balance grows as an investment, the calculation may at first seem daunting. But it's simple. Think of the inflation compensation earmark as a ladder of zero-coupon bonds, the ith rung of which pays $C(1+r)^i - C$. The cost of this ladder—its present value (Appendix A.7.1)—is the amount that should be earmarked for inflation compensation. It is (A.12) with $C_i = C(1+r)^i - C$.

You may not actually want to build such a ladder, but instead mingle this earmark with the rest of your investments. But computing the cost of the ladder lets you know the amount of savings to be excluded from what is otherwise available for expenses. One advantage of not building an actual ladder is that you can adjust the earmark periodically for changes in the rate of inflation and for the required term n simply by recalculating its value.

If you expect to be able to achieve an appreciation rate R on investments, then you can compute a simple formula for the present value P of the inflation compensation earmark. If your rung yields are all assumed to be the same rate R, then for inflation rate r and flat payout C, the cost of the inflation compensation earmark, based on (A.12), is

$$P = C \left(\frac{1+r}{1+R} + \cdots + \frac{(1+r)^n}{(1+R)^n} - \left(\frac{1}{1+R} + \cdots + \frac{1}{(1+R)^n} \right) \right).$$

Note that

$$\frac{1+r}{1+R} = \frac{1}{1 + \frac{R-r}{1+r}}$$

so by (A.3), for $X = \frac{R-r}{1+r}$,

$$P = C \left(\frac{(1+X)^n - 1}{X(1+X)^n} - \frac{(1+R)^n - 1}{R(1+R)^n} \right).$$

One might set $R = 2r$, expecting conservatively that investments appreciate at a rate that is at least double that of inflation. If $r = 0.025$ and $n = 25$, then

$$P = 4.5C$$

(approximately). Thus, for a 25-year retirement with 2.5% annual inflation, earmark 4 1/2 year's worth of non-adjusting income.

A.11 Buyout Value of a U.S. Pension

There is a diminishing population of true "pensioners": those receiving a pension from a previous employer. It is important for these pensioners to be able to evaluate the value of their pension in case their pension provider offers a lump sum buyout of the pension, that is, offering a single lump sum payout in exchange for agreeing to cancel the pension.

Such offers have become increasingly common, as companies seek to transfer their investment risk to that of the pensioner. The decision to accept or reject such an offer is fraught and complex (Sect. 17.2.9). Here, I simply explain how to calculate the price that the U.S. Government mandates for a flat (not inflation-adjusting) pension buyout offer.

The government mandate depends only on the terms of the pension and does not take into account individual considerations such as the recipient's health and risk preferences. Therefore, this buyout pricing does not necessarily reflect the value of the pension to the individual.

In a sense, this calculation has already been described. In terms of the value of its payouts, a pension is no different from a fixed rate immediate annuity, if the pension already is paying, and a fixed rate deferred annuity if the pension starts paying at some time in the future. We have seen how to evaluate each of these in terms of the value of a comparable ladder of bonds (Appendix A.9).

However, here I describe a different and simpler metric designed by the U.S. Government for setting the value that a private pension provider must use when offering a lump sum buyout. When using a bond ladder to evaluate an annuity, we sought to create a ladder with the best possible return for comparable risk, based on corporate bonds whose risk was comparable to that of the insurance company that offered the annuity. The risk of a private sector pension default is mostly much smaller than the risk of default of an insurance company, on account of multiple layers of protection mandated by the U.S. Government (Sect. 17.2). Until recently, the U. S. Government had mandated that the benchmark for computing the value of a private pension buyout must use (risk-free) U.S. Treasury bonds. This was good for the pensioner, as it required the payout to be larger than if the value were based on higher yield (riskier) corporate bonds. However, under pressure from companies to make buyout offers less expensive to them, this standard was downgraded to a rate determined by a selection of higher-yielding corporate bonds.

348   R. P. Kurshan

The U.S. Government formula for determining the value of a flat pension avoids the complexities of building a ladder altogether. It is simplified to three rates, mandated by the Pension Protection Act of 2006. It requires that a lump sum pension buyout offer be no less than an amount calculated using three different corporate interest rates. The first is a short-term corporate bond interest rate meant to cover the forthcoming 5 years of pension payments. The second is a medium-term corporate bond interest rate meant to cover the following 5–20 years. The last is a long-term corporate bond interest rate meant to cover payments for the years past the first 20. The rates apply for as long as the pension is expected to last, that is, as long as the annuitant's and any survivor's benefits are expected to be active, based on IRS longevity tables. The lump sum buyout offer must be large enough so that it can, in theory, be used to build a bond ladder with bonds with those yields for the years involved.

While this simplifies the calculation, it provides an unrealistic comparison. It doesn't capture the costs of building an actual ladder and the inevitable "holes" in such a ladder. It is unlikely that the government formula allows for a direct replacement with a ladder of comparable-risk bonds.

Nonetheless, there can be other reasons (not all sound) to accept a buyout:

- You do not expect to live long, and therefore the lump sum benefit will exceed the pension benefit.
- You worry that the pension issuer will default and that other layers of government protection discussed in Sect. 17.2 will prove to be inadequate.
- You think you can do better than the benchmark by investing the payout sum yourself (but, *cf.* Sect. 17.2.9).

The government formula in essence breaks a pension into three fixed rate annuity-like investments. Their costs are determined by (A.13). The first is like an immediate annuity with yield r_1 that lasts 5 years. The second is like a deferred annuity with yield r_2 and deferral period of 5 years that lasts 20 years. The last is like a deferred annuity with deferral period of 20 years. As soon as you die, the payments stop. Here, "as soon as you die" is a deterministic number, determined by IRS longevity tables. These tables give numbers that are close to those in the Social Security and the Society of Actuaries tables, which predict a sooner death than the insurance company tables (Appendix A.9.1—**longevity tables**). This sooner prediction of death, of course, works to the advantage of the pension provider, as the formula provides for a lesser lump sum than had the insurance company tables been used.

At any rate, here's how to compute the pension buyout value based on the government formula. Let n be the number of years that the actuarial tables

Appendix A   Some Simple Math   **349**

give you to live. For a simple pension without survivor benefits, if $n < 5$, only the first annuity is relevant; if $5 < n < 20$, only the first two annuities are relevant; otherwise, all three come into play.

If your pension does have survivor benefits, it's a little more complicated, because once you die, your spouse continues to receive benefits but may only receive a part of the benefit that you received. An example should make it all clear.

Define the function F as

$$F(C, r, n, d) = C \frac{(1+r)^n - 1}{r(1+r)^{n+d}} \tag{A.14}$$

The F gives the value of a deferred annuity with periodic payouts C, yield r, deferral period d, and term n, derived in (A.13).

As an example, suppose the primary pension holder M receives a pension of $C_1 = \$30,000$ per year, and when M dies, if M's partner N is still alive, N receives a reduced survivor benefit of $C_2 = \$15,000$ per year (a 50% survivor benefit is pretty typical).

Suppose the Social Security tables give M another $L_1 = 16.32$ years to live and N $L_2 = 22.13$ years, from the date of a buyout offer.

Then the fair value (according to the IRS) for a buyout offer is $P = P_1 + P_2 + P_3 + P_4$, where

$$P_1 = F(C_1, r_1, 5, 0)$$

the value of M's annuity in the first period,

$$P_2 = F(C_1, r_2, L_1 - 5, 5)$$

the value of M's annuity in the second period, until M's death,

$$P_3 = F(C_2, r_2, 20 - L_1, L_1)$$

the value of N's (reduced) annuity benefits in the remainder of the second period after M's death, and

$$P_4 = F(C_2, r_3, L_2 - 20, 20)$$

N's annuity benefits in the third (and last) period, until N's death.

The function F is valid also for fractional values of n and d.

350   **R. P. Kurshan**

The three yields r_1, r_2, r_3 can be hard to find from IRS sources, but they are required to be stated in a buyout offer.

There are more complex situations that this calculation does not cover, such as "pop-up" options, where if the secondary annuitant dies first, the primary annuitant begins to receive larger pension payments that were forgone by adding a surviving spouse option. Such options make a pension more valuable, so using the above calculation gives a lower bound on the value of the pension.

This takes some of the mystery out of how lump sum buyout offers are derived. Some people erroneously believe that if the employer is offering a buyout, it must be under-valued, while in fact its value is controlled by the IRS. Whether it is a *good* value for you is the subject of Sect. 17.2.9.

References

Aliber, R. Z., & Kindleberger, C. P. (2015). *Manias, panics, and crashes: A history of financial crises*. London: Palgrave Macmillan.

Altman, E. I. (1989). Measuring corporate bond mortality and performance. *The Journal of Finance, 44*(4), 909–922.

Bauer, S. (2020). An Unstoppable Force. *The New Yorker*, 28–35. https://www.newyorker.com/magazine/2020/11/23/how-a-deadly-police-force-ruled-a-city.

Bengen, W. P. (1994). Determining withdrawal rates using historical data. *Journal of Financial Planing, 7*(4), 171–180.

Bengen, W. P. (1996). Asset allocation for a lifetime. *Journal of Financial Planing, 9*(4), 58–67.

Bierwirth, L. (1994). Investing for retirement: Using the past to model the future. *Journal of Financial Planing, 7*(1), 14–24. as cited in Bengen (1994), Cooley et al. (1998).

Bodie, Z. (1995). On the risks of stocks in the long run. *Financial Analysts Journal, 51*(3), 18–22.

Bodie, Z., Merton, R.C. (2000). *Finance*. Prentice Hall: Hoboken.

Bogle, J. C. (2010). *Common sense on mutual funds*. Wiley: New York.

Charupat, N., Milevsky, M. A., & Kamstra, M.J. (2015). The sluggish and asymmetric reaction of life annuity prices to changes in interest rates. *Journal of Risk and Insurance, 83*(3), 519–555.

Cooley, P. L., Hubbard, C. M., & Walz, D. T. (1998). Retirement savings: Choosing a withdrawal rate that is sustainable. *AAII Journal*, 16–21. the "Trinity Study".

De Bondt, W. F. M., & Thaler, R. (1985). Does the stock market overreact? *Journal of Finance, 40*(3), 793–805.

Edesess, M. (2007). *The Big Investment Lie: What Your Financial Advisor Doesn't Want You to Know*. Berrett-Koehler: California.

© The Author(s), under exclusive license to Springer Nature Switzerland AG 2022
R. P. Kurshan, *Investment Industry Claims Debunked*,
https://doi.org/10.1007/978-3-030-76709-9

352 **References**

Ellis, C. D. (2012). Investment management fees are (much) higher than you think. *Financial Analysts Journal, 68*(3), 4–6.

Ellis, C. D., Munnell, A. H., & Eschtruth, A. D. (2014). *Falling Short: The Coming Retirement Crisis and What to Do About It.* Oxford University: Oxford.

Fama, E. F. (1970). Efficient capital markets: A review of theory and empirical work. *The Journal of Finance, 25*(2), 383–417.

Fama, E. F., & French, K. R. (1993). Common risk factors in the returns on stocks and bonds. *Journal of Financial Economics, 33*(1), 3–56.

Fama, E. F., & French, K. R. (2010). Luck versus skill in the cross-section of mutual fund returns. *Journal of Finance, 65*(5), 1915–47.

FRED (2015a). 10-Year Treasury Constant Maturity Rate. In *Federal Reserve Bank of St. Louis.* https://research.stlouisfed.org/fred2/series/GS10.

FRED (2015b). Federal Funds Rate. In *Federal Reserve Bank of St. Louis.* https://research.stlouisfed.org/fred2/series/DFF.

Goyal, A., & Wahal, S. (2008). The selection and termination of investment management firms by plan sponsors. *Journal of Finance, 64*(4), 1841. Table 10.

Greszler, R. (2015). Bankrupt Pensions and Insolvent Pension Insurance. In *BACKGROUNDER*(3029). http://report.heritage.org/bg3029.

Hebner, M. T. (2006). *Index funds: The 12-step program for active investors.* IFA Publishing Inc.: Bristol.

Homer, S., & Sylla, R. (2005). *A history of interest rates.* Wiley: New York.

Horneff, W. J., Maurer, R. H., & Stamos, M. Z. (2008). Lifecycle asset allocation with annuity markets. *Journal of Economic Dynamics and Control, 32*(11), 3590–3612.

Huang, H., & Milevsky, M. A. (2011). Lifetime ruin minimization: should retirees hedge inflation or just worry about it? *Journal of Pension Economics and Finance, 10*(3), 363–387.

Huang, H., Milevsky, M. A., & Young, V. R. (2017). Optimal purchasing of deferred income annuities when payout yields are mean-reverting. *Review of Finance, 21*(1), 327–361.

James, T., & Ghilarducci, T. (2016). *Rescuing retirement: A plan to guarantee retirement security for all Americans.* Disruption Books: New York.

Jegadeesh, N., & Titman, S. (1993). Returns to buying winners and selling losers: Implications for stock market efficiency. *Journal of Finance, 48*(1), 65–91.

Kahneman, D. (2011). *Thinking, Fast and Slow.* Farrar, Straus and Giroux: New York. see also http://www.nytimes.com/2011/10/23/magazine/dont-blink-the-hazards-of-confidence.html.

Kahneman, D., & Tversky, A. (1979). Prospect theory: An analysis of decision under risk. *Econometrica, 47*(2), 263–291.

Keen, S. (2011). *Debunking economics: The Naked emperor dethroned?.* Zen Books: New York. Revised and Expanded Edition.

Kurshan, R. P. (2019). *Should one roll over to a roth in retirement?.* doi: 10.6084/m9.figshare.13783993. tinyurl.com/wbqpuygn.

References 353

Leland, H. E. (1980). Who should buy Portfolio Insurance?. *Journal of Finance, 35*(2), 581–594.

Malkiel, B. G. (2015). *A random walk down wall street.* W. W. Norton & Co.: New York.

Mandelbrot, B., & Taleb, N. N. (2005). How the finance gurus get risk all wrong. *Fortune Magazine, 152*(1), 99–100. tinyurl.com/w5jxuq6.

Markowitz, H. (1952). Portfolio selection. *The Journal of Finance, 7*(1), 77–91.

Marotta, D. (2012). The false promises of annuities and annuity calculators. *Forbes Investing.* http://www.forbes.com/sites/davidmarotta/2012/08/27/the-false-promises-of-annuities-and-annuity-calculators/#74b360856e03.

Merton, R. C. (2014). The crisis in retirement planning. *Harvard Business Review, 92*(7-8), 43–50.

Milevsky, M. A. (2012). *The 7 most important equations for your retirement.* Wiley: New York.

Milevsky, M. A., & Posner, S. P. (2014). Can collars reduce retirement sequencing risk? *Journal of Retirement, 1*(4), 46–56.

Peters, O., & Gell-Mann, M. (2016). Evaluating gambles using dynamics. *Chaos, 26,* 023103.

Poundstone, W. (2006). *Fortune's Formula.* Farrar, Straus and Giroux: New York.

Reinsdorf, M. B., & Lenze, D. G. (2009). Defined benefit pensions and household income and wealth. *Survey of Current Business, 89,* 50–62. https://www.bea.gov/scb/pdf/2009/08%20August/0806_benefits.pdf.

Robinson, J. (1962). *Economic Philosophy.* Penguin Books: New York.

Ross, S. A. (1999). Adding risks: Samuelson's fallacy of large numbers revisited. *Journal of Financial and Quantitative Analysis, 34*(3), 323–339.

Saari, D. G. (1990). A visit to the Newtonian N-body problem via elementary complex variables. *American Mathematical Monthly, 97*(2), 105–119.

Samuelson, P. A. (1963). Risk and uncertainty: A fallacy of large numbers. *Scientia* **98**(4), 108–113.

Schondelmeyer, S. W., & Purvis, L. (2019). Trends in retail prices of prescription drugs widely used by older americans: 2017 Year-End Update. *AARP.* https://www.aarp.org/content/dam/aarp/ppi/2019/06/trends-in-retail-prices-of-specialty-prescription-drugs-year-end-update.doi.10.26419-2Fppi.00073.001.pdf.

Scott, J. S., Sharpe, W. F., & Watson, J. G. (2009). The 4% Rule–At What Price?. *Journal of Investment Management, 7*(3), 31–48.

Seburn, P. W. (1991). Evolution of employer-provided defined benefit pensions. *Monthly Labor Review,* 16–23. http://www.bls.gov/mlr/1991/12/art3full.pdf.

Sharpe, W. F. (1964). Capital asset prices: A theory of market equilibrium under conditions of risk. *The Journal of Finance, 19*(3), 425–442.

Sharpe, W. F. (1975). Likely gains from market timing. *Financial Analysts Journal, 31*(2), 60–69.

354 References

Sharpe, W. F. (1991). The arithmetic of active management. *Financial Analysts Journal, 47*(1), 7–9.

Sharpe, W. F. (2013). The arithmetic of investment expenses. *Financial Analysts Journal, 69*(2), 34–41.

Shiller, R. J. (2015). *Irrational exuberance*. Princeton University: Princeton.

Sholar, B. (2018). *FireCalc*. http://www.firecalc.com/.

Stanley, T. J., & Danko, W. D. (1996). *The Millionaire Next Door*. Longstreet Press: New York. There is a new edition published by Taylor Trade Publishing in 2010.

Sutton, G. D. (2002). Explaining changes in house prices. In *BIS Quarterly Review* (pp. 46–55).

Taleb, N. N. (2007). *The Black Swan*. Random House: New York.

Tobias, A. (2016). *The only investment guide you'll ever need*. Mariner Books: New York. 2nd updated edition, paperback.

Tsatsaronis, K., & Zhu, H. (2004). What drives housing price dynamics: cross-country evidence. In *BIS Quarterly Review* (pp. 65–78).

U.S. Department Labor (2016a) Private pension plan bulletin abstract of 2014 form 5500 annual reports, data extracted on 6/30/2016. In *Employee Benefits Security Administration*. https://www.dol.gov/sites/default/files/ebsa/researchers/statistics/retirement-bulletins/private-pension-plan-bulletins-abstract-2014.pdf.

U.S. Department Labor (2016b). Private pension plan bulletin historical tables and graphs 1975–2014. In *Employee Benefits Security Administration*. https://www.dol.gov/sites/default/files/ebsa/researchers/statistics/retirement-bulletins/private-pension-plan-bulletin-historical-tables-and-graphs.pdf.

Vanguard (2000). *Plan for a long retirement*. https://personal.vanguard.com/us/insights/retirement/plan-for-a-long-retirement-tool.

von Neumann, J., & Morgenstern, O. (1944). *Theory of games and economic behavior* Princeton University: Princeton.

Waring, M. B., & Siegel, L. B. (2015). The only spending rule article you will ever need. *Financial Analysts Journal, 71*(1), 91–107.

Wismer, D. (2014). Warren Buffett: 'Investing advice for you—and my wife' (and other quotes of the week). *Forbes Investing*, 171–180. http://www.forbes.com/sites/davidwismer/2014/03/02/warren-buffett-investing-advice-for-you-and-my-wife-and-other-quotes-of-the-week/.

Index

Symbols
1031 exchange, 63
3.8% medicare surtax, 233
401(k), **222**, 226, 239
    catchup contribution, 222
403(k), 221
409(a) plan, 230
4% rule, xi
4% rule, **202**
529 ABLE plan, 256
529 education fund, 255

A
AARP, 204
Ackman, William A., 14
Active management, 7, 41
Actual tax rate, 231
Adjusted gross income (AGI), **230**
Alimony, 230
Alpha, 8, 43
Altman, Edward I., 70
American Association of Individual
    Investors (AAII), 6
American Can Co., 282
American Opportunity tax credit, 257

Annual funding notice, 299
Annual payout rate, 56, 340
Annual percentage rate (APR), 327, 331
Annual percentage yield (APY), 326,
    327, 331
Annuity, **49**, 55, 56, 150, **339**
    deferred, **53**, 56, 57, 150, 339, **344**,
        345, 348, 349
    fixed rate, 51
    fixed term, **51**, 93, 104
    immediate, **52**, 56, 57, 339, 348
    indexed, 51
    MYGA, 51
    variable rate, 50
AT&T, 282
Automated Clearing House (ACH), 138
Avaya, 297
Ax, James, 4

B
Back-door Roth IRA, 228
Balance, vii, 40, 94, 98, 100
Bankruptcy, 5, 33, 53, 54, 57, 155, 171,
    230, 288–290, 295, 297, 301,
    305, 307, 310

© The Author(s), under exclusive license to Springer Nature Switzerland AG 2022
R. P. Kurshan, *Investment Industry Claims Debunked*,
https://doi.org/10.1007/978-3-030-76709-9

356   Index

Barclays Aggregate Bond Index, 180
Bauer, Shane, 307
Bear market, 19, 23, 112, **120**
Beat the market, 16
Bengen, William, 202
Berkshire Hathaway, 17
Berlekamp, Elwyn, 4
Beta, 8
Bethlehem Steel, 282, 288, 301
Bill, 32
Bipartisan American Miners Act, 291
Bipartisan Budget Act, 284
Blackjack, 3
Blackrock, 65
Black-Scholes, 3
Black-Scholes-Merton formula, 83
Bloomberg, 59, 64
BND, 35, 64
BNDX, 64
Boat, 174
Bodie, Zvi, 8, 44, 83, 95, 115
Bogle, John C., 40, 41
Bond, **30**
   callable, **31**, 37
   convertible, 31
   coupon, 31, 325, 328
   discount, 31, 34, **320**, 325
   duration, 35
   investment grade, 33, 37, **336**
   junk, 33
   maturity, 30, **31**, 34, 35, 37, 90, 321, 336
   municipal, 33, 35
   par value, 321, **325**, 330
   rating, 32, 33, 70, 87, 336, 340, 344
   risk-free, 1, 32, 37, 83, 90, 204, 306, 347
   speculative grade, 33
   straight, 31, 321, 324
   term, 31
   yield, **31**, 33, 330
   zero-coupon, 31, **34**, 83, 104, **319**, 335

Bond ladder, **36**, 335, 338
Break the buck, 48
Brighthouse Financial, 52, 53
Buffett, Warren, 2, 5, 6, 8, 15, 17, 41, 95
Bull market, 19, 23
Bypass trust, 152

C

Callable, 32, 338
Capital Asset Pricing Model, 43, 84, 87
Carlson, Ben, 180
Cash, 46, 93
Cash inflow, 334
Catchup contribution, 222, 225
C-CPI-U, 50, 233
CD, 27, 29, 46, 93, 104
CDARS, 47
Central Falls, Rhode Island, 310
Central State Teamsters, 291
Chained urban consumer price index, 50, 233
Charitable contributions, 258
Charupat, Narat, 57
Civil Service Retirement System, 284
COBRA, **271**, 275
COLA, 263, **265**, 266
Compound annual growth rate (CAGR), **184**, 197
Community Bankers, 48
Confirmation bias, 80
Consumer price index, 49, 52, 184, 233
Continuous compounding, 327
Convertible, 31
Counterparty risk, 37, 52, 53, 68, 70, 90, 155, 256
Coupon, 31, 325, 328
Coverdell education savings account, 257
COVID-19, 88, 125
CPI-U, 49, 52, 184, 233
CPI-W, 266
Craig's List, 213

Index   **357**

Credit default swaps, 5
Credit report freeze, 159
Credit union, 47
CRSP, 29, 64, 65
Cum-ex, 5
Current yield, 330

D
Deferred compensation, 230
Defined benefit plan, **281**, 315
Defined contribution plan, **222**, 230,
    238, 284, 293, 315
Degradation, x, 49, 93, 99–101, 104,
    183, 185, 188, **189**, 190–194, 196,
    197, 200, 201, 214, 249, 334
Delphi, 288
Delta Airlines, 288
Dental insurance, 278
De-risking, **283**, 305, 315
Descriptive models, 78
Detroit, 310
Deutsche Bank, 60
Dirty bomb, 176
Discounted cash flow, 330
Discount price, 31, 34, **320**, 321, 325
Discount pricing, 321, 325, 330
Discount rate, 320
Divorce benefit, 264
Dollar cost averaging, 57, 177–179, 193
Dot com bubble, 120
DQYDJ, xiii
Duration, 35

E
Eaglevale Partners, 15
Eastern Airlines, 301
Eastman Kodak Co., 282
Edesess, Michael, 23
Education savings bonds, 257
Educator expenses, 230

Effective long-term capital gains tax
    rate, 233
Effective ordinary income tax rate, 231
Efficient market, 2
Emergency fund, **107**, 209
Employee Benefits Security
    Administration, 292
Employee Retirement Income Security
    Act (ERISA), 288, 292
Epicycle, 80
Equifax, 159
Equity, 27
Equity risk, 68
ETF, 44
Eton Park, 15
EU, 40
Euclid of Alexandria, 323
Euler number e, 327
Expected utility theory, 75, 78, 80
Expense ratio, 42–44, 64, 65, 115, 116,
    172–174
Experian, 159

F
Face value, **30**, 31, 32, 34, 320–322,
    324, 326, 330, 335, 337, 339,
    340
Fama, Eugene, 2, 18
FDIC, 47
Federal Funds Rate, 48
Federal Reserve, 32, 34, 48
Federal taxation, 230
Fees, 36, 172
Fidelity, 19, 42, 64, 196
Fidelity Retirement Income Planner,
    196
File and suspend, 264
Financial Accounting Standards Board,
    283
Financial advisor, vii, ix, x, 9, 86, 87,
    89, 174, 257

358   Index

Financial Industry Regulatory Authority (FINRA), 257
FIRECalc, 203
FireEye, 165
Fixed income investment risk, 68
Fixed income investments, 28, 32, 86, 88, **93**, 95, 98, 100, 102, 105, **112**, 117, 232, 245, 247
FLPSX, 19
Fraud deterrence, 159
French, Kenneth, 18
FTSE, 64
Funding ratio, 287, 289, **299**
FZROX, 64

G

Gates, William H. III, 17
Gell-Mann, Murray, 192
General Electric Co., 282
Geocentric theory, 80
Geometric series, 322
Goodyear Tire and Rubber Co., 282
Government Accountability Office (GAO), 313
Great Depression, 47, 237, 281, 314
Great Recession, 17, 32, 237, 286
Great Society, 274
Gross income, 230
Guaranteed Retirement Account, 315

H

Harvesting capital gains, 233
Healthcare, 269
Hebner, Mark, 44
Heliocentric theory, 80
Highway and Transportation Funding Act, 300
Housing bubble, 61
Huang, Huaxiong, 49, 57, 206, 265

I

Ibbotson, Roger G., 196
Imputed growth rate, **191**, 193, 194, 197, 214
Indexed annuity, 51
Index funds, 29, **41**, 42
Inflation compensation, 345
Innovis, 161
Insurance, 147
  disability, 156
  long-term care, 154, 278
  longevity, 53, 57, **150**, 157, 344
  medical, 153
  term life, 151
  whole life, 152
Internal rate of return (IRR), 330
Investment Advisers Act, 9
Investment grade, 37, **336**
IRA, **224**, 226, 247, 249
  catchup contribution, 225
  Kay Hutchison Spousal Limit, 228
  nondeductible, **221**, 224, 225
  SIMPLE, 224
IRMAA, **234**, 277
Iron Workers Local 17, 298
IRS form 5329, 228
IRS identity protection pin, 165

J

Johnson, Lyndon Baines, 274
Juggling ladder rung payouts, 337
Junk bonds, 33

K

Kahneman, Daniel, 7, 12, 71, 78, 80, 84
Kamstra, Mark J., 57
Kepler, Johannes, 80
Kicking the can down the road, 299, 300
Kierkegaard, Søren, 117
Kindleberger, Charles P., 122

Index **359**

Kitces, Michael, 9, 233
Kiting, 309
Koch, Ed, 209
Krugman, Paul, 70, 205

L
Lehman Brothers, 48, 54
Lieber, Ron, 51, 160, 161
Life insurance, 151
Lifetime learning credit, 257
Limit order, 45
Liquidity risk, 31, 37, **90**, 207
Load, 45
Load fee, 44
Logarithm, 184
Long-term bond, 35
Long-term capital gains, 232
Long-Term Capital Management, 83
Long-term care, 154, 278
Longevity insurance, 53, 57, **150**, 157, 344
Longevity tables, 183, **342**, 343, 348
Lost decade, 120
LTV Steel, 288
Lynch, Peter, 6

M
Malkiel, Burton G., 83
Mandelbrot, Benoit, 208
MAP-21, 299
Marginal tax rate, 231
Market capitalization, **19**, 29, 65
Market crashes, 122
Market timing, 23, 135
Markowitz, Harry, 43, 84
Marotta, David, 58
Maturity, **30**, 34, 35, 37, 90, 104, 321, 336
Mean reversion, 82
Medallion hedge fund, 16
Medicaid, 155, 272, 273

Medicaid planning, 279
Medicare, 153, 229, 234, 243, 271, 272, **273**, 273, 275–278
Medicare surtax, 233
Medigap, 153, 272, 275, **276**, 277
Merton, Robert C., 8, 44, 82, 83, 187, 205
MetLife, 53
Milevsky, Moshe A., 49, 57, 185, 201, 206, 265
Miller, Merton, 43
Mindich, Eric, 15
Modern Portfolio Theory (MPT), 84, 87
Modified adjusted gross income (MAGI), 225, 228, **230**, 233, 265, 278
Money market, 48
Morgan, J. P., 2
Morgenstern, Oskar, 76
Mortgage, 175, 331
Mortgage formula, 63, 184, 214, 319, **331**, 331, 332, 334, 337, 340, 341
Mortgage payoff amount, 334
MSCI, 65
Multi-employer pension plan, 289
Multi-employer Pension Reform Act, 284, 298
Multi-Year Guaranteed Annuity (MYGA), 51, 104
Municipal bond, 32, 35

N
Nasdaq, 29, 41
National Credit Union Administration (NCUA), 47
National Retiree Legislative Network, 301
Net investment income tax, 229, **233**, 243
Net unrealized appreciation (NUA), 243

360 Index

New Deal, 267, 281, 314
Newsletters, 6
Newton, Isaac, 80
New York Stock Exchange, 29
Nixon, Richard M., 47
No load fund, 45
Nondeductible IRA, **221**, 224, 225
Non-qualified deferred compensation, 230
Normative models, 78
Note, 32, 46
NYC pension funds, 12

O

Optimal window length, 128, 133
Ordinary income, 230, 231
Orwell, George, 299, 309
OTC bond, 36, 38, 329

P

Pan Am, 288, 301
Par value, **31**, 321, **325**, 330
Passive management, 10, 41
Pay-as-you-go, **267**, 267, 272, 273, 311
Penn Treaty, 155
Pension, 281
   private sector, 287
   public sector, 307
Pension Benefit Guaranty Corporation (PBGC), 284, 288–290, **292**, 295–302, 316
Pension buyout, 303, 347
Pension Protection Act, 283, 292, 299, 348
Pension Rights Center, 298
Perry Capital, 15
Pershing Square, 14
Persistence, 9, **14**
Peters, Ole, 192
The Pew Charitable Trusts, 307, 313
Phantom income, 320

Phantom interest, 34, 320
Portfolio insurance, 104, **201**
Posner, Steven, 201
Poundstone, William, 5
Powerball, 77, 81
PRBC, 161
Preferred stock, 338
Premium pricing, 321, 325, 330
Present value, 31, 32, 35, 183, **320**, 322, 324, 329, 330, 332, 334, 338, 339, 345, 346
Prichard, Alabama, 310
Prime investment question, 119
Principal, **33**, 46, 50, 51, 235, **320**, 322, 324–326, 328, 330–332, 334–336, 338–340
Prospect theory, 78, 80, 84

Q

Qualified business income, 230
Qualified distribution, 230
Qualified tuition program, 255
Quantitative easing, 34

R

Reagan, Ronald, 273, 315
Real estate, **58**, 120, 232
Real estate investment trust (REIT), 58
Real rate, **183**, **184**, 185, 206, 214, 332, 345
Rebalancing, 94, **180**
Renaissance Technologies, 16
Retirement cash buffer, **198**, 199, 201, 209, 210
Retirement crisis, 313
Retirement expenses fund, **183**, 188, 198, 200, 209, 214, 216, 250, 252, 253
Reverse dollar cost averaging, 189, 193
Risk, 67
Risk-reward tradeoff, 87

Index

361

Risk aversion, 84
Risk transfer, **283**, 305
RMD, 142, 201, 208, 224, 226, 229, 240, 249, **250**, 251, 252
Robinson, Joan, 84
Robocalls, 169
Rollover, **224**, 228, 229, 242, 252
Roosevelt, Franklin Delano, 47, 281
Ross, Stephen A., 75
Roth, 223, 227, 238, 239
   back-door IRA, 228
Rothschild, Mayer, 2
Russell 3000, 65

S
S&P 500, xiii, 1, 6, 7, 14, 15, 17, 19, 29, 39, 41, 43, 44, 52, 53, 59, 64, **65**, 82, 89, 95, 96, **97**, 97, 98, 100, 101, 103, 112, 113, 120, 122, 124, 125, 127, 128, 174, 180, 185, 193, 196–201, 223, 230, 236, 246, 248, 304
Saari, Donald G., 80
Samuelson, Paul A., 36, 75, 83
Savings bank, 47, 49, 334
Schwab, 65
Scott, Jason S., 204, 205
SECURE Act, 54
SEC yield, 49, 65
Sequence of returns, 192
Sharpe, William F., 13, 23, 43, 72, 204, 205
Sharpe ratio, 71, **72**, 179
Shiller, Robert, xiii
Shock absorber, 102, **198**
Sholar, Bill, 203
Short-term capital gains, 232
Short sale, 4
Siegel, Laurence B., 50, 207
Simons, James, 4, 16
SIMPLE IRA, 224
Single-employer pension plan, 287

Sinquefield, Rex A., 196
Slocum, Joshua, 111
Small cap, 19
Social Security, **261**, 262, 265, 301, 316
Solar panels, 63
SolarWinds, 165
Sommer, Jeff, 6
Sortino, Frank, 72
Spending, 137
SPIVA, 9, 18
Stability, 86, 87, 94, 96, 97, 194, 198
Standard deduction, 230
Standard Oil of New Jersey, 282
Stock picking, 25
Stocks, 29
Stocks, Bonds, Bills, and Inflation (SBBI), 196
Stockton, California, 310
Straight bond, 31, **321**, 324
STRIPS, 34

T
Taleb, Nassim Nicholas, 208
Target-date fund, 93, **115**
Task Rabbit, 213
Taxable income, 230
Tax-advantaged accounts, 221
Tax bracket, 231
Tax rate, 231
Term, 320
Thorp, Edward O., 3, 16
Timing market, 23, 135
Tobias, Andy, 7
Tort, 4
Total income, 230
Transunion, 159
Treasury Inflation-Protected Securities (TIPS), 31, 34, 90, 205, 263
Trigger condition, **103**, 105, 106, 112, 117, 124, 126–133, 198, 199, 201
   pre-retirement, 124
   retirement, 125

362   Index

Trinity study, 202
Trump, Donald J., 59, 271, 291
Tversky, Amos, 78, 80, 84
TWA, 288
Two-factor authentication, 164

U
Underperform, how to, 23
Unearned income medicare
    contribution tax, 233
Uniform Gifts to Minors Act (UGMA),
    258
Uniform Transfers to Minors Act
    (UTMA), 258
United Airlines, 288, 296, 301
United Mine Workers, 291
Urban consumer price index, 49, 52,
    184, 233
US Airways, 288
U.S. Steel Corp., 282
Utility function, 75
Utility theory, 75, 84

V
Valeant Pharmaceuticals, 14
Vallejo, California, 307, 310
Vanguard, 6, 10, 14, 18–20, 23, 35,
    41–43, 48, 58, 64, 65, 83, 86, 94,
    99, 113–115, 172, 174, 178, 204,
    214, 258, 304
VBMFX, 115
Vesting period, 282
VFIAX, 41, 95
VFINX, 41
VGSIX, 58

VGTSX, 115
Vietnam War, 274
Vision insurance, 278
VMFXX, 49
VMRXX, 49
VNQ, 58
von Neumann, John, 76
VOO, 64
VTBIX, 115
VTI, 64
VTIBX, 115
VTSAX, 115
VTSMX, 115
VWIUX, 64
VXUS, 64, 115

W
Walker, Gov. Scott, 309
Waring, M. Barton, 50, 207
Wash sale, 233, **247**
Watson, John G., 204, 205
Welfare queen, 309
Wilshire 5000, 65
Workplace sectors, 284

Y
Yahoo Finance, xiii
Yield, 19, 31, 33, 320, 330
Yield curve inversion, 32, 36
Yield to maturity, 330

Z
Zero-coupon bond, 31, **34**, 83, 104,
    319, 335

Printed in the United States
by Baker & Taylor Publisher Services